S0-ANP-615

Practical Performance Profiling

Improving the efficiency of .NET code

By Jean-Philippe Gouigoux

Published by Simple Talk Publishing February 2012

Copyright February 2012
ISBN 978-1-906434-82-3

The right of Jean-Philippe Gouigoux to be identified as the author of this work has been asserted by him in accordance with the Copyright, Designs and Patents Act 1988.

All rights reserved. No part of this publication may be reproduced, stored or introduced into a retrieval system, or transmitted, in any form, or by any means (electronic, mechanical, photocopying, recording or otherwise) without the prior written consent of the publisher. Any person who does any unauthorized act in relation to this publication may be liable to criminal prosecution and civil claims for damages.

This book is sold subject to the condition that it shall not, by way of trade or otherwise, be lent, re-sold, hired out, or otherwise circulated without the publisher's prior consent in any form other than that in which it is published and without a similar condition including this condition being imposed on the subsequent publisher. All product names mentioned are the trademarks of their respective holders.

Technical Review by Paul Glavich
Cover Image by Andy Martin
Edited by Marianne Crowder
Typeset & Designed by Matthew Tye, Peter Woodhouse & Gower Associates

Table of Contents

Chapter 2: Profiling a .NET Application 49

Chapter 5: Profiling the Sample Application – Client Side   205

Chapter 7: Beyond Profiling   475

About the author

JP Gouigoux is a MCTS/MCPD Enterprise Architect, and MVP "Connected System Developer," with an Engineering degree in Mechanical Systems from the Université de Technologie de Compiègne (France) and a Master of Science in Advanced Automation and Design from Cranfield University (UK). JP works as a software architect, and is a board member at MGDIS, an innovative software company based in Vannes (France). His role includes responsibility for platform architecture for a customer base of ~850, as well as R&D, internal and external training, and expertise in .NET.

Having always been involved in education, JP teaches algorithms, security, software tests and Application Lifestyle Management at the Université de Bretagne Sud. He is a regular lecturer at Agile Tour and other IT conferences, and writes articles for programming magazines as well as regular entries on his website and blog, the first editorial of which dates back to 1996, at a time when people talked about "programming web pages"! His interest in teaching has recently led him to start writing technical books; this book was born out of years of performance-oriented audits and profiling campaigns.

In addition to passing on knowledge, JP's main drive is to help integrate research and new technologies into real-world software. He tries to maintain his "once a mechanical engineer" point of view to address problems with a realistic and practical approach. As a strong supporter of pragmatism in IT, he particularly enjoys the Agile approaches to his job.

When he is not developing software, JP can be found writing short stories, going on long bike trips, renovating his stone house and (most often) playing Lego with his two kids.

Acknowledgements

First of all, my thanks go to the wonderful editorial team I had at Simple Talk: Laïla Lofti put me in the starting blocks, Alice Smith supervised the whole process, and Marianne had admirable patience when explaining the subtleties of the English language to me, even citing Shakespeare! If you like reading this book, it is mostly down to her.

I often called the three of them "Charlie's Angels," and I really felt like Bosley, comfortably relying on their skills.

It can't be often that authors thank their boss but, then again, I don't have an average boss. You will no doubt know how IT people always wish their boss would trust them, while still being technical enough to offer a sound judgment on strategic architecture decisions. You know how we often wish our boss would respect us, while still having the authority to get a team going? Well, I have found that kind of boss in Frank Mosser, CTO of MGDIS.

Thanks, Frank, for letting me make my own way through my job, research, and teaching.

Also, my thanks go to my dear colleagues, who, in addition to putting up with my daily mutterings about following best practices, writing maintainable code, and learning new techniques, felt obliged to read the French edition of this book. I am doing this for you guys too!

It may sound all too common to say that a book would have not been written without the support of a lovely wife and kids. Still, nothing is more true... Clémence, Mathieu, during these months working crazy hours, with both of you sleeping in the next room, my motivation has always been to show you that you can do anything in life as long as you are ready to work enough to obtain it. Gwen, I live for this spark of pride in your eye.

About the Technical Reviewer

Paul Glavich has been an ASP.NET MVP for the last six years, and works as a solution architect for Datacom. Past roles have included technical architect for EDS Australia, and senior consultant for Readify. He has accumulated 20 years of industry experience ranging all the way from PICK, C, C++, Delphi, and Visual Basic 3/4/5/6 to his current specialty in .NET with ASP.NET.

Paul has been developing in .NET technologies since .NET was first in Beta. He was technical architect for one of the world's first Internet Banking solutions using .NET technology.

He can be found on various .NET-related newsgroups, and has presented at TechEd Australia on numerous occasions. He is also a member of ASPInsiders (WWW.ASPINSIDERS.COM) with direct lines of communication to the ASP.NET team.

He has co-authored two books on ASP.NET Ajax, has written technical articles which can be seen on community sites such as ASPAlliance.com (HTTP://WWW.ASPALLIANCE.COM), and has his own blog at HTTP://WEBLOGS.ASP.NET/PGLAVICH. Paul has also released several Open Source projects on Nuget (HTTP://NUGET.ORG).

His current interests in technology revolve around anything in ASP.NET, but he also has a strong interest in Windows Communication Foundation, on which he is a Microsoft Certified Technical Specialist. Naturally, performance testing and optimization have both been a major focus throughout this entire period.

On a more personal note, he is married, with three children and two grandkids, and he holds a 5th Degree black belt in a form of martial arts known as Budo-Jitsu, a free-style eclectic method of close quarter combat.

Preface

Software optimization means returning to the fundamentals of programming, which many developers may have forgotten about. Let us remember that the 640 kilobytes limit in the first x86 processors led programmers to accomplish miracles!

Resources have become easy to use and almost unlimited, but they still have a price. Of course, hardware acquisition costs do not reflect this, but we can measure the energy consumption of code in production, and work out the relationship between the resources used and what this amounts to in terms of energy or even carbon.

Optimization of code attempts to reduce the quantity of resources used, thus improving the execution speed. This difference will be more or less noticeable to a user. The impact is more significant on a server farm. If a program is optimized by 20%, the effects on a laptop are quite limited (better reactivity, maybe longer battery life). But in a server farm, a gain of 20% means one machine out of five can be spared! Facebook's Project HipHop springs to mind: generating C++ from their PHP code brought an average improvement of 50%. Half of the servers for Facebook equates to 60,000 tons of carbon dioxide. Now, we're talking!

Optimization is also about taking into account the architecture of new machines. In the past few years, clock frequency has reached physical limits and Moore's law has been prolonged by multiplying cores. To remain efficient, we must today produce parallelized code that is able to use multicore hyper-threaded platforms. Parallelized code will tend to use more energy, but in a shorter timespan than its mono-thread equivalent. There again, the improvement can reach 30–50% and become an appreciable source of savings.

Emergence of cloud computing and giant datacenters will stress the fact that performance is not an optional extra or an intellectual whim, but has a strong economic and environmental impact. The profitability of these datacenters is directly linked to the quality and performance of the code that is executed inside of them. These are fundamental issues for developers and our industry.

Code optimization is no longer optional on a planet with finite resources.

Beyond choices and solutions that large IT players will put in place, any developer can write efficient code and improve overall performance. Just as every citizen is encouraged to adopt ecological practices, it is time for developers to focus on writing code that is more efficient and requires fewer resources. There is no need to become an expert at the language used. Most of the time, common sense and good habits will suffice, as Jean-Philippe Gouigoux demonstrates in this book. I am convinced that readers will discover effective techniques for programming differently and engaging in sustainable development.

Eric Mittelette – Microsoft France
Technical team lead – Developers technical relations team
Head of sustainable development

Introduction

When was the last time you used a performance testing tool on your application? Were the results analyzed, and did you identify bottlenecks in software processes? What steps were taken following this analysis?

If you can answer these three questions, congratulations! And, to be honest, you do not necessarily need this book, even if you will certainly find in it a few methods and tricks that will help you progress further.

If you have not given these questions any thought before, or if you know their importance but do not know how to deal with them, you have nothing to feel ashamed of; you are simply among the majority of developers, software architects or companies for whom the performance analysis step is not routinely included in the software production process.

This book does not explain in depth how .NET works. It will not take the reader up the grueling slopes of algorithm tuning. It simply deals with the 20% of defects in the code that account for 80% of performance loss. Generally, no software is fully optimized. Doing so is theoretically impossible and, most of all, absurd from a commercial point of view.

When an application takes 20 seconds to perform a user interaction, unless the process is extremely complex, there is a good chance that our performance problems simply come from a few programming errors somewhere in the code. A careful profiling session will often identify the faulty parts and the problem can then be solved quite quickly by a change to the code, dividing the process time by an appreciable factor, sometimes even beyond our expectations.

Don't be too hard on developers: between unit tests, naming conventions, quality norms and delivery processes, it is impossible to give one's complete attention to the consequences of every line of code. A developer can sometimes spend days optimizing just a few lines of code. Think, for example, of the list-sorting algorithms that were optimized by researchers for years before the invention of QuickSort. On a 100,000- or even 1,000,000-line piece of software, optimizing everything from the start is clearly not realistic.

Optimizing every part of an application is not a good idea anyway. It would mean spending a lot of time on analyzing code that, depending on new versions, will change anyway. Code is alive, and performance optimization needs stability. That does not mean software performance should not be tested during the whole development cycle. On the contrary, it is good practice to integrate some dedicated tests into the development process, in order to detect code modifications that would cause performance to drop significantly. This should even be done as soon as possible, so as to throw an alert as soon as any suboptimal code is added.

Performance optimization, on the other hand, does not form part of the development cycle, but takes place after it. Profiling and correction should be performed on a stable version, on which neither processes nor algorithms will be further modified, to avoid having to repeat the whole profiling process.

The other trap in optimization lies in its overuse. Let us come back to our example application where a user interaction takes 20 seconds. Obviously the ease of use, and thus the commercial impact, will be excellent if we succeed in lowering this to 1 or 2 seconds only. And we can reasonably hope that it will only take us a few days to reach this level of performance. But we are not going to sell more licenses if we then lower this time to half a second. In addition, we would certainly need quite some time to achieve this, maybe months. This is the second rule of performance optimization: the more we progress, the harder the next step is, because we identify the bottlenecks in the order of size, starting with the largest. This makes it essential to know when to stop. Ideally, before each optimization campaign, objectives should be set that are precise and measurable.

This, of course, brings us to the necessity of calculating time spent in processes. This can be manual, using a stopwatch. Let us not underestimate this method: this is the one that is closest to how our customers experience our product. But we can also put in place automatic test scenarios, load tests and everything needed for a complete test architecture that will enable us to work out, as quickly as possible, the performance gains obtained by a code modification.

It is also important to set time limits on an optimization campaign. The experiences of development teams, particularly those working with Agile methods, allow us to predict better and better the time needed to add features. But optimization is much more difficult to plan. Sometimes, an hour of analysis will help us discover a huge bottleneck that can be corrected quite simply. Sometimes, profiling will not help us and the only way to improve the speed of the scenario will be to completely rewrite, or even re-architect the module. The good news is that a scenario can always be accelerated. The bad news is that, when starting a profiling analysis, we have no guarantee of the time necessary to achieve our objectives.

Many tools will help us with profiling, but it will be years before any are able to understand what is commonly called the "intent of the developer." Several profilers, as long as we provide them with debugging files, are able to show the functions in the source code where the most time is spent: which function takes the maximum amount of time, which line of code is called the most times, etc. But only a human analyst can determine whether these times are justified by the complexity of the business process behind the code. Three seconds is often considered the maximum amount of time a user interaction should take, but when the only visible result is the display of a short piece of text, that already sounds awfully long. On the contrary, nobody could criticize an application for taking longer than this to perform a complex bulk process on each of the business objects contained in a massive database.

All this means that it is essential to find the points of execution in the code that are called most often, and not necessarily the longest ones. Several approaches can be taken to lower the time spent in a function, but they do not all have the same yield. These can be ranked in order of preference.

• Removing a useless function: there is no better improvement to effort ratio. If the target code calculates a value that has already been processed at some other point of the software, and we modify it so that it reads the existing result, we can simply remove the code, and replace it with a single reading operation. The yield makes the effort an excellent investment. This is the principle of a cache: creating once and reading many times.

- Accelerating a function that is massively used: when it is impossible to completely remove a call, we can sometimes modify its content so that it executes in a quicker way. Of course, the functions that are called most often should be dealt with first. Profilers can tell us which these are.

- As a last resort, we could turn to functions that are called less often, and try to improve them. But generally, the first two steps allow sufficient improvements.

When talking about profiling, we start from the hypothesis that, one way or another, the only way to spend less time on an atomic process is to do it with fewer processor cycles. This is not true for performance in its more global sense. Therefore we have several other approaches at our disposal.

- Adding resources, by scale-up (a quicker processor or more RAM, for example) or scale-out (typically, adding more machines). After all, the price of hardware, for now, is still lower than a good developer. But, as this book will show, there are lots of times when the yield from a software improvement is much better. And, in an environment with increasingly limited resources, the ratio could tend to favor the software approach more and more in the future.

- Using existing resources more efficiently. Sadly, examples of resource waste are quite numerous, even if virtualizing has allowed for major improvements. A decade ago, it was quite common to see a server being used at only a few percent of its capacity for long periods. Even today, far from all applications are able to take advantage of multicore machines, even though multicore is quite common nowadays. This subject will be introduced briefly, since some optimization techniques need multithreading, even on single-core machines. But this book will not go into parallel programming in depth.

- Modifying the software architecture. Sometimes, adding resources or rewriting code will not enable us to reach the level of performance requested for our software usage, and we will have to rethink the technical concepts at the heart of the application. For example, if no database can be tuned to be quick enough, maybe it is time to bring in-memory databases to the game. Or, even better, to place our whole business tier in memory, using mechanisms like object prevalence.

This book primarily talks about profiling, demonstrating how to use profiling tools and providing the technical grounding necessary to understand the results they provide us with. Then, it will examine practical cases of scenario performance profiling, using a sample application. For each of these cases, we will show how the bottlenecks appear in the profilers, how to detect the root cause, and several ways of correcting them.

How to read this book

*In order to get the most out of this book, I recommend that you follow the approach described in Section E, **Recommended methods**, at the end of Chapter 3, **Sample Application**. The book can be read in any order, but I am convinced that readers will do best by following this advice.*

Go to WWW.SIMPLE-TALK.COM/REDGATEBOOKS/JPGOUIGOUX/CODEDOWNLOAD.ZIP to download the code accompanying this book.

Chapter 1: Profiling Principles

A A strictly structured activity

There are three steps in software performance improvement.

- **Profiling**: using test strategies and a specialized toolset, a developer attempts to find all the bottlenecks in the code, and corrects them. This book will focus on profiling, as it is very often overlooked, despite the fact that it generally leads to very useful results. At this stage of the analysis, all improvements add up and (within the course of an optimization campaign) it is extremely rare for a subsequent improvement to undo the effects of a previous one.

- **Fine-tuning**: this second step starts when profiling no longer identifies any bottlenecks. The application is working correctly in terms of the code but, if the performance is not as high as expected, you can play with the configuration to improve performance by a few more percent. Tuning is highly dependent on the context, and different improvements can interact with each other. Lowering the memory use can lead to higher CPU (central processing unit) consumption or a modification that leads to better results for a given scenario could slow down another one. This makes fine-tuning an art, and this is the source of performance improvement's reputation for complexity. By contrast, the first step generally delivers very good results without requiring much knowledge.

- **Re-architecture**: if you have not managed to squeeze the last drops of performance out of the tuning stage, you will have to resort to re-architecting the software or the hardware. This is generally extremely bad news if the cycles are long but, provided the project team work in short iteration cycles and can quickly loop on conception, analysis, coding, and testing, re-architecting is feasible.

As I said above, this book mainly focuses on the first step. Profiling consists of using software to record metrics during the execution of a target application following a given scenario. The goal is to analyze these metrics to find possible improvements to the code that would result in better performance.

All the terms in the previous paragraph are important, and they should be explained carefully.

While profiling can be performed without specialized toolset and software, profiling tools provide an easy and accurate way to profile all aspects of your code. We will be using software tools dedicated to finding performance problems in applications. In our case, these tools are adapted to .NET, and will be introduced in a later chapter.

Next, we talk about metrics because profiling is mainly about measuring. Whether it be time, number of method calls, or percentage of time spent in a given method, profilers basically produce values. In some cases, they can provide a developer with an initial analysis of these metrics, and propose a few hints, but one should not expect much from these tools in terms of active help. Analyzing the metrics remains the job of a human, and this book aims to offer intellectual tools in addition to these software tools, in order to help developers diagnose the reason behind a bottleneck.

Also, the term "scenario" is used to stress one of the fundamental characteristics of profiling: it is always applied to given scenarios of use of the target application, not to the application itself. Profilers do not analyze the code: they only record the behavior of the application when executing a chain of interactions. Talking about application performance improvement is a misnomer, since we will only be improving particular scenarios. Of course, optimizing different scenarios affects all uses of the application, but it is the developer's job to optimize the scenarios that best cover the uses of the program.

Finally, the goal of profiling is improving the performance of an application. But what kind of performance are we talking about? Light use of memory? Robustness? These goals are, of course, important, but users generally only pay attention to display speed and how quickly processes react. On a server application, in addition to latency, throughput (number of transactions processed in a given time) is of major interest. In short, a lean application is an appreciable quality, but what is really required is speed. Although there are some tools dedicated to memory profiling (and this could fill a book in itself), we will only talk about speed here.

By the way, what kind of speed should we reach? What are our goals? Are they measurable? The answer depends so much on context that the definition can only be technical (and arguably vague): an application is fast enough when customers and users consider that additional performance will not bring them additional value. This may seem indeterminate, but I must stress the importance of pragmatism in profiling: the goal is certainly not to reach the ultimate speed of an algorithm, but to maximize the ratio between the time spent in profiling and the result in terms of additional usability for the customer. A word of warning: profiling is an activity in which, even more so than when coding, it is easy to get caught up in the search for perfection and to lose sight of the customer's interest and, therefore, our own.

The graph in Figure 1-1 illustrates this clearly: except in particular cases where an application is already of excellent quality, the first modifications are quite simple and bring large improvements. The yield is thus very good. But, step by step, the solutions will become more complex, and the yield will go down. At the end of the profiling cycles, we reach the tuning phase, where efforts have to be substantial in order to gain these last few milliseconds.

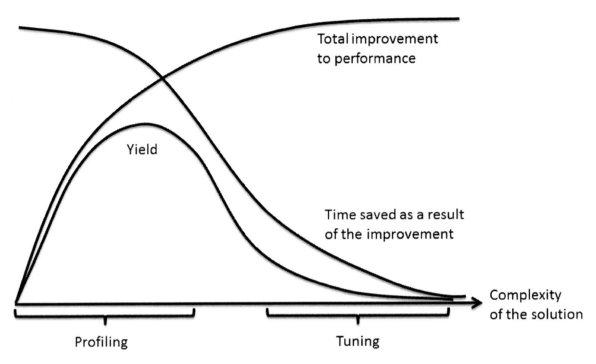

Figure 1-1: The relationship between performance gain and time invested.

Without going as far as saying that the second phase is not useful, the present book focuses on the first step. I will demonstrate that this step can be taken by any developer, whereas tuning really is an expert domain. This common misconception explains why profiling is often neglected. Yet, this first step shows a much better ratio between performance gain and time invested.

In the rest of this book, a sample application will serve as a reference for two scenarios that we are gradually going to bring to the desired level of performance. This will lead us to show the different aspects of profiling, as well as explaining in depth how it should be done and, particularly, with which tools. This work is traditionally left to a few experts in a team of developers. In practice, however, providing a few fundamental rules are followed, a non-expert developer, without any particular knowledge of .NET runtime internals, can carry out useful profiling. There are two main reasons for this.

- Firstly, many improvements to performance can be made simply by removing common code mistakes, and there is no need to use complex technical solutions to achieve this. For example, running a loop that sends many SQL queries, instead of running only one query and then looping through the results, is a coding mistake. This kind of problem should be obvious from looking at the trace, and any developer is capable of finding this problem and solving it.

- Secondly, experience shows that, very often, the simpler the optimization, the more it improves performance. It is very common to reduce the execution time of a given scenario by one, sometimes two, orders of magnitude by solving its three main problem areas. On the other hand, if one wishes to optimize the process further, it becomes necessary to engage in more complex tuning, involving expert knowledge of .NET internals. For example, the position of variable instantiation in the code can influence the behavior of the garbage collection mechanism, but this kind of high-end profiling requires expert measures and often brings small improvements, making it only necessary as a second phase of the optimization process.

The purpose of the present book is to show that the performance of code is the responsibility of each and every developer working on it, and there is no reason, most of the time, for leaving this to a single technical expert. The cost associated with leaving profiling to later stages of software development is also a good incentive for putting developers in charge of their code's performance.

But this is only possible if each developer knows and follows a few basic rules, without which profiling can quickly become a waste of time or, even worse, counterproductive. I propose five rules:

1. platform stability
2. environment neutrality
3. goals set before analysis
4. measurable improvements
5. descending granularity.

These five rules are explained in more detail in the following sections.

B   Platform stability

B.1   Why such a rule?

It is essential when profiling an application to agree the details of the platform on which we will be working: exact version of the target software, type and version of database, operating system version and main settings, machine specifications, etc.

The reasons behind this are quantitative: to compare analyses taken at different points in time and, in particular, to see if modifications actually improve a scenario, it is essential to be able to trust the numbers, and thus compare them on a level playing field.

Platform stability is particularly important when optimizing code. If, for example, we start using a new version of hardware, it may be useful to run identical tests on the target software using both the old and new versions of the hardware, so that we know the difference that the new hardware makes to performance. We can then account for this change to the platform when comparing new metrics with previous results, and thus measure fairly how our optimizations have improved the code over time. However, once we have recorded metrics on our new platform, we should stick to this platform to keep the tests fair.

B.2   How to apply this rule

A completely integrated software factory, performing source control, compilation, deployment on dedicated hardware, and testing is, of course, the ideal situation in which to apply this rule. This way, a branch of code can be created especially for performance optimization in the exact same platform. This brings two advantages.

First, as with any source control software that supports branching, a team can continue to develop the code while another team takes charge of optimizing a given release. The optimization team will thus stay on stable code, without any risk of the metrics being affected because a bug correction has slipped in unnoticed and altered the test environment.

Second, when you have finished optimizing it is easier to merge branches or cherry-pick code modifications back into the code database. One must be careful when choosing to merge a modification: as a general rule, modifications that apply to any version, and hence will be more likely to be merged back to the main branch, will often be the most complex in terms of the number of lines of code affected.

Generally speaking though, most of the performance-optimizing code modifications will have to be merged back to the main branch, in order to benefit all future versions of the product. The rare occasions when this is not wanted are particular cases in which the improvement makes no sense on versions other than the one it was originally written for. A typical example is a version that has been optimized in a Beta phase with a particular customer, with little or no success. If performance improvements are not high enough or have caused functional regressions, the branch will simply be tagged as dead and never merged back to the main branch of source code. (For more information about branching, see, for example, HTTP://MSDN.MICROSOFT.COM/EN-US/LIBRARY/BB668955.ASPX.)

B.3   Particular cases

It is important not to confuse general software optimization with tuning, which is platform-specific. Stability of the software platform does not remove the need for testing in multiple environments. The software version must definitely be fixed for profiling, but sample customers' setups will vary. We could, and this often happens, improve performance for a customer with a big database, while slightly lowering it for a customer with less data. In this case, the absolute loss on the "light" environment is generally very limited, while it is a very appreciable gain for the "large" environment. In this case, we will of course consider this an improvement and keep it. Having metrics on small environments will allow us to choose the best optimization methods for large ones, while limiting the possible loss of performance on small ones. This might well not affect our choice, but it is important to make that choice in an informed manner.

A good example is the addition of indexes on a database system: on a table with a few dozen lines and very frequent modifications, the time needed to create and update the index would far outweigh the reduction in time when searching the data. But the loss in this case would be only a few milliseconds, whereas the improvement to performance from such an index on a table with a million lines would be huge. So there really is no question as to the utility of the index.

Other cases may appear less clear cut, and this is often the case when deciding whether to use a cache. The threshold of profitability is generally much higher than it is with database indexes, and the usefulness of caches will be the subject of further discussion.

The best way to deal with this kind of situation can be to simply give the customer the option to activate the performance improvement and, if necessary, to adjust the settings. This way, our customers can choose whether to activate it or not, depending on their needs. This is where testing multiple environments using a software integration platform (which, as a reminder, should remain unchanged throughout the optimization process) really gets interesting. Ideally, this would be done for each type of customer. This way, not only do we give administrators options to set the level of an optimization, but in addition we give them the metrics necessary to choose the right setup.

If we push this method even further and carry out optimization tests in a very wide range of possible environments and usages of our application, we could go so far as to provide default settings, adapting the way the application functions to the way it is used, in order to always get the best speed for functionality. This could be done at installation, or even at runtime. This last case is even more sophisticated, because it promises a customer the best benefits at any time of running, without them having to adjust the settings themselves.

B.4   A real-life example

Let's take the example of an extraction and transformation mechanism manipulating XML data and, in particular, of a sorting action. Depending on the size of XML, on the CPU used, and the available RAM, we could achieve better performance using a memory-based sorting algorithm, manipulating directly an XML DOM with a QuickSort algorithm, or even using the `xsl:sort` function included in the XSL/T parser. After numerous tests in different conditions, we are able to determine the best choice in light of the context, and thus it is possible to include this choice in our data manipulating algorithm.

But what can we do when no visible pattern emerges from our analyses? The answer could be to use an Artificial Intelligence algorithm, like neural networks or, more suited to this particular case, fuzzy logic.

Creating such a system from scratch is highly complex, and the time necessary for the algorithm to choose the right method for manipulating the data could be longer than the advantage given by making the right choice. At this point in the process, the choice will, without any doubt, be to use the method that gives the best performance on higher volumes of data, for the reasons discussed above. Whatever we choose, one thing is important: appreciating that, while these advanced algorithms are complex to use, the step is far from being as big as is generally thought. To explain this, we have to separate the theoretical part of these systems from their application.

Behind genetic algorithms or Bayesian networks stand mathematical theories that are not accessible without serious study, even if the main concepts are relatively easy to grasp. The real difficulty is in constructing frameworks using these concepts. But we are seeing more and more complete Software Development Kits (SDKs), which encapsulate all the theory behind easy-to-use, simple Application Programming Interfaces (APIs). Open source .NET libraries like AForge make it possible for non-expert users to use advanced genetic algorithms or Bayesian networks in their applications. They are only a few hundred kilobytes in size, and come with examples that show how extremely simple they are to use. In short, a developer should not be put off by the complex and academic appearance of these technologies. They certainly are sophisticated tools, but Open Source developers have put a lot of effort into masking their complexity behind simple APIs. If one adds that these frameworks are free and available in .NET, it would be a shame to do without. In addition to bringing technical solutions for better (sometimes extraordinarily better) performance, they also offer a great marketing advantage.

B.5   Link to maintainability

Maintainability of the code should be taken into account when optimizing. The worst case scenario would be to optimize a process by a few percent, but at the same time introduce a showstopper bug. And if this functionality is so complex that it would take a lot of time to analyze and correct each of its side effects, we will have to revert to the original code. This kind of bad code should be something of the past if you have adopted modern methods of code analysis and you carry out regular reviews. However, in heavy, industrial applications that have been running for a long time, examples of bad code definitely remain, and one has to bear this technical debt as long as it has not been refactored out. Any developer will have heard, at least once in his or her career, something like "this part of the code is really complex, and only X or Y is able to make corrections to it." This situation should be avoided if possible, because there is always the danger that X or Y will break a leg, become ill, or go to work in another company, leaving you in an uncomfortable situation.

It appears from experience that this kind of situation is over-represented in the field of performance optimization. Thinking about it, this should not be surprising: writing quick-executing code is sometimes a daunting task.

We should forget as quickly as possible the idea that what is simple should run fast. Let's take the example of a cache: the simplest approach would be to always compute the value that we need, and not use a cache. Integrating a cache to the code, even in its simplest form, will require additional lines of code, deferred function calls, etc.

Simple code is often much easier to maintain, as well as being quicker to write. Apart from highly obscure code, understanding 10 lines of code will always be easier than understanding 100 lines. All this leads us to the conclusion that optimized code will always be more difficult to maintain, as is noticed every day by numerous teams of developers.

Luckily, this problem is mostly solved by the principle of platform stability: we should always optimize stable code, typically at the very end of the programming process, just before the release. We should never start analyzing performance of code in which we know there are still bugs to be corrected. It is possible that the corrections will stop the optimized code from working or even lead to the reverse, slowing down execution. Let's imagine that we have optimized some code that calculates a complex financial computation every second, and that a change in the specification results in the function being called only once a day. All efforts made in order to improve the execution time of the function by a few milliseconds will be rendered useless, since the function will now only be called once in the morning and kept in cache for the rest of the day.

Thus, maintenance complexity of optimized code is not really an issue: if the rule of platform stability is respected, only code upon which there will not be any further development will be optimized. The fact that maintenance of the code becomes more complex is less important because we should not need to edit this code anymore. This rule is also an advantage during the optimization process. When using stable code, we are supposed to have good test coverage, which is nice because there is no other time when we will need this safety net more than when optimizing code, which sometimes results in massive refactoring.

To put it in a nutshell: "Premature optimization is the root of all evil" (Donald Knuth).

C   Environment neutrality

C.1   The principle

Environment neutrality is the second basic rule in software performance optimization. It can look similar to the first rule about platform stability, but it is in fact quite different. The previous principle concerned keeping the code, and the software and hardware on which it is being profiled, stable so that metrics can be compared fairly over time. The present principle, by contrast, is about controlling any extraneous factors (such as other applications running on the machine) that may affect the environment (or rather the environments, as explained above) in which the code is executed and profiled.

It is, of course, important that there are several environments, and that these cover the field of application of our piece of software. For example, if our product can be installed on several brands of database engine, and we want to improve the performance of a SQL query generator, we will have to ensure that the improvements are tested on all the database engines we are compatible with. We could indeed realize, during the tests, that a change to the code leads to an improvement to performance on one database engine and to the opposite on another one.

On the other hand, each environment should be as neutral as possible, which means it should have the smallest, or at least a stable, impact on the performance metrics. This point should be explained in more detail: it is impossible for the environment not to have an effect on performance. The CPU we use, the amount of available RAM, even the operating system used, will all have an impact on the measured performance of our application. But it is of paramount importance that this impact remains as stable as possible over time. For example, if our application uses Internet Information Services (IIS), it is logical that fewer resources are available when IIS answers to requests, but this is part of the measured system and, moreover, these resources will be used in a more or less deterministic way during our test scenario.

Taking this to the extreme, we could carry out performance tests on a machine where the CPU is twice as powerful during the first half of an hour as it is in the second, provided that we always start our performance tests at the same point in the hour. Getting caught in such extreme situations is obviously not recommended. Below, we discuss a few things which should be checked to ensure as neutral an environment as possible.

C.2   Virtualization

Many platform editors give assurances that virtualizing has only a tiny impact on systems' and applications' performance, most of the time providing studies to prove this. This is true, but only in the conditions set up for those studies. First of all, the performance of a virtual machine is comparable to its physical equivalent (the host machine) if considered as an average, as is the case when considering the number of transactions per hour on a web server, or the number of SQL queries served in a minute. In some cases, performance may even be higher.

Furthermore, virtualization is indeed performance-equivalent if the whole of a physical machine is dedicated to a virtual machine. This makes sense if you're trying to show a good return on investment by consolidating servers. However, this is not usually what happens in performance profiling, where virtualization is often used to set up new environments quickly, which will be independent from other environments and, moreover, as neutral as possible (see above). Sadly, resources are always shared by hypervisors like Microsoft Hyper-V or VMWare ESX.

And this is where virtualization affects the second principle of performance profiling: when the hypervisor dedicates a complete physical CPU to the virtual test machine, results can indeed be quite stable. But if we use more virtual CPU than what is physically available, the hypervisor will be in charge of balancing the CPU slots between the machines and it will at times give less CPU power to our test machine, in an unpredictable way. The tests will be affected, and the quality of the metrics will be insufficient for us to analyze them.

Another intrinsic feature of virtualization can be a source of problems on performance tests, depending on how the profiler measures the time. Indeed, contrary to a physical machine where an oscillating crystal regulates the processor ticks, a virtual machine can only count on an emulated clock which, depending on the use of resources, can sometimes get behind reference time by a few milliseconds, or even more. When simply using an application, this will be of no importance, but when profiling, with every millisecond being important, this is a potential problem.

C.3   Remote desktop

Care should be taken never to profile a Graphical User Interface (GUI) application through a remote desktop application, using Remote Desktop Protocol or a similar system. When connecting to a machine remotely, the screen render that we see is a copy of the screen render that has been computed on another machine. But the display server will not consider the rendering complete when the last part of the content has been rendered. Instead, it will wait for a reply from the client confirming that the last pixel has been updated remotely.

In .NET terms, this means that the time taken by the `Paint` method will take into account the transit of the screen description from server to client. If the Remote Desktop Protocol is sent on a Virtual Private Network running at 512 Kilobytes per second, what will happen? Put simply, the `Paint` method will be measured as taking almost a second, instead of 30 milliseconds or so when profiling locally. Since the network speed can be highly variable, it becomes impossible to get a precise idea of the time needed to refresh the display. We will see later that there are other reasons that make display speed profiling complex, but this is already a good reason in itself for not using a remote desktop when profiling a GUI application.

C.4   Effects from external caches

IIS and ASP.NET, among other servers, have a slow start compared to their normal speed of operation. The first call to a website on an ASP.NET server, for example, may require C# compilation, followed by JIT (Just In Time) compiling to create the machine code from the Microsoft Intermediate Language, and finally the loading in memory. The time required to set up the request pipeline should also be added to this initialization time.

In short, one given operation can take a lot more time if it is run just after the server has been booted up rather than after some previous calls. Two solutions are possible.

We could decide that the first call is part of the user experience, and it is important to reproduce this behavior in our tests. Thus, performance trials will start with a reset phase that will put the context in its initial state. For example, in the case of a web service, we could kill the ASPNET_WP.exe or W3WP.exe process.

We could also consider that this time should never be taken into account in our tests, as the server is supposed to work 24 hours a day. Thus, we should always make an initial function call that will be excluded from the measurements. This is typically done in initialization scripts, paying particular attention not to forget any web services.

The cache effects we are talking about in the present chapter are effects we can work on a bit. It is indeed quite simple to run or stop processes corresponding to ASP.NET or IIS. But there are several levels of cache over which we have no control, in particular operating system caches (such as I/O, RAM, and SWAP). Going even further into the architecture, there are also caches inside the CPU, on the server bus, and so on. Short of a complete reboot between tests, it seems difficult to purge all of these cache mechanisms. Luckily, the deeper into the computer architecture we go, the smoother the effects of the cache are on our scenarios. CPU time is usually measured in nanoseconds, so a discrepancy at this level is insignificant when analyzing performance measured in seconds.

C.5   Antivirus software

Antivirus systems are the plague of performance profiling. Their unpredictable behavior, the fact that they call kernel functions, and their relative instability in terms of resource use make it very hard to perform profiling on a system containing one.

We can only recommend not installing any antivirus software on a server used for profiling, rather than just deactivating it. Indeed, most antivirus systems automatically reactivate for security reasons. The rationale behind this is that while the user should be able to disable the antivirus temporarily for particular tasks, there is a risk that the user will then forget to reactivate the system. Even uninstalling an antivirus can cause problems, so it is best to never install them on performance test servers. Obviously, this means that this server should be independent from the rest of the LAN, or at least made inaccessible from the outside by the firewall configuration. Anyway, it is generally speaking good that the profiling system should be as isolated as possible.

C.6   Other profiling tools

This may sound obvious, but one should not use another profiling tool when a profiler is running. Of course, most developers would not think of running two profilers at once, but there are some other tools, the functioning of which we are not necessarily aware of.

Using too many Windows performance counters can change the profiler's measurements. They generally do not cause huge slowdowns, but enough to affect the consistency of performance tests.

IntelliTrace can be a much bigger problem. IntelliTrace is a mechanism that appeared in Visual Studio 2010. To put it briefly, it allows a developer to debug an application after an interaction has been executed. Standard debugging is about controlling the state of memory during the execution of the code. IntelliTrace allows one to see where the code went, what were the values of variables, etc. *after* the execution.

IntelliTrace works by collecting data about the execution of every method, recording every change of every variable. All this can seriously slow down execution. It is not unusual to notice execution times going up two-fold or more.

When using Visual Studio 2010, debugging is done through IntelliTrace by default (note, though, that it is only present in the Ultimate version). If a profiler attaches to a process that runs under the control of IntelliTrace, the metrics may be radically different from an independent profiling session. As a result, it is recommended that you disable IntelliTrace when profiling from Visual Studio.

C.7   Miscellaneous services

A profiling environment is not necessarily a system in which all services should be stopped if they have no relation to the target application. But we do have to control the use of resources by these services.

For example, it is no use deactivating remote access on such a machine, as this can be very helpful for setting up test environments, gathering reports, etc. When running tests, since we will always be connected locally (see reasons above), this service will not consume any resource.

By contrast, care should be taken with other services like those supporting index-based search, as we never know when they are going to start crawling our system, or how much resource they are going to consume. Those are enemies of a truly neutral environment.

In cases where services cannot be disabled, for example because of lack of administrative rights, their effects can be countered by running the same test as many times as necessary to get stable metrics, or even to detect abnormal results and exclude or smooth them.

C.8   A comparison with nanotechnology

A parallel can be drawn between platform neutrality and nano-engineering. In the past, it was accepted that too many factors came into play in the finish of the machining of a mechanical part, and that ultimately it was impossible to achieve micrometer range. Even with diamond tools and highly-rigid machine bodies, the vibration from a truck passing a hundred meters away would be enough to make the machining irregular.

A very talented scientist, Richard P. Feynman, then claimed in a famous speech given in 1959 ("There is plenty of room at the bottom") that there was no scientific reason why machining could not be absolutely perfect, providing that one finds all the sources of disturbance and eliminates them. A complete range of technologies emerged in the following years, including air-cushion mounted machines, vacuum machining, harder-than-diamond materials like CBN (Cubic Boron Nitride), among others. As predicted by Feynman, it became possible to machine parts with near-atomic precision. To describe such a finish in layman's terms, consider that two such parts would be welded together irreversibly simply by pressing their faces against each other.

In my view there is absolutely no reason why what has been achieved in mechanical engineering could not be achieved in computer science. If we suppress all the side effects described above, as well as all others that might arise when profiling, we could obtain metrics that would be absolutely precise in one test, without a need for averaging these results over numerous tests.

Considering that high levels of predictability in computing are sometimes a problem, for example, when trying to generate a random number, it would be a shame not to take advantage of this predictability when it can serve our needs.

D   Goals set before analysis

Out of the five performance profiling principles, the third could be considered the least important. After all, we can run a performance improvement program without fixing specific goals, and simply state that we are to do our best in a certain amount of time. We would then simply decide on the time to be spent instead of the percentage of time-reduction to be achieved in a particular use case. Even in the case where we wish to take all the time necessary to improve the performance of our application, we will need to plan for a release before our customers decide it has taken too long and go to our competitors. In short, whichever way we go, we have limits to take into account.

As for any software development, we can act on three parameters.

1. Quantity of improvement: what are your goals in terms of time spent on given scenarios? Do you want to reach less than three seconds between launching the application and seeing the login form? Should a given process be run in less than one second? Should the GUI stay reactive when the user opens a page that is going to take half a second to appear?

2. Time: how much developer time do we want to use to achieve a set of goals, and how are we going to sort them by order of priority in this case? Do we accept that some of those with low priority may stay unresolved?

3. Quality: this is generally the last criterion one should play with, and it is good practice to leave it untouched. But we have all had to compromise at some point on testing, documentation or code maintainability to release a long-awaited performance improvement to our customers. This should, of course, be done as a last resort, and we should reserve enough time to bring the quality back up to our normal standards as soon as possible after the release.

No sensible developer would start working on a task without having a precise idea of what they should achieve, and how long they have to do so. The same holds true for performance improvement, since it is a development activity like any other. Of course, objectives appear to be easier to describe. The function already exists; it is only a matter of making it quicker. But how much quicker? How far should we take the optimization? Typically, three seconds is a rule of thumb for a user interaction. Should we go lower? How much lower? What about bulk treatments? What do we consider to be the right time per unit?

It is always tempting for a project leader to define a goal, not in terms of performance gain, but in terms of time invested: "reduce the time of this function, but spend no more than three days on it." This approach is flawed, primarily because the very first improvement could take only a few hours to be more than enough to satisfy even our most demanding customer. What is the point of keeping a developer digging in the code, trying other methods, at the risk of introducing regressions to the code? Should they not start working on some other, more productive, task instead?

The inverse is also true: optimizing a software application, even if some simple recipes exist (and this book is here to show that such recipes are not restricted to experts), remains a question of finding the faulty code. In an application with a million lines of code, it takes a good profiler, trained eyes and a bit of luck to find the right correction quickly. It is much more difficult to predict how much time will be required to correct code rather than write it. To continue with the example above, it would be a waste of time stopping a developer after three days when the profiling and analysis have been done, and the diagnostics are 80% complete. The solution is almost certainly just a few hours away.

These examples are to remind project managers and product managers of a truth that they have great difficulty in listening to: it is particularly difficult to keep performance improvements within a timeframe and, for optimization to be successful, goals must be set in terms of how long a particular use case should take. Whatever happens, an optimization process will be stopped when the time allocated to it has passed, but this limit must not become the goal per se. Most of the time, results are quick to come: this whole book is based on the fact that a few standard mistakes, relatively easy to find, account for a big part of performance problems. The stereotype of an expert exploring the code for months to unearth some fine-tuning to improve performance by a few percent is only true for software that has already received long-running attention. On any standard data

Chapter 1: Profiling Principles

management application, a well-equipped developer can produce miracles in a few weeks. And they will always be proud to announce that they have reached the goal in four hours instead of three days, at which point we can challenge them to reach another step or add some functionality in the remaining time.

But the rule is important: we should never start an optimization campaign without quantified goals. At best, we would be losing time and, at worst, we would get mediocre results.

E   Measurable improvements

E.1   The reason for this rule

Quantified goals require tools to measure them. This rule is certainly the simplest of the five principles, at least to explain: when conducting the performance test for an application, we have to establish what we will be measuring, and how.

The "what" relates to scenarios: which user interactions take the longest? What bulk treatments get on your users' nerves, or have them leaving their desks to go and have a coffee while your software crunches numbers? Often, your Quality Assurance team will give you the answer, and help you to identify the scenario. Sometimes, your customers will tell you directly, and in this case it is obvious that the improvement should be made even more quickly.

41

E.2 How to apply this rule

The "how" is up to us: we can choose to add software timers between a button click and the results appearing on screen, or we can ask a QA tester to use a manual stopwatch and run a few tests on our application. Let's not underestimate the latter solution: it is obviously less precise, but profiling is not perfect either. And when a customer complains about an interaction being slow, they are generally talking about seconds and not milliseconds. Manual stopwatches also have other advantages that more than compensate for their smaller degree of precision.

- Profiling is made very simple: there is no need to instrument the software, activate traces, use a profiler or attach a debugger. We simply run the application as is, and we time it. The scenario may be run several times to check whether subsequent tries are quicker (which is often the case, because of cache mechanisms), and in order to gain more precise metrics, by averaging them. It does not get much easier than that!

- "Human eye" watching is also interesting, in that it captures the feel for slowness. When instrumenting the code for a given computation, for example, the time recorded only relates to the actual number crunching, and a server developer may overlook that the results have to be sent to the network, and then displayed on the GUI, which takes additional time, particularly if the volume of the answer is not well constrained. How do we know this is not precisely where our performance problem lies? A human tester with a manual stopwatch will be closer to what the customer feels, as they will only hit **Stop** when everything is displayed and they have regained control. Maybe, as developers, we would have forgotten to take into account display time, but the tester will not. It always pays to put oneself in the customer's shoes.

E.3   A real-life example

When analyzing a particularly long business-related software process, a conversation with a developer in the server team, illustrated with a demonstration of his unit tests, convinced me that the problem lay somewhere else. Maybe a slow network on customer premises? Apparently not, because the QA team had successfully reproduced the problem at our own site. After putting traces in the GUI application, it was confirmed that the client indeed received the process log a few seconds after the process execution. But this log was sent in XML, and a complex process in XSL/T on the client side was taking some time before letting the rest of the process go on. Overall, the server process was taking a minute or so, but the tester had to wait over 180 seconds before being able to scroll through the log. The improvement of the client-side process was done by using streamed XML instead of loading the logs in a RAM-based DOM.

F   Descending granularity

F.1   A short story

The reader may have already heard the story that life is like a jar of rocks. When we start filling a jar with sand and pebbles (the least important things in life), there is no more space for big rocks (the important things in life). Whereas when we start by putting rocks in the jar, we can then fit a few pebbles around them, and then pour sand into the remaining cracks.

The same goes for profiling: when a developer starts by improving the least-used functions, or functions that account for a small amount of time in the scenario, they will sometimes find that all this work is undone by the next improvement to the code. Conversely, if they optimize the code starting with the main issues, they will come across the smaller ones step by step, without compromising what has already been done.

F.2   Example

Let's take the example of an application that takes too much time to load. Profiling indicates that library loading is too slow, by two seconds. We start optimizing this part of the code, and after a lot of work, succeed in bringing it down to one second. But this is not enough and we decide to load the libraries in a parallel thread when the user enters his or her details in the login form. The last login is suggested and often used, but the user always has to enter his or her password, and the security requires that it is at least eight characters long. On average, this takes three seconds, which means we have three seconds for library loading, and the time spent reducing the initial two seconds to only one has simply been wasted.

This does not mean that this work should be trashed: maybe one day we will load many more libraries and will be happy to have found a way to get this done in less time. But if we have spent three days analyzing the loading of libraries and optimizing the code, and we have risked delaying an important release to our customers, this was clearly a mistake. In performance optimization, as in any other area of computer science or even more so, perfection is sometimes the enemy of good.

F.3   A word of warning

This rule may well be the most difficult to follow of the five principles. All these principles are about common sense, but this one in particular necessitates a critical eye, and should be borne in mind throughout the analysis. The principle of a fixed platform can be satisfied by good organization at the start, with the help of automated tools, and we will not have to think about it when actually profiling. By contrast, the present rule is difficult to apply because we sometimes have no idea beforehand about the granularity of the code. It is sometimes discovered alongside the actual profiling process.

Something to take care of before optimizing a particular method is to find all its callers, and to see how the calls are made. If it is called in a loop, the first thing to check is whether the loop can be reduced. It is a common code mistake to call a function that will send the same result in a loop, instead of storing the result in a variable at the beginning of the loop and using it for the rest of the process. If this is the case then, even if the function is abnormally lengthy, we will get better results by suppressing calls rather than shortening execution time. And we can always reduce the execution time afterwards if necessary.

In order to accomplish this recommendation in the code, which enables us, when applied iteratively, to reach the most granular level, we have to start by examining the function declaration. If it is `private` or `internal`, it's our lucky day: we will only have to look in the class or assembly, respectively, to find the callers. In this case, a simple text search or use of the **Find All References** command in the context menu of Visual Studio will be enough to find a complete list of callers.

If the method is marked as `public` or `protected`, we will have to load all the projects that could call the method. Alternatively, if this is too heavy or complex, we could use a tool like NDepend (see Figure 1-2), which is able to analyze all references in our code down to function level, and send back information on the calls between functions (see Figure 1-3).

This rule, although the most complex to apply, is the one that helps the most with getting more benefits from a profiling campaign. To return to the previous example, let us imagine that we have spent three days optimizing the execution time of a function by a factor of three. Suddenly, we realize this function is called ten times in the exact same way, and a few lines of code to store its value would have been enough to divide the complete execution time by ten. Frustrating... and potentially stressful if our customer has been calling every evening to check on our progress. And that is without mentioning the possible bugs introduced into the code because we modified the function itself, instead of just its calls.

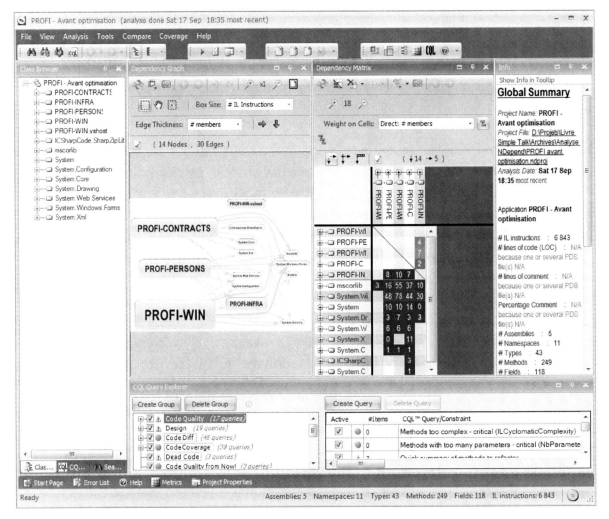

Figure 1-2: NDepend global view.

Some of our readers, in particular project managers who have never been developers, or developers who have only worked on critical applications where high quality is achieved by spending ten times more on development resources, may have a hard time imagining that such an error is possible. Not only is it possible, but I dare say that, sadly, it is quite common, for several connected reasons. The policy that developers should not be overly specialized, so that several people understand the same part of code, is important for maintaining the software. Each developer should be able to take on the task of another and bring continuity to development. But the flip side of the coin is that the code loses homogeneity, because fewer people have a high-level view of the business process and data stream. This, linked with the notion of reusability, which is also good per se, causes problems. A developer may use a function created by someone else without worrying about the way it works internally. On simple business management software, we cannot honestly criticize them for this. But what if this function in a subsequent version calls a web service, or any other time-consuming operation? The callers will still be persuaded a simple call to a read function could not be a performance problem, although it definitely is, in reality. If another developer joins the project and adds a loop around this process without fully analyzing its behavior, the code can quickly become a performance mess.

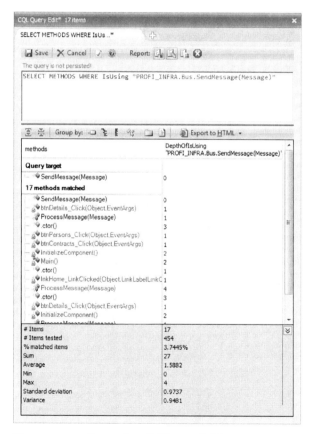

Figure 1-3: Example of NDepend CQL query to retrieve callers.

F.4   Who's the culprit?

Who is responsible for a function that is too slow for standard usage? The developer, clearly. Developers are responsible for the quality of what they write, and this includes performance. It is their duty to test carefully any new function they plan to call. Referencing it in their own code makes them jointly responsible for the content of the function. Even if the source code is not available to the developer, they should benchmark the function by creating unit tests that will also help in detecting potential bugs introduced by future versions in the scenarios.

But establishing responsibility is not enough to incur liability. Developers should be responsible for what they produce, but only within the limit of the time that has been given to reach the required quality level. If we give a developer two days to create a text-box component with automatic spell-checking, they will obviously not create a high-performance system from scratch, but rather use an existing off-the-shelf component. We cannot reproach them for not running a full set of performance tests on it in this time frame.

It is also the responsibility of the project manager to organize their team in such a way that the person responsible for a given component always has an overall understanding of the component, even if not in detail. That person will never know all the code contained by the module if several developers commit code to it, but they will at least keep a critical view of the added functionalities and ensure that the module does not slowly slip outside the initial architecture it has been designed inside. Ideally, every developer should have a day, from time to time, to perform code reviews and remove technical debt. Code quality can also be improved through peer programming. The time required for this is obviously considerable but, again, there is a balance to be struck between functionality and quality, all resources being equal.

Chapter 2: Profiling a .NET Application

A   .NET memory management

A.1   Principles

The .NET platform includes a memory management system, which is in charge of allocating and releasing memory. These two functions work together, but in a very different way to C++ or other languages. Indeed, instead of letting the developer deal with these two operations, .NET takes care of releasing memory. The user allocates memory by explicitly creating instances of a class, using the new keyword, but never explicitly releases it. That is the role of a .NET module called the garbage collector (GC). The GC analyzes and frees memory when it is no longer being used, making it available for the application to use. Such systems use complex heuristics to accomplish this in an efficient manner. We are going to explain how it works in the following sections.

A.2   Automatic memory management and performance

As with any technology that simplifies the work of a developer, the loss of performance associated with the use of garbage collectors has been the subject of controversy. Rather than go into these discussions, let us return to the simple principles of performance improvement in software applications, as discussed at the beginning of this book. It is possible to make slight gains in performance by managing memory manually, but it takes expertise. Even seasoned developers make memory management errors in C++, and memory management can take up a considerable amount of development time. In short, yield is bad and, in most cases, we will benefit from using automated memory management and GCs.

A.3   Real time: a case apart

A.3.a   Remedying a misunderstanding

However, there is one area in which GCs cause real issues: real-time applications. It is important to discuss this, because confusion between speed and real time is partly to blame for the negative press regarding performance of languages with automatic memory management.

Real-time programming is defined by the fact that the time required to perform functions is precisely known in advance. A particular call will have a predictable execution time. This way, when a function is called, the system will know how long it will take to perform it by adding up all the individual times. The concept of real time stops there, and does not extend to performance in terms of quickness of execution.

Risk management theory

Real-time programming has strong links to risk management theory. A given risk, in mathematical terms, is described by the equation: Risk = Probability × Severity. Let us apply this to the case of a program that must react in a given time, and suppose there is one chance in a thousand that in the course of a day it will not happen. This is the probability. If severity is weak (for example, the user just has to wait half a second longer), the total risk is acceptable. If, by contrast, lives are at stake, the risk would obviously be too high.

Again, a misunderstanding is the source of the false connection between real time and performance. Real time is used a lot in the aeronautic and satellite industries, but not for reasons of performance. It is a source of surprise for many non-specialists to learn that industrial processors are often run at a much lower clock speed than general-purpose computers. In a mainstream laptop, the CPU operates at a few billions of operations per second (we talk in gigahertz), but at the price of a thermal envelope that needs dedicated fans to bring fresh air for cooling. Indeed, the heat of a processor increases exponentially with the frequency of operation. In an industrial environment, where robots are exposed to dust and debris, it is obviously essential that the processor is in a sealed case. As a result, these processors work at a much lower clock speed, typically a few tens or hundreds of megahertz. This way, much less heat is generated and the processor can be kept in a safe casing.

The risk of overheating is also connected to material failure, but modern processors are able to warn the system automatically, or at least shut down, before they melt. This sort of behavior would obviously not be acceptable on an airplane. The processors embedded in airplane commands run at a low clock speed so as to ensure they do not overheat from normal functioning. The only way the processor could reach such high temperatures is if the plane were on fire. And in that case, it is better to keep the flight controls (a vital function) for as long as possible, until the processor melts anyway, from internal or external heat.

We are at the heart of the concept of real time: whatever the situation, real-time applications must go on working in a predictable way, as planned. But again, performance is not really an issue in this case: an airplane will not be safer with a processor running at 1 GHz rather than 1 MHz. Quite the contrary, in fact. In terms of speed of reactions, supposing for example that it takes ten operations or so to send a command, the difference in execution time will only be in the order of a millionth of a second. Absolutely negligible. Conversely, even if there were only a one in a million chance per hour that a high-speed processor would automatically shut down because the sun was shining too hard on its casing, would we be willing to board a plane with such a processor, knowing that a modern airplane flies for around 100,000 hours in its lifetime?

A.3.b   Unpredictability of garbage collection

This is why the technology behind garbage collection is incompatible with real time, and why one will never see a "Powered by .NET" label on airplane controls. Since memory management is in the hands of the system instead of the developer, it is impossible to know in advance when the garbage collection will be activated. .NET may choose to run a garbage collection because the operating system indicates that it requires memory, or because its own algorithms predict that memory needs to be freed.

The time sequence in Figure 2-1 shows memory allocation (white rectangles) and memory release operations (filled rectangles) in an application where the developer is in charge of memory management, and incorporates release operations in the code.

Figure 2-1:   Memory allocation and release in an explicit memory management system.

Every time the application or process is run, the position of the release operations stays the same.

By contrast, Figure 2-2 shows the same treatment coded in an environment where the runtime is responsible for freeing up the memory. Filled rectangles, in this case, represent the GC firing up.

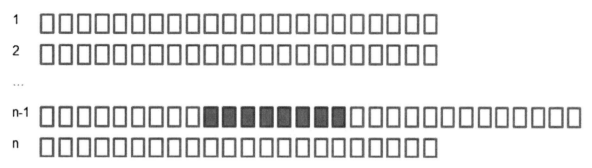

Figure 2-2: Memory allocation and release in a garbage collection based system.

Memory recycling is unpredictable: the GC executes when the runtime decides it should. During some processes, it will not start at all. At other times, it may operate at the end of the process, or at the start, or even right in the middle of it if necessary.

The garbage collecting mechanism is much more complex than it may appear at first. Despite being fundamentally unpredictable, it will always try to execute at the best time: sometimes waiting for the end of a user interaction, sometimes when the CPU is being used less. It will even launch itself in a separate thread in order to have the least possible impact on the current application. Finally, sophisticated mechanisms (which we will cover in detail later) allow it to execute as fast as possible, by scanning only the parts of the memory that are most likely to contain spaces which could be freed.

Despite all this, a small risk remains that the GC will kick in right in the middle of the user interaction and slow it down. Most of the time, the user of a typical application will not even notice that the server has taken a second longer to run a command. By contrast, there cannot be even the smallest risk of a plane not reacting to flight commands during that same second.

Clearly, real-time applications are extremely different from standard ones. Test and validation levels for them are obviously much higher, specific software and hardware platforms are used to develop them and, moreover, their development takes much longer and is more costly.

To return to "normal" applications (those that do not need to operate in real time), the reader can be assured that loss of performance due to automatic memory management is a myth. There are indeed slowdowns, but they are almost never noticeable to the user. Moreover, the use of the GC greatly reduces memory leaks, whereas only an excellent level of coding or additional expertise would guarantee the same in C++, both of which carry high costs.

GC quicker than explicit memory release?

Analysis of Figure 2-2 can lead to the following observation: since the application in most cases does not recycle memory during the normal execution of a simple interaction or command, is it possible that a .NET application could be quicker than a C++ application? Well, this is indeed the case: benchmarks have shown that, in operations limited in time and consuming lots of memory, processes can occasionally be quicker in .NET than in C++. And if the application has some periods of relative inactivity that the GC can use, this can be achieved throughout the application. Conversely, if the application is used intensely over a continuous period of time, C++ will perform better. Of course, this is only true if the coding is absolutely perfect in terms of memory management.

A.4   Memory allocation

Having justified automatic memory release, we will now analyze the opposite operation, namely memory allocation. How does a C# developer reserve memory in .NET?

The `new` keyword is extremely simple to use, although its internal functioning is relatively complex, as we will see below. Let us pretend we have two classes called `Animal` and `Dog` and that the second inherits from the first (see Figure 2-3).

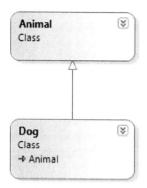

Figure 2-3:   A simple class hierarchy.

The equivalent C# code is shown below:

```
class Animal
{
    public Int16 Mass;

    protected virtual void Eat()
    {
        throw new NotImplementedException();
    }
}
```
Listing 2-1

```
class Dog : Animal
{
    public bool WithCollar;

    protected override void Eat()
    {
        throw new NotImplementedException();
    }
}
```
Listing 2-2

The simplest code to create an instance of **Dog** in memory is the following:

```
Dog test = new Dog();
```

Listing 2-3

To spice this up a little bit (and more importantly, because this will ease comprehension of the following chapter), let us use code that is a little more complex:

```
Animal test = new Dog();
```

Listing 2-4

This line of code is valid because **Dog** inherits from **Animal**. This would also stand true if **Animal** were an interface that **Dog** implements.

Let us now take a closer look at what happens when this particular line of code is executed by .NET. Imagine that we are right at the start of the application. Despite some initializations performed by the CLR (Common Language Runtime), which is .NET's execution engine, we can consider the memory to be empty. The CLR will request memory from the operating system, and place two pointers on it, which will become the starting points of the stack and the heap. The heap is the space in memory where instances of classes will be located, whereas the stack is a short-life, reduced-size memory space used to chain the commands that are executed by the runtime. I will explain these two notions in much more detail below.

For our example, we will represent RAM as a ribbon containing 32-bit (4-byte) spaces (see Figure 2-4).

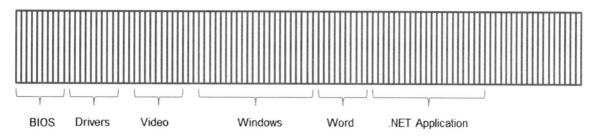

Figure 2-4: Typical occupation of the physical RAM.

The computer BIOS uses one part of the memory, typically at the very beginning of the ribbon, in order to start the system. Hardware drivers are loaded on top, in particular for display and networking. Finally, the operating system (OS from now on) reserves some memory space for itself and allocates the remainder to applications, including .NET applications, which are viewed by the OS like any other process. The only difference being that the OS (and this is the case for Windows too) does not natively recognize MSIL (Microsoft Intermediate Language, the binary content of a .NET assembly). The process is simply a CLR host process, and it is in turn responsible for running the .NET application itself, by compiling MSIL to machine language on the fly. This mechanism is known as JIT compilation.

Let us now take a detailed look at the content of this .NET application (see Figure 2-5).

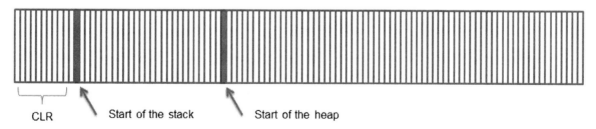

Figure 2-5: Typical occupation of the memory allocated to a .NET process.

The CLR uses a bit of memory at the beginning of the space allocated by the OS, then positions a pointer in memory to represent the stack, and another one to represent the heap. Note that a stack is allocated for each thread.

Coming back to our first sample line of code:

```
Animal test = new Dog();
```

Listing 2-5

The `test` **variable** is a **reference** of type `Animal` to an **instance** of type `Dog`. This simple sentence contains all the concepts we need to describe memory allocation. Let's unpack each word.

- A **reference** is an address in memory. It can be thought of as a metaphorical arrow pointing to a memory slot, but the following section, "How .NET helps us," will explain that a reference is in fact much more than a simple pointer.

- A **variable** is the simple name given to a reference in order to facilitate the developer's work: it allows him to remember an English word instead of a number corresponding to a position in memory. The term "offset" is generally used to identify this position in memory because, depending on the available memory and the other applications running, the OS can allocate any place in the physical memory to a given application. Thus, the only thing that remains unchanged is the distance from the start of the memory pages allocated to this application.

- An **instance** corresponds to the total amount of memory used by an object created by the CLR.

Once again, let us take a closer look at the memory (see Figure 2-6) to see the result of "creating and allocating an instance to a reference" (every word counts).

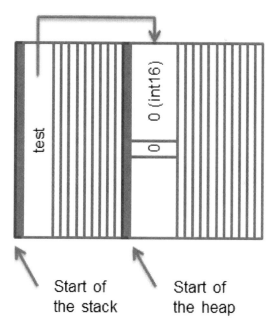

Figure 2-6: Creating an instance and referencing it.

The 16-bit integer corresponding to the mass of an `Animal` uses half of a 4-byte slot. As for the Boolean containing the `WithCollar` member, it uses only a single bit, and is placed immediately after it. Since the `Dog` class inherits from the `Animal` class, an instance of the former logically contains all the members defined by both classes. It is the CLR's job to take care of this. Section A.7 of this chapter, *Working out how much memory is used*, will explain this mechanism in more detail.

The `test` variable uses one slot in the stack. It simply contains the address of the instance itself. Once the CLR has allocated some space in the heap and positioned the stack content on it, it moves the pointer to the next slot (see Figure 2-7). This way, the CLR is ready for the next allocation request.

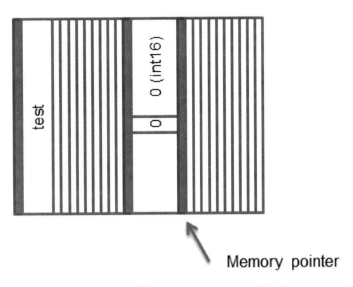

Memory pointer

Figure 2-7: Position of the memory pointer after the process of instantiation.

This simple example of memory allocation already raises several questions about the performance of applications.

- Memory allocation shifts the memory pointer to the right. But memory cannot be released by simply moving it to the left, because different instances do not have the same life cycle. An object instantiated before another could become useless before or after the other, depending on what use is made of it. Yet this pointer cannot continually shift to the right, because no application has unlimited resources.

- In our example, the memory slot is not full: 17 bits out of 32 have been used (a 16-bit integer + a 1-bit Boolean), and the pointer has been moved one slot farther along, as if all 32 bits had been used. This overconsumption can become a problem.

- If the stack is not used much, memory slots will be wasted between the stack and the heap. On the other hand, an application that uses lots of slots on the stack should never overflow onto the heap, as this would overwrite some heap data.

We will see in the following sections how the CLR takes care of all these issues which are related to the performance of a .NET application. We mean performance in the wide sense, because it is not just about speed of execution, but also unreasonable use of memory resources which can slow down an application.

A.5   How .NET helps us

We will now explain further the concept of reference that was introduced above. It is not, as the use of arrows might suggest, a simple pointer to an instance, as would be the case in any language like C or C++ where the developer has complete control over the memory.

By contrast to a reference, a pointer is nothing more than a memory address. If an object uses 4 bytes for a 32-bit integer member, then 2 more bytes for another member, and finally 4 more bytes for a third and final member, the pointer to this object will only contain the memory address of the very first byte, and the application will have to know it should load the first 4 bytes to retrieve the first member, then the fifth and sixth to load the second member, etc. If this object belongs to a list, it will be simpler to reach the next object in the list by offsetting the pointer by 4+2+4 = 10 bytes (see Figure 2-8).

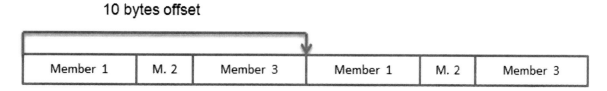

Figure 2-8:   Using a correct offset to read the next object in an array.

What if, instead of pointing to the beginning of an object in memory, a pointer were to point at the next memory slot, as in Figure 2-9? When reading the first member, which is an integer coded on 4 bytes, the last 3 bytes would be used together with the first byte of the second member that follows it, and the values would make no sense. With C++ or any other language using pointers, this mistake is very easy to make, because the developer can move the pointer as they please.

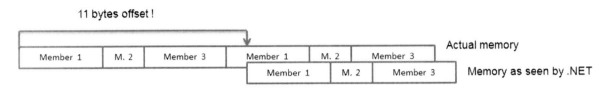

Figure 2-9: Effects of an incorrect offset (this cannot happen in the CLR).

The main difference with .NET is that, unlike C++, it does not allow us to manipulate pointers, only references. Just like pointers, references designate a slot in memory, but they have an additional feature: they know the structure of the type they are pointing to. When the first member is accessed, the CLR takes care of reading the bytes from 0 to 3 and confirming that these 4 bytes really represent a 32-bit integer. In other words, a reference is a type-safe pointer.

This is not something very complex per se, like the garbage collection mechanism, but it is one of the key characteristics of .NET. It makes coding simpler, less prone to bugs, and contributes to better performance of .NET development in general, as algorithms linked to memory use are not at the mercy of poor development.

A.6   Value types and reference types

Discussions about the difference between value types and reference types often lead to confused assertions such as "value types are on the stack, reference types are on the heap" or "values correspond to structures, whereas references correspond to classes." There is truth in both these sentences, but a developer who needs better performance must understand these differences more precisely.

A.6.a   How a stack works

We will start by looking at how a stack works in .NET, using the overly-simplistic example in Listing 2-6.

```
namespace MemoryManagement
{
    class Program
    {
        private static int a = 2;
        private static int b = 3;

        static void Main(string[] args)
        {
            int total = a + b;
        }
    }
}
```

Listing 2-6

To help us understand how the CLR works, and also gain experience with reading MSIL, we are going to use the MSIL Disassembler (ILDASM) tool that comes with .NET SDK. On a standard Vista / Windows 7 installation, you will find it in `C:\Program Files\ Microsoft SDKs\Windows\v7.0A\bin\ildasm.exe`.

Once the application is started, on the **File** menu select **Open** to load the executable containing the code above, in its compiled form. We can also use drag and drop to put the `MemoryManagement.exe` file in the tool. A window similar to Figure 2-10 will then appear.

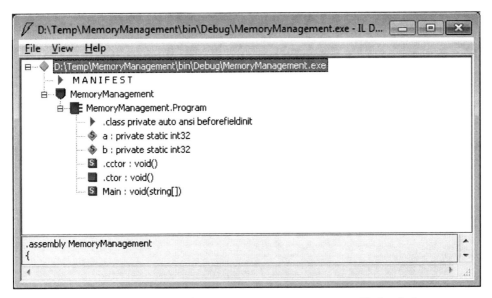

Figure 2-10: ILDASM.exe with the `MemoryManagement` assembly loaded.

Double-click on **Main** to open a window with the disassembled IL code. We use the word "disassembled," because this does not show us the exact binary IL code as it is contained in the executable or library file, but displays it in a form with names corresponding to operations, making it easier to read.

If this code does not look very clear, there is no need to worry: this is the case for most .NET developers, even some extremely proficient ones, and we will unpick the content enough to find out how it relates to the corresponding C# code.

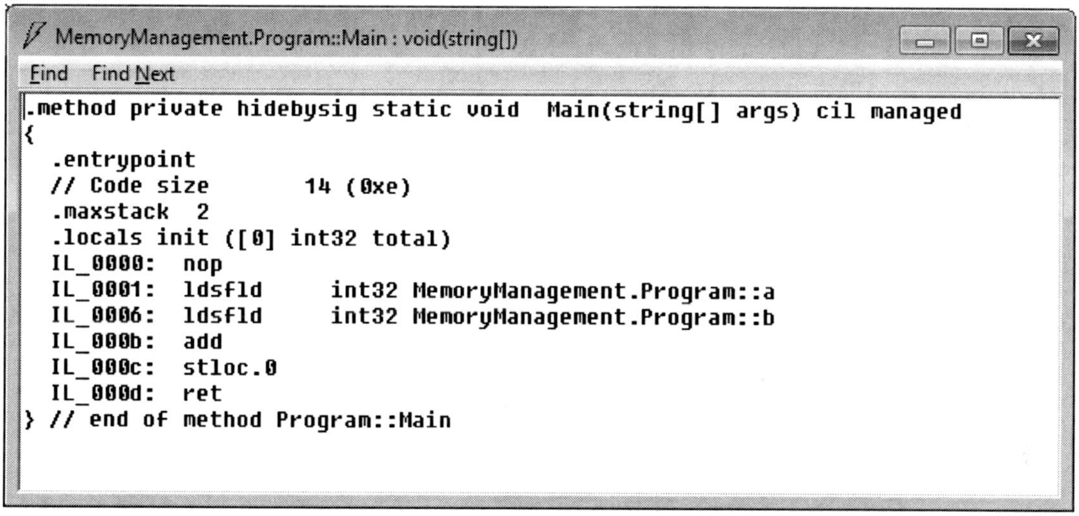

```
MemoryManagement.Program::Main : void(string[])
Find   Find Next
.method private hidebysig static void  Main(string[] args) cil managed
{
  .entrypoint
  // Code size       14 (0xe)
  .maxstack  2
  .locals init ([0] int32 total)
  IL_0000:  nop
  IL_0001:  ldsfld       int32 MemoryManagement.Program::a
  IL_0006:  ldsfld       int32 MemoryManagement.Program::b
  IL_000b:  add
  IL_000c:  stloc.0
  IL_000d:  ret
} // end of method Program::Main
```

Figure 2-11:   Disassembled IL Code for the Main() function.

To understand the stack well enough (it can be puzzling at first), we must explain in a few words how a computer's CPU works. When an application asks the processor to sum two 32-bit integers, a specific instruction must be given to the processor.

In an ideal world, a CPU would have enough pins to accept all input bits and send all the output bits, including the pins necessary to write the instruction to be run (see Figure 2-12).

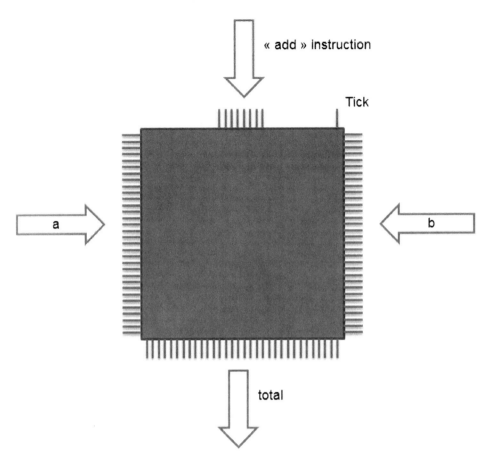

Figure 2-12: Configuration of an ideal processor, adding two 32-bit integers.

But, despite much effort, the ideal processor does not exist, for the simple reason that if we have to double the size of the bus (the "width" of the data accepted) for operations with two parameters, more complex ones with eight parameters would need a 256-bit bus, which would be extremely difficult to manage.

The solution to this problem is to pass the different values in a sequence, one for each tick of the CPU clock, hence the presence of a "Tick" pin. The process starts with storing the first value in a processor register (a "memory slot," but which is located right in the CPU itself, and not in the RAM). See Figure 2-13.

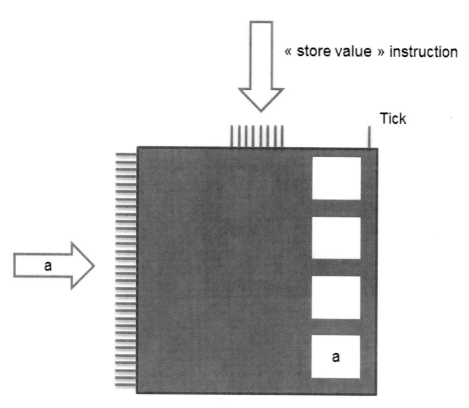

Figure 2-13: Storing value a.

Then, the RAM controller has up until the next clock signal (the "tick" we talked about above) to position the right values on the bus pins (Figure 2-14).

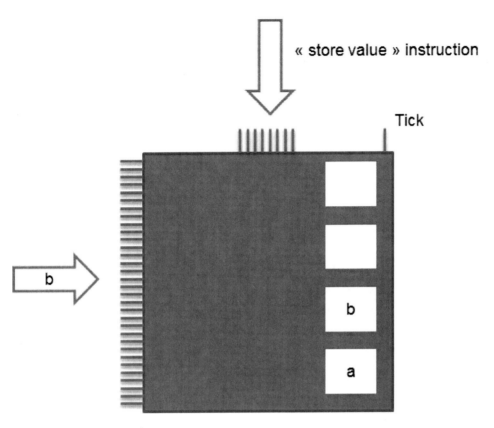

Figure 2-14: Storing value b.

The two values being in the registers, the processor can now receive the **add** instruction. To be more precise, this instruction is a 32-bit code asking it to compute the addition of the two registers that have been used (a CPU typically contains more than two registers). The result is then produced on the bus, as an output. To optimize performance, not only are registers not emptied but, in some cases, the content of one of the registers is replaced with the result, in order to accelerate use of this value in the next step of an algorithm, by not having to reload it from memory and thus sparing one CPU cycle (see Figure 2-15).

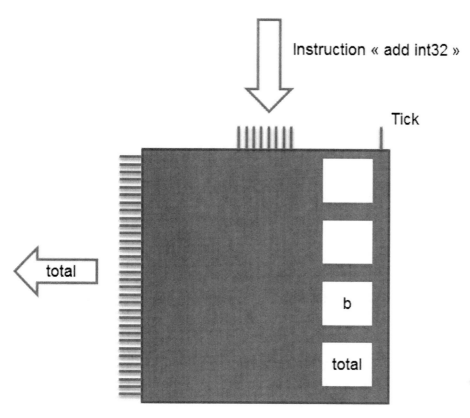

Figure 2-15: Running the add instruction.

A.6.b   Back to the IL code

The principle of a stack is not intuitive, but its existence is made necessary by the fact that the processor can only take one piece of data at a time.

The same mechanism is found in the IL code, which is logical since the IL is quite close to the binary code that is executed by the processor. Returning to the second window of ILDASM, let's break down the lines starting with IL_. Those are the ones containing instructions.

```
.method private hidebysig static void  Main(string[] args) cil managed
{
  .entrypoint
  // Code size       14 (0xe)
  .maxstack  2
  .locals init ([0] int32 total)
  IL_0000:  nop
  IL_0001:  ldsfld     int32 MemoryManagement.Program::a
  IL_0006:  ldsfld     int32 MemoryManagement.Program::b
  IL_000b:  add
  IL_000c:  stloc.0
  IL_000d:  ret
} // end of method Program::Main
```

Listing 2-7

At offset 0, nop means "no operation." This instruction simply does nothing (and, yes, there is a good reason for having such a "do nothing" operation, but the explanation is outside of the scope of this book).

One byte further, we find the first instruction responsible for loading the value of a. This code asks the CPU to take the value of variable a, which is a 32-bit integer, and place it on the stack.

Since this instruction takes 5 bytes, we are now at offset 0006 to load the value of the second variable, b, which will come on top of the preceding value in the stack.

At this point, the content of the memory is as shown in Figure 2-16.

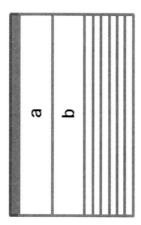

Figure 2-16: Content of the memory before the call to add.

At offset 000b (which is 11 in hexadecimal) one finds the entry for the **add** instruction. This operation code (opcode) corresponds to the addition of the last two integers on the stack (see Figure 2-17). It should be noted that this instruction is coded on only one byte. Once this instruction has been executed, the stack will go down by one level, and will only contain the result, which is also a 32-bit integer.

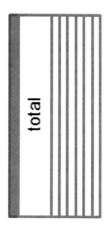

Figure 2-17: Content of the memory after the call to add.

This is when the result is stored. Indeed, at this point of the code, the resulting total is still in the .NET stack, and it should be stored in the memory slot designated by the variable called `total`. In order to achieve this, the instruction `stloc.0` is used. The zero used as a suffix of this instruction corresponds to the index of the local variable as defined in the line `.locals init ([0] int32 total)` shown above. Had we used two local variables, we would for example have seen `.locals init ([0] string result, [1] int32 total)`, and we could have used the instruction `stloc.1`.

The last instruction is simply `ret`, which exits the method.

Maxstack

The IL code also contains a definition of the maximal size of the stack, which in our case is 2 (see maxstack in the IL code above). Actually, this is not the size of the stack itself, but the maximum level of stacking reached by this particular method. In this very simple example, the stack had grown by two memory slots at the peak of stack use by the function. This information helps the CLR when creating the stack.

A.6.c   Difference between value and reference

We can now revert to our initial question, namely the difference between value types and reference types, equipped with a better understanding of the stack mechanism.

When local variables are passed as parameters to a function, we have seen that these variables are stored on the stack. But since the size of a memory slot on the stack is limited, it is impossible to store too complex a piece of data on it. If, instead of an `add` function on two `Int32` variables, we now want to call a method such as `Associate(Person a, Contract b)`, only the memory addresses of these two instances will be stored on the stack for reasons of space.

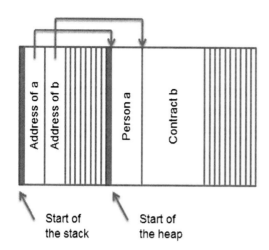

Figure 2-18: Memory state in a function call with two reference parameters.

It is of course possible to mix both modes. For example, let us imagine a function defined as `Duplicate(Person a, int n)`. The state of the stack before execution would be as shown in Figure 2-19.

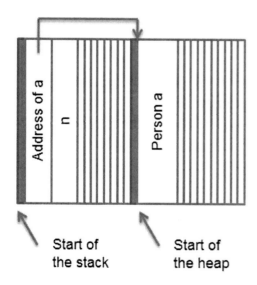

Figure 2-19: Memory state in a function call with a reference and a value parameter.

Value types are simple types that can be represented in memory concisely. Conversely, reference types are those that shouldn't be put on the stack. As a result, the stack will contain just a reference to these objects, the content of which is located on the heap.

This has a profound impact on the way that variables can be modified by the function calls. When a value type is used, it is the value itself that is contained on the stack. Yet this value still exists in the variable that has been used, and the contents have just been copied. Hence, when the data is modified inside the function call, the original variable content will remain unchanged.

```
public void ValueNotModified()
{
    int value = 2;
    Double(value);
    // value is still equal to 2
}

public void Double(int number)
{
    number = number * 2;
}
```

Listing 2-8

When using a complex type (such as a class), the address of the variable is also copied and, of course, its modification would only have a local effect, just like the value above. But since there is a level of indirection, nothing prevents the code of the function from modifying the content of the object pointed at by this address, since it knows its location.

```
class Animal
{
    public Int16 Mass;

    public void ReferenceModified()
    {
        Animal bobby = new Animal();
        bobby.Mass = 10;
```

```
        DoubleMass(bobby);
        // bobby.Mass is now equal to 20
    }

    public void DoubleMass(Animal candidate)
    {
        candidate.Mass *= 2;
    }
}
```

Listing 2-9

Nevertheless, it is not possible to change the address of the variable, as the address itself is copied, so changing it inside the function will not change the original variable.

```
class Animal
{
    public Int16 Mass;

    public void ReferenceModified()
    {
        Animal lucky = new Animal();
        lucky.Mass = 10;
        DoubleMass(lucky);
        // lucky.Mass is unmodified
    }

    public void DoubleMass(Animal candidate)
    {
        candidate = new Animal();
        candidate.Mass = 20;
        // The local reference now points to another instance of Animal,
        // and it is this new instance that we modify. But when returning
        // from the function, the local variable lucky of the calling code
        // will still point to the original instance, which has remained
        // unchanged by the present code.
    }
}
```

Listing 2-10

75

Of course, there is nothing to stop a developer from passing a simple type as a reference. A mechanism called boxing, which we will cover in detail later in this chapter, allows a developer to convert a value from the stack to the heap. In a way, this is what happens when a parameter is preceded by the `ref` keyword, for example, in a function like `ApplyReduction(decimal amount, ref int percent)`(see Figure 2-20).

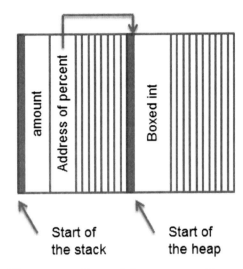

Figure 2-20: State of the memory with a parameter passed using the `ref` keyword.

In this case, the integer can be returned modified:

```
public void ValueModified()
{
    int value = 2;
    Double(ref value);
    // value is now equal to 4
}

public void Double(ref int number)
{
    number = number * 2;
}
```

Listing 2-11

Generally, it is better to use the default mode defined by .NET, which has of, course, been chosen for performance reasons: the fact that the data is available directly in the stack, thus avoiding the need for dereferencing (follow the arrows at the top of Figures 2-18, 2-19, and 2-20) to retrieve the content in the heap, avoids a complex operation, thus reducing processing time. In fact, the advantages are such that a dedicated mechanism has been put in place to execute the inverse operation, namely to make it possible to fit a complex type in the stack in order to gain performance. This is what happens inside structures.

A.6.d   The particular case of structures

Structures (objects defined by the keyword `struct`) are very similar to classes, in that they have members, methods, and, subject to a few restrictions, can have constructors.

The difference is that they are represented in memory as value types: the entirety of their data is stored in the stack. Of course, this approach should be limited to small entities, where it makes sense to speed things up, while staying within a limited memory size. These particular cases do exist. For example, the coordinates of a point represented by two floating point numbers, or a color defined by three short integers (the typical RGB format).

```
public struct Coordinate
{
    float X;
    float Y;

    public Coordinate(float X, float Y)
    {
        this.X = X;
        this.Y = Y;
    }
}
```

Listing 2-12

In terms of memory use, everything is on the stack and nothing on the heap, with all the associated consequences. In particular, the memory contains the values describing the object, and not a reference to an object, which means the object cannot be modified.

Figure 2-21:   Representation of a structure in memory.

This is the main way of making immutable objects, which significantly improve the quality of the code. Indeed, since immutable objects cannot, as their name indicates, be modified after they have been created, they suffer far fewer side effects and bugs due to uncontrolled modification of their members.

A.6.e   Relationship to performance

The improvement to performance from replacing classes with structures should be weighed up carefully. The use case is obviously a factor, but it also depends on the size of structures in memory, and on the amount of modification the business logic will apply to them.

To explain these three parameters further:

- the more intensely a structure is used, or the larger the lists they are in, or if they are read in a loop, the more advantageous a structure will be in terms of performance

- the larger the structure, the more expensive it is to manipulate on the stack; in most cases, a class will still be more advantageous as it can be addressed through a single address block, even though an additional step is required to access the data

- finally, a structure benefits from being immutable, but this is a high price to pay in cases where the content has to be modified, since we will have to create a completely new object with its members defined as needed; this kind of operation is very demanding on the GC.

A.7   Working out how much memory is used

Before studying the main part of memory management from the performance point of view, namely the garbage collection, there is one last point to make on memory allocation, from a quantitative point of view. In some scenarios, it can be useful to have an exact understanding of how the CLR reserves memory when creating an object, in order to try and reduce how much it reserves, or at least analyze it.

Let's start by putting static variables to one side, as these are trivial. Indeed, .NET will allocate a unique memory space for these variables when loading the class that contains them. Nothing worthy of note except, of course, when these variables are decorated with the `[ThreadStatic]` attribute, which means this process of memory allocation will be executed for each and every thread using the class.

The way .NET takes inheritance into account when working out the size of memory needed does not pose any problems either. When an instance of an object is requested, the CLR will analyze the whole dependency tree to come up with a list of all members for each type. No need to use recursion there, since only value types need to refer to the type definition. As far as reference types are concerned, the memory content will simply be the one for a reference.

The only real difficulty in calculating the size of memory to allocate comes from the way .NET organizes memory. By default, it decides the layout of the different members in order to reduce overconsumption. Let's use an example to demonstrate this:

```
public class Set
{
    public short A; // 2 bytes, or 16 bits
    public int B; // 4 bytes, or 32 bits
    public short C; // 2 bytes, or 16 bits
}
```
Listing 2-13

On a 32-bit architecture, memory blocks are 4 bytes in size, and .NET knows how to lay out the members of the class to use the fewest blocks possible. The problem with this mechanism is that the positions of members may change if another member is added in the future. However, when working with external software written in native code, we have to set the layout of the class (or, more commonly, the structure) in a stable way, because their way of reading data from managed code is based on memory pointers. This is achieved by using the attributes [StructLayout] and [FieldOffset]. These two attributes can be found in the System.Runtime.InteropServices namespace.

The minimum required to achieve a fixed memory layout is the following code:

```
[StructLayout(LayoutKind.Sequential)]
public class Set
{
    public short A; // 2 bytes, or 16 bits
    public int B; // 4 bytes, or 32 bits
    public short C; // 2 bytes, or 16 bits
}
```
Listing 2-14

With this code, we are guaranteed that members will be placed in memory blocks in the order in which they are written. As a result, they will not move when we add other members to the end of the definition, and we eliminate the risk of misalignment.

The flip side of the coin is that, since data cannot overlap memory slots, we will have a problem of space optimization. As Figure 2-22 shows, the members sit on three blocks, where in theory two would suffice.

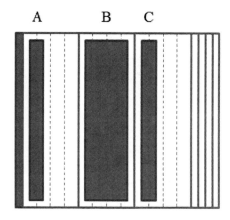

Figure 2-22: Memory occupation in sequential mode.

Luckily, this can be optimized by using the explicit layout mode, which lets us control the positioning of members in memory (Listing 2-15).

```
[StructLayout(LayoutKind.Explicit, Size=8)]
public class Set
{
    [FieldOffset(0)]
    public short A; // 2 bytes, or 16 bits
    [FieldOffset(4)]
    public int B; // 4 bytes, or 32 bits
    [FieldOffset(2)]
    public short C; // 2 bytes, or 16 bits
}
```

Listing 2-15

The result is that we have saved a memory block, while still keeping a fixed memory layout (see Figure 2-23).

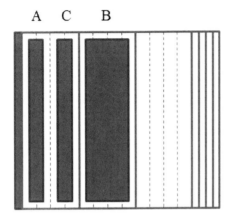

Figure 2-23: Optimized memory occupation using explicit layout.

A.8   Garbage collection

After talking at length in the previous sections about the way memory is allocated by the CLR, it is time to address the more complex part, which is how this memory is freed up by the GC when the CLR decides that it is not being used anymore and should be made available for other uses.

A.8.a   Criteria for memory collection

Before studying the way a GC frees up memory, we should understand the rules that apply when determining whether a particular slot of memory has become useless. As a reminder, the developer is not in charge of memory recycling with .NET; the CLR is. Which means the system must use precise rules to decide when memory is no longer in use.

First, the GC starts with the heap and, for each object found in memory, it will step through every reference. If no references point to this object, then no instructions can reach it. In this case, this is memory we can free up.

But what exactly do we mean by "stepping through references?" There are lots of ways for an object to be referenced:

- it can be referenced by a local variable that sits in the stack

- it can be referenced by a member of another object

- it can be referenced by a static member of a given class.

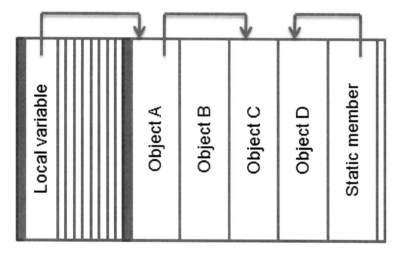

Figure 2-24: Different ways an object can be referenced (or not).

In the example illustrated in Figure 2-24, Object B is not referenced by any variables or members, and is therefore eligible for memory recycling.

There are a number of ways in which an object can lose a reference:

- the code has allocated a null value to the variable that once referenced the object

- the local variable is no longer in the scope of the process that referenced it.

On the other hand, what happens when an object was referenced by another one, and that one is no longer referenced itself? The GC is not concerned by this, as it treats every single object separately, by walking through the whole tree of references, starting from what are called the roots. Roots are variables that are active, typically static members of classes that have been loaded by the CLR, or local variables for the method currently executing. The first step of memory recycling consists of stepping through the tree of references from these roots, and marking as "live" all the objects that are met along the way.

Objects marked as live cannot be recycled, whereas every object that has not been marked is considered unreachable, and therefore can be recycled.

A.8.b   Compacting mechanism

Once objects have been recycled from random locations in the heap, the memory will be left with a lot of gaps, which does not seem very efficient. This is where the second step of garbage collection, called compaction, comes into play. So far, the GC has only marked the unused memory, but the memory allocation pointer (where the next object would be created in memory) is still at the end of the last item on the heap.

The GC then proceeds with compaction, by successively bringing every object on the heap back as close as possible to the beginning of the heap. In our example, Object A will not move, but Object C will move next to A, and D will shift in the same way, and so on (see Figure 2-25).

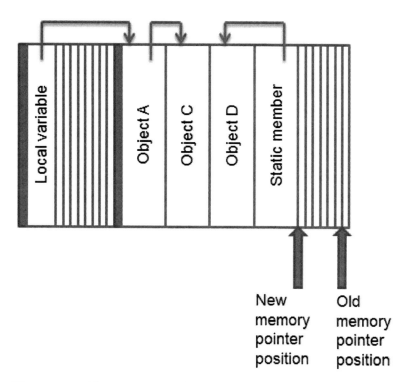

Figure 2-25: Memory compaction.

The space saved by Object B disappearing corresponds to the shift of the memory allocation pointer in the heap. Since this pointer is the place where the next object will be created in memory, we will start again with a compact memory, without any holes. In other words, the memory is not fragmented.

Behind the scenes of defragmentation

The defragmentation process is more complicated than it may seem, since all memory addresses managed by the CLR have to move according to the way the objects shift. In our example, Object C moves, but A has a reference to this object, so this reference has to be updated accordingly. Of course, all this is done by the GC without the developer having to do anything.

A.8.c   Fixed memory and fragmentation

It is not completely true that all memory fragmentation is eliminated by the second step of garbage collection. There exists a particular case of objects stored in the heap that cannot be moved: we call them pinned objects.

An object has to be pinned in memory when it is needed for the purpose of interoperability with a piece of software which is not compatible with .NET. For example, when communicating with COM objects (Component Object Model is an older Microsoft architecture, which uses pointers, usually coded in C++), we have to provide the application with memory addresses. That means we cannot let the GC move these objects around. They should be pinned in memory right from their creation for the external application to be able to read and write to them.

Of course, this leads to gaps in memory. Imagine a memory layout as illustrated in Figure 2-26, with Object C pinned, and Objects A, D and E marked as live (by a star).

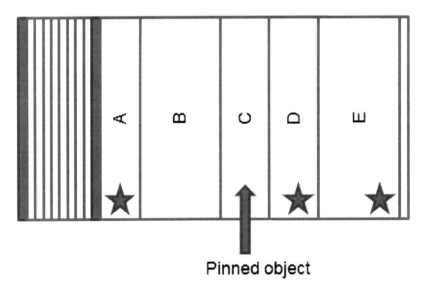

Figure 2-26: Pinned objects.

The compaction step will result in the memory layout illustrated in Figure 2-27.

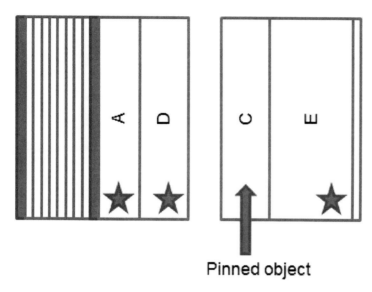

Pinned object

Figure 2-27: Memory layout after compaction.

Object D was small enough to be moved into the gap, but the remaining space could not accommodate E as well. There is now a hole between D and C, because the latter could not be moved to fill it.

This has a considerable impact on performance, because a highly-fragmented memory will cause resource allocation problems. The higher the level of fragmentation, the more additional memory will be used on top of what is actually needed; hence the importance of releasing pinned objects as soon as possible.

We will see in the next sections how to use tools to identify this rate of fragmentation, analyze its value and its evolution and, in particular, to find out which classes are responsible for the fragmentation.

A.8.d Start and execution of the garbage collector

Caution

It is very difficult to predict when the GC will start running. Depending on the context in which the machine is used, a GC pass may be launched every minute, or the whole application may be run without any memory recycling being necessary, simply because there is enough memory for all processes.

From a performance point of view, the GC does as much as it can to reduce its impact on the execution of the application, by running in a separate thread from the main application thread, and under a lower priority. It aims to run when the application is not in much demand from users.

However, when pressure on memory becomes too high, the GC operation will be executed and will temporarily reduce performance. The first rule for high-performing memory management is not to overload the GC. In particular, it is essential to reuse large objects when possible. For example, do not re-create a connection to a database for every request sent to it.

An unrealistic example?

This example of a database connection might sound absurd, but calls to a common function, which is a few levels deeper in the call stack, are enough for an inattentive developer to fall into this trap. Nobody would write code that loops on creation of a connection followed by execution of a command, but it is possible to write a function that executes these two operations at once and, one day or another, someone may call it several times, without necessarily worrying about how it works, or wrongly assuming that it must keep the connection in a cache. A pool mechanism is usually used to mitigate this risk.

The second rule to help garbage collection performance is to reduce the lifetime of objects as much as possible. The reason for this rule is explained in the following section.

A.8.e   Concept of generation

The concept of generation is the most sophisticated process in the .NET GC. Stepping through every reference in the tree (the first step of garbage collection, as explained above) is a potentially long process if a large amount of memory is in use.

Yet, a lot of objects in a .NET application have a life cycle that is basically equivalent to the one of the application process itself. Take, for example, the main window in a WinForms or Windows Presentation Foundation (WPF) application. Also, on ASP.NET servers, objects in charge of session management typically have a very long life. This means that a mechanism that would avoid retesting objects that are still live when the GC runs could be interesting.

Within .NET, this mechanism is called generations. As a general rule, when the GC starts it will only test objects that were not marked as live the previous time. This is what we call a Generation 0 collection. All objects still marked as live are promoted to Generation 1, and they will not be tested the next time we run a Generation 0 collection. This saves a lot of time, because only the objects created since the last garbage collection will be tested.

If the application has retrieved enough free memory through this process, it stops there. But if not enough memory was freed, the CLR will run a higher level collection, which will also test the objects marked as Generation 1. If the Generation 1 object is not live anymore, it will be recycled. If the object is still live, it will be promoted to Generation 2.

A Generation 2 collection (which is a "full" garbage collection, as .NET in its current version only uses three levels, 0 to 2) will only be run as a last resort, when even a Generation 1 collection does not free up enough memory.

This system ensures that long-living objects are moved to the higher generations quickly, where they will rarely be tested. On the other hand, objects with short lives, typically those created and referenced by a local variable inside a low-level function, will soon be removed, as soon as the next Generation 0 collection happens.

A good indicator of the GC's performance is the ratio between the numbers of passes for the different generations. In general, for one Generation 2 collection, it is normal to count tens of Generation 1 collections, and up to a thousand Generation 0 collections. Very often, simple programs may only use Generation 0 for the duration of their process.

A.8.f   Impact of coding over memory recycling performance

The inner workings of the GC have a potentially high impact on performance, not only because it is designed to reduce the time spent on analyzing objects, but also because it gives the developer an opportunity to help the GC get the best out of Generation 0 collections, by the way they allocate new objects and free references.

Indeed, a late instantiation and an early release of objects will limit the probability of an instance moving up the generations, and it will therefore spend less time in memory.

Let us first illustrate the concept of late instantiation, with a block of code that I often come across during audits:

```
public void FunctionNotOptimalForGC()
{
    Animal fido = new Dog();
    Contract help = new Contract();

    #region A

    // Numerous operations on fido

    # endregion

    help.CreateInsuranceOver(fido);
}
```

Listing 2-16

As far as pure execution is concerned, this code does not cause any problems. But let us suppose that the GC fires when the application is executing the code in region A. The instance referenced by the variable help will be found to be live when the roots are analyzed, since this local variable points to it. Therefore, this object will be promoted to Generation 1. If the GC had fired just a bit later, after the end of the function then, because the object of type Contract was only referenced by a local variable, it would have been considered recyclable. Thus it would have had a very short life, freeing memory as soon as possible. Instead, it is in Generation 1 and will stay in memory much longer, despite the fact that we do not need it anymore (and we cannot even access it as we exited the function that contained the only reference to it).

Of course, there is nothing to indicate that the GC will fire when the process executes the code in region A. But let us take a look at a variant of the previous code, which does exactly the same thing (Listing 2-17).

```
public void FunctionBetterForGC()
{
    Animal fido = new Dog();

    #region A

    // Numerous operations on fido

    # endregion

    Contract help = new Contract();
    help.CreateInsuranceOver(fido);
}
```

Listing 2-17

There is still a chance that the GC will run in the middle of the last two lines, and that the instance of Contract will be promoted to Generation 1, but it is a much slimmer chance than in the first version of the code. And in this particular case, we can improve the situation further by removing the local variable help.

```
public void FunctionOptimalForGC()
{
    Animal fido = new Dog();

    #region A

    // Numerous operations on fido

    # endregion

    new Contract().CreateInsuranceOver(fido);
}
```

Listing 2-18

This type of code optimization can be applied the other way around. The performance of the GC will also improve if references to an object that is not going to be used anymore are removed as soon as possible. Let us look at a slightly different example (Listing 2-19).

```
public void FunctionNotOptimalForGC()
{
    Animal fido = new Dog();
    Contract help = new Contract();
    help.CreateInsuranceOver(fido);

    #region A

    // Numerous operations on fido

    # endregion
}
```

Listing 2-19

In the code above, during all the time spent in region A, we had no further use for the instance of `Contract`. It would be a pity to risk the object being moved up to Generation 1 during this time. Therefore, it is good practice to set the variable `help` to `null`, in order to ensure that no object points to the instance of type `Contract`.

This way, if the GC fires when the code is in region A, the instance will be recycled immediately. The code in Listing 2-20 achieves this.

```
public void FunctionOptimalForGC()
{
    Animal fido = new Dog();
    Contract help = new Contract();
    help.CreateInsuranceOver(fido);
    help = null;

    #region A

    // Numerous operations on fido

    # endregion

}
```

Listing 2-20

Keeping expectations low

There is no point expecting miracles from this optimization method. It is basically a coding technique that is relatively easy to learn and get used to, and can only improve the performance of the GC. But there will be little to be gained from rewriting portions of code of a slow application after tracing early instantiations or late releases. At best, the improvements will be hardly visible. This is why this technique is discussed in a theoretical chapter and will not be studied in the practical chapters that form the second part of this book. As explained in the introduction, it is essential when auditing an application for performance to deal as a priority with the few basic errors that will bring the biggest improvements in time. The techniques explained in this section will only be applied as a last resort, when the budget and time available justify spending quite a lot of time on saving the last tenth of a second.

A.8.g   Choice of garbage collector

Not only does .NET come with a low-priority, high-performance GC, but in addition it offers two flavors of it: one for servers and one for client-side applications.

The server version allows us to benefit from a GC tuned specifically to reduce impact on memory, whereas the workstation version is configured in a way that reduces as much as possible the chances of the GC executing in the middle of a user interaction. Indeed, there is no problem in a server-side function taking three seconds instead of two once in a while. But an interface freezing randomly for a second, right in the middle of a user interaction, for example, when scrolling through a form, is a real problem for the user.

To activate the server version of the GC, add the lines in Listing 2-21 to the configuration file for the application.

```
<configuration>
  <runtime>
    <gcServer enabled="true"/>
  </runtime>
</configuration>
```

Listing 2-21

In this case, the GC is not concurrent anymore. Two other additional parameters exist to fine-tune the GC's behavior:

```
<gcConcurrent enabled="false" />
<gcTrimCommitOnLowMemory enabled="true" />
```

Listing 2-22

The first one allows the user to specify whether the GC runs concurrently (in server mode, it never does). For an extremely detailed account of this setting, please refer to Tess Ferrandez's blog post, *How does the GC work and what are the sizes of the different* generations? at HTTP://BLOGS.MSDN.COM/B/TESS/ARCHIVE/2008/04/17/HOW-DOES-THE-GC-WORK-AND-WHAT-ARE-THE-SIZES-OF-THE-DIFFERENT-GENERATIONS.ASPX. Tess is an escalation engineer in the ASP.NET developer support team at Microsoft, and she is an expert at GC tuning.

The second parameter can be activated to help reduce the memory footprint of the GC, and is thus particularly useful on servers with lots of small websites.

A.8.h   Garbage collection in .NET 4.0

The GC has undergone some major changes in .NET 4.0. It is not my aim to go over those changes in detail here: they are extremely technical and will not change the way you profile performance, or even memory use, at all. At most, they may slightly increase the threshold after which the rate of memory consumption affects the performance of the application. But the way the GC works has not changed in depth.

The main improvement is the introduction of an ephemeral segment, which works as a buffer to make it possible to have a background GC. You may reply that we already had a background GC in .NET 2.0, and that was true for the workstation GC. However, the server GC was a "blocking" one, which meant all operations were stopped when the GC kicked in. As we explained, latency is not much of a problem in this case, but it definitely may be on a client GUI.

What .NET 4.0 offers is a GC that will be able to do more operations in the background. Indeed, even in the workstation GC where the analysis of the unreferenced objects was concurrent, there were periods when memory allocation had to be blocked. The improvement reduces this time and thus the associated latency. Also, the improved GC allows for true concurrency: lower-generation collections will be allowed while a full-generation collection is executing. This will also reduce latency, as a Generation 0 collection is generally very quick.

New overload `GC.Collect(int, GCCollectionMode)`

An additional signature will appear on `GC.Collect`. *But the cases where one has a good reason to call this function are so rare that I am not even going to list them here. This may be a good opportunity to recall one of the main recommendations in .NET memory management: do not call* `GC.Collect` *unless you know exactly what you are doing. And since memory management is such a complex field, chances are only Microsoft experts will know what they are doing. In conclusion:* **do not call** `GC.Collect`... *ever!*

.NET 4.0 will also introduce functions to notify the code of a garbage collection. The **GC notification** functionality is based on `GC.RegisterForFullGCNotification`, `GC.WaitForFullGCApproach` and `GC.RegisterForFullGCComplete` methods. Although very few developers may need this, these functions could be used to prevent interactions from happening when a garbage collection is approaching. The relationship to performance management certainly lies more in the fact that profilers will be able to benefit from these APIs to follow GC activity more precisely. A bit like the fact that the new process hooking was of great benefit to profilers to help them connect to .NET 4.0 processes easily, without needing elaborate techniques sometimes including code instrumentation to do so.

A.9 Boxing, unboxing and associated performance

A.9.a What is the problem?

Let's start with some basic code:

```
using System;

namespace BoxingUnboxing
{
    class Program
    {
        static void Main(string[] args)
        {
            int value = 10;
            object content = value;
            Console.WriteLine(content);
        }
    }
}
```

Listing 2-23

This code compiles and works perfectly in .NET: it prints out 10 at the command line when executing. We are calling the `Console.WriteLine` method, passing a reference to an **object**. We are thus using a reference, contained in the heap, whereas an integer is a value type, contained in the stack (see Figure 2-28).

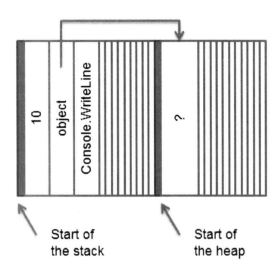

Start of
the stack

Start of
the heap

Figure 2-28: Pointing to a value in the heap seems absurd.

How does the CLR manage to make the function point to a reference containing the value 10, and in a way that is transparent for the developer? Again, the answer is found in the IL code (see Figure 2-29).

```
BoxingUnboxing.Program::Main : void(string[])
Find   Find Next
.method private hidebysig static void  Main(string[] args) cil managed
{
  .entrypoint
  // Code size       19 (0x13)
  .maxstack  1
  .locals init ([0] int32 integer,
           [1] object content)
  IL_0000:  nop
  IL_0001:  ldc.i4.s   10
  IL_0003:  stloc.0
  IL_0004:  ldloc.0
  IL_0005:  box        [mscorlib]System.Int32
  IL_000a:  stloc.1
  IL_000b:  ldloc.1
  IL_000c:  call       void [mscorlib]System.Console::WriteLine(object)
  IL_0011:  nop
  IL_0012:  ret
} // end of method Program::Main
```

Figure 2-29: Finding the box instruction in the IL code.

The instruction at Line 0005 is called **box**: this is the one responsible for placing the value inside a memory slot on the heap, and sending a reference back to this slot.

The content of memory (stack and heap) now becomes something like Figure 2-30.

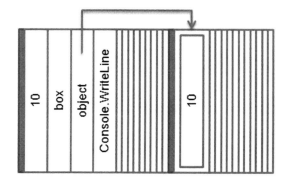

Figure 2-30: Representing the boxing of a value as a reference object.

The instruction **box** transforms value 10 into a reference to a memory slot that has been tailor-made in the heap (and normally, the instruction and value are unstacked, but they are included in the diagram to aid understanding). Then, the function `Console.WriteLine` can use a reference to an **object** as planned.

The opposite function is **unbox**. In C#, it is written in the same way as a cast operation, even if these two operations are actually different. The code in Listing 2-24 shows an example of unboxing.

```
using System;

namespace BoxingUnboxing
{
    class Program
    {
        static void Main(string[] args)
        {
            int value = 10;
```

```
            Function(value);
    }

    public static void Function(object content)
    {
        int value = (int)content;
        Console.WriteLine(value);
    }
  }
}
```

Listing 2-24

Spying on the IL corresponding to the function Main, we find the instruction box again (see Figure 2-31).

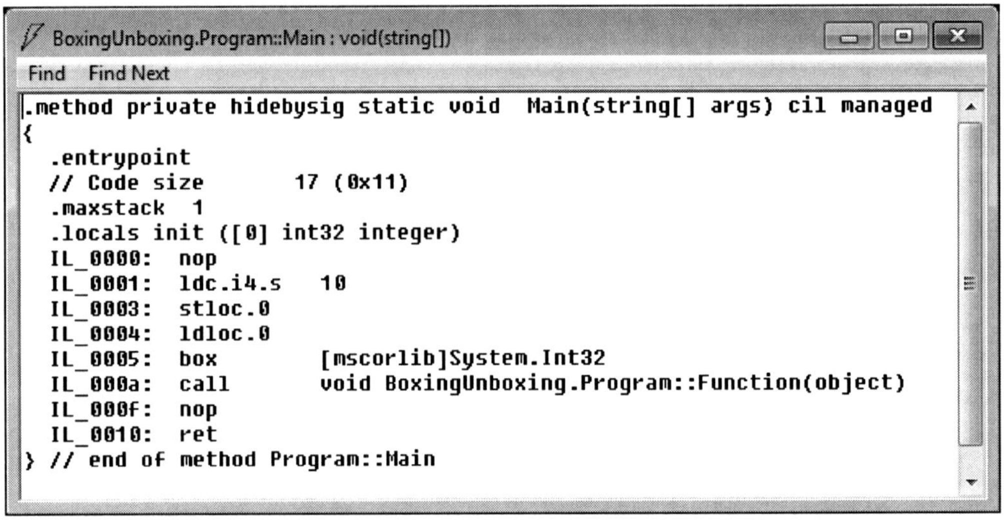

```
BoxingUnboxing.Program::Main : void(string[])                    _ □ ✖
 Find   Find Next
.method private hidebysig static void  Main(string[] args) cil managed
{
  .entrypoint
  // Code size       17 (0x11)
  .maxstack  1
  .locals init ([0] int32 integer)
  IL_0000:  nop
  IL_0001:  ldc.i4.s    10
  IL_0003:  stloc.0
  IL_0004:  ldloc.0
  IL_0005:  box         [mscorlib]System.Int32
  IL_000a:  call        void BoxingUnboxing.Program::Function(object)
  IL_000f:  nop
  IL_0010:  ret
} // end of method Program::Main
```

Figure 2-31: box instruction.

The integer that corresponds to local variable at index 0 is actually boxed before being passed as the argument of Function.

Now let us look at the IL code for this function (see Figure 2-32).

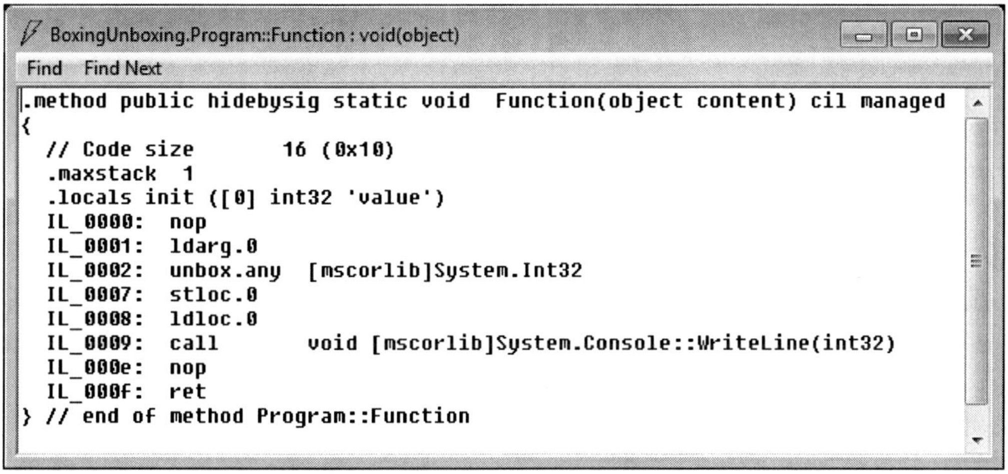

```
BoxingUnboxing.Program::Function : void(object)                    _  □  ✕

Find    Find Next

.method public hidebysig static void  Function(object content) cil managed
{
  // Code size        16 (0x10)
  .maxstack  1
  .locals init ([0] int32 'value')
  IL_0000:  nop
  IL_0001:  ldarg.0
  IL_0002:  unbox.any   [mscorlib]System.Int32
  IL_0007:  stloc.0
  IL_0008:  ldloc.0
  IL_0009:  call        void [mscorlib]System.Console::WriteLine(int32)
  IL_000e:  nop
  IL_000f:  ret
} // end of method Program::Function
```

Figure 2-32: unbox instruction.

The first, and unique, argument for the function is loaded into memory, unboxed by the unbox.any instruction in the form of a System.Int32 (equivalent to int), then the result is stored in a local variable at index 0, namely value.

A.9.b   Boxing/unboxing and performance

Obviously, and this is the reason for this chapter, boxing and unboxing do not happen for free: they have a cost in terms of memory and time spent by the CPU executing them. In fact, these costs are quite high: to box a value, memory has to be allocated, then the content has to be copied to this memory slot. The inverse operation needs to verify the type contained in order to know whether unboxing is possible with the value type in which we want to retrieve the content of the box. And finally, the memory will have to be freed, as there will no longer be any references pointing to it at the end of these processes. In short, this process is transparent but far from cost free and, as soon as it is called repetitively (in a loop, for example), costs in memory and time will go up quickly; it is not rare to find badly-written algorithms in which half the time is spent on boxing/unboxing.

Listing 2-25 provides a small benchmark to convince the reader of the interest of paying particular attention to boxing and unboxing processes.

```
using System;
using System.Diagnostics;

namespace BoxingUnboxing
{
    class Program
    {
        private static int _Total = 0;

        static void Main(string[] args)
        {
            int value = 1;
            int nbIterations = 2500000;

            Stopwatch chrono = Stopwatch.StartNew();
            for (int index = 0; index < nbIterations; index++)
                Function(value);
            Console.WriteLine("Elapsed time with boxing and unboxing : {0} ms",
                            chrono.ElapsedMilliseconds);

            chrono.Reset();
            chrono.Start();
            for (int index = 0; index < nbIterations; index++)
                OptimizedFunction(value);
            Console.WriteLine("Elapsed time without boxing or unboxing : {0} ms",
                            chrono.ElapsedMilliseconds);
        }

        public static void Function(object content)
        {
            _Total += (int)content;
        }

        public static void OptimizedFunction(int content)
        {
            _Total += content;
        }
    }
}
```

Listing 2-25

A loop executes a few million iterations on a simple integer incrementing operation. The only difference is that the reference function takes an `object` as a parameter, whereas the optimized function uses an `int`. Does such a small difference lead to noticeable consequences? Indeed, the time is more than twice as long (see Figure 2-33), and that's without mentioning memory consumption.

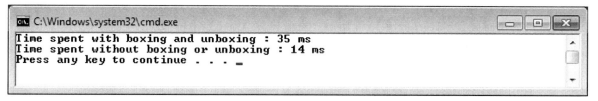

Figure 2-33: The impact of boxing and unboxing on performance.

***

Dependence on the context

Replaying this benchmark on my (much less powerful) old computer led to an increase by a factor of more than four, so do not take these figures literally.

***

Therefore, there is a lot to be gained from controlling the frequency of boxing and unboxing. The bad news is that this is quite complex for a developer, and one must pay particular attention to one's code to clearly identify these operations. I thus recommend systematically sending the relevant code through ILDASM, and then counting the number of **box** and **unbox.any** instructions. If masses of code need to be analyzed, a small tool can be programmed to call ILDASM and generate statistics from the textual content, in order to make the analysis easier.

A.9.c   The cure

Getting rid of boxing and unboxing operations does not happen without putting a lot of effort into programming. In the sample code above, we have shown that passing an `int` parameter instead of an `object` was enough to solve the problem. But in the real world, if a developer chose to use an **object** type, that was precisely because they wanted the function to be able to handle all possible types, not just integers. Does this mean that we should create an overloaded signature for each of the possible simple types? Yes, and this is indeed the case in some functions provided by the .NET Base Class Library (BCL).

If we take a look at the code that was used to demonstrate the concept of unboxing, we can see that the integer was passed as an argument to a particular signature of the `System.Console.WriteLine` function, namely `WriteLine(Int32)` (see Figure 2-34).

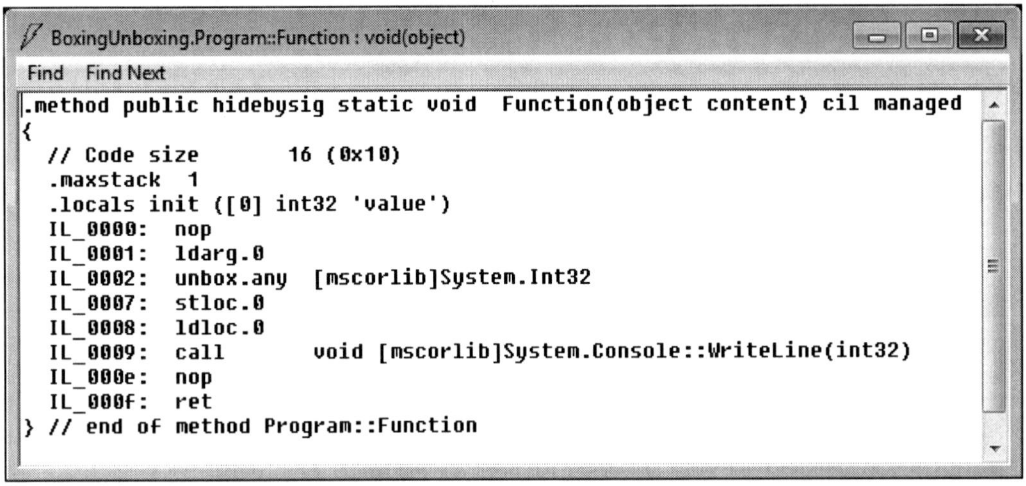

```
 BoxingUnboxing.Program::Function : void(object)                        _  □  ✕
Find   Find Next
.method public hidebysig static void  Function(object content) cil managed
{
  // Code size        16 (0x10)
  .maxstack   1
  .locals init ([0] int32 'value')
  IL_0000:  nop
  IL_0001:  ldarg.0
  IL_0002:  unbox.any  [mscorlib]System.Int32
  IL_0007:  stloc.0
  IL_0008:  ldloc.0
  IL_0009:  call        void [mscorlib]System.Console::WriteLine(int32)
  IL_000e:  nop
  IL_000f:  ret
} // end of method Program::Function
```

Figure 2-34: A code without boxing.

A quick look at Microsoft's documentation shows the possible overloads for the method `WriteLine` of the class `Console`. There are 18 of them in .NET 3.5, and we find every possible simple type (see Figure 2-35).

Name
WriteLine()
WriteLine(Boolean)
WriteLine(Char)
WriteLine(Char[])
WriteLine(Decimal)
WriteLine(Double)
WriteLine(Int32)
WriteLine(Int64)
WriteLine(Object)
WriteLine(Single)
WriteLine(String)
WriteLine(UInt32)
WriteLine(UInt64)
WriteLine(String, Object)
WriteLine(String, Object[])
WriteLine(Char[], Int32, Int32)
WriteLine(String, Object, Object)
WriteLine(String, Object, Object, Object)
WriteLine(String, Object, Object, Object, Object)

Figure 2-35: Possible overloaded signatures for `Console.WriteLine`.

If a function that takes an `object` as a parameter is exposed, it is strongly recommended to also provide an equivalent signature for each of the simple types it will be used with.

```
System.Int32 vs int
```

In .NET there is no difference between `System.Int32` *and* `int`. *The keyword* `int` *is directly translated by the compiler into* `Int32`. *This, as well as the notion of automatic boxing and unboxing, can be a source of confusion for Java developers, who are used to the difference between* `Double` *and* `double`, *for example. With Java,* `double` *corresponds to a value type in the stack, whereas* `Double` *is a reference type contained in the heap. Going from one to the other is not automatic as it is with .NET, and one should use the* `Double` *constructor to incorporate a* `double` *into a* `Double`. *The inverse operation is done through the use of* `GetValue()` *on a* `Double`. *This approach may seem better, because it explicitly shows the developer the necessary operations, whereas .NET hides them a bit more with the automatic boxing and unboxing (even if, for the latter, an explicit instruction with the same syntax as casting is necessary). Microsoft has chosen to simplify the syntax in the 90% of cases where this will not be a performance issue, while leaving it to the developer to handle the remaining 10% of cases where it can cause a problem.*

To conclude with these performance issues, it should be noted that the problem also arises with the `ArrayList` class, which corresponds to lists of `object`. One should be particularly careful when `ArrayList` are created on value types. Luckily, generic `List<T>` lists solve this problem by removing the need for boxing and unboxing, and they are, anyway, the preferred classes for managing lists.

A.10 Memory management and finalization

A.10.a Let .NET do it!

The `System.GC` class provides access to several methods related to memory management. Unless you have a great deal of experience in .NET memory management and know precisely what you are doing, it is strongly recommended that you simply forget about its very existence.

There is a lot of temptation for beginner developers to explicitly call the `Collect` method at the end of a process which they know is memory-intensive. Of all the cases I am aware of since the early versions of .NET, none has ever shown that calling the GC mechanism explicitly could give better results in memory consumption or performance than simply letting the GC do its job.

Of course, in use cases where the memory consumption does not vary at all, explicit garbage collection can allow control of memory use in one's application, but this comes with a high price tag.

- Sooner or later, the use of the application will change, and the memory consumption will vary.

- Explicit GC calls at regular intervals have the natural consequence of increasing the number of garbage collections. In the end, this increases processing time.

- As a general rule, there is no need to limit memory consumption of an application as long as the system keeps enough memory available. In the case of a system where the memory is under a lot of pressure, the GC will adapt by running passes more frequently than on a system well equipped with RAM.

In short (and this may be the most important recommendation of this first section about memory management), it is essential to let the GC do its job, and not try to improve memory use by directing the collection process in any way.

We can have much more impact by helping the GC to recycle memory efficiently, by taking care of resources as explained below.

The question of high memory use

A question is often asked by beginner developers: is it normal that such and such a .NET process uses so much memory? The feeling that the CLR does not release enough of the memory used is very common, but one must understand that, as long as memory is available, it is normal for .NET to use it. And why would it do any differently? As long as the OS can provide it with memory, there is no sense in .NET limiting its use of it: running the GC more often would take time and thus slow down the application. The only important point to check is that the same process can also run in a smaller memory set. We will come back to this in more detail later in this chapter.

A.10.b Releasing external resources when the GC is fired

Firstly, let us make it clear that we are only talking about external resources here, such as connections to a database, memory spaces not controlled by managed code (typically in COM interoperability), or any other resources that are not controlled directly by the CLR. Indeed, contrary to what happens with C++, an object in .NET does not need to worry about whether the managed objects it references should be recycled or not. The CLR will check whether this object is referenced by any others and, if not, it will free them as well.

By contrast, in the examples below, it is important to release resources correctly. In the case of a database connection, this means calling the closing method on the corresponding API. But in most cases, as below, this operation is explicit, and there is no need to wait for the end of the object's life to close the connection.

```
using System;
using System.Data;
using System.Data.SqlClient;

namespace FreeingResources
{
    class Program
    {
        static void Main(string[] args)
        {
```

```
            SqlConnection connection = new SqlConnection();
            SqlCommand command = new SqlCommand("SELECT * FROM TEST", connection);
            IDataReader reader = null;
            try
            {
                connection.Open();
                reader = command.ExecuteReader(CommandBehavior.CloseConnection);
                if (reader.Read())
                    Console.WriteLine(reader.GetString(0));
            }
            finally
            {
                if (reader != null && !reader.IsClosed)
                    reader.Close();
            }
        }
    }
}
```

Listing 2-26

In the example above, the `CommandBehavior.CloseConnection` parameter used in
the `ExecuteReader` method guarantees that the connection closing operation will be
called automatically upon closure of the associated reader.

By contrast, we can imagine a .NET object for which we would need to initialize a
connection during construction, and to close the connection only when the object is at
the end of its life. To do so, there exists a way of informing the CLR that it should execute
an action when freeing an object. Typically, this works as shown in Listing 2-27.

```
using System;
using System.Data;
using System.Data.SqlClient;

namespace FreeingResources
{
    public class Tracer
    {
        SqlConnection connection = null;
```

```
    public Tracer()
    {
        connection = new SqlConnection();
        connection.Open();
    }

    ~Tracer()
    {
        connection.Close();
    }

    public void Log()
    {
        SqlCommand command = new SqlCommand("UPDATE TABLE SET nb = nb + 1",
                          connection);
        command.ExecuteNonQuery();
    }
    }
}
```

Listing 2-27

Obviously, this example is oversimplified: keeping the connection open throughout the life of this object would only make sense if it was destined to be called extremely frequently on the Log() method. In the more plausible case of the method being called irregularly, it would definitely be better to open the connection and close it at the end of the function call.

This would remove the need to deal with closing the connection upon disposing of the instance, and would also free database connections for other uses, making the code more capable of handling high loads. But this is not the end of the matter, and one should remember that performance handling is often about choosing where to strike the balance between two extremes. In this example, one could argue that opening and closing the connection at each call takes processing time and slows the process down. In particular, opening a database connection is a heavy operation, which involves starting a new thread, calculating authorization levels, and several other complex operations.

So, how does one choose? Quite simply, by knowing the mechanisms used in database connection management. In practice, SQL Server will pool the connections, bringing better performance even if they are opened and closed frequently. When the `Close` instruction is called on an ADO.NET connection, the underlying object that deals with the actual database connection is in fact not abandoned, but only deactivated, and marked as available for another user. If the object is then taken from the pool, the opening of a connection is much less complex, since the object exists and the code only has to reactivate it for another use, usually only having to reauthorize it. In short, since we have no need to deal with the object finalizer, we can write as shown in Listing 2-28.

```
using System;
using System.Data;
using System.Data.SqlClient;

namespace FreeingResources
{
    public class Tracer
    {
        SqlConnection connection = null;

        public Tracer()
        {
            connection = new SqlConnection();
        }

        public void Log()
        {
            SqlCommand command = new SqlCommand("UPDATE TABLE SET nb = nb + 1",
                            connection);
            try
            {
                Connection.Open();
                Command.ExecuteNonQuery();
            }
            finally
            {
                Connection.Close();
            }
        }
    }
}
```

Listing 2-28

A.10.c   Early release of resources

The method described above (releasing a resource upon object recycling) still has a major drawback: if the resource is precious, it is a waste to wait minutes or even hours for the GC to release it.

This is the reason behind yet another .NET mechanism: the IDisposable interface. Implementing this interface forces a class to have a Dispose() method, allowing the class instances to release resources as soon as the developer calls the method, whether it be explicitly or through the using keyword. Listing 2-29 provides an example of this.

```
using System;
using System.Data;
using System.Data.SqlClient;

namespace FreeingResources
{
    public class Tracer : IDisposable
    {
        SqlConnection connection = null;

        public Tracer()
        {
            connection = new SqlConnection();
            connection.Open();
        }

        public void Log()
        {
            SqlCommand command = new SqlCommand("UPDATE TABLE SET nb = nb + 1",
                            connection);
            command.ExecuteNonQuery();
        }

        #region IDisposable Members

        public void Dispose()
        {
            connection.Close();
        }
```

```
        #endregion
    }
}
```

Listing 2-29

The user of such an object would work with a code that calls the method like in Listing 2-30.

```csharp
using System;

namespace FreeingResources
{
    class Program
    {
        static void Main(string[] args)
        {
            using (Tracer logger = new Tracer())
            {
                logger.Log();
            }
        }
    }
}
```

Listing 2-30

For readers who are not used to the using keyword, the code above is exactly equivalent to Listing 2-31.

```csharp
using System;

namespace FreeingResources
{
    class Program
    {
        static void Main(string[] args)
        {
            Tracer logger = new Tracer();
```

```
            try
            {
                logger.Log();
            }
            finally
            {
                logger.Dispose();
            }
        }
    }
}
```

Listing 2-31

By using `Dispose` the caller guarantees that the resources will be released as soon as possible.

A.10.d Combining both operations

At this point in the evolution of our example code, something is still missing: what happens if the caller does not use the `Dispose` mechanism, by forgetting to include the `using` keyword or to call the equivalent method? Resources will not be released, even when the GC recycles the object, and there will be a resource leak.

It is thus necessary to apply both of the mechanisms we have described above, in a combined way (see Listing 2-32).

```
using System;
using System.Data;
using System.Data.SqlClient;

namespace FreeingResources
{
    public class Tracer : IDisposable
    {
        SqlConnection connection = null;
```

```
    public Tracer()
    {
        connection = new SqlConnection();
        connection.Open();
    }

    ~Tracer()
    {
        connection.Close();
    }

    public void Log()
    {
        SqlCommand command = new SqlCommand("UPDATE TABLE SET nb = nb + 1",
                        connection);
        command.ExecuteNonQuery();
    }

    #region IDisposable Members

    public void Dispose()
    {
        connection.Close();
    }

    #endregion
    }
}
```

Listing 2-32

This way, the `Dispose` mechanism can be called explicitly to release the associated resource as soon as possible, but if for some reason this is overlooked, the GC will eventually call the finalizer. This will be done later, but it is still better than never.

Nonetheless, a seasoned developer will notice the code duplication: the finalizer and the `Dispose` function use the same code, which is contrary to a well-known best practice. As a result, we should combine the resource freeing code, as in Listing 2-33.

```csharp
using System;
using System.Data;
using System.Data.SqlClient;

namespace FreeingResources
{
    public class Tracer : IDisposable
    {
        SqlConnection connection = null;

        public Tracer()
        {
            connection = new SqlConnection();
            connection.Open();
        }

        ~Tracer()
        {
            FreeResources();
        }

        private void FreeResources()
        {
            connection.Close();
        }

        public void Log()
        {
            SqlCommand command = new SqlCommand("UPDATE TABLE SET nb = nb + 1",
                            connection);
            command.ExecuteNonQuery();
        }

        #region IDisposable Members

        public void Dispose()
        {
            FreeResources();
        }

        #endregion
    }
}
```

Listing 2-33

We are getting there, but there are still a few potential problems we have to deal with.

- If Dispose is called explicitly, there is no use for the finalizer anymore, because we know it will not do anything: the resource has already been freed.

- We should make sure that calling the method to free resources several times will not cause any problems.

- We should take into account the fact that, when Dispose is called, the Dispose method for other managed resources should be called as well. Generally, the CLR takes care of this by using the finalizer, but in this case, we have to do it ourselves.

The final code is given in Listing 2-34.

```
using System;
using System.Data;
using System.Data.SqlClient;

namespace FreeingResources
{
    public class Tracer : IDisposable
    {
        SqlConnection connection = null;

        public Tracer()
        {
            connection = new SqlConnection();
            connection.Open();
        }

        ~Tracer()
        {
            FreeResources(false);
        }

        private bool _Disposed = false;

        private void FreeResources(bool Disposing)
        {
```

```
                // If the object has already released its resources,
                // there is no need to continue
                if (_Disposed) return;

                if (Disposing)
                {
                    // This is where the Dispose would be called if there
                    // were managed resources in this class
                }

                connection.Close();

                // To avoid coming back to this code several times
                _Disposed = true;
        }

        public void Log()
        {
            SqlCommand command = new SqlCommand("UPDATE TABLE SET nb = nb + 1",
                            connection);
            command.ExecuteNonQuery();
        }

        #region IDisposable Members

        public void Dispose()
        {
            FreeResources(true);
            // The following lines tell the GC that there is no use
            // in calling the finalizer, when it recycles the current object
            GC.SuppressFinalize(this);
        }

        #endregion
    }
}
```

Listing 2-34

This code structure is known as the "Dispose pattern", and is quite a standard form. Despite all the effort we have put into it, it is still not 100% complete. If we want to take care of all the possible situations, we should add one more safety feature: once Dispose has been called, the object cannot have its `Log` method called. A traditional modification is to set the connection to `null`, and then check its value in `Log` or any method that could use it.

Further details can be found by searching for "Dispose" and "Pattern" on the Internet. There are numerous discussions on side effects and how to avoid them, memory performance of each variant of the pattern, etc. The goal of the present book is not to provide the reader with a state-of-the-art summary of these discussions, but to show the link between this pattern and the performance of an application. If it is not correctly implemented, there are risks of massively reducing the access to unmanaged resources. It should be noted that having many objects implementing finalizers can adversely affect the performance of the GC. See HTTP://MSDN.MICROSOFT.COM/EN-US/LIBRARY/0S7IX93I.ASPX for more information.

A.10.e   A last note

It is essential to stress that the memory use of a process has absolutely nothing to do with the fact it cannot release it. This is a common misunderstanding of .NET memory management. As long as the OS does not restrict the CLR in its memory consumption, .NET has no reason whatsoever to run the GC at the risk of generating a drop in performance in the application.

It is perfectly normal for an application to grow in memory up until it reaches hundreds of megabytes. Even if one pass of the GC could make this drop to ten megabytes, as long as no other process needs memory, the CLR should not sacrifice even a small percentage of its time to freeing this memory. This is the origin of the reputation of .NET and Java as "memory hogs." In fact, they are only using available resources as much as possible, while still maintaining a process to release them as much and as quickly as possible, should the OS ask for them.

In real life

A developer in my team created an application that processed XML in bulk. Each file was a few hundred kilobytes at most, and the corresponding instance of XmlDocument *around one megabyte. The developer, who was watching memory consumption out of curiosity, was alarmed by the fact that it was growing consistently, for each file processed, and asked me whether he should cancel the process before reaching an* OutOfMemoryException. *After growing to 700 megabytes or so, it suddenly dropped to around 100 megabytes, and this cycle repeated itself like clockwork until the end of the application. This case is a good example of how .NET works: on this machine, which had 2 gigabytes of RAM and almost no other active applications, it would have been counterproductive to have more GC activity, since the whole process would have taken a few more minutes, whereas reducing peak memory use would have made no difference at all. It is also revealing about the difficulty of grasping the GC mechanism for a developer who has not had it explained, which can cause performance issues, as explained above.*

B   The particular case of inline functions

B.1   The inlining mechanism

The inlining mechanism is a feature of .NET as well as many other platforms. In short, this means copying the code of the function to the place where the function is called, instead of having to jump from one to the other in the stack. Of course, this only makes sense if the amount of code copied is very short.

The example in Listing 2-35 shows two functions that make the same calculation, but in two ways. Function1 directly computes the requested result, whereas Function2 uses an intermediary function.

```
using System;

namespace Inlining
{
    class Program
    {
        static void Main(string[] args)
        {
            int result = Function1(1);
            result = Function2(1);
        }

        private static int Function1(int parameter)
        {
            int result = parameter * 2;
            return result + 1;
        }

        private static int Function2(int parameter)
        {
            int result = IntermediaryFunction(parameter);
            return result + 1;
        }

        private static int IntermediaryFunction(int parameter)
        {
            return parameter * 2;
        }
    }
}
```

Listing 2-35

Figure 2-36 shows the corresponding IL code, which we obtained for Function1.

```
Inlining.Program::Function1 : int32(int32)

Find   Find Next
.method private hidebysig static int32  Function1(int32 parameter) cil managed
{
  // Code size       13 (0xd)
  .maxstack  2
  .locals init ([0] int32 result,
           [1] int32 CS$1$0000)
  IL_0000:  nop
  IL_0001:  ldarg.0
  IL_0002:  ldc.i4.2
  IL_0003:  mul
  IL_0004:  stloc.0
  IL_0005:  ldloc.0
  IL_0006:  ldc.i4.1
  IL_0007:  add
  IL_0008:  stloc.1
  IL_0009:  br.s       IL_000b
  IL_000b:  ldloc.1
  IL_000c:  ret
} // end of method Program::Function1
```

Figure 2-36: Function1 IL code.

Even if the previous examples of IL code have not made the reader completely familiar with this syntax, the structural similarities with C# are quite easy to find:

- at IL_0001, the code loads the first parameter of the function in the stack

- at IL_0002, it loads value 2 as a 32-bit integer in the stack

- at IL_0003, it performs a multiplication

- and so on.

If we now compare this to the IL code for Function2 (see Figure 2-37), we see differences in terms of process.

```
Inlining.Program::Function2 : int32(int32)                                    [_][□][✕]
Find   Find Next
.method private hidebysig static int32  Function2(int32 parameter) cil managed
{
  // Code size        16 (0x10)
  .maxstack  2
  .locals init ([0] int32 result,
           [1] int32 CS$1$0000)
  IL_0000:  nop
  IL_0001:  ldarg.0
  IL_0002:  call           int32 Inlining.Program::IntermediaryFunction(int32)
  IL_0007:  stloc.0
  IL_0008:  ldloc.0
  IL_0009:  ldc.i4.1
  IL_000a:  add
  IL_000b:  stloc.1
  IL_000c:  br.s           IL_000e
  IL_000e:  ldloc.1
  IL_000f:  ret
} // end of method Program::Function2
```

Figure 2-37: Function2 IL code.

This time, we go through a call to `IntermediaryFunction`. Why are we studying this code, since it does not show inlining? Inlining is indeed not performed by the compiler, but by Just In Time compiling. JIT compiling is named after its purpose, which is transforming IL code to executable machine code only when this code is reached in the execution. For this reason, we cannot observe inlining in IL code. But lines `IL_0002` and `IL_0007` are still very interesting, because they show how .NET works when calling a function.

- The call definition takes 5 bytes, which is much more than simply storing a value or variable in memory (these instructions do not contain an address to a method, and thus can be coded in less space).

- In addition, this example does not show the complexity behind the call operation. The CLR will pass through a function table that will provide it with the actual method address, then execute the associated code, place the result in the stack and eventually call the return operation.

- Line IL_0007 shows that, once the function has been called, the stack contains the return value, and that this is stored as planned in the zero-index local variable, in our case, Result.

The most important thing to realize is that the 5 bytes needed for call could be replaced with 2 bytes for ldc.i4.2 and mul, without the resulting behavior being affected in any way. These two codes are precisely what the IntermediaryFunction contains in its IL (see Figure 2-38).

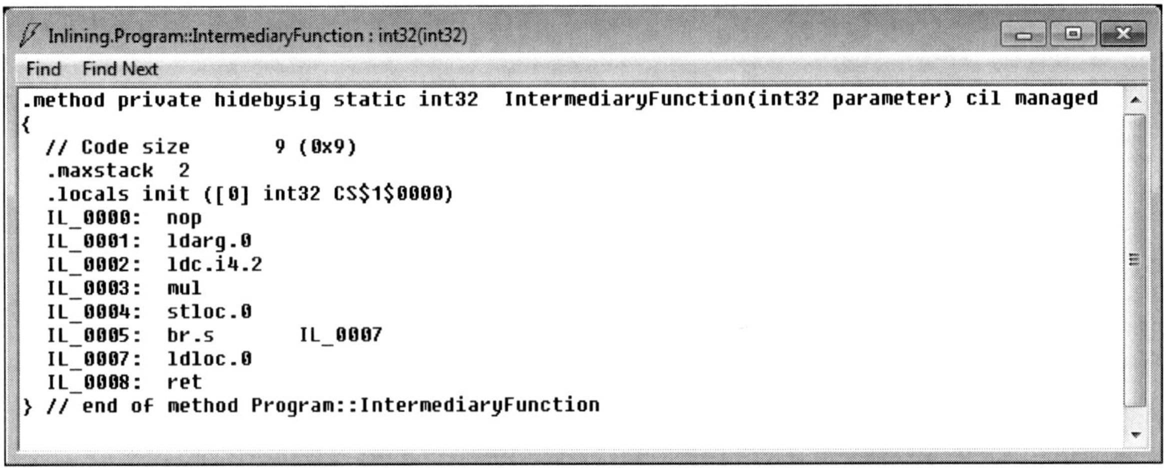

```
Inlining.Program::IntermediaryFunction : int32(int32)                          □  □  ✕

Find   Find Next

.method private hidebysig static int32  IntermediaryFunction(int32 parameter) cil managed
{
  // Code size       9 (0x9)
  .maxstack  2
  .locals init ([0] int32 CS$1$0000)
  IL_0000:  nop
  IL_0001:  ldarg.0
  IL_0002:  ldc.i4.2
  IL_0003:  mul
  IL_0004:  stloc.0
  IL_0005:  br.s        IL_0007
  IL_0007:  ldloc.0
  IL_0008:  ret
} // end of method Program::IntermediaryFunction
```

Figure 2-38: IntermediaryFunction IL code.

So why would the CLR waste some operation codes instead of replacing the code in all callers with the code it will execute? In fact, there is no good reason, and this is precisely what happens when .NET optimizes the process through inlining of the function.

B.2 Inlining and performance

As in many aspects of performance optimization, one should strike a balance between two extremes. Not inlining any functions would result in lots of `call` operations and reduced performance but, on the other hand, inlining everything would result in massive machine code redundancy, thus increasing the size of code in memory.

One of the basic rules of development is to avoid duplicating code as much as possible. Yet, .NET decides, at execution time, to duplicate the code of any functions that it inlines. Thus, it deliberately increases the size of machine code, and goes against this rule. This is why a function will not be inlined unless its size in IL code is smaller than 32 bytes.

The JIT compiler uses a particular heuristic to determine whether a function should be inlined or not. Such a decision is not predictable, and it is not possible to force the CLR to inline a given function. By contrast, it is possible to prevent a function from being inlined, as the code in Listing 2-36 shows.

```
using System.Runtime.CompilerServices;

[MethodImpl(MethodImplOptions.NoInlining)]
private static int IntermediaryFunction(int parameter)
{
    return parameter * 2;
}
```

Listing 2-36

The corresponding IL code shows the `NoInlining` keyword, which will inform the CLR of the characteristics requested by the developer (see Figure 2-39).

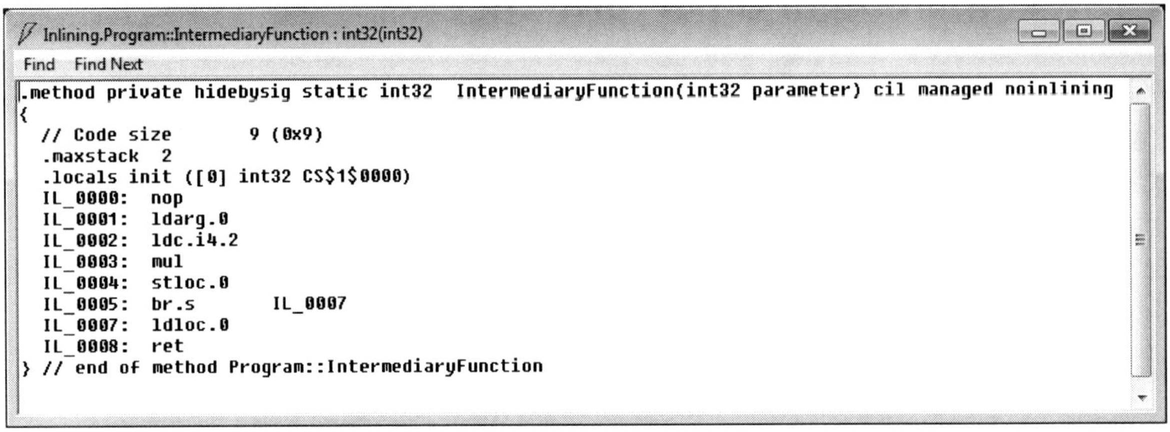

```
Inlining.Program::IntermediaryFunction : int32(int32)                    [ _ ][ □ ][ X ]
Find   Find Next
.method private hidebysig static int32  IntermediaryFunction(int32 parameter) cil managed noinlining
{
  // Code size       9 (0x9)
  .maxstack  2
  .locals init ([0] int32 CS$1$0000)
  IL_0000:  nop
  IL_0001:  ldarg.0
  IL_0002:  ldc.i4.2
  IL_0003:  mul
  IL_0004:  stloc.0
  IL_0005:  br.s        IL_0007
  IL_0007:  ldloc.0
  IL_0008:  ret
} // end of method Program::IntermediaryFunction
```

Figure 2-39: `IntermediaryFunction` IL code compiled in `NoInlining` mode.

It is quite interesting to notice that the **MethodImplOptions** enumeration does not have any member values such as `Inlining` or `ForceInlining` (or any other name that would convey the same meaning: see Figure 2-40).

In C++, most modern compilers support the `inline` keyword, for compatibility reasons, but still make their own decision as to whether or not to inline a function. In C#, where there is no such keyword, it is recommended to leave it to the CLR to obtain the best performance. In the same way as with the GC, most of the attempts at hand-tuning inlining will result in performance at best equal, and most of the time worse, than by leaving .NET to take care of it.

Member name
Unmanaged
ForwardRef
PreserveSig
InternalCall
Synchronized
NoInlining
NoOptimization

Figure 2-40: Enumeration values for `MethodImplOptions`.

Let .NET do it... really!

This last remark is very important in the .NET world, where particular attention has been given by Microsoft to using adaptive mechanisms that will find the best choice in most cases. Let us leave the experts to do their work. This book is about improvements to performance that we can make to our code, and not to .NET itself. Searching the Internet will come up with few articles about performance improvements through .NET tuning (explicitly calling the GC, disabling inlining, etc.). Furthermore, these micro-optimizations are so sensitive to context (CLR version, OS version, modification – however slight – of the source code, etc.) that it generally does not make sense to apply them to software that is not completely stable.

In addition to the 32-bytes limit, the JIT forces additional constraints on inlining a function (source: *JIT Optimizations: Inlining (II)*, David Notario, HTTP://BLOGS.MSDN.COM/B/DAVIDNOTARIO/ARCHIVE/2004/11/01/250398.ASPX).

- Functions marked as virtual cannot be inlined, of course, since their implementation will depend on the exact type of the calling class (which will only be known at runtime) and the corresponding functions marked as override.

- All functions using a complex flow, with loops, try…catch zones, switch operators, etc. will also be rejected.

- Methods where one parameter or more is a struct will not be inlined as well.

- Calls to classes marked as `MarshalByRef` cannot be inlined (apparently, this is not the case anymore since Visual Studio 2005, but Microsoft has kept fairly quiet on this subject).

- All security calls block inlining.

- Finally, when the CLR detects rare calls, inlining will not be used. Typically, a static constructor will only be called once at class initialization, and in this case, it is not useful to inline them.

These conditions can seem very restrictive, but they are justified by technical difficulties. One should remember, again, that inlining is a question of finding the right balance between speeding up calls and increasing the size of machine code.

B.3   Impacts on profilers

Inlining allows .NET to reach actual performance improvements, and the following blog post can be consulted with great interest: *Inlining – yes, it happens*, Bart De Smet, HTTP://BARTDESMET.NET/BLOGS/BART/ARCHIVE/2007/02/19/INLINING-YES-IT-HAPPENS.ASPX. It benchmarks inlining in great detail.

On the other hand, a profiler can be deceived by this mechanism. When a function is inlined at execution time, a profiler could report zero calls to the function, even if we know for sure that our test scenario contains several calls to it.

Listing 2-37 is a test code.

```
using System;
using System.Runtime.CompilerServices;

namespace InliningBenchmark
{
    class Program
    {
        static void Main(string[] args)
        {
            LoopWithoutInlining();
            LoopWithInlining();
        }

        #region Without INLINING

        private static void LoopWithoutInlining()
        {
            for (int index = 0; index < 1000000; index++)
                GlobalFunctionWithoutInlining(1);
        }

        private static int GlobalFunctionWithoutInlining(int parameter)
        {
            int result = FunctionWithoutInlining(parameter);
            return result + 1;
        }

        [MethodImpl(MethodImplOptions.NoInlining)]
        private static int FunctionWithoutInlining(int parameter)
        {
            return parameter * 2;
        }

        #endregion
```

```
    #region With INLINING

    private static void LoopWithInlining()
    {
        for (int index = 0; index < 1000000; index++)
            GlobalFunctionWithInlining(1);
    }

    private static int GlobalFunctionWithInlining(int parameter)
    {
        int result = FunctionWithInlining(parameter);
        return result + 1;
    }

    private static int FunctionWithInlining(int parameter)
    {
        return parameter * 2;
    }

    #endregion
    }
}
```

Listing 2-37

Two sets of three functions calling each other appear in this code. The two sets are exactly the same, except for the names and the fact that, in one case, the last function explicitly disables inlining.

Caution

For the inlining to be visible on this code, one should remember to compile the code in Release mode, in order to activate .NET code optimizations. If a debug version is used, one will not see any difference in performance, and the behavior we are talking about below will not be reproduced.

Analyzing this code with Red Gate's ANTS Performance Profiler (the tool will be introduced in detail in Chapter 4, *Profilers*) produces the time allocation graph in Figure 2-41.

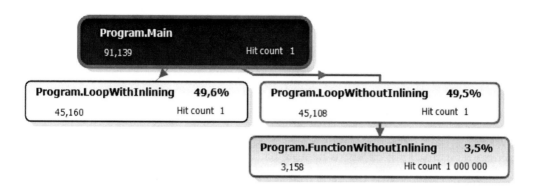

Figure 2-41: Call graph for the inlining benchmark.

This type of graph will be explained in detail later in this book, but we can clearly see the two branches that correspond to the two regions of code in our benchmark. The issue here is not performance in itself. A difference is visible, but the code is so different from an actual application that nothing can be deduced from it. What is interesting to see, however, is that FunctionWithInlining does not appear by default in the graph. Even when the **Hide insignificant methods** option is cleared, it remains invisible (see Figure 2-42).

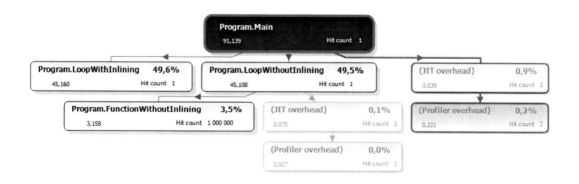

Figure 2-42: Expanded call graph for the inlining benchmark.

It is important to remember this option of ANTS Performance Profiler which, by default, will not display functions that take less than one percent of the time, in order to reduce display clutter. Incidentally, we see here that the functions that were left out were really not significant.

The function we talked about is actually absent, even if this option is disabled, since it has been inlined. Thus, the profiler cannot see it. The need to profile such a function is generally rare, since they are so reduced in code size. However, in some cases it is necessary to disable inlining in order to be able to compare variations of time. We could decorate all functions with the required attribute, but it is much simpler to use the dedicated option in the profiler. In ANTS Performance Profiler, it can be set in the **Options** dialog box (see Figure 2-43).

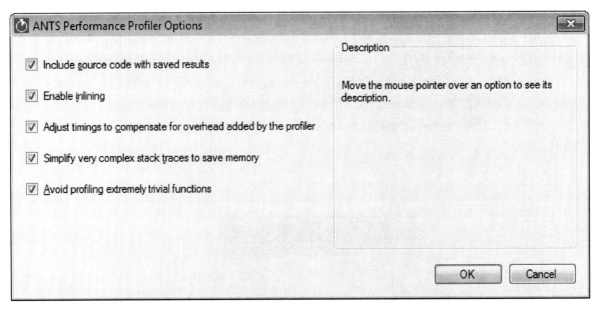

Figure 2-43: Options in ANTS Performance Profiler with Enable inlining selected.

Of course, other profilers show an equivalent option (see Figure 2-44).

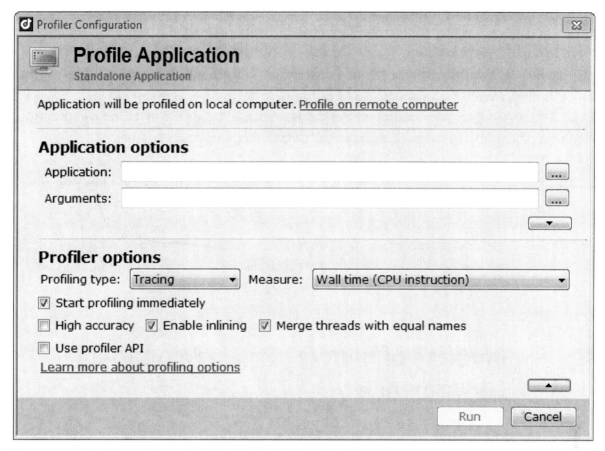

Figure 2-44: Profiler configuration in JetBrains dotTrace Profiler 4.0.

It should be noted that, when dotTrace talks about activating inlining, it is actually talking about activating its own way of handling inlining. The documentation explains that the default behavior consists of activating this option, and thus disabling the inlining through the CLR, in order to see the functions in the results. This can be a trap in the case of a pure performance analysis, because the profiler's default behavior will reduce execution speed. Of course, this issue is theoretical, as profilers slow execution down anyway. Most profilers provide options to adjust the ratio between performance loss and the completeness of the metrics. Using this inlining option by default is astonishing, but

JetBrains' position on this particular point is that it would be more disorienting for developers not to see functions that they know for sure have been executed in the reports.

In conclusion, choosing whether or not to activate such an option depends on the metrics sought. If we are open to any performance problem, it can be interesting to leave the option activated and then modify it afterwards, in order to find out whether the function itself was the problem or the number of calls that have been placed inline.

Inlining should not be seen as a significant source of performance gain

Generally speaking, one should not spend too much time studying inlining. Profilers take it into account because they are supposed to accommodate all possible situations. But in a normal session of performance improvement, we will never use this option. Material improvements are to be found elsewhere.

C   Impacts of memory management on performance

C.1   A large variety of impacts

We have talked at length about memory management, but what impacts does it have on the performance of a .NET application? There are several.

Of course, overloaded memory has the largest impact on performance: the bigger the amount of memory used, the more time the system will take to manage it. Most importantly, when the limits of physical memory are reached, the system performance will drop dramatically. At some point, it will stop responding and throw an exception like `OutOfMemoryException`.

You may also come across long-term effects. Typically, resources that are not freed will slowly clutter memory until complete saturation. Also, it is possible to notice a drop in performance simply because of memory fragmentation. In short, there are several ways in which memory issues can affect performance, and we are going to study them in detail in the following sections.

C.2   Virtual memory use

From a strictly quantitative point of view, memory occupation greater than the amount of RAM actually available will reduce the performance of the system because it will be obliged to use virtual memory, and then partially depend on the hard disk speed instead of keeping all necessary objects in physical memory. The impact in this case is extremely high, and immediately noticeable to the user.

This happens long before an `OutOfMemoryException`. Indeed, in most operating systems, a program uses a memory space that looks contiguous, but in the background the OS in fact combines the RAM with a space known as swap. Swap is a reserve of memory, with extremely degraded performance, but low cost. This memory is slow because it generally sits on a hard disk. Yet, it allows the system to temporarily use more memory than is available in physical RAM, instead of stopping applications with an error. Operating systems have been highly optimized to know which memory page should be put in swap to reduce impact, but the effect is still very noticeable.

`OutOfMemoryException`-type exceptions happen when all the virtual memory (the physical memory and the memory from the swap space) has been used. Obviously, given the difference in performance between RAM and hard disk memory (even the fastest hard disks are at least ten times slower than an old RAM stick), performance drops dramatically as soon as swap is used.

Operating systems, whether they be Windows, Linux or any other modern system, can manage memory in a very efficient manner, by allocating frequently-used pages to physical memory, and less-used ones to swap. This is done dynamically during concurrent execution of applications. This is why, if we leave an application running in the background while we work intensely with other applications, it will take a while to get it back in the foreground, and even longer for it to become as reactive as it was before. After a few operations, the OS swaps the memory pages and those corresponding to this application will progressively go back to physical memory, whereas others will go to the hard disk.

Yet, despite all the effort OSs or the CLR put into managing memory in an optimal way, they cannot do much if a given process uses most of the memory available and runs across the entire domain frequently: in this case, the system spends most of its time exchanging memory blocks from the RAM to the swap space and vice versa. That's when the user experiences a massive slowdown.

To understand precisely how all this works, let us imagine an application whose memory use (and we are not talking about memory allocation, but actual memory use) grows progressively. This application will go through all the different phases depicted in Figures 2-45 to 2-49.

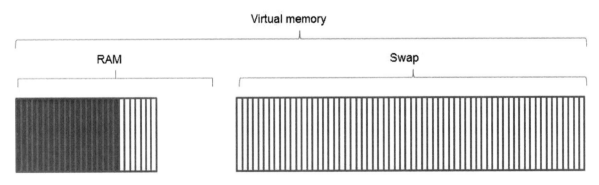

Figure 2-45: Standard occupation.

During the "standard occupation" phase (see Figure 2-45), the application only uses part of the memory that has been provisioned for its use. Of course, the OS will favor physical memory over swap space, in order to optimize performance. This is the normal state of execution for an application.

 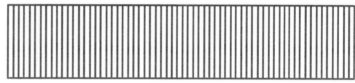

Figure 2-46: Extended standard occupation.

When the application needs more memory, the OS may have enough RAM available to simply allocate more physical memory to the process (see Figure 2-46). It may also decide to allocate more virtual memory, by preparing some swap pages. At this point, performance is still optimal, since everything is running in RAM.

 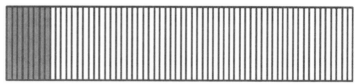

Figure 2-47: Long swap use.

If the memory needs go on up, the OS will start sorting the pages that are frequently accessed (in writing or reading) from those that are used less often. The latter ones will be sent to swap space (see Figure 2-47). As long as things stay the same, the performance will remain acceptable. Of course, it will not be optimal, but the rare cases of pages placed in the swap will not be a problem. That is, of course, unless all the pages have the same probability of being accessed (which is quite common on server applications, since each part of the memory corresponds to a given request, and there is no reason for some places to remain almost unused).

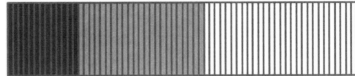

Figure 2-48: Quick swap use.

At some point, we suffer actual performance problems: this is when the physical memory could not be increased by the system, and the swap now contains some pages that the application has a quite frequent use for (see Figure 2-48). The consequence is that the system spends its time swapping pages from RAM to disk (hence the name "swap"). This takes a huge amount of time and the performance drops by a factor of ten or more.

Figure 2-49: Memory overflow.

At some point (and if the dissatisfied user has not already stopped the process), the whole virtual memory is used by the application, and the CLR will throw an `OutOfMemoryException` (see Figure 2-49). The CLR keeps just a bit of memory at any time to inform the user about this status and give the application a last chance to close properly. Do not pin high hopes on this exception, though: when it happens, there is not much we can do. Saving data on persistent memory may be possible, but it takes some memory, and we do not have any. If we try, the corresponding code will certainly reach another `OutOfMemoryException`. This is why it is recommended never to catch an `OutOfMemoryException` or `StackOverflowException`: we cannot do much with them. The most scrupulous programmers even say `SystemException` should, in general, never be caught.

C.3   Memory leaks

Readers will no doubt have heard the following assertion at least a few times: memory leaks do not exist in .NET, because memory is managed by .NET, and thus all cases of memory leaks are taken into account by the CLR. This is partly true and partly false. If an application only deals with managed memory, we have no need to worry about memory leaks: there will not be any. But this is not the way all applications work. The .NET platform allows for the use of COM objects, for example, and in particular the BCL provides wrappers to these unmanaged resources.

This is when problems start to appear. If a .NET object owns an external resource that has not been freed correctly and lives on somewhere in memory, there is no way the .NET object can be released.

Let us imagine a very simple application that is composed of two forms. The first form is there simply to allow for simulating a memory leak at the requested moment (see Figure 2-50).

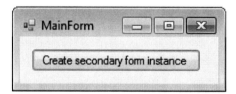

Figure 2-50: Main window of the memory-leaking test application.

The actual memory leak comes from the second form (see Figure 2-51).

Figure 2-51: Secondary window of the memory-leaking test application.

The content of this form is not important, and has no impact on the presence of a memory leak.

The code for the main form (except for the code that generates the graphical objects, which is of no interest to us) is as shown in Listing 2-38.

```
using System;
using System.Windows.Forms;

namespace MemoryLeak
{
    /// <summary>
    /// The main form is there only to run instances of the second form.
    /// The main form does not leak any resource.
    /// </summary>
    public partial class MainForm : Form
    {
        public MainForm()
        {
            InitializeComponent();
        }
```

```
        private void button1_Click(object sender, EventArgs e)
        {
            // Instantiation and display of the second form
            SecondaryForm dialog = new SecondaryForm();
            dialog.ShowDialog();

            // The best practice that consists of calling Dispose on the form
            // will not have any effect on the memory leak in the secondary form
            dialog.Dispose();

            // It is essential in our test to call the GC in order to be sure
            // that the memory is actually lost (leaked) and not only
            // kept for later recycling
            GC.Collect(GC.MaxGeneration);
        }
    }
}
```

Listing 2-38

Listing 2-39 shows the code for the second form.

```
using System.Collections.Generic;
using System.Windows.Forms;
using Microsoft.Win32;

namespace MemoryLeak
{
    /// <summary>
    /// The secondary form is the one that leaks memory
    /// </summary>
    public partial class SecondaryForm : Form
    {
        List<decimal> Content = new List<decimal>();

        public SecondaryForm()
        {
            // Initialization of the form, with the filling of a list of numbers,
            // just to artificially increase the amount of memory used,
            // which will help us see the increases in memory in the
            // performance monitor
```

```
        InitializeComponent();
        for (int index = 0; index < 100000; index++)
            Content.Add(0M);


        // The memory leak comes from the fact that, when hooking to a
        // system event and never unhooking it, the current form
        // makes it impossible for the GC to recycle it
        SystemEvents.PowerModeChanged += new PowerModeChangedEventHandler
                                        (SystemEvents_PowerModeChanged);
    }


    void SystemEvents_PowerModeChanged(object sender,
                                    PowerModeChangedEventArgs e)
    {
        // What is actually done here has no importance
    }


    private void SecondaryForm_FormClosed(object sender, FormClosedEventArgs e)
    {
        // If one wishes to correct the memory leak problem demonstrated
        // here, the best way to do so is to uncomment the line below;
        // if this is done, nothing will prevent the form from being recycled
        // SystemEvents.PowerModeChanged -= new PowerModeChangedEventHandler
        // (SystemEvents_PowerModeChanged);
    }
}
}
```

Listing 2-39

The code above has been heavily commented, and there should be no need to repeat the explanation of the leak. Yet, it is interesting to follow it through. To do that, we execute the program **perfmon**, which is Windows' performance monitor, and we add a counter on private memory used by the process (see Figure 2-52).

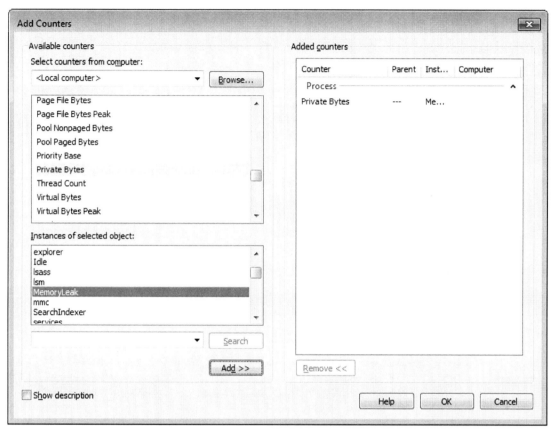

Figure 2-52: Setting a counter to watch memory leaks.

The screen capture does not show it because of the large number of counters, but this particular one is part of the **Process** category. This is not a .NET related counter, but a system counter that can be watched on any application, even if it is not managed by the CLR. It should be noted that the analysis is restricted to one given application, in our case the test **MemoryLeak** process.

If we start the application and open a secondary form several times by clicking on the button of the main form, we can close the windows, call the **Dispose** method indirectly, and even force a GC pass, but the memory will still increase at every new instance of the form, as shown in Figure 2-53. This graph is typical of a memory leak.

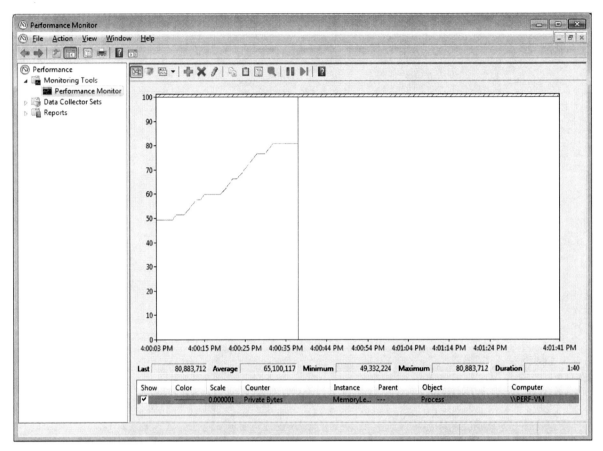

Figure 2-53: Graph of the private memory used when memory is leaking.

Once we correct the application code by uncommenting the line that releases the `SystemEvents.PowerModeChanged` resource properly, we get a graph that shows a normal use of memory (see Figure 2-54).

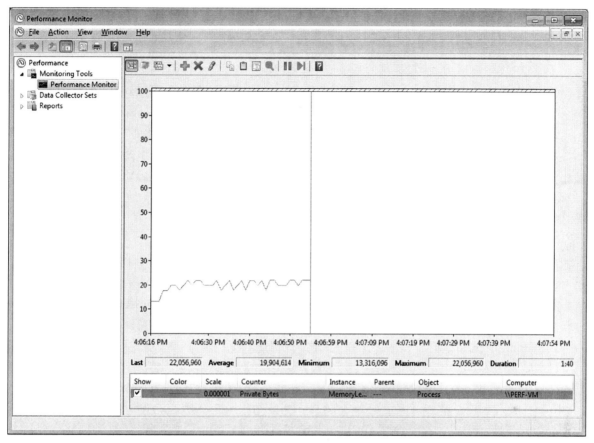

Figure 2-54: Graph of the private memory used when no leaks appear.

This shows that memory leaks do indeed exist in .NET, even if they are limited to particular circumstances. However, simply following conventions for resource releasing should ensure we avoid them.

C.4 Special heap for big objects, and memory fragmentation

Memory allocation has been discussed in great detail at the beginning of this chapter, because it is essential to understand the GC mechanism well and, in particular, the role of generations, in order to anticipate potential performance problems. Nevertheless, not everything has been covered, and there is a type of memory management designed specifically for large objects (the limit being set at 85 kilobytes in versions 2.0 to 3.5 of .NET). These objects are indeed managed in a separate heap, called the Large Object Heap (we will use the acronym LOH in the following section).

This heap is different because it is not compacted. The objects it contains are generally images or binary fragments, or even objects managing arrays, which take a lot of memory space. This means that moving them around during compaction would take quite some time, and the CLR decides to leave them where they are, and remembers the free slots in which it will be possible to put some other objects later.

In general, this is not a problem because on an application life cycle (the running of a client application from process start to its closing, or the length of time between two process recycles for an ASP.NET application), few large objects are created. These tend to be big objects that have roughly the same life cycle as the application that contains them. But there are particular cases, for example, an application dealing with bitmaps, in which the CLR will have to manipulate many instances of such objects. Since the memory space is not compacted after each GC pass, it will get more and more fragmented except in the particular case where the instances all have the same size. If it becomes too fragmented, there comes a time where it becomes impossible to allocate large objects, and the CLR throws an OutOfMemoryException-type exception.

The case is rare enough not to be covered in depth in the present book, which concentrates on "traditional" errors that bear the largest impact on performance.

Readers who are interested in this subject can refer to the scarce documentation available on the Internet, in particular *The Large Object Heap*, Mohammad Jalloul, HTTP://BLOG. MOHAMMADJALLOUL.COM/BLOGS/MO/ARCHIVE/2010/02/21/THE-LARGE-OBJECT-HEAP.ASPX and *Trouble with the Large Object Heap*, Keith Vinson, HTTP://WWW.CODEPROJECT.COM/ KB/CS/LARGE_OBJECTS_____TROUBLE.ASPX (there are four underscores between "Objects" and "Trouble"). I will only suggest a few solutions to avoid the problem.

- Generally speaking (and this advice applies to garbage collection in general), the developer should let .NET CLR do its work. Most of the time, it knows how to deal with these objects better. Fragmentation of the LOH is one of the main reasons why one should not call `GC.Collect` explicitly: one call per code execution will inevitably lead to more frequent execution of the GC, thus accelerating the fragmentation if it is bound to appear.

- In the particular case of large objects, several possibilities are offered to us in order to make the work of the CLR on the LOH more efficient:

- This can seem overly simplistic, but there are cases where it is possible to cut a large object into several smaller ones. In the case of arrays or lists of value types, the solution can be to point to instances of reference types, which will reduce the size, by keeping only the reference instead of the content. Of course this only defers the problem, but it can be enough in some cases.

- In the (not so rare) case where large objects are of the same type and thus, under certain circumstances, may be the same size, this fact can help reduce fragmentation because the spaces released will be exactly the same size as the space requested by the next allocation processes.

- The most elegant way to solve this fragmentation problem at the object level is to implement a pooling architecture: instead of re-creating an object every time one is allocated, we will only create a few instances of a class that will be coded so that it can be used by several successive calls. The code will, of course, be more complex in order to deal with re-entrance, but this is the best solution, because the number of instances on the whole application life cycle will be limited to the size of the pool, thus making it impossible to reach the memory limit, or even to generate fragmentation because of this class.

- Finally, and this may not be the most elegant solution, but it is certainly the simplest one (and one that is largely accepted on server applications): we can recycle the process from time to time. Memory is thus completely released, and we start again with zero fragmentation. In addition, memory leaks are reset. The wait for the process restarting and the loss of state can generally be dealt with by rotating processes and ensuring that sessions are ended cleanly. Developers often tend to reject this kind of solution because it lacks elegance. Yet, in an Agile context, where pragmatism is of utmost importance, this approach is justified. Indeed, it achieves its goal with a large economy of means. Customers are generally much more open to this kind of solution than we think they are, particularly when they realize even Microsoft uses this trick in IIS.

Caution

The fact that the LOH is not compacted leads some developers to not pin objects in memory for interoperability. One should do so, though. Microsoft documentation is clear on the fact that this may change in future versions of .NET. It is thus essential to use the pinning mechanism if this is the expected result, and not rely on the fact that the instances do not move, which is actually just a side-effect of the current lack of compaction.

D   Other resources to look after

D.1   Memory is not everything

The previous sections have explained at length how memory consumption could affect the performance of a .NET application. Although problems linked to RAM are the major source of slowdowns, they are far from being the only ones. All resources of a system can become bottlenecks at some point.

D.2   CPU

First comes the processor consumption. This is the most common limiting factor in an application's performance. It is also the hardest criterion to study. On the graph in Figure 2-55, would you say the processor is being used correctly?

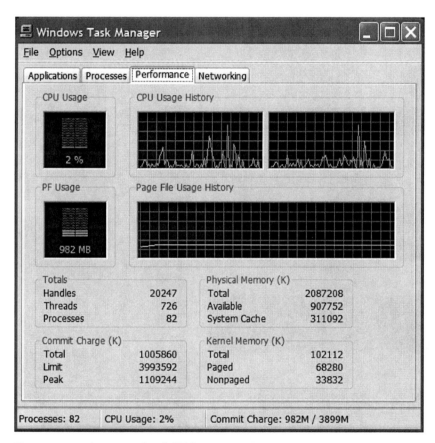

Figure 2-55:   An example of CPU consumption.

Let us first notice that the two cores are being used, which is the sign of a multithreaded application. Although this is standard practice for professional software which is widely distributed, it is far from being guaranteed on any tailor-made piece of software that comes from a small software development company. Lots of small utility programs only use one core, and bringing the power of multicore programming to non-expert programmers is one of the major challenges of the coming years.

What can we say about the fact that the CPU consumption spikes? What about the fact that its average level is well under half of what is available? Is it a good thing that the application is not too greedy with the CPU? We could also argue that it does not use all the resources that are available…

The answer depends on the context. Let us take another example (see Figure 2-56).

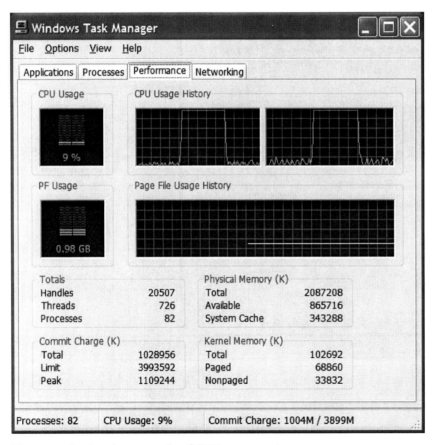

Figure 2-56: Another example of CPU consumption.

This time, we notice that the processor is used at almost 100% for a considerable period of time. A developer could say that the application is running "flat out." Again, is this good or not?

The context is essential to determine whether CPU consumption is correct or not. In the second example, the computer was calculating a 3D render, which is an operation needing lots of mathematical operations. In this situation, it makes sense that CPU use is 100%. Had it been only 80%, this would have been the sign of a bottleneck in the loading of data from the hard disk, for example. If troughs appeared in the graph, this could have meant that the render operation needed some data from the disk. It would then be necessary to load it into memory, which would be bad practice: in order for a render to be as quick as possible, everything should already be placed in RAM.

On the other hand, the first example also shows a normal use of the processor, because it relates to the start of an office application: the major work in this case is reading from the hard disk, and it is normal that the CPU does not have much to do. It can serve other processes in the meantime.

In short, CPU use for a task is not a very useful indicator. In fact, it only makes sense on a set of parallel tasks, and in this case informs more on the health of the system as a whole rather than on a given application. If a 3D render occupies 100% of the processor, any new process will only get allocated a part of what it would have received, had it been the only process running on the machine. In the same way, on a web server that deals with hundreds of requests in parallel, each request uses a fraction of the CPU but globally, when the whole reaches 80%, care should be taken because a sudden request peak could seriously increase the average answering time and lower the throughput.

Multicore programming

Despite multicore processors becoming more and more common, the notion of processor time will stay as long as the number of cores remains lower than the number of processes run in parallel on a machine, and certainly beyond to ensure a good distribution of resource. On a machine with two cores for three processes, or with only one core, the applications have to share the CPU power. The OS is in charge of sharing the CPU, and allocates a slot of computing time to such or such an application, depending on its priority. During this timeslot, the CPU will only process operations for this application. The capacity of the OS to carefully balance these timeslots determines its reactivity. If the slots are too big, it will feel as though the application has been suspended. If they are too small, the CPU will waste too much time switching from one application to the other.

D.3   Inputs/outputs

As soon as an application reads or writes to the disk, the time taken for an operation is considerably longer. Still, it seems quite difficult to imagine getting rid of persistent memory, which is necessary at least for loading an application when it starts up.

Hard disk speed and access time are clearly an important criterion, but controllers are also important. However, this is a hardware question, which has nothing to do with .NET process performance optimization.

On the other hand, an application that was programmed to generate a temporary file for every operation would be confronted by a serious bottleneck, and would benefit, for example, from grouping its writing activities in one file, with the additional help of a buffering architecture.

Temporary files generation – a word of warning

I have noticed several times on .NET 2.0 / Windows XP platforms that a call to System.
IO.GetTempFileName() *did not always send a new filename. In some cases where calls were made in very quick succession, the function could return the same name twice which, of course, causes a problem when the second process is prevented from writing to the file, since the first one has locked it. A safety code, verifying the pre-existence and running the function another time after a small wait, was enough to provide a reliable solution. The code in Listing 2-40 shows this solution.*

```csharp
private static readonly int _MaximumTrialsNumber = 8;
private static readonly int _DelayBetweenTrialsInMilliseconds = 50;

public static string GenerateTempFile()
{
    string tempFile = string.Empty;
    int numberTrials = 0;
    bool succeeded = false;
    while (numberTrials++ < _MaximumTrialsNumber && !succeeded)
    {
        try
        {
            tempFile = Path.GetTempFileName();
            succeeded = !File.Exists(tempFile);
            if (!succeeded)
                Thread.Sleep(_DelayBetweenTrialsInMilliseconds);
        }
        catch (IOException)
        {
            Thread.Sleep(_DelayBetweenTrialsInMilliseconds);
        }
    }
    if (!succeeded)
        throw new ApplicationException("Impossible to generate a temporary file");
    return tempFile;
}
```

Listing 2-40

It is particularly on a server application, dealing with lots of individual requests, that I/O should be watched carefully, in addition with the code using them being thread-safe.

Figure 2-57 shows a screenshot of the Windows Performance Monitor (running and use of this tool are discussed in detail later) when starting OpenOffice Calc.

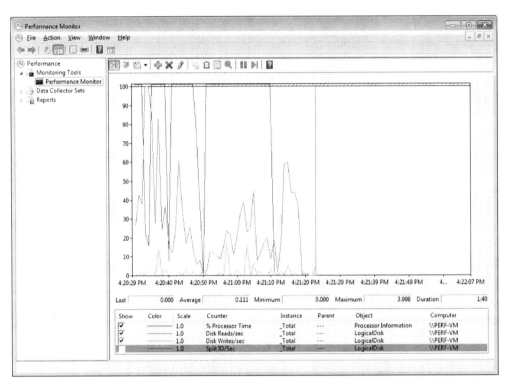

Figure 2-57: Performance Monitor included in Microsoft Windows.

We clearly see the blue line (hard disk readings) spiking and, as expected in this kind of operation, when this curve is at the top, the curve for the CPU and the one tracking disk writing stay quite low. This is quite logical: since we are loading an application, there is little reason for writing to the disk, except for some small activity logs. As for the CPU, it is not insignificant because running an application needs some calculation as well as reading libraries. But the hard disk remains the limiting factor in such cases, and the CPU can serve several other applications at the same time.

D.4   Available hard disk space

There exists another case when non-volatile memory can limit an application in its execution. We have talked about the qualitative aspect of using hard disk space (limits in I/O), but we should also take into account the quantitative aspect.

Given the sizes of current disks, it seems hardly possible that an application could be limited by lack of available space, but several factors mean this situation is more likely to arise in industry than on a home computer.

- SAS hard disks for servers are more expensive than SATA disks for home computers, and have smaller capacity. At the time of writing this book, a 15,000 RPM SAS disk with 148 gigabyte capacity was three times the price of an equivalent 1 terabyte SATA disk.

- Virtual machines often use tens of gigabytes, and a server can be filled with virtual disks very quickly when duplicating machines for test purposes.

- In industry, it is common to restrict user space with quotas. This means that, even if the disk has plenty of free space, it may be possible to reach a situation where an application run by a given user does not have any available space.

An overconsumption of hard disk space most of the time reveals simple mistakes, the majority of which are:

- traces activated in verbose mode and left active by mistake on a production server under heavy load; in addition to slowing down the application, this can quickly lead to a full disk

- bad practice in the removal of temporary files can also lead to an overconsumption that will be slower, but just as problematic as the previous case; as a rule of thumb, the process that creates a temporary file should always be held responsible for its removal.

In real life

When installing an XML-based ETL (Extract, Transform, Load) application, a debugging function had been created that would dump the data content at each step of the transformation workflow. On a workflow with 10 actions, each running on the 1,000 lines / 20 columns, each execution could report up to 10 megabytes of traces. This ETL was called several times per hour and per user, and the application was used by 75 to 200 users per server. A small calculation leads to a potential of 10 gigabytes on the hard disk every hour. Luckily, we have never sent an incorrect configuration file with this setting enabled...

D.5   Network bandwidth

Often, the trio composed of CPU, RAM and ROM is seen as representing all the resources of a computer. This was historically true on systems that were not connected, but we now live in a world of interconnected machines, and the first resource everyone is aware of is the speed of their Internet connection. This is particularly important because the network is almost always much slower than the hard disk.

In short, one should take care to use the network bandwidth sparingly in an application. This is of utmost importance when the network is the Internet, the speed being far lower than on an internal network.

This recommendation applies particularly to ASP.NET applications, where developers should be careful with the size of requests as well as responses.

Caution

Be careful with the facility provided by ASP.NET to create web services. Simply placing a `[WebMethod]` *attribute on top of a method generates everything that is necessary to transform it into a web service. But, by default, every object returned by this method will have its whole content serialized in XML and sent through as a response to a SOAP request. If this object has numerous instances associated as list members, it will quickly increase in size. More importantly, much more data is often sent than what was really necessary. Best practices, based on Data Transfer Objects, use of* `XmlIgnore` *attributes, etc. are detailed later in this book.*

Chapter 3: Sample Application

A   Criteria

A.1   Why use a real application?

As has already been explained, this book's philosophy is not about understanding the detailed inner workings of .NET and analyzing every possible minute optimization, but rather showing the usual causes of degraded performance in .NET applications. Causes are sometimes simple, but finding the exact location of the bug from the symptoms is generally more complex. In short, the goal here is not to go into performance tuning, but to show the typical coding errors that cause performance degradation.

With this in mind, it quickly became clear when writing this book that the associated sample application could be nothing less than an actual industrial-grade piece of software. Having stressed the importance of dealing with real problems and moving away from an academic point of view, it would have been out of place to propose applying profiling methods to limited code samples without any link to reality.

A.2   Using experience

The use of a real application also made my life easier, as I did not have to create artificial problems and so avoided all the validation associated with doing this. Past experience of trying to demonstrate a problem to an outside developer, has shown that it is sometimes difficult to re-create a performance-related problem with sample code.

The idea behind the present book started to form after several years of analyses and performance-related audits of an industrial application, today used by hundreds of customers and thousands of end-users, some of them with extremely demanding performance requirements. Having been the software architect behind this platform, I decided (with the agreement of my managers) to base the sample application on this experience.

After 10 years and up to 35 developers working on this platform, I think I have collected enough material to recognize the most statistically recurrent performance-related coding errors.

A.3   The choice of transparency

Since I am using a real application to demonstrate performance improvement scenarios, I am implicitly recognizing actual errors in implementing code, or even analysis errors in some cases. It is, of course, not easy to recognize your own errors in public, particularly in a commercial piece of software, but I believe that a degree of humility is necessary to improve a software application as well as your own practices.

By contrast, a software editor who denies the presence of any more-than-small-sized bugs in their application would definitely not be credible. Confusion between computer-based processes (which are not prone to errors due to the highly deterministic nature of electronics) and code development (much more prone to bugs) is largely responsible for the common belief that a software program should always "just work."

A well-designed and long-debugged piece of software will work very robustly in all situations for which it has been validated. In particular cases where a great deal of effort has been put into testing or establishing mathematical proofs of algorithms, it can even be possible to guarantee that the software will function correctly, but generally with a price tag that will efficiently deter most customers.

In short, once the program is in working order, its functioning will be robust and the developer can be very confident in its capacity to execute processes according to the business requirements. But it is impossible to have a high-performance program after each release iteration, short of spending lots of time profiling, and thus increasing its cost.

Let us take an example as simple as list sorting. Any beginner developer can find the insertion algorithm by themselves in just a few minutes. On the other hand, it has taken researchers months to agree on an effective algorithm, namely QuickSort. Traditional algorithms had a serious performance limitation: their execution time was proportional to the size of the list squared. These methods were said to be of order n^2. The huge benefit of QuickSort has been to reduce this order to n log(n). On large lists, the gain can reach a hundred-fold. Further information can be found at HTTP://COMJNL.OXFORDJOURNALS. ORG/CONTENT/5/1/10.SHORT.

This should make it obvious that all applications with millions of lines of code contain numerous sections that are suboptimal. Pretending the contrary and hiding code-related performance problems from customers or users is counterproductive. In an Agile approach, a more cooperative relationship should be sought with customers.

A.4   The limits of transparency

For copyright reasons, the code used here as an example could not be taken directly from the actual industrial application source code. Also, it was not possible to use screen captures of this product.

This means I had to create a kind of mock-up of the reference application, only reproducing the code areas that would show actual performance problems. Of course, this results in a miscellany of anti-patterns, an anthology of worst practices.

Some of the errors put into this sample application come directly from the industrial application on which this book is based, others have been added deliberately to increase the load and fit, into one single application, all the examples of code that can harm performance. In the first case, the names of classes, functions and variables have been changed, but the structure is otherwise identical. As for the architecture, I have tried to stick to what had been put in place at the beginning of the reference application's life cycle, in order to show how the architecture itself has evolved to improve overall performance.

B   Sample application

B.1   Field of use

The application (or rather platform, because it is used by several business applications) chosen for demonstration is based on .NET 2.0. The first application using this platform is a plain old records-management application, with forms and workflows, reporting, bulk processing, etc. The second one uses the same architecture to provide users with tools to model complex budget calculations.

B.2   Architecture

From a high-level point of view, the platform enables developers to create applications with a WinForms-based client that communicates with an ASP.NET server through web services. The back-end is linked to heterogeneous databases through ADO.NET. Business applications are based on this platform, and additional modules such as reporting are integrated.

B.3   Graphical User Interface

This book is about showing code structure and architecture solutions that lead to performance loss. This means it was out of the question to clutter up the code with lines relating to aesthetics or even ergonomics.

The GUI, as bland as can be borne, is accepted as such: the buttons are gray, the interface does not use any color and there is no layout to speak of. The only aspects of a GUI that are present are those necessary for the purposes of demonstration. For example, loading dynamic content required WinForms containers, which have thus been used here. Lots more code would be necessary to make this application user-friendly, but this could lead to confusion.

B.4   Business description

The purpose of the sample application has been extremely simplified in comparison with the original application, in order to better demonstrate the performance problems, and make profiling easier, as well as relating it to this book.

The business involves persons and contracts. A list of persons is stored in a database, with their first name, last name, and a description. A list of contracts with date, amount, and discount code is stored in another table. Each contract is linked to one and only one person, who is a party to the contract.

The GUI only allows navigation of the data, starting from either persons or contracts. An entry can be selected from the lists displayed, in order to view its details. In the case of contracts, it is also possible to launch a merged Word file, or a text file containing an XML summary of the contract data.

When the list of contracts is displayed from a person, only the contracts to which this person is a party are displayed. Finally, a specific interface control provides breadcrumbs to navigate the display history.

C   Application details

C.1   Finding the application

In order to fully understand what follows, I recommend that you take a few minutes to get used to the sample application. It's called PROFI, and it can be downloaded from the Simple Talk website at:
WWW.SIMPLE-TALK.COM/RedGateBooks/JPGouigoux/CodeDownload.zip.

A horrible application

At the risk of repetition, the sample application we will be using is a kind of global performance anti-pattern. A seasoned developer will soon realize that it is coded in a catastrophic manner. But this is the goal of this application, which is supposed to show the most common performance-related problems that have been found during several years of use of an industrial application, as well as some additional ones. The reader is thus invited to curb their potential indignation. This is absolutely normal: PROFI should reflect all performance-related evil practices.

C.2   Why PROFI?

Such a name may sound strange. Rest assured that it has nothing to do with "profit," as the application is published under a Creative Commons license BY-NC-SA.

There are a couple of reasons behind this name:

- PROFI is the beginning of "profiling," which is one of the main subjects of the present book

- PROFI is the abbreviation of "professional" in German; I like to think readers will be professionals or developers interested in becoming more professional.

C.3   Database setup

In order to simplify installing the associated database, I have provided several methods to choose from.

Support files

All necessary files referred to below are available on the Simple Talk website at:
WWW.SIMPLE-TALK.COM/REDGATEBOOKS/JPGOUIGOUX/CODEDOWNLOAD.ZIP.

C.3.a   Attaching the database files

The easiest method is to copy the `PROFI.mdf` and `PROFI_log.LDF` files into `C:\ Program Files\Microsoft SQL Server\MSSQL10.SQLEXPRESS\MSSQL\DATA`, then attach the database.

C.3.b   Restoring the backup

The second method is to simply restore the PROFI database by using the `PROFI.bak` backup file.

C.3.c   Using scripts

The third method is to execute the script called `PROFI-Creation.sql`. To do so, you just need to connect to SQL Server Management Studio, open the script and execute it.

File location

Depending on SQL Server installation options, the user may have to modify the locations of the MDF and LDF files in the script. By default, they are placed in `C:\Program Files\Microsoft SQL Server\MSSQL10.SQLEXPRESS\MSSQL\DATA` *for a SQL Express version of SQL Server.*

C.3.d   Manual creation

The final method, which is the best way of understanding the data structure, is to manually create the database, by following the simple instructions below.

1. In SQL Server Management Studio or in the Server Manager in Visual Studio .NET, create a database and name it PROFI. Use the Windows Integrated Authentication method.

2. There is no need to create a particular user; we will use dbo.

3. Add a table called PERSON, with the following fields:

    a. uid, with type nchar(32), declared as primary key

    b. lastname, with type nvarchar(60), declared as mandatory field (NOT NULL)

    c. firstname, with type nvarchar(60), with NULL allowed

    d. description, with type nvarchar(500), with NULL allowed.

4. Add a table called CONTRACT, with the following fields:

    a. uid, with type nchar(32), declared as primary key

    b. owner, with type nchar(32), with NULL allowed, and declared as a foreign key on the uid field of the PERSON table

    c. amount, with type numeric(9,0), declared as mandatory field (NOT NULL)

    d. start, with type datetime, with NULL allowed

    e. discount, with type nvarchar(8), with NULL allowed.

5. Use the data import capability of SQL Server (accessible in the Management Studio) to incorporate data from files PROFI-CONTRACT.csv and PROFI-PERSON.csv if you want to use a text format, and PROFI-DATA.xls if you prefer to use an Excel file.

Adding data manually

It is also possible to add only a few lines of data manually to the two tables. The only important thing is to take care to put, in the contracts table, owners that correspond to persons that exist in the other table. The quantity is not really important. Anyway, the times obtained when profiling will differ from those in the book because of the difference of computers, context, etc. If this approach is chosen, the tests will have to be modified accordingly (search for "Assert" in the PROFI source code).

C.4 Installing the application

C.4.a Opening the solution

The files supplied with the present book contain a directory called `SampleApplica-tionPROFI` with a Visual Studio 2010 solution, which is self-sufficient. When launching `SampleApplicationPROFI.sln`, you will get a set of projects as in Figure 3-1 in the Solution Explorer of Visual Studio.

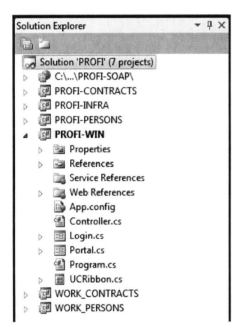

Figure 3-1:   Solution Explorer of Visual Studio for the PROFI application.

Readers using the Express version of Visual Studio may experience difficulties with the web project, because some versions apparently do not embed a web development server. The simplest thing to do in this case is to install IIS Express (which is also free and available at HTTP://WWW.MICROSOFT.COM/DOWNLOAD/EN/DETAILS.ASPX?ID=1038), then create a web application and copy the content of PROFI-SOAP into it.

The reader can also simply copy the directory PROFI-IIS (which sits in the Setup directory supplied with the book), then declare it as a web application in IIS or IIS Express. The corresponding URL should then be used to configure the PROFI-WIN client.

C.4.b   Solution compiling

If the web references are out of date, you should build the solution, refresh them, and then build the solution again. It is a good idea to update the server configuration as soon as possible. To do so, let us open the web.config file in the PROFI-SOAP project. This is the web services server project, particularly interesting extracts of which are shown in Listing 3-1.

```xml
<?xml version="1.0" encoding="utf-8"?>
<configuration>
  [...]
  <appSettings>
    <add key="PROFI.Authentication.Mode" value="LoginForm"/>
    <add key="PROFI.ServerDescription" value="Test server — Local mode"/>
  </appSettings>
  <connectionStrings>
    <add name="DBConnection" connectionString="Data Source=ALDEBARAN\
SQLExpress;Initial Catalog=PROFI;Integrated Security=True"/>
  </connectionStrings>
  <system.web>
    <compilation debug="true">
      [...]
    </compilation>
    <authentication mode="Windows" />
    [...]
    <identity impersonate="true" userName="jp-gouigoux"
password="UnobfuscatedPassword" />
    [...]
  </system.web>
  [...]
</configuration>
```

Listing 3-1

The first line that needs to be modified is the connection string: it should reflect your database configuration. The example above shows a SQL Express instance, ALDEBARAN being my computer name, and PROFI being the name given to the database itself.

The other line to be modified in the configuration file is the one about impersonation: it is possible to use any user, provided that it has sufficient rights to access SQL Server. Other rights are needed, like writing to the temporary files directory, but these are normally in place, unless the configuration is particularly unusual.

Impersonation

Using impersonation is, of course, not mandatory. It is also possible to give the necessary rights to the default user under which the web server works. In the case of the web development server integrated in Visual Studio (also known as Cassini), this is the user that ran Visual Studio. If the connected user is the one who created the database as its creator-owner, impersonation will not be necessary.

All references in the solution are project references, in order to make building it easier. The only external reference is `ICSharpCode.SharpZipLib.dll`, which is supplied in the `Refs` sub-directory of the solution. Should the case arise, it could be necessary to renew the reference to this library in the PROFI-CONTRACTS and WORK-CONTRACTS projects.

The solution is quite simple in terms of code, and should compile out of the box. The only issue that has been detected by some testers (and for which we have not found any root cause) is an error message on a `*.XmlSerializers.dll` assembly when building. The way round this is to activate **Generate serialization assembly** in the properties of the project in question.

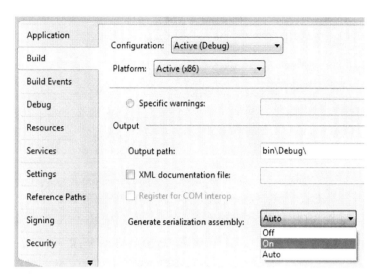

Figure 3-2:   Compiling directives.

C.4.c   Running the application

Similarly, running the application should not require any particular modifications. You should just check the following points in case of difficulties.

The start-up project should be PROFI-WIN.

The four projects corresponding to the client-side part of the application (namely those prefixed with PROFI-) should be compiled with automatic test scenario mode activated, as per Figure 3-3. We will explain the need for this in more detail in Chapter 5, Section B.2.c, *Compiling options*. For now, suffice it to say that these build options automate the running of tests, right inside the application.

If the user wishes to run the application in "normal" mode (without executing automated GUI tests), they should remove these two options from the four client-side projects and recompile. In "normal" mode, the application displays a login form. One can connect using "admin" as a user name and "hiya" as the password. It is also possible to use any other user name. In this case, the password is the user name in reverse order. For example, a login combination could be gouigoux/xuogiuog.

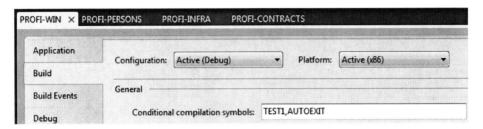

Figure 3-3:   Compiling directives.

If, at the start-up of the application, a `WebException` error appears, indicating that the process is "unable to connect to remote server," the user may have to modify the web server address in the `app.config` file of PROFI-WIN. To find the right address, one should first select the PROFI-SOAP project (this runs on a local web development server), then retrieve the port number from the project properties (see Figure 3-4).

Figure 3-4:   The port number can be found in the Properties pane.

Using this value, we can then update the following parameter in the application configuration file (the `App.config` file in project PROFI-WIN):

```
<add key="PROFI:Stubs:BaseURL" value="http://127.0.0.1:49166/PROFI-SOAP/"/>
```

Listing 3-2

Troubleshooting

Due to problems with the handling of IPv6 by the web development server when using `localhost`*, it is preferable to use the corresponding IPv4 address, which is 127.0.0.1. This issue does not arise when using IIS instead of Cassini.*

The other reference to a web server address (a bit further down in the configuration file) is not important for now. We will explain in the next chapter what this line is for.

Normally, the port number chosen should be the same as in the book, since it is related to the files supplied with it, but Visual Studio can decide to change it, and in this case you should update web references in the projects that contain them, namely PROFI-WIN, PROFI-CONTRACTS and PROFI-PERSONS.

C.5   Description of the assemblies

I have already explained in the previous paragraphs the role of some of these projects, but I list them again in full here. First, for the server-side part of the application:

- PROFI-SOAP contains the web services; this module does not contain any business-related methods, but only exposes existing ones as web methods

- PROFI-CONTRACTS contains the methods related to the business of contracts, which means database requests and the code to create associated documents

- PROFI-PERSONS contains the method related to the business of persons, as well as a reference to contracts, that are associated with persons as their owner.

As far as the client side is concerned, we have the same division in business-related domains:

- PROFI-CONTRACTS has all the classes necessary to display contract-related information

- PROFI-PERSONS is the equivalent for persons

- PROFI-WIN is the client application, in other words the start-up project and the only executable project

- PROFI-INFRA contains infrastructure methods that are useful to the three preceding projects, and thus is used as a reference by each one of them.

The reader may notice that the two business-related libraries on the client side are not directly referenced by any project. As we will explain later, those are loaded by reflection, from the execution directory by convention. This is the reason for the following line in the build events properties of projects PROFI-PERSONS and PROFI-CONTRACTS:

```
copy "$(ProjectDir)bin\$(ConfigurationName)\*.*" "$(SolutionDir)PROFI-WIN\
bin\$(ConfigurationName)\"
```

Listing 3-3

C.6   Client-side architecture

The client is based on a message bus architecture. The class **Portal** in PROFI-WIN is the main window for the WinForms application, but all interactions happen through an instance of the **Bus** class of PROFI-INFRA.

This bus distributes instances of the **Message** class to all instances of classes that implement interface **IController** (these two definitions are also located in PROFI-INFRA). When launching the application, all these instances, called controllers, are created dynamically by reflection on the business-related libraries, which contain classes named **Controller**. The first message emitted by the bus runs the authentication process.

Then, each user interaction generates another message. For example:

```
private void btnPersons_Click(object sender, EventArgs e)
{
    PROFI_INFRA.Message msgPersons = new PROFI_INFRA.Message("PERSONSLIST");
    Bus.Current.SendMessage(msgPersons);
}
```

Listing 3-4

Eventually, the controllers process the messages they are concerned with (See Listing 3-5).

```
public void ProcessMessage(PROFI_INFRA.Message message)
{
    switch (message.Order)
    {
        case "HOME":
            // Command to return to the beginning of the application history
            _DisplayContentHistory.Clear();
            Portal.Current.Reset();
            break;

            [...]
    }
}
```

Listing 3-5

The way the client works will not be explained in detail for now, since we are going to study it in lots more detail in the next chapters.

C.7 Web services architecture

For the same reason, there is no use in explaining in depth how the web services work, as the profiling process will lead us into that in the main chapters of this book.

For now it is enough to point out that the three web services contained in the project are for general-purpose (`Service.svc`), contracts related (`ServiceContracts.svc`) and persons related (`ServicePersons.svc`) methods.

C.8 Database architecture

The database only contains two tables: one for persons and one for contracts. All types are simple, unique identifiers are used as primary keys, and a foreign key is put in place between the uid field of PERSON and the owner field of CONTRACT (see Figure 3-5).

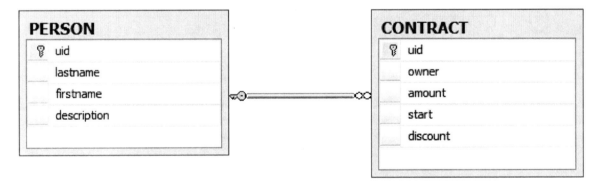

Figure 3-5: PROFI's (simple) database structure.

D   Why such a heavy application?

The reader may wonder why a sample application needs such heavy project partitioning, a message bus based architecture for the client, dynamic loading of components and so on. We seem to be far from the Agile best practices of simplicity.

It is absolutely true that, had we simply had to create an application that provides the features requested for PROFI, we could have hard-coded a simple executable with everything in it, including database access. In fact, we could even have done without any database, storing data in flat files. If the goals of the application were only to provide the features shown here, namely displaying contracts and persons, Agile methods would lead to a much simpler version of PROFI and, clearly, the present code would represent a case of huge over-architecture.

But there is a reason behind this apparently over-weighted code: as has been explained at the beginning of this chapter, PROFI is derived from an actual industrial application, in order to show realistic performance-related problems. It was out of the question to rewrite a new application. I wanted to remove everything unnecessary from the original application, only leaving in architectures and sections of code that were involved in performance problems found over the years in both test and production.

This also explains why, when reading the sample application code, one might be astonished by how obvious redundancies are: they are so because the rest of the application has been cleaned of 99.9% of its code, in order to produce a concentrate of all the mistakes that have been corrected over years of development. In the real word, with almost one thousand times more lines of code, it is of course much more difficult to find redundancies, multiple requests, etc.

By starting with a real application, our goal was to show the reader actual performance problems.

E   Recommended methods

In the next chapters, we are going to analyze in depth all the points that are performance-sensitive in the target application. When doing so, it is important to keep in mind a few basic profiling principles, as they have been explained at the beginning of this book.

One of these principles is not to trust one's developer instinct for performance. It will be shown time and again in the following chapters that what we think is a bottleneck may not be a problem or vice versa, and that performance improvement must be led by blind faith in profiling results.

Another principle, when solving the issues that have been found through the use of profilers, is to always think in terms of simplicity. Most performance problems come from the fact that, in order to execute a given process, the computer has to go through more atomic steps than is absolutely necessary. One should remain conscious of the difference between algorithmic and inherent complexities. The former should not be much higher than the latter. Faced with a performance problem, our instinct is to re-architect. If we think in terms of refactoring, which means keeping the same behavior while simplifying internal operations, this is not a problem: it generally leads to better performance as an additional benefit. But if we design a new architecture to better solve a problem, it is difficult to prevent the complexity from increasing, and we may achieve the opposite of what we wanted.

Important note

The whole principle of this book relies on a good acceptance of the recommendations below. The practices of this book have come about from rigorous testing, years of experience and ongoing efforts at dealing with performance issues. For this reason, I recommend that you follow the instructions quite closely.

To fully benefit from the exercise, the reader is invited, even if this sounds like a lot of effort, to read the entire source code of the sample application with a critical eye, and to try and find all the points that are sources of performance problems. The files supplied with the book include an unmodified and an optimized version of the application. Of course, you should study the first version, in order to appreciate that simply reviewing code is generally quite useless for performance: often, some points are identified as problems when they are not and, inversely, code that appears harmless may be a huge problem. Sometimes, the problem is not in the coding, but in the code being inappropriate for the use cases.

A typical case is data loaded but not displayed: strong use of bandwidth and resource for nothing, just in order for the GUI to be ready to display more details. In practice, there may be lots of cases where the user does not need this piece of data, and we could spare its loading. This kind of problem is typically almost impossible to find in the code, since it is not the result of some technical mistake. It is only a problem because it is heavier than the simplest acceptable use case. Only a profiler tool will show where we are spending too much time, track down these unnecessary slowdowns and, most importantly, help us to judge if the correction is worth analyzing, depending on the time spent in the faulty code. To follow up on our example, there would be no use putting in place a two-phase data retrieval process if the rarely-used data is very small.

It is essential for you to realize by yourself these difficulties, which are inherent to performance studies, by reading the source code of the sample application before optimization, and trying to find all the problematic lines of code (I recommend that you write them down). Only then should you read on. Unless you are an expert, you will certainly learn about performance issues that you had not thought of, because only a profiler can see some issues, as explained above.

Chapter 4: Profilers

A   Choice of tool

This chapter gives a detailed overview of several profilers which may be of interest to the reader. This book is aimed at developers who want to learn enough to be able to deal with the most common performance problems, rather than at profiling experts. More complete solutions are available but they are complex to use and, moreover, very expensive. Therefore this chapter is deliberately limited to commercial products that are affordable, which will be more useful to the target audience.

To make things easier, all the examples in the following chapters use the same profiler, Red Gate ANTS Performance Profiler. This choice was not easy, and you may prefer a different tool. I will therefore introduce a range of options, all of which could be used to reproduce the analyses in the following chapters, even though it would be easier to use ANTS Performance Profiler.

This chapter includes a section on Open Source profilers, even though these tools are not as advanced as the commercial products. Nevertheless, they have been in progress for several months and the possibility of using them for professional software development will, no doubt, arise again in the not-too-distant future.

B   Red Gate ANTS Performance Profiler

B.1   Overview

Red Gate produces a performance profiler as well as a memory profiler. These two products have long been sold as a single application, but nowadays they are two separate tools, even if they share a common logic of use and appearance. In this book, we will be using only the first tool.

At the time of publishing, ANTS Performance Profiler was in version 6.3, but version 7.0 is due to be released soon. The new version will let you decompile methods without source directly from the ANTS interface, allowing you to navigate the decompiled source as if it were your own code. If you have the PDB file, you will even be able to view line-level timings for the decompiled code, letting you identify the exact code that caused the bottleneck. Version 7.0 will offer support for SharePoint 2010 and IIS Express applications, as well as full support for Windows Azure and Amazon EC2, letting you profile applications running in the cloud.

The screen captures here are based on version 6.3. The welcome screen that appears when running the software is shown in Figure 4-1.

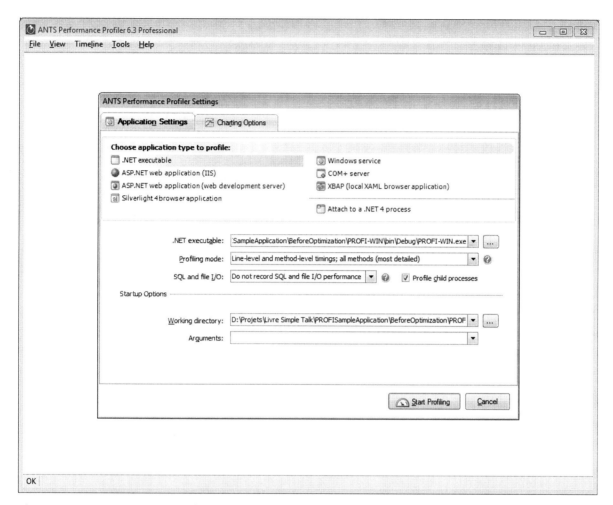

Figure 4-1: Starting ANTS Performance Profiler.

When the target application is an executable project, the profiler can be started directly from Visual Studio, using the ANTS / Profile Performance menu. When the target application ends, the results are displayed by default in a tree-based form (see Figure 4-2).

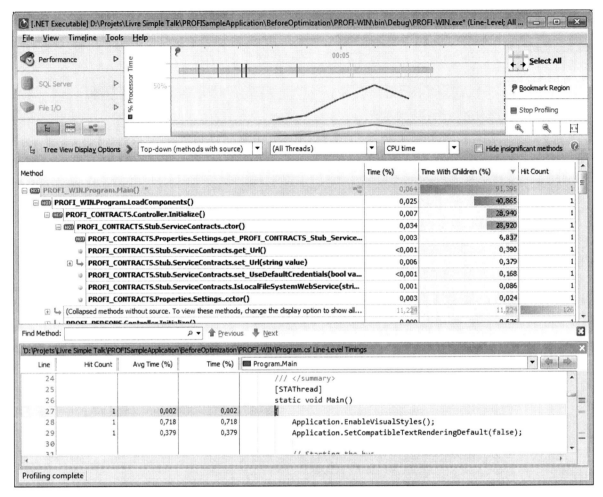

Figure 4-2: Results are displayed by default using the call tree.

The timeline in the top pane allows the user to select a position in the profiled scenario, and the table in the middle of the interface (the call tree) shows the corresponding times spent in different functions, putting the longest ("hottest") stack trace at the top. The lower pane shows the source code of the application, allowing problems to be located more precisely.

B.2 Advantages

The main advantage of ANTS Performance Profiler is that it is really easy to get used to. It is ideal for a developer who is a beginner at profiling applications, because it presents the metrics very clearly, and it does not take expert handling to identify bottlenecks.

Exploring the call stack up or down is made a breeze, through the use of visual graphs (see Figure 4-3).

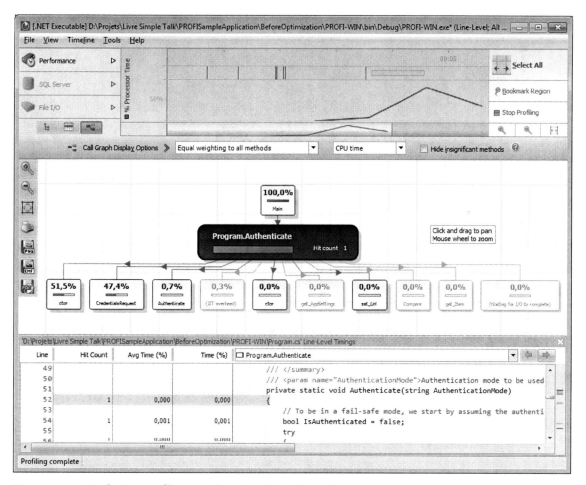

Figure 4-3: Exploring profiling results using the call graph.

This product will be explored in more detail in the rest of this book, as this is the profiler that has been chosen to show the profiling techniques on the sample application.

Other strong points of the Red Gate profiler are the richness and quality of documentation, as well as the excellent support.

Lastly, the application can be called from the command line, which enables integration in a software factory. For a truly industrial approach to performance, this feature is essential, and luckily integration has been treated with great care by Red Gate: the command line gives access to all necessary details.

B.3   Use in server analysis

B.3.a   How the profiler manages web servers

Unlike when profiling an executable application, using a profiler on an ASP.NET application needs a few preliminary adjustments, or even changes to the server configuration itself. First, it is important to know that profilers can work in several ways: they can connect directly to the IIS process, or they can use a different port that will provide the same response as the original IIS port. In the first case, it is often necessary to restart IIS, but we will not have to modify the client configuration. In the second case, we need to modify the port number used by the client, but this way avoids restarting IIS.

It should be noted that most modern profilers allow profiling on the web development server (also known as Cassini). This is the solution used by Visual Studio when a web project is created on the file system instead of a web address, as shown in Figure 4-4.

Figure 4-4: The Visual Studio New Web Site dialog box.

However, this forces us to use a virtual directory redirection.

As a consequence, we have three possible options to profile web services. These will be detailed in the following three sections about using ANTS Performance Profiler, but other profilers generally offer approximately the same options.

Performance impact of profilers

Be aware that, depending on the way they are used, profilers can have a major impact on the performance of an application. Profiling an application in production is therefore strongly discouraged.

187

B.3.b Using IIS without specifying a new port

The first method, which is the simplest if the web project has been created on an IIS virtual directory (choosing **HTTP** in the **Location** box when creating the web project in Visual Studio), consists of using the **ASP.NET web application (IIS)** option (see Figure 4-5).

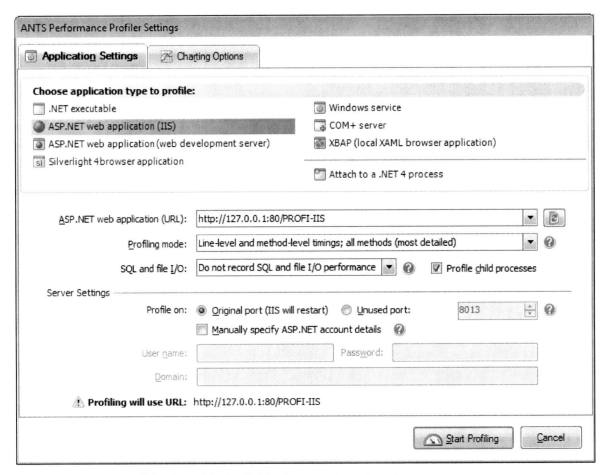

Figure 4-5: Settings dialog box with the Original port option selected.

The first profiling option is to keep the same port number, in order to avoid changing the client configuration when we profile the server. But this means restarting IIS.

Caution: by default, ANTS Performance Profiler uses the `LocalSystem` account. To use another account, you have to select the option **Manually specify ASP.NET account details** and specify a user name, password, and domain. It is highly recommended that this user has local administrator rights.

B.3.c   Using IIS by specifying a new port

The second option available when using IIS is to specify an unused port. This tells IIS to open a new instance of the application on the nominated port. The profiler then watches the new instance of the application at the specified, different URL.

ANTS Performance Profiler informs us of the modified URL that the client should call, and you will need to change the client configuration accordingly (see Figure 4-6).

This mode also supports using a specific user account.

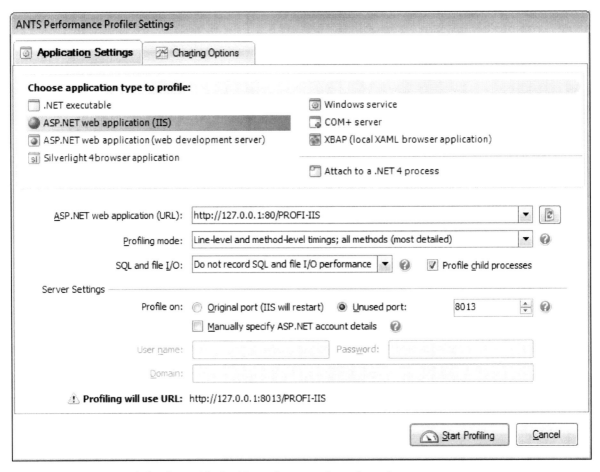

Figure 4-6: Settings dialog box with the Unused port option selected.

B.3.d   Using the web development server

If you are using Cassini, Microsoft's web development server, rather than IIS, most profilers will still be capable of running by using a dedicated option. ANTS Performance Profiler provides the **ASP.NET web application (web development server)** mode for this purpose (see Figure 4-7).

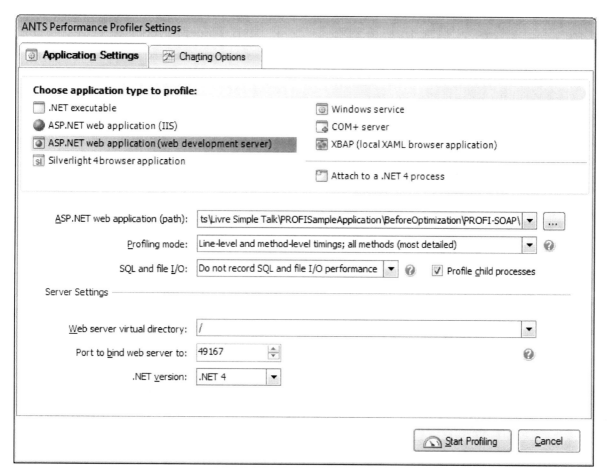

Figure 4-7: Settings dialog box showing options for using Cassini.

When this option is selected, the configuration options change to reflect that the user account cannot be changed when Cassini is used, as it always uses the current user. Incidentally, this is the main role of this simple web server: to provide a solution so that a developer who does not have administrative rights (which is always the case, right?) can still create websites to test their work.

If the application is already running, you will need to specify a different port. We show here a case where ANTS Performance Profiler will listen to port number 49167, while the web development server on D:\...\PROFI-SOAP\ remains positioned on port number 49166 by Visual Studio .NET. We should then modify the client configuration to point to the new port number instead of the original one.

If we take a look at the icon tray in Windows, Cassini is indeed working on Port 49166 (see Figure 4-8).

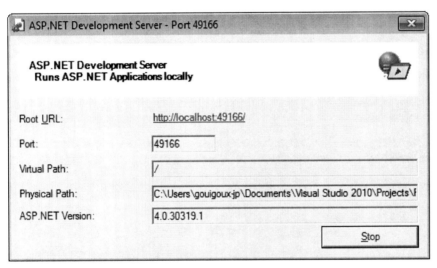

Figure 4-8:   The web development server dialog box shows which port is being used.

But if we start the server profiling with ANTS, it will start a browser on Port 49167, and we can see in Figure 4-9 that it correctly serves the pages generated by Cassini.

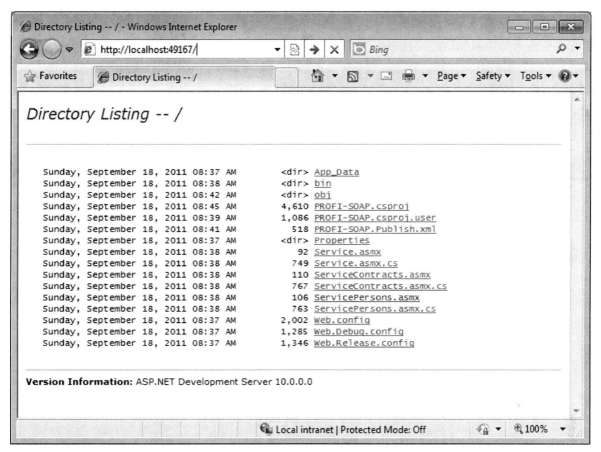

Figure 4-9: Content of the virtual directory for PROFI-SOAP.

This window must remain open throughout the profiling operation, even if we use another application as the client to the web application that is profiled. Closing it is a signal for ANTS that the profiling session is finished.

B.3.e   The particular case of .NET 4

The three methods above can be used for applications compiled and run under any version of the .NET runtime, but .NET 4.0 introduces new hooking functions in the Common Language Runtime, which can be used by ANTS Performance Profiler to attach in an easier way to the application process that is to be analyzed (see Figure 4-10).

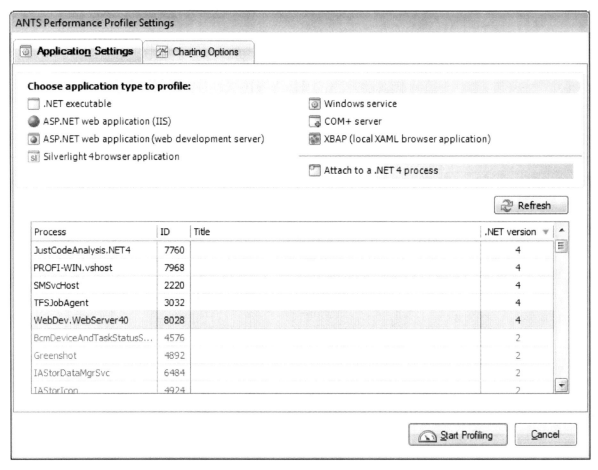

Figure 4-10: Attaching to a .NET 4 process.

Process name for Cassini

While you're looking at this screenshot, notice that the name of the process matches the web development server. In .NET 2.0 (or 3.0 or 3.5, since these versions use the same runtime), the name is the same except for the final "40."

The dialog box for Cassini shows the version used, which can be useful when debugging several applications that use different versions of .NET at the same time (see Figure 4-11).

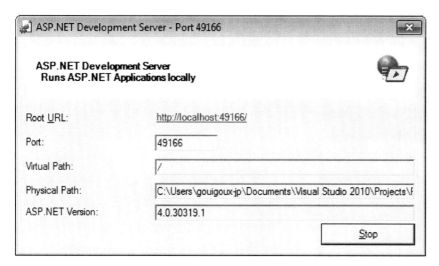

Figure 4-11: The web development server dialog box shows the version of .NET in use.

B.4   Conclusion

The preceding paragraphs may lead readers to think that ANTS Performance Profiler is difficult to set up when profiling a server application. In fact, this is the case with all profilers, because the process of hooking to IIS is not straightforward.

ANTS Performance Profiler is certainly the most accessible profiler in our selection. This is why it has been chosen to illustrate the chapters on profiling the sample application.

C   JetBrains dotTrace Performance

C.1   Overview

JetBrains dotTrace Performance 4.0 is close in functionality to ANTS Performance Profiler, but with an interface that may appear a bit more difficult for a beginner to understand. It can also be run right from Visual Studio .NET, using the **dotTrace** menu and the **Profile startup application** command, but the results shown by default at the end of the profiling session are a bit harder to digest (see Figure 4-12).

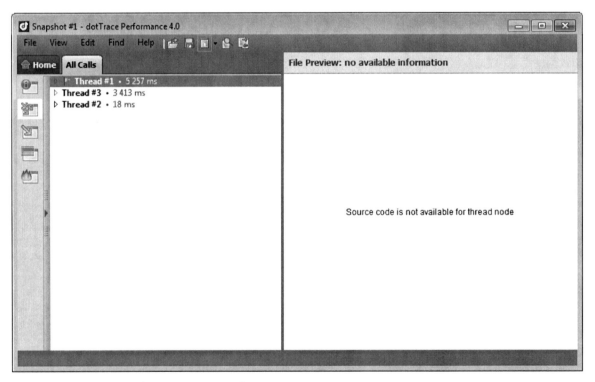

Figure 4-12:   JetBrains dotTrace user interface.

One has to expand the thread content to see the actual results (see Figure 4-13).

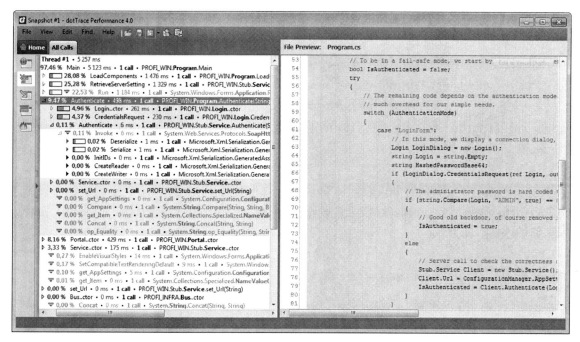

Figure 4-13: Expand the thread to view the results.

DotTrace also includes a function to identify hot spots (functions that take the longest time to perform). But, since its default behavior takes into account all classes, including system ones, the results are quite difficult to exploit.

C.2   Advantages

DotTrace offers a fairly sophisticated functionality for comparing two different analyses of the same application. This can be useful for checking whether a code modification improves performance. In practice, analyzing the associated metrics remains complex.

DotTrace also enables us to use a profiling API directly inside an application code, which is a very nice feature if we need to take snapshots at precise moments in the executed scenarios.

C.3   Aside on profiling modes

Like most profilers, dotTrace provides a choice of profiling methods. The balance can be adjusted between very complete profiling, that will slow down the execution considerably, and a coarse approach with a light impact on the execution. It is good practice to use the second method to perform a quick and dirty analysis, and then concentrate on bottlenecks, using more precise metrics.

To give an idea of the difference in time between the profiling modes, here are the times recorded for a reference method (`LoadComponents`, which will be discussed later), using different options.

- Tracing / WallTime (perf counter): 1,820ms.

- Tracing / WallTime (CPU instruction): 1,056ms.

- Line by Line / WallTime (perf counter): 1,854ms.

- Line by Line / WallTime (CPU instruction): 1,102ms.

- Sampling / WallTime (perf counter): 109ms.

- Sampling / Thread time: 47ms.

- Sampling / WallTime (CPU instruction): 57ms.

The differences are quite important, and one should be careful not to profile a long scenario using the most detailed mode, otherwise the analysis will take too long to run. This advice is also applicable to all other profilers, which offer similar options, even if they have different names.

The expert explanation (Oleg Stepanov, from JetBrains, on the difference between tracing and sampling)

The difference is in how we collect data. For tracing mode, a hook is called each time a function execution starts and finishes. We record the time on entry and time on leaving, and use the difference to calculate the total execution time of the function. The issue with that is that we have to account for the time needed to switch from the application code to the profiler code. We have special handling for that ("High accuracy" mode in the profiler), but it requires even more time measurements and slows down the application. Sampling mode is a completely different story: we just pause the application once in a while and record the current stacks of all threads. Then we collect statistics on this information and this forms the snapshot.

C.4   Conclusion

The product from JetBrains lacked just a bit of clarity in the presentation of resulting metrics to be the reference profiler in this book, but it deals very well with what is expected from a good profiler. The presence of an API can be a huge advantage, should the case arise. Since this book was written, version 4.5 has been released.

D   Eqatec Profiler

D.1   Overview

Eqatec takes a different approach to the other profilers, through code injection. It starts by rebuilding the target application (see Figure 4-19).

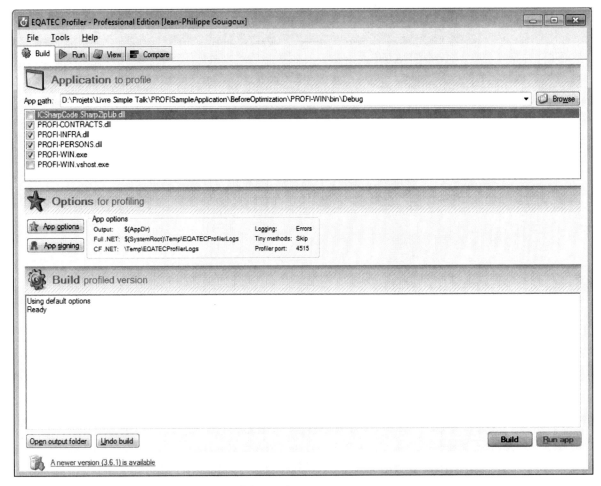

Figure 4-14: Building a profiled version of the application.

The application can then be executed and the metrics are collected in a report that will be analyzed in a third separate tab, the fourth tab being used to compare analyses (see Figure 4-20).

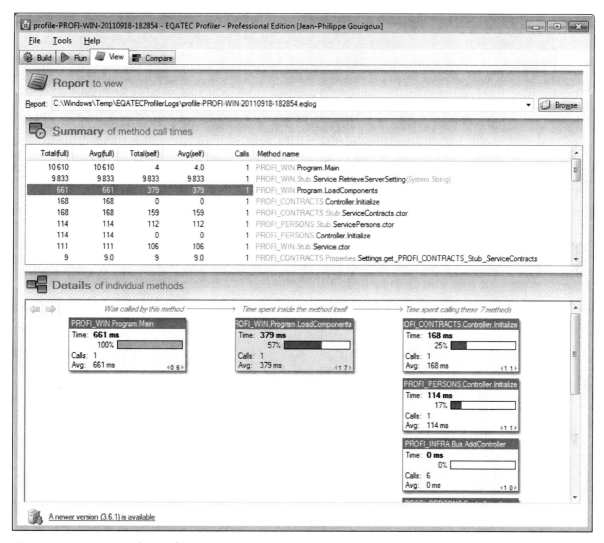

Figure 4-15: Viewing the profiling report.

The visual report is quite complete, and the data set out in a very clear manner. It should be particularly stressed that the product from Eqatec is the only one to avoid the traditional approach with a tree for the methods and a grid for metrics. It uses a map-based visualization, where the method in question is always placed in the center, with the callers on the left, and the callees on the right. The result is quite interesting.

D.2   Advantages

The design and workflow are particularly valuable when it is not obvious which way the problem should be approached.

Eqatec should also be applauded for offering a free version of their product.

D.3   Conclusion

Eqatec Profiler is a good product, which is easy to access, but a few features are missing for industrial use. It should be mentioned, though, that at the time of writing Eqatec may be the only company that provides tools for profiling .NET Compact Framework applications.

E   Open Source profilers

A list of tools cannot be complete without at least one Open Source product. One such product used to exist, but it was quite limited in function, and disappeared a few years ago: its name was **NProf**. It is still available on SourceForge, but in a 0.10 version that has not evolved since October 2010. The product has been moved to Google Code, where it is officially classified as abandoned. For the most nostalgic of readers, Figure 4-21 shows what the product looked like.

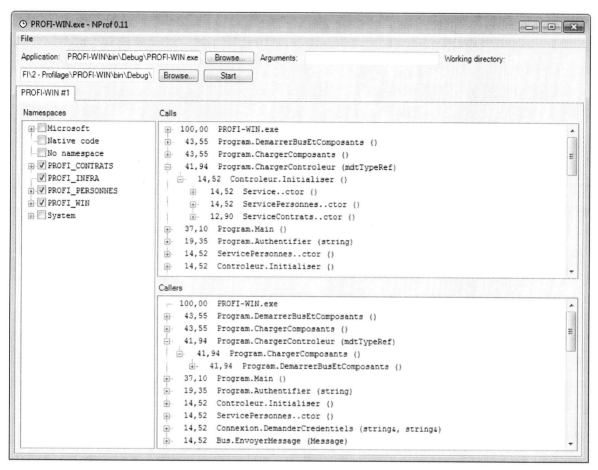

Figure 4-16: The NProf user interface.

The least we can say is that the interface was dry. After a profiling process without any options, the user would obtain two tree-based lists, the first one sorted in ascending call stack order, and the other one in reverse order. Numbers showed the percentage of time spent in the function, and that was pretty much it.

Running NProf on a 64-bit computer

The screenshot above shows PROFI in French, because the French version of this book was written before the English one, and I had a 32-bit system at that time. The computer I used for this book in English was running a 64-bit system, and NProf did not show any results in this case.

SlimTune is an Open Source profiler that can be found on Google Code and seems a bit more advanced. Visual C++ 2008 redistributable packages, internally based on SQL Server Compact edition, profiling wizard, remote server profiling: SlimTune seemed to have lots of interesting features. Alas, the product is still in Beta and at the time of writing it really was not usable.

Lastly, and this is becoming more and more of a habit when a functionality is missing in the official .NET stack or in commercial products, we should take a look at the extremely rich ecosystem growing around **Mono**, the Open Source implementation of .NET. There is a nice surprise there: the various profilers that used to exist have merged into a powerful application, which seems more likely to last.

F   A word on memory profilers

As was said at the beginning of this chapter, in addition to pure performance profilers, memory profilers are also available. That is not to say that memory has nothing to do with performance; when you have found a performance problem caused by high use of the GC, you will certainly use a memory profiler to identify the root of the problem. However, this book concentrates on basic performance problems and will only use the basic functions of performance profilers. In fact, every step carried out on the samples that follow could be done with more basic tools, but commercial tools are not expensive and much more user-friendly.

Chapter 5: Profiling the Sample Application – Client Side

A   Aim

In this chapter and the next, we are going to concentrate on an applied approach, using the sample application to identify slow interactions, which means portions of C# code that represent a performance problem during a call, without taking into account external causes. In this chapter, we will study the client-side part of the sample application. Since the application is composed of a WinForms client and an ASP.NET server, it is a good idea to analyze the slow behavior of both modules. It makes sense to start with the client because a first round of analysis will help us determine whether bottlenecks are its responsibility or if they ultimately come from a lack of server responsiveness. The bottlenecks classified as the latter will be studied in the following chapter on server-side profiling.

B   Configuration

B.1   Profiling scenarios

As we explained in Chapter 1, *Profiling Principles*, it is important to base our analyses on well-defined scenarios, whose speed of execution we wish to improve. We will use two scenarios here, with the goal of lowering their execution time below one second per user interaction.

Given the limited complexity of our sample application, these two scenarios basically cover all available interactions.

B.1.a   Scenario on persons

This first profiling scenario will execute a short series of simple interactions. Let's start by connecting to the application (see Figure 5-1).

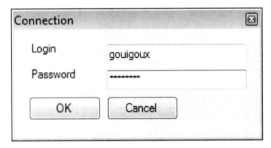

Figure 5-1:   Login dialog box.

The authentication is extremely simple: the password is simply the reverse of the user name. For example, the password for the user *gouigoux* will be *xuogiuog*.

We will see a dialog box similar to that in Figure 5-2, and click **Persons** to populate the list on the right-hand side.

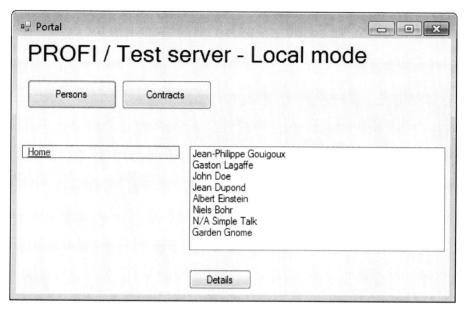

Figure 5-2:   List of persons.

The next step is to select the first person on the list and display the details, which will bring us to a dialog box as in Figure 5-3.

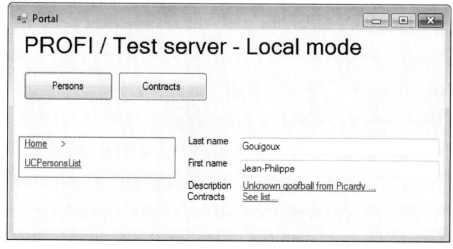

Figure 5-3:   Details of a person.

We click the link to the person description, modify the text that gets displayed, and confirm the changes by clicking **OK** (see Figure 5-4) which takes us back to the previous dialog box.

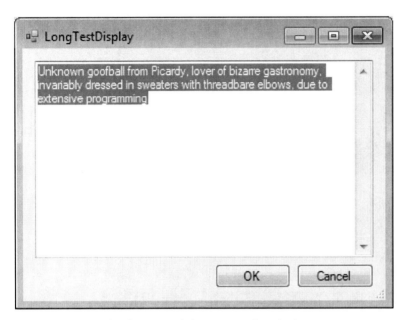

Figure 5-4:   Dialog box containing person description.

Lastly, we click the second link, which displays the list of contracts associated with the selected person. As we will focus on contracts in the second scenario, we will stop the user interactions here for this scenario.

To conclude this scenario, we close the application. If we had been running the profiler, the tool would then stop and display the metrics, which will help us to visualize what happened in terms of method calls. If everything worked well, we should see the following web method calls: `RetrieveServerSettings` twice, then `GetPersonsList`, and lastly `GetPerson`.

B.1.b   Scenario on contracts

The second scenario is no more complex: again, the user starts by logging in but, this time, we click **Contracts**, and the dialog box in Figure 5-5 displays.

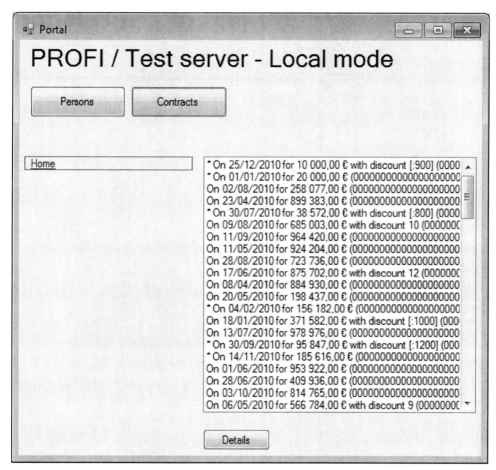

Figure 5-5:   List of contracts.

Selecting the first contract and clicking **Details** produces the dialog box in Figure 5-6.

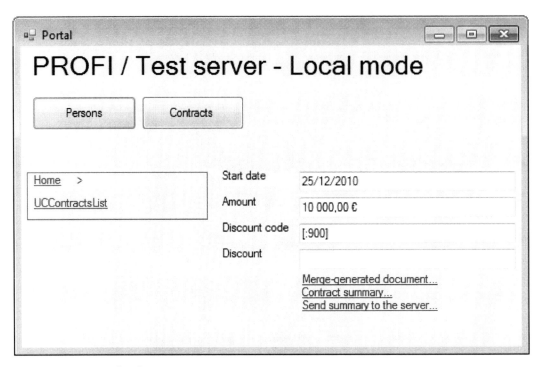

Figure 5-6: Details of a contract.

At this point of the scenario, we click each of the three links in turn. The first link opens a Word document, and the second opens a text file, each in default editors. We close these two applications, and then click the third link, which does not display a dialog or open other software, but simply sends an activity summary to the server. Lastly, we close the application, which concludes our second scenario.

B.2 The need for scenario automation

I have automated replay of the test scenarios in order to avoid variation in the waiting times between user interactions interfering with metrics (and this is even truer for the client-side part of the application). This approach is often used in industrial contexts in order to repeat integration tests easily without using human testers, who are precious resources, on such a trivial activity. As always in the field of testing, automation also brings stability to metrics, in addition to the option to replay whenever you want to, in a short space of time.

Lastly, automation allows us to use periods of low resource consumption (generally at night) to perform tests on heterogeneous environments. In short, it is clearly useful to let a machine replay user scenarios instead of asking a person to carry out the same set of interactions. In light of this, there are two approaches for the server side.

- Either we record the HTTP or SOAP messages sent during a scenario, and we use this data to replay server calls. This approach has the advantage that it prepares the ground very well for load tests.

- Or we record the scenario on the client side, and we replay the interaction on the client every time, using the calls to the server induced by these interactions. The advantage of this solution is that it facilitates configuration of the server, and also allows you to test the client side at the same time.

The second approach has been chosen in this book, because we will be able to benefit from the client-side automation for the server, without needing to introduce a new technique that is not directly related to performance improvements.

This leads us to the question of which technology to use. Tools like TestComplete exist to record and replay scenarios on Windows applications. However, not every reader can afford a commercial tool, so I have decided to try and show how we can design a home-made automation system. The different methods that have been tested are explained below.

B.2.a   NUnitForms

The NUnit extension called NUnitForms enables developers to write unit tests that manipulate a WinForms interface with a very simple syntax. Let us imagine a basic program like the one in Figure 5-7.

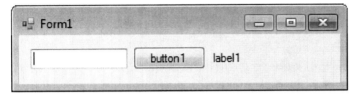

Figure 5-7:   A basic program.

Clicking the button copies the content of the text-box to the label on the opposite side, as in Figure 5-8.

Figure 5-8:   Using the basic program.

We can then generate a perfectly readable unit test that reproduces the steps of interacting with the application and validating the result using code like that shown in Listing 5-1.

```
using System;
using System.Windows.Forms;

using NUnit.Framework;
using NUnit.Extensions.Forms;
```

```
using TestNUnitForms;

namespace TestingNUnitForms
{
    public class Assert
    {
    }

    [TestFixture]
    public class TestClass
    {
        [Test]
        public void Test()
        {
            Form1 dialog = new Form1();
            dialog.Show();

            TextBoxTester textBox1 = new TextBoxTester("textBox1");
            ButtonTester form1_button1 = new ButtonTester("button1", "Form1");
            LabelTester label1 = new LabelTester("label1");
            FormTester Form1 = new FormTester("Form1");

            textBox1.Enter("123");
            form1_button1.Click();
            Assert.AreEqual("123", label1.Properties.Text);
            Form1.Close();
        }
    }
}
```

Listing 5-1

The only additional step needed for this method to work is to add references to NUnit and NUnitForms, both Open Source products that the reader will find at HTTP://WWW.NUNIT.ORG and HTTP://NUNITFORMS.SOURCEFORGE.NET respectively.

This method is well suited to integration in a software factory, where developers are already applying Test First, or even Test Driven programming.

B.2.b   UI Automation

The automation approach through UI Automation is a bit more complex, but will teach users a lot, in particular about accessibility. This method is based on the use of proxies behind all of the GUI interactions, with the goal of routing all events and operations to a Braille display, a speech synthesizer or any other peripheral that is specially designed for people with a disability. In addition to opening the world of IT to people who are usually excluded from it, it offers an additional solution in automating Windows interactions. The principle is to place our code precisely at the level of indirection provided by the proxies in order to automate test scenarios.

How to use UI Automation

*We are not going to go into much detail, because it is outside the main scope of this book. Readers wanting to learn more may find it useful to refer to the UI Automation documentation or the relevant section of my blog (*HTTP://WWW.GOUIGOUX.COM/BLOG-FR/?TAG=UIAUTOMATION*). For the most advanced readers, I have set out the bases of an XML framework aimed at piloting Windows applications using UI Automation, and published this as an Open Source project hosted by CodePlex at* HTTP:// UIAUTOTESTXML.CODEPLEX.COM/. *Please note that my blog is mainly in French. However, the UIAutoTestXML project is documented in English.*

B.2.c   Compiling options

In order to reduce the impact on the sample application, and also to facilitate the delivery of a complete and easy-to-install source code so that every reader can benefit as much as possible from the examples, a third method has been chosen. It is quite limited, but extremely easy to apply, since the principle is to write additional code that directs the execution of the application each time a user interaction would have been waited for.

In practice, this means adding code that, at the end of the loading of a form or user control, will run the next interaction. Let us take an example: when the list of persons displays, we might want the first entry to be selected and clicking **Details** to be simulated. This can be done with the code in Listing 5-2.

```
namespace PROFI_PERSONS
{
    public partial class UCPersonsList : UserControl
    {
        [...]

        public UCPersonsList()
        {
            InitializeComponent();

#if TEST1
            this.Load += new EventHandler(delegate(object sender, EventArgs e)
                { lstPersons.SelectedIndex = 0; btnDetails_Click(null, null); });
#endif
        }

        [...]
    }
}
```

Listing 5-2

In order to activate this mode of automatic functioning, one simply has to use the compiling option TEST1 in the properties of the project containing UCPersonsList (see Figure 5-9).

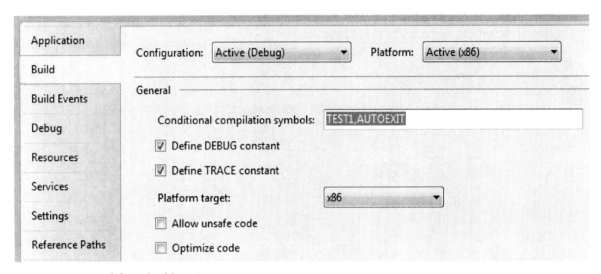

Figure 5-9: Modifying build options.

Of course, in certain cases, it is better to use the `Activated` event, or `Enter` or `Shown`, depending on the exact sequence we wish to produce.

What could be the purpose of the second compiling option (`AUTOEXIT`)? It is related to the last part of the automated scenario, namely exiting the application. In some cases, we would like the program to stop automatically, for example when profiling, since the profiler tool generally waits for the process to stop before calculating metrics of time spent in the different methods. We might as well help it to do that instead of waiting for a user interaction. The code in Listing 5-3 allows us to implement this behavior just after displaying the list of persons in our example.

```
namespace PROFI_PERSONS
{
    public partial class UCPersonsList : UserControl
    {
        [...]

        public UCPersonsList()
        {
            InitializeComponent();
```

```
#if TEST1 && AUTOEXIT
            this.Load += new EventHandler(delegate(object sender, EventArgs e) {
Application.Exit(); });
#endif
        }

        [...]
    }
}
```

Listing 5-3

On the other hand, when debugging test scenarios, it is useful to keep the application open at the end of the session. We thus remove the `AUTOEXIT` compiling option (or set it to `AUTOEXITOFF` or another value that is different from the initial one, which makes it easier to reverse the behavior later on).

The projects in question

When modifying compiling options, it is important to enter the project properties for PROFI-WIN, PROFI-PERSONS, PROFI-CONTRACTS and PROFI-INFRA. Not all these projects will need the complete set of options but, in order to reduce the risk of mistakes, it is advisable to keep the values the same for all four projects.

It can be helpful, when running these automated tests, to use the same notion of "assertion" as within unit tests. This can be achieved in our example as shown in Listing 5-4.

```
        internal void Fill(string restrictionOnPersonUID)
        {
            [...]

#if TEST2
            if (lstContracts.Items.Count != 102)
            {
```

```
                    MessageBox.Show("Error in TEST2 : an incorrect number of
                                    contracts has been found");
                Application.Exit();
        }
#endif
        }
```

Listing 5-4

Limits with numerous test scenarios

The use of several options (TEST1, TEST2, etc.) allows for the use of several test scenarios. The options should be cumulated with OR operators in the code (for example #if TEST1 || TEST2). Of course, this will only work with limited numbers of scenarios. If this number increases too much, there will be more reason to use other automation methods, or even a dedicated tool.

In the case of the second scenario, it has been necessary to write slightly more complex code (Listing 5-5).

```
public UCContract()
{
    InitializeComponent();

#if TEST2
    this.Load += new EventHandler(delegate(object sender, EventArgs e)
    {
        // We store references to any pre-existing WinWord process, and then launch
        // the WinWord file associated with the current contract
        Process[] preexistingProcesses = Process.GetProcessesByName("winword");
        lnkDocument_LinkClicked(null, null);

        // Then, we wait in a loop for the new process to appear, using a timeout
        // in case of problems preventing it from appearing
        Process newProcess = null;
        Stopwatch chrono = Stopwatch.StartNew();
        do
        {
            Thread.Sleep(100);
            foreach (Process p in Process.GetProcessesByName("winword"))
```

```
                    if (!preexistingProcesses.Contains(p))
                    {
                        newProcess = p;
                        break;
                    }
            }
        while (newProcess == null && chrono.ElapsedMilliseconds < 10000);

        // We suppress the new WinWord process if it has appeared
        if (newProcess!= null)
            newProcess.Kill();

        // We use the same method to run the summary file
        preexistingProcesses = Process.GetProcessesByName("notepad");
        lnkSummary_LinkClicked(null, null);

        // Same looping method with a delay before retrying in order not to
        // overload the processor
        newProcess = null;
        chrono = Stopwatch.StartNew();
        do
        {
            Thread.Sleep(100);
            foreach (Process p in Process.GetProcessesByName("notepad"))
                if (!preexistingProcesses.Contains(p))
                {
                    newProcess = p;
                    break;
                }
        }
        while (newProcess == null && chrono.ElapsedMilliseconds < 10000);

        // We attempt to modify the content of the text file and close the notepad,
        // saving the modifications
        Thread.Sleep(500);
        SendKeys.SendWait("File modification");
        SendKeys.SendWait("%{F4}");
        SendKeys.SendWait("e");

        // Finally, the modified file is sent to the server
        lnkUpload_LinkClicked(null, null);
    });
#endif
```

```
#if TEST2 && AUTOEXIT
    this.Load += new EventHandler(delegate(object sender, EventArgs e) {
Application.Exit(); });
#endif
}
```

Listing 5-5

The comments in the code should be enough to make clear what the code is supposed to do but, in a nutshell, it automates opening (which is easy) and closing (a little more complicated) of external applications that will be started from the target application, namely Word and the Windows text editor, Notepad. Running these applications is quite easy, since we only have to simulate clicking the corresponding links in the GUI. But as far as closing them is concerned, things are less straightforward. For Word, we decide to kill the process, whereas exiting Notepad will be done by sending the ALT+F4 command to the window, then confirming saving the data by simulating pressing the **e** key. We use a small delay in case the application has been found as a process, but is not yet ready to receive commands. Given the simplicity of the Notepad application, 500 milliseconds should be more than enough.

In both cases, it is important not to kill processes of the same application that existed before running the automated test. This is why we store them prior to running the command.

One should also take into account that these processes will not necessarily appear immediately, particularly Word, which is a bigger application. We allow ten seconds for them to appear, while checking ten times per second whether they are there. The use of a timeout is necessary to avoid an infinite loop in the program, should one of the expected processes never appear, for any reason. The pause between each attempt is a good practice to give the CPU a breather, allowing it to perform other tasks in the meantime.

Warning on SendKeys

SendKeys *commands are sent to the foreground application: it is thus very important not to bring any other application to the foreground while tests are executing, as this could interfere with their functioning.*

B.3   Profiler configuration

When profiling a client application, there is no need to configure the profiler, at least with ANTS Performance Profiler. Once the Visual Studio .NET solution is configured with the right compiling options for test and automatic exit, one only has to run a profiling session from the **ANTS** menu, using the **Profile Performance** command (see Figure 5-10). Care should be taken not to select **Launch ANTS Performance Profiler**, which would start the profiler but would not run the application automatically, as we want in this case.

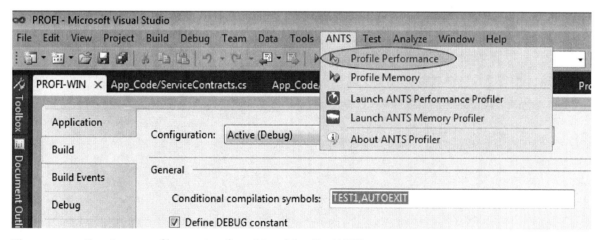

Figure 5-10: Starting a profiler session from Visual Studio ANTS menu.

The profiler is then run, and the start-up application launched. Since the latter is configured to run automatically, one should simply let the scenario run, and then let the profiler take control back when the application has closed, analyze collected metrics, and display them. The main program window is then displayed (see Figure 5-11).

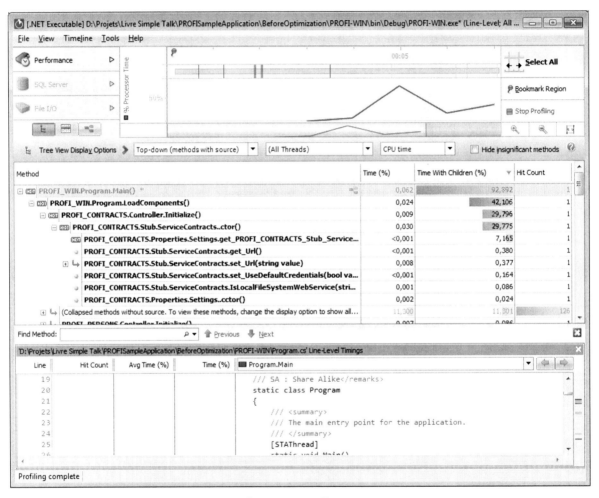

Figure 5-11: Results displayed in ANTS Performance Profiler.

> **Warning on** SendKeys **(*again*)**
>
> *At the risk of repetition, it is essential not to run any other operation on the test computer while executing the automated scenario. If the* SendKeys *are sent to other processes, the scenario will not finish correctly, and we could cause data loss in the other applications.*

Of course, exact values will vary with the machine, and the reader should not take the content shown above at face value. However, a lot of effort has been put in so that the sample application behaves as deterministically as possible, and the percentage should remain fairly stable.

C   Analysis of results from the first scenario

From now on, we are actually profiling the application. This consists of iterating over the points below.

- Analyzing outstanding metrics values. Most profilers help the user by putting the methods that take up the main part of the time of the scenario at the top of the list. ANTS Performance Profiler, for example, uses orange "HOT" text to identify the functions that deserve attention.

- Modifying the code in order to remove the bottleneck found by the profiler. At this stage, it is important not to modify anything else, in order to avoid distorting the next set of metrics.

- Profiling the same scenario again and checking the improvement to performance. In the best-case scenario, the bottleneck will be removed completely, and we can move on to the next method in the list. At worst, the drop in execution time will be insufficient, and we will have to try something else to improve performance. As a general rule, however, since the profiler shows an atomic method, it is quite easy to spot the problem.

The sections below relate to iterations performed on the client side of the sample application and the levels of improvement to the code in which they resulted.

C.1   Loading components

C.1.a   Metrics analysis

The first point to note on the stack of hotspots (this is the term used to refer to methods using the most resource or taking the longest time to execute in a scenario; in short, bottlenecks) is that the `Main` method appears at the top of the list, with an execution time almost equal to 100%. This is quite logical, since the scenario is automated, which means there is little time spent outside the main execution thread.

The second point to note is that loading the components takes almost half of the time spent in `Main`. A click on the line which corresponds to `LoadComponents` allows us to start analyzing the problem by displaying the relevant source code in the lower pane (see Figure 5-12).

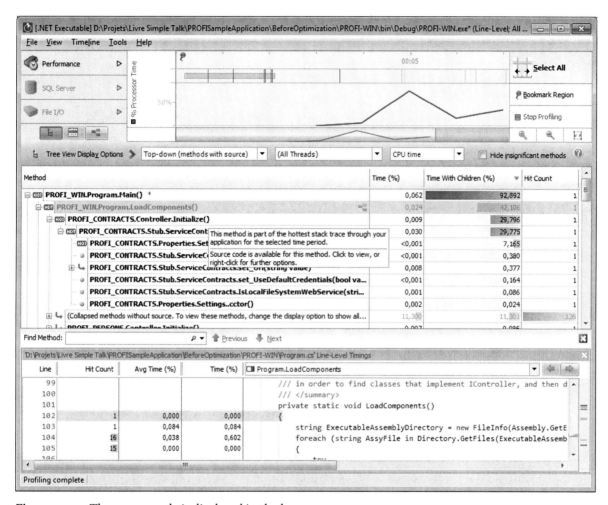

Figure 5-12: The source code is displayed in the lower pane.

As we are interested in the actual time spent, we start by setting the profiler to display time in milliseconds instead of percent, which is the default mode (see Figure 5-13).

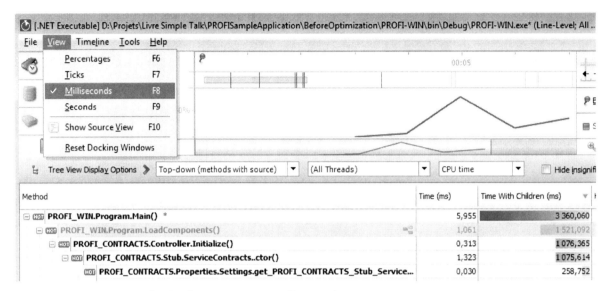

Figure 5-13: Changing the display time unit to milliseconds.

The modified interface is a bit clearer: the main bottleneck is the `LoadComponents` function. It takes 1,521ms out of the total execution time for the scenario of 3,360ms.

ANTS Performance Profiler displays in bold the methods for which we have access to source code. In our case, this means those corresponding to our application. First, we are going to study the .NET functions that are called directly by `LoadComponents`. By doing this, we stand a better chance of finding something easy to correct than if we have to study a complete stack of method calls, particularly as the .NET BCL classes are, generally speaking, extremely quick.

Viewing all methods

To see all the methods and not only those we have created, change the **Tree View Display Options** *to use* **Any method**.

Doing so, we notice that 353ms are spent in the `Assembly.LoadFrom` method, which is quite a lot (see Figure 5-14). The red highlighting also identifies the lines that take the most time (we also have this visual indicator in the source code when it is available). The **Hit Count** column shows that we called the `Assembly.LoadFrom` function 15 times. This is a sufficient explanation for our performance problem: we repeat this quite complex operation 15 times, whereas we only have 3 controllers to load.

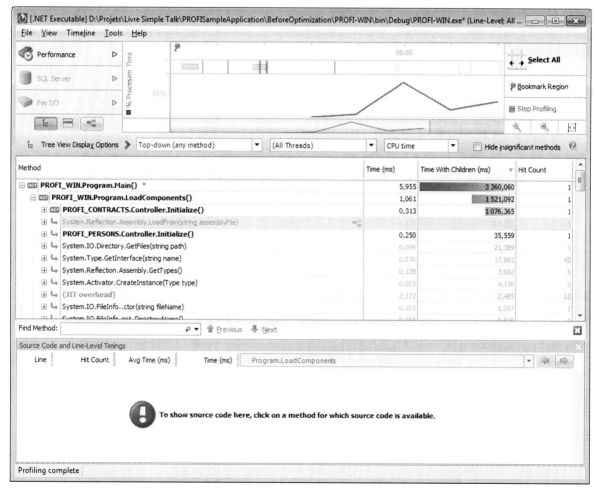

Figure 5-14: Source code is available for methods shown in bold.

To view this information in a format which is more accessible when several levels are involved, we can click the new call graph icon on the right-hand side of the LoadComponents method (this icon only appears when the line is selected; see Figure 5-15).

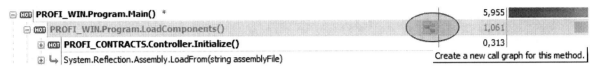

Figure 5-15: The new call graph icon.

This brings up another pane, namely the call graph (see Figure 5-16).

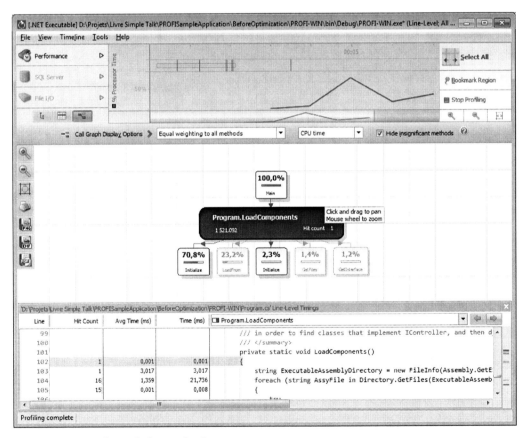

Figure 5-16: Call graph for method LoadComponents.

It should be noted that the third icon at the top left of the form is now orange, because it corresponds to this particular mode of the GUI, the first one being the sorted list of methods we started with (the call tree), and the second displaying a list of all functions (the Methods Grid – we will come back to this mode later on, for other analyses).

The callers of the targeted function being limited to `Main`, we will gain more from studying the callees. Gray blocks indicate functions without any associated source code, typically .NET functions like `Assembly.LoadFrom` and `Directory.GetFiles`. Other blocks are those for which we have `.pdb` files. This does not mean we are only interested in one kind of block. In this particular example, we are going to start by studying a gray block, namely the one corresponding to `Assembly.LoadFrom` (see Figure 5-17). We click on it to expand it and get more information.

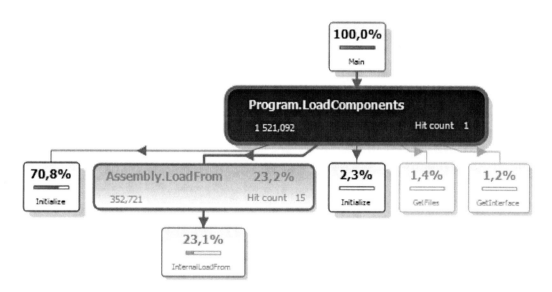

Figure 5-17: The expanded call graph.

The function `Assembly.LoadFrom` is called 15 times, despite the fact it is only supposed to load .NET assemblies in order to retrieve business-related controllers. It just so happens that our test application has only two business domains: persons and contracts. We can count three business domains if we take into account the controller associated to the display portal.

C.1.b   Diagnosis

By running in debug mode and stopping on the **Program.LoadComponents** method, we are able to retrieve all values passed to **Assembly.LoadFrom** (Listing 5-6).

```
foreach (string assyFile in Directory.GetFiles(executableAssemblyDirectory))
{
    try
    {
        Assembly currentAssy = Assembly.LoadFrom(assyFile);

        […]
    }
    catch
    {
    }
}
```

Listing 5-6

The results include all the files returned by **Directory.GetFiles** (see Figure 5-18).

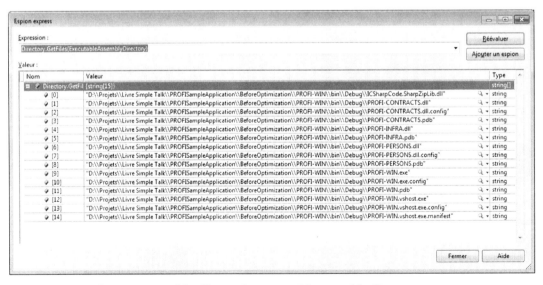

Figure 5-18: Debugger view of the files in the executable assembly directory.

Visibly, numerous files have been loaded despite the fact there was no chance of them containing a `Controller` class. However, the goal of this function is to find the particular classes that allow for dynamic loading of a new business domain in the application. Nevertheless, it was obvious that files with an extension other than `.dll` could not contain such a class.

C.1.c   First optimization attempt

A first attempt at code optimization consists of simply filtering out files which do not end with `.dll` (Listing 5-7).

```
foreach (string assyFile in Directory.GetFiles(executableAssemblyDirectory,
".dll"))
{
    try
    {
        Assembly currentAssy = Assembly.LoadFrom(assyFile);

        [...]
    }
    catch
    {
    }
}
```

Listing 5-7

We rebuild, and run the profiling operation again to check for improvement. Sadly, this code cannot work, and the scenario will not execute correctly. Indeed, the executable file PROFI-WIN.exe contains a controller, and a particularly important one, since it is responsible for displaying the portal. Let us note in passing that the message bus architecture makes the application very robust, since no exception is thrown. The application simply displays nothing.

The right code modification is shown in Listing 5-8.

```
foreach (string assyFile in Directory.GetFiles(executableAssemblyDirectory))
{
    try
    {
        FileInfo lib = new FileInfo(assyFile);
        if (string.Compare(lib.Extension, ".exe", true) != 0 &&
                        string.Compare(lib.Extension, ".dll", true) != 0) continue;

        Assembly currentAssy = Assembly.LoadFrom(assyFile);
        [...]
    }
    catch
    {
    }
}
```

Listing 5-8

Modification tags in the code

To help the reader make his way through the sample application code, all performance-related modifications have been tagged with lines starting with "PERF – [the modification that has been done]" and finishing with "PERF – End of modifications." The tags contain a code for the chapter and the number of the corresponding section. The code contains this reference to the book so that the user can easily match up the optimized code with the book. The book always uses the modified code in order to avoid unnecessary to-ing and fro-ing between the book and the code. Modifications from this chapter about client-side performance start with CLIENT. In the next section, the code will be SERVER. This is necessary, not only because the naming of sections inside different chapters could lead to indistinguishable situations, but also because there is no strict separation of optimization operations. For example, a code modification on the client could result from a problem seen on the server, or vice versa. A third chapter will cover optimization outside profiling, and the corresponding code will be SUP.

The results show that the number of calls to the `Assembly.LoadFrom` function has dropped to six (see Figure 5-19).

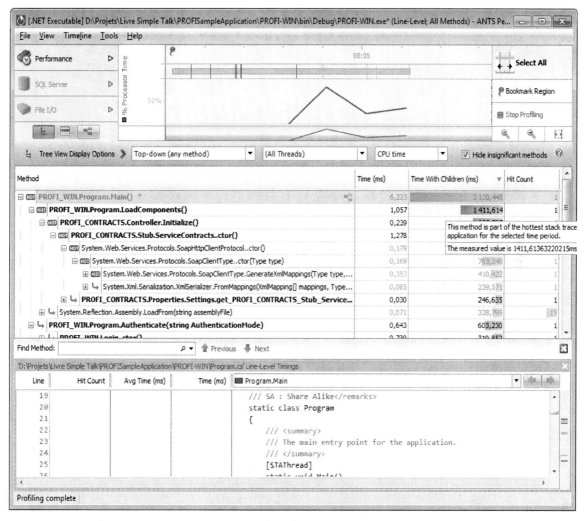

Figure 5-19: Calls to `Assembly.LoadFrom` reduced to six.

Despite this, the time spent in the function does not really change. We are now at 328ms instead of 353ms. Why such a small difference, when we have more than halved the number of function calls? The answer lies in the nature of the files: since most other files (`.pdb`, `.config`) could not be loaded as an assembly anyway, the code immediately threw an exception and spent very little time on these files. Since those that remain are the ones actually loaded, the overall time does not change much.

C.1.d   Second optimization step

To validate this hypothesis, we will push the optimization further with code that is a little more intelligent, and which will prevent libraries that are not part of PROFI from being loaded, simply by using the naming convention PROFl.* (Listing 5-9).

```
foreach (string assyFile in Directory.GetFiles(executableAssemblyDirectory))
{
    try
    {
        FileInfo lib = new FileInfo(assyFile);
        if (string.Compare(lib.Extension, ".exe", true) != 0 &&
                    string.Compare(lib.Extension, ".dll", true) != 0) continue;

        if (!lib.Name.StartsWith("PROFI")) continue;

        Assembly currentAssy = Assembly.LoadFrom(assyFile);

        [...]
    }
    catch
    {
    }
}
```

Listing 5-9

The profiling results confirm the hypothesis. Adding the restriction above avoids the unnecessary loading of ICSharpCode.SharpZipLib.dll, and thus reduces the time spent to only 26ms. This corresponds to a considerable performance gain, as this library was much bigger than the other ones. There now are only five calls to Assembly.LoadFrom (see Figure 5-20).

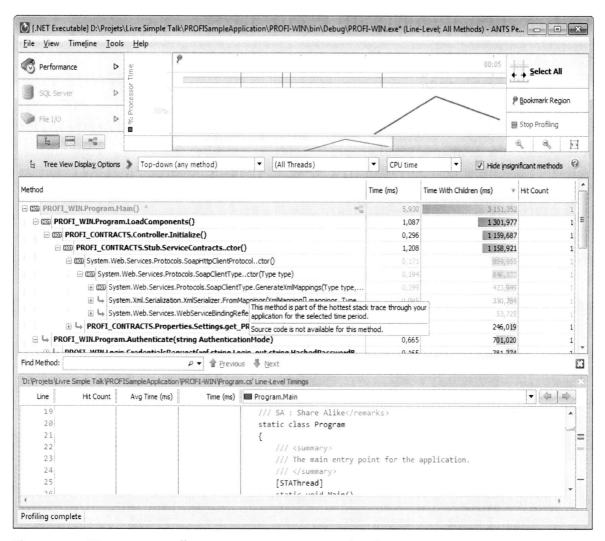

Figure 5-20: Time spent on calls to `Assembly.LoadFrom` reduced.

C.2   Instantiation of controllers

C.2.a   Analysis

If we were to follow a purely logical approach, we should now analyze the next hotspot identified by the profiler as a bottleneck. It is good practice to start always by optimizing code that can bring the highest gains. However, it is equally important to think in terms of yield ratio between this gain and the work necessary, and this hotspot seems quite complex. Meanwhile, there is a method that can be dealt with as simply as the previous one, because it is a .NET one. This is `Type.GetInterface`, and it is called 43 times (see Figure 5-21).

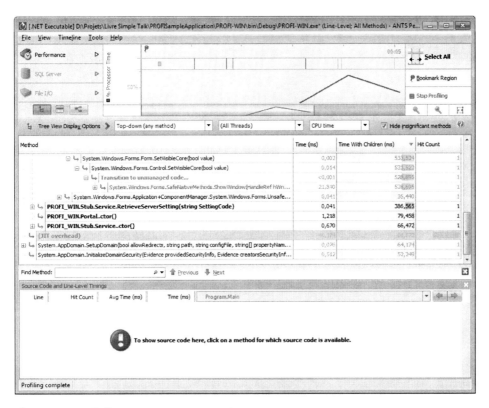

Figure 5-21:   Calls to `Type.GetInterface`.

C.2.b   Diagnosis

A quick search in the code shows the only place where this function is called, which is the function LoadComponents (Listing 5-10).

```
// Walk through the types, in order to retrieve and instantiate those implementing
// the interface defining a business-related controller
foreach (Type TypeInAssembly in currentAssy.GetTypes())
   if (TypeInAssembly.GetInterface(typeof(IController).FullName) != null)
   {
       // Instantiation of the controller
       IController controller = Activator.CreateInstance(TypeInAssembly)
                         as IController;

       // If initializing the controller works fine, we hook the instance to the
       // bus, in order for it to listen to the messages that the bus dispatches
       if (controller.Initialize())
          Bus.Current.AddController(controller);

   }
```
Listing 5-10

This code contains one of the most classic errors from the performance point of view: the loop continues after the successful iteration, whereas it could be stopped without changing the results in any way. Indeed, in our case, one PROFI assembly can only contain a single controller. It is thus no use continuing the foreach loop once the class that implements IController has been found.

C.2.c   Optimization

The proposed code is shown in Listing 5-11.

```
// Walk through the types, in order to retrieve and instantiate those implementing
// the interface defining a business-related controller
foreach (Type TypeInAssembly in currentAssy.GetTypes())
   if (TypeInAssembly.GetInterface(typeof(IController).FullName) != null)
```

```
    {
        // Instantiation of the controller
        IController controller = Activator.CreateInstance(TypeInAssembly)
                            as IController;

        // If initializing the controller works fine, we hook the instance to the
        // bus, in order for it to listen to the messages that the bus dispatches
        if (controller.Initialize())
            Bus.Current.AddController(controller);

        break;
    }
```

Listing 5-11

C.2.d   Results

There are now only 40 calls to **GetInterface** (see Figure 5-22).

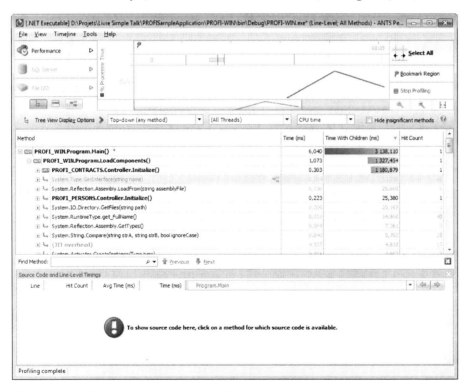

Figure 5-22:   Calls to Type.GetInterface reduced.

C.2.e   Pushing the optimization further

Why are there still 40 calls, when we only load three different controllers? We have the same type of problem as in the preceding section: we trust the interface retrieval function to find the right class, although we could considerably accelerate the process by using a naming convention so that the class we seek is always called `Controller`.

We can imagine a sort of code short cut: we start processing the `Controller` class if it exists. If it does, and if this class implements `IController`, we will not even have to loop on the other classes, and we can thus avoid calling `GetTypes` altogether.

First, we refactor the code by extracting lines that use the class once it has been detected (see Figure 5-23).

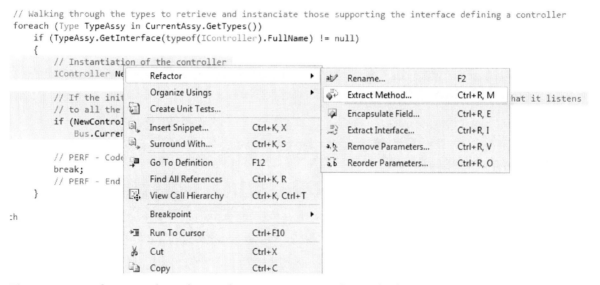

Figure 5-23:   Refactoring the code in order to extract particular methods.

Listing 5-12 shows the resulting code.

```
// Walking through the types to retrieve and instantiate those supporting the
// interface defining a controller
foreach (Type typeAssy in currentAssy.GetTypes())
    if (typeAssy.GetInterface(typeof(IController).FullName) != null)
    {
        LoadController(typeAssy);
        break;
    }
  [...]
}

private static void LoadController(Type typeAssembly)
{
    // Instantiation of the controller
    IController newController = Activator.CreateInstance(typeInAssembly)
                        as IController;

    // If initializing the controller works fine, we hook the instance to the bus,
    // in order for it to listen to the messages that the bus dispatches
    if (newController.Initialize())
        Bus.Current.AddController(newController);
}
```

Listing 5-12

Delimiting the modifications

Inside the PERF tags, I use "Original code" and "End of modifications" respectively to signal the old code that has been replaced by the optimization process (here the code moved out by refactoring), and the end of the replacement modifications. When several code modifications are applied, the internal modification tags are chained one after the other, and the code that was previously added is then commented out like the original one.

240

Then we can carry out the optimization itself, as explained in Listing 5-13.

```
string nspace = currentAssy.GetName().Name.Replace("-", "_");
Type typeController = currentAssy.GetType(nspace + ".Controller");
if (typeController != null && typeController.GetInterface(typeof(IController).
                 FullName) != null)
{
    LoadController(typeController);
    continue;
}

// Walking through the types to retrieve and instantiate those supporting the
// interface defining a controller
foreach (Type typeAssy in currentAssy.GetTypes())
    if (typeAssy.GetInterface(typeof(IController).FullName) != null)
        [...]
```

Listing 5-13

Since Visual Studio replaces hyphens (-) in the assembly name by underscores (_) when setting the default namespace, we have to reverse the operation to generate the full name of the type that we are looking for.

C.2.f   Results

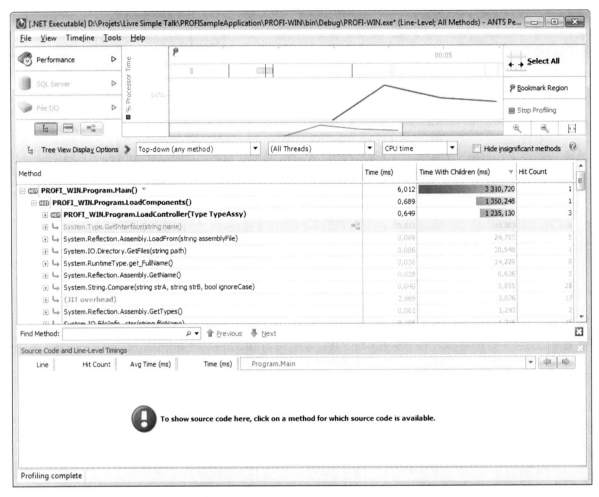

Figure 5-24:   Updated profiling results.

As expected, we now only go through the `GetInterface` function eight times (see Figure 5-24). In fact, the total time spent in these calls is so low we have to clear the **Hide insignificant methods** option to see the relevant line!

In a real application, we could also have used a convention to identify assemblies that expose a business domain to the client, in order to improve the performance further. In the same way as above, we would have extracted the command that checks if a class implements IController.

Is using conventions justified?

Given the number of times conventions are used to improve performance, the reader is justified in questioning the usefulness of pushing this method too far: the code should be robust enough to tolerate missed conventions. This is true, but there are many examples where such tolerant conventions have progressively been turned into strict rules, thus favoring performance without any risk associated: indentation in Python, conventions in Ruby, etc. All the conventions here have a business-related meaning. In addition, they bring more code standardization, which is especially important when people other than its creators maintain the code. Given how little effort is needed to respect code conventions and the advantages associated with them, using them a lot is justified. The compromise is that possible lack of robustness must be met by correct handling of their absence (as above), and by adding test procedures at compilation to enforce their use.

C.3   Creating web service clients

C.3.a   Analysis

At this point of the profiling iterations, we move on to the second biggest bottleneck. If we expand the function tree marked as HOT, we notice that one single call to a .NET function takes a lot of time: instantiating the web service client for contracts.

Let us take a more detailed look at the data displayed by the profiler (see Figure 5-25).

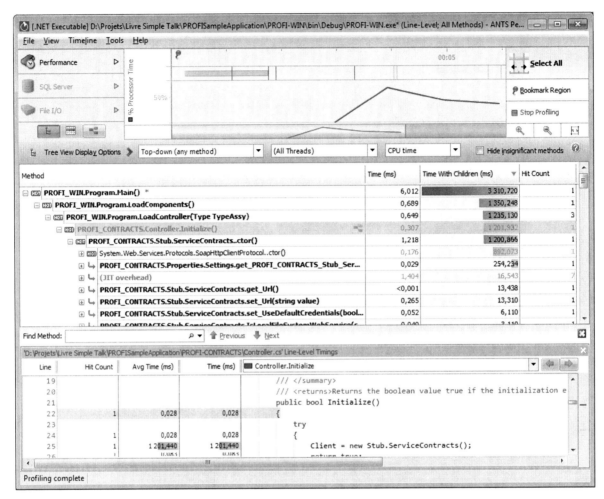

Figure 5-25:   Profiler results, showing a "HOT" path.

All the time used by this function is in fact spent in the constructor of the underlying class `SoapHttpClientProtocol`. This means the solution is unlikely to be easy. Instead of reducing the number of calls as we have done before (there is only one here), we will have to understand why this particular call is taking so much time.

C.3.b   Diagnosis

If we take a look through the list of functions, we see the constructor of the web service client associated to persons. It is also quite long (25ms), but still much quicker than the one for the contracts (1,200ms). A quick look at the functions called by these classes (which were generated from the WSDL by the .NET SDK) shows many calls to classes in charge of serialization, reflection, etc., in other words, methods that are generally resource- and time-intensive (see Figure 5-26).

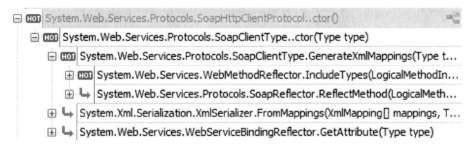

Figure 5-26:   Details of the classes associated to web service client.

Overall, it seems logical that these calls are relatively slow, given the number of operations they perform. It is important to appreciate all the work that goes on behind these classes, in order to realize that optimization will not come from modifying the calls themselves.

- Generation of an HTTP client

- Security considerations

- Deserializing the input parameters

- Dynamic invocation of a function

- Serializing the results to be returned

- Support for asynchrony

- Use of settings and resources

- And more.

In conclusion, these classes perform operations that are as complex as what an ASP.NET server does when executing a web method. The fact that they are generated by a generic tool from any WSDL (by adding a web reference in Visual Studio .NET or using the `wsdl.exe` command-line utility) also contributes to suboptimal performance: it is difficult to be flexible and quick at the same time, even if this should always remain a goal for developers.

C.3.c   Decision

We propose to drop this problem for now, since we have no immediate solution. Of course this does not mean we are not going to do anything to speed this code up. But it is just not a glaring programming error that we could correct in a few minutes. We have to use more sophisticated means in this case, and these will be demonstrated a bit later.

As far as the difference in creation time for the two instances (contracts and persons) is concerned, we will nevertheless check that there is nothing more we can do to ensure they are created as quickly as possible. To do so, we start analyzing the content of each call in more detail (see Figure 5-27).

PROFI_CONTRACTS.Controller.Initialize()	0,256	1 189,937	1
PROFI_CONTRACTS.Stub.ServiceContracts..ctor()	1,184	1 188,915	1
System.Web.Services.Protocols.SoapHttpClientProtocol..ctor()	0,171	881,626	1
PROFI_CONTRACTS.Properties.Settings.get_PROFI_CONTRACTS_Stub_Ser...	0,029	252,797	1
(JIT overhead)	1,438	16,268	7
PROFI_CONTRACTS.Stub.ServiceContracts.get_Url()	<0,001	13,797	1
PROFI_CONTRACTS.Stub.ServiceContracts.set_Url(string value)	0,234	13,325	1
PROFI_CONTRACTS.Stub.ServiceContracts.set_UseDefaultCredentials(bool...	0,029	5,975	1
PROFI_CONTRACTS.Stub.ServiceContracts.IsLocalFileSystemWebService(s...	0,049	3,059	1
PROFI_CONTRACTS.Properties.Settings..cctor()	0,064	0,883	1
(Waiting for I/O to complete)	<0,001	<0,001	3
(JIT overhead)	0,586	0,766	1
(Waiting for I/O to complete)	<0,001	<0,001	3
PROFI_PERSONS.Controller.Initialize()	0,238	26,388	1
PROFI_PERSONS.Stub.ServicePersons..ctor()	0,737	25,614	1
System.Web.Services.Protocols.SoapHttpClientProtocol..ctor()	0,003	19,245	1
PROFI_PERSONS.Properties.Settings.get_PROFI_PERSONS_stub_ServicePe...	<0,001	2,875	1
(JIT overhead)	0,959	1,481	6
PROFI_PERSONS.Stub.ServicePersons.set_Url(string value)	0,192	1,040	1
PROFI_PERSONS.Properties.Settings..cctor()	0,134	0,216	1
PROFI_PERSONS.Stub.ServicePersons.IsLocalFileSystemWebService(string...	0,001	0,008	1
PROFI_PERSONS.Stub.ServicePersons.get_Url()	<0,001	0,006	1
PROFI_PERSONS.Stub.ServicePersons.set_UseDefaultCredentials(bool valu...	<0,001	0,006	1
(Waiting for I/O to complete)	<0,001	<0,001	3

Figure 5-27: Profiler results for the two calls to web methods.

The function called `GenerateXmlMappings`, which takes a fair amount of time, is absent from the persons-related code. Could it be that this information is put in cache at first call, and thus takes time to perform only for the first business domain that is called? To confirm this hypothesis, we are going to code a quick test, by simply reversing the order in which libraries are processed when loading the controllers. Listing 5-14 shows the modification in `LoadComponents`.

```
private static void LoadComponents()
{
        string executingAssemblyDirectory = new FileInfo(Assembly.
            GetExecutingAssembly().Location).DirectoryName;
        string[] libsList = Directory.GetFiles(executableAssemblyDirectory);
        Array.Sort(libsList);
        Array.Reverse(libsList);
        foreach (string assyFile in libsList)
```

Listing 5-14

Once the profiler is launched again, we indeed notice that the function in question now lies in the persons domain instead of the one dealing with contracts (see Figure 5-28).

PROFI_PERSONS.Controller.Initialize()	0,276	1 190,825	1
PROFI_PERSONS.Stub.ServicePersons..ctor()	1,281	1 189,797	1
System.Web.Services.Protocols.SoapHttpClientProtocol..ctor()	0,182	881,774	1
PROFI_PERSONS.Properties.Settings.get_PROFI_PERSONS_stub_ServicePe...	0,052	252,499	1
(JIT overhead)	1,366	16,503	7
PROFI_PERSONS.Stub.ServicePersons.get_Url()	<0,001	14,326	1
PROFI_PERSONS.Stub.ServicePersons.set_Url(string value)	0,277	13,365	1
PROFI_PERSONS.Stub.ServicePersons.set_UseDefaultCredentials(bool valu...	0,068	6,198	1
PROFI_PERSONS.Stub.ServicePersons.IsLocalFileSystemWebService(string...	0,049	3,041	1
PROFI_PERSONS.Properties.Settings..cctor()	0,084	0,809	1
(Waiting for I/O to complete)	<0,001	<0,001	8
(JIT overhead)	0,579	0,752	1
(Waiting for I/O to complete)	<0,001	<0,001	3
PROFI_CONTRACTS.Controller.Initialize()	0,264	28,329	1
PROFI_CONTRACTS.Stub.ServiceContracts..ctor()	0,740	27,544	1
System.Web.Services.Protocols.SoapHttpClientProtocol..ctor()	0,003	21,968	1
PROFI_CONTRACTS.Properties.Settings.get_PROFI_CONTRACTS_Stub_Ser...	<0,001	2,445	1
(JIT overhead)	0,939	1,391	6
PROFI_CONTRACTS.Stub.ServiceContracts.set_Url(string value)	0,182	0,872	1
PROFI_CONTRACTS.Properties.Settings..cctor()	0,035	0,112	1
PROFI_CONTRACTS.Stub.ServiceContracts.IsLocalFileSystemWebService(s...	0,001	0,006	1
PROFI_CONTRACTS.Stub.ServiceContracts.get_Url()	<0,001	0,005	1
PROFI_CONTRACTS.Stub.ServiceContracts.set_UseDefaultCredentials(bool...	<0,001	0,005	1

Figure 5-28: Profiler results when inverting the two calls.

We have validated our hypothesis, and are now able to proceed to the next steps, since there is nothing to do to these calls for now.

248

C.4   Attempt at optimizing authentication

As we have put the previous problem to one side, because the amount of time it would take to analyze and correct the code would outweigh the improvement to performance we could expect to achieve, we are going to study the next call in the list sorted by total execution time, namely `Program.Authenticate`.

Alas, this function poses exactly the same problem as the previous one: the slow points are all .NET function calls (see Figure 5-29).

PROFI_WIN.Program.Authenticate(string AuthenticationMode)	0,797	747,896	1
PROFI_WIN.Login.CredentialsRequest(ref string Login, out string HashedPasswordB...	0,136	405,010	1
System.Windows.Forms.Form.ShowDialog()	0,033	374,302	1
System.Security.Cryptography.SHA256.Create()	0,030	22,134	1
System.Security.Cryptography.HashAlgorithm.ComputeHash(byte[] buffer)	0,098	4,168	1
System.Convert.ToBase64String(byte[] inArray)	0,038	1,725	1
System.Runtime.InteropServices.Marshal.SecureStringToBSTR(SecureString s)	0,025	1,401	1
(JIT overhead)	1,078	1,078	6
System.Security.SecureString.Dispose()	<0,001	0,060	1
System.Runtime.InteropServices.Marshal.PtrToStringUni(IntPtr ptr)	0,003	0,004	1
System.Text.Encoding.GetBytes(string s)	<0,001	0,003	1
System.Windows.Forms.TextBox.get_Text()	<0,001	<0,001	1
PROFI_WIN.Login..ctor()	0,752	335,507	1
PROFI_WIN.Login.InitializeComponent()	1,075	230,255	1
System.Windows.Forms.Form..ctor()	0,007	87,413	1
(JIT overhead)	11,539	17,082	3
System.Security.SecureString..ctor()	<0,001	0,005	1
System.Windows.Forms.Form.add_Activated(EventHandler value)	<0,001	<0,001	1

Figure 5-29:   Profiler results for the `Authenticate` function.

As far as the `Connection` class constructor is concerned, the `InitializeComponent` method is the one created by Visual Studio to group together code related to the graphical interface generation. Logically, we only find WinForms method calls (see Figure 5-30) in there.

PROFI_WIN.Login.InitializeComponent()	1,075	230,255	1
System.Windows.Forms.Control.PerformLayout()	<0,001	67,421	1
System.Windows.Forms.TextBox..ctor()	0,024	43,598	2
System.Windows.Forms.Control.ResumeLayout(bool performLayout)	0,053	30,975	2
System.Windows.Forms.Control.set_Location(Point value)	0,043	23,229	7
System.Windows.Forms.TableLayoutControlCollection.Add(Control control, int column, int …	0,045	15,583	6
System.Windows.Forms.Form.set_ClientSize(Size value)	0,006	8,607	1
(JIT overhead)	7,153	7,375	36
System.Windows.Forms.Label..ctor()	0,013	5,933	2
System.Windows.Forms.Control.set_Size(Size value)	<0,001	5,671	7
System.Windows.Forms.TableLayoutPanel.set_ColumnCount(int value)	0,025	2,544	1
System.Windows.Forms.Label.set_Text(string value)	0,024	2,389	2
System.Windows.Forms.Button..ctor()	0,026	2,121	2
System.Windows.Forms.Form.set_FormBorderStyle(FormBorderStyle value)	0,044	2,104	1
System.Windows.Forms.Label.set_AutoSize(bool value)	0,032	1,875	2
System.Windows.Forms.ContainerControl.set_AutoScaleDimensions(SizeF value)	0,006	1,477	1
System.Windows.Forms.TableLayoutPanel.get_RowStyles()	0,005	1,405	3
System.Windows.Forms.Form+ControlCollection.Add(Control value)	<0,001	1,165	1
System.Windows.Forms.TableLayoutColumnStyleCollection.Add(ColumnStyle columnStyle)	0,032	0,844	2
System.Windows.Forms.TableLayoutPanel.get_ColumnStyles()	0,005	0,762	2
System.Windows.Forms.ButtonBase.set_Text(string value)	<0,001	0,741	2
System.Windows.Forms.TableLayoutPanel..ctor()	0,006	0,561	1
System.Windows.Forms.Form.set_Text(string value)	<0,001	0,555	1
System.Windows.Forms.TableLayoutPanel.set_RowCount(int value)	0,025	0,532	1
System.Windows.Forms.TableLayoutPanel.get_Controls()	0,007	0,488	6
System.Windows.Forms.ContainerControl.set_AutoScaleMode(AutoScaleMode value)	0,024	0,387	1
System.Windows.Forms.Control.add_KeyPress(KeyPressEventHandler value)	0,005	0,330	1
System.Windows.Forms.Control.set_TabIndex(int value)	0,034	0,271	7

Figure 5-30: Profiler results for the `InitializeComponent` method.

As far as the second function, `AskForCredentials`, is concerned, the same problem arises, but this time directly. In short, apart from using something other than WinForms, there is not much we can do to improve on the 748ms taken for authentication. We need to keep in mind that we are in an automated scenario: this would be quite fast if it were a real user interaction, but it is, in fact, slow.

250

The case with WinForms

The last point about WinForms should not to be taken lightly: we will see later that the visibility manage-ment in this technology can be very slow. We could also say the same about layout management (which also produces a flicker that can be awkward). Generally speaking, any GUI technology has its perfor-mance traps. Migrating to WPF may help in some cases, owing to the use of hardware acceleration, but should not be seen as a panacea. There is no such thing as a free lunch.

C.5   Retrieving server settings

C.5.a   Analysis

The next candidate for performance improvement is the call to the client function that was automatically generated to correspond to the web method `RetrieveServer-Setting` (see Figure 5-31).

This single call takes almost half a second, which seems like a possible source of improvement. A look at the source code displayed in the bottom pane shows this method is called to retrieve the authentication mode. The `Authenticate` function code indicates that this mode can be `LoginForm` or `WindowsIntegrated`. This relates to how the user will need to log in.

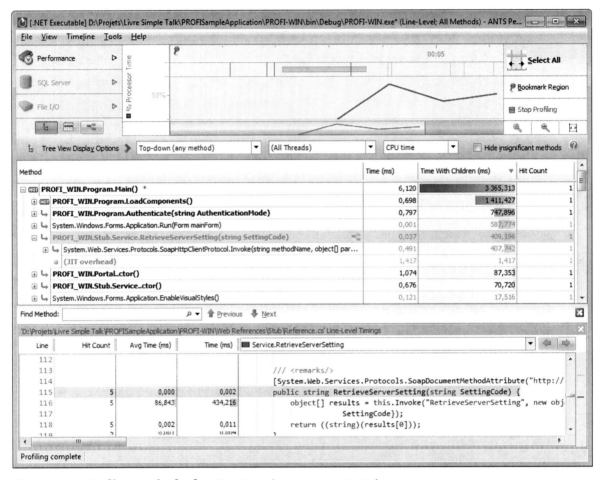

Figure 5-31: Profilers results for function `RetrieveServerSetting`.

For security reasons, it makes sense that this parameter should be the responsibility of the server: the client should not be allowed to choose the degree of security it will use to access the server. The server should decide this. Yet why did the developer jump to the conclusion that this mode should be brought back every time from the server to the client? It is possible to place this setting in the client configuration, while still leaving it on the server for use during the actual authentication process.

Similarity to validation

The same trick is used with validation. The server must validate parameters that are passed to it, in order to avoid canonicalization errors (SQL injection, Cross Site Scripting, arguments duplication, and so on). But there is nothing to stop the client from pre-validating these values in order to reject them in advance, thus avoiding costly trips back and forth to the server just for validation purposes.

C.5.b   Code optimization

We add the following line to the client configuration file:

```
<add key="PROFI.Authentication.Mode" value="LoginForm"/>
```

Listing 5-15

As far as the code retrieving the authentication mode is concerned, the simplification is radical. The original version is shown here:

```
Stub.Service client = new Stub.Service();
client.Url = ConfigurationManager.AppSettings["PROFI.Stubs.BaseURL"]
            + "Service.asmx";
string authenticationMode = client.RetrieveServerSetting
            ("PROFI.Authentication.Mode");
```

Listing 5-16

The modified version uses only one line:

```
string authenticationMode = ConfigurationManager.AppSettings
                            ["PROFI.Authentication.Mode"];
```

Listing 5-17

C.5.c   Results

The new profiler results obviously do not show the call anymore (see Figure 5-32), but it is also important to check that the overall behavior is quicker. It hardly seems possible that a single setting read operation could take longer than a call to a web service, but it is essential when optimizing to substantiate the actual improvement with irrefutable metrics every time. In my experience surprises can be numerous... and everywhere!

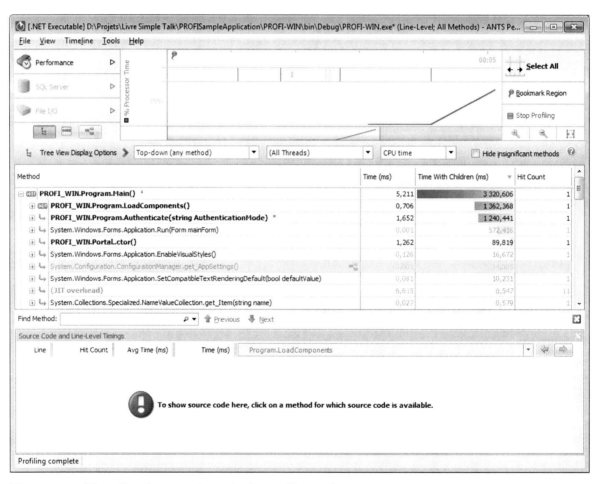

Figure 5-32:   The call to the server is not in the profiler results anymore.

Retrieving the setting only takes 14ms (`get_AppSettings` property in `Configura-tionManager`), which means that performance has clearly been improved. Even if half a second seems like a small gain, when added to similar optimizations, and repeated on numerous interactions performed by a large number of users, the global time saved can amount to hours.

C.5.d   Freeing resources

While we are in this section of code, let's look at an optimization method that is not related to execution time itself, but rather resource use. The previous code in fact had a problem in the releasing of resources:

```
Stub.Service client = new Stub.Service();
client.Url = ConfigurationManager.AppSettings["PROFI.Stubs.BaseURL"]
            + "Service.asmx";
string authenticationMode = client.RetrieveServerSetting
                        ("PROFI.Authentication.Mode");
```

Listing 5-18

Indeed, the `Dispose` function was never called on the `Client` instance. Given how simple it is to free resources in this case, it would be a shame not to perform this operation. We call the `Dispose` function using a pattern that is designed to ensure it will be done even in the case of an exception (Listing 5-19).

```
string authenticationMode = null;
Stub.Service client = null;
try
{
    client = new Stub.Service();
    client.Url = ConfigurationManager.AppSettings["PROFI.Stubs.BaseURL"]
                + "Service.asmx";
    authenticationMode = client.RetrieveServerSetting("PROFI.Authentication.Mode");
}
```

```
finally
{
    if (client != null) client.Dispose();
}
```

Listing 5-19

Testing the null value is, of course, not necessary in this simple code, but it is better to keep it anyway; this operation is almost immediate, and this is good practice in case an amendment to the code were to lead to an exception before the web service client is instantiated.

By the way, this code is completely equivalent to the shorter form in Listing 5-20.

```
string authenticationMode = null;
using (Stub.Service client = new Stub.Service())
{
    client.Url = ConfigurationManager.AppSettings["PROFI.Stubs.BaseURL"]
                + "Service.asmx";
    authenticationMode = client.RetrieveServerSetting("PROFI.Authentication.Mode");
}
```

Listing 5-20

C.5.e   Memory use

While we are studying a web service stub, let's look at the memory use of the instance we are working with.

We can use CLRProfiler (a memory diagnostic tool created by Microsoft and available at HTTP://MSDN.MICROSOFT.COM/EN-US/NETFRAMEWORK/AA569269) to take a memory snapshot immediately after the call to RetrieveServerSetting. The simplest way of doing this precisely is to add a line of code to stop the application. We notice from the snapshot that the stack memory is entirely used by the instance of Stub.Service that we have created to perform the operation (see Figure 5-33).

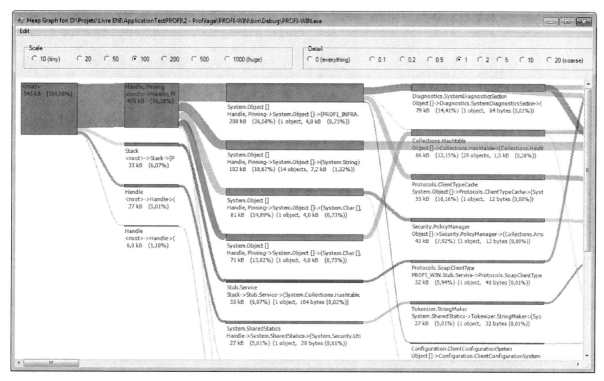

Figure 5-33: CLRProfiler.

33 kilobytes may not look like much memory, but one should recall that the corresponding web service only contains two methods with very simple parameters as inputs as well as outputs. Let us now imagine an industrial-grade web service with dozens of methods, each of them with complex parameters, thus using complex and resource-greedy XML serialization; the level of memory use will be much higher, and can even become an issue if we do not take particular care to keep it limited. To look into memory consumption further, you could use a tool such as ANTS Memory Profiler, which will give you much more than memory allocation metrics. However memory profiling could fill another book, and is outside the scope of this one.

C.6 Message traffic

C.6.a Preliminary note on call counting

We start our iterative process again. The profiler shows that the next function taking most time is the one that corresponds to creating the **Portal**-type form. This is the object passed as input to the **Application.Run** method, and the target for Win32 events loop. Inside this instance is the most "business-related" part of the scenario.

At this stage of our analysis, let us describe in more detail the concept of a "hit." These differ according to whether we are in the function call tree or in the source code.

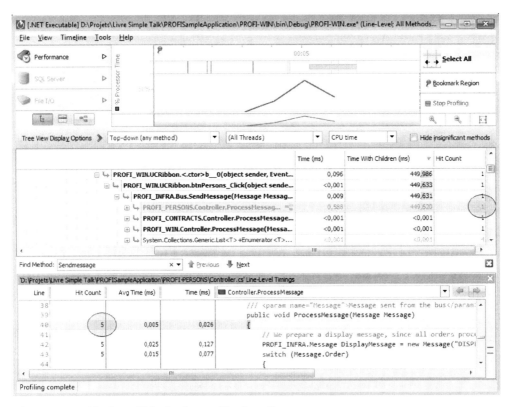

Figure 5-34: Notion of hits in the profiler interface.

The screenshot in Figure 5-34 shows 1 in the **Hit Count** column on the right-hand side of the call tree, and corresponds to the call of function `ProcessMessage` in `SendMessage`. As for the column of the same name in the source code, the value is 5 for the same command.

This is not an error, but reflects the presence of two different metrics. The function call tree shows a chain of calls: `ProcessMessage` is indeed only called once by `SendMessage` when the latter is called from the `Portal` constructor. But nothing prevents it from being called by other chains of calls. In the bottom pane, the count is the total number of calls to this function, wherever they have come from.

Should any doubt arise, the simplest thing to do is to use the second display mode of ANTS Performance Profiler, namely the Methods Grid, which displays the complete list of methods. It can be accessed using the middle button of the three in the top left of the window (see Figure 5-35).

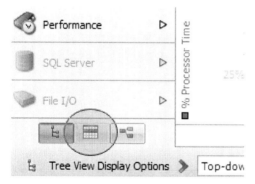

Figure 5-35:   Accessing the Methods Grid.

The display then changes and the functions are shown with the sum of all calls (see Figure 5-36).

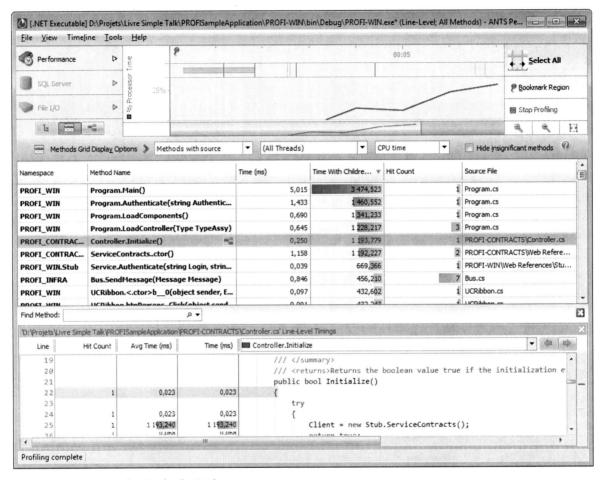

Figure 5-36: Using the Methods Grid.

For now, it will be more useful to focus on this grid rather than the call tree, since the tree gives more importance to the longest path of functions instead of the time spent in functions in general.

First profiler execution

The first time the profiler is run for a particular scenario, the loading of the libraries (and some other effects) can affect the metrics. In order to keep the results stable, it is always advisable to start by running the scenario once without recording the metrics, and then analyze the time values from the second execution.

C.6.b   Analysis

So as to take into account only the functions for which we have the most chance of finding improvements, we change the first filter in **Methods Grid Display Options** to **Methods with source**.

Figure 5-37 shows the results. I have decided to concentrate on methods that take more than 30ms, the others having less potential for performance improvement. As was indicated in the first chapter about profiling rules, it is important to always set clear limits to optimization. Having said that, 30ms is an arbitrary choice, as it depends on the machine, the level of performance demanded by the users, etc. I could have been a little less ambitious and set a goal of 100ms, or tried to push it to just 20ms: the important thing is to set a limit.

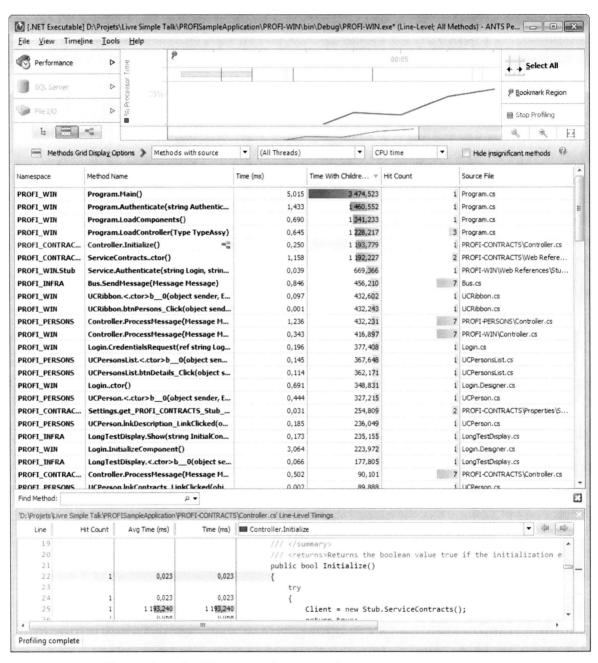

Figure 5-37: Profiler results with all functions taking more than 30ms.

Of course, in the first lines we see the methods on which we have worked beforehand. They remain high because they are inherently complex. The next method on the list is `Bus.SendMessage`. This function is called seven times during our reference scenario.

To investigate a bit deeper into what happens in these seven calls, we will use ANTS Performance Profiler's graph generation functionality. To do so, we click the icon that appears when we select the line in question (see Figure 5-38).

.C...	Controller.Initialize()	0,250	1 1
.C...	ServiceContracts..ctor()	1,158	1 1
b	Service.Authenticate(string Login, strin...	0,039	6(
	Bus.SendMessage(Message Messag...	0,846	4!
	UCRibbon.<.ctor>b__0(object sender, E...	0,097	4:
	UCRibbon.btnPersons_Click(object send..Create a new call graph for this method.		4:
S	Controller.ProcessMessage(Message M...	1,236	4:

Figure 5-38: Create new call graph button.

This takes us to the call graph (see Figure 5-39).

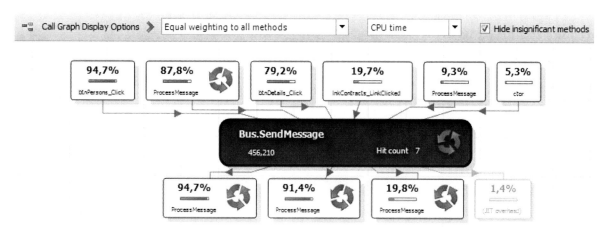

Figure 5-39: The call graph.

It should be noted that options have been selected in order to emphasize methods for which we have source code (for the reasons explained before), and to hide methods that are too short to be significant in our performance quest.

The symbol with three red arrows in a circle means that function calls are recursive. This is explained by the fact that our sample application uses a message bus. We are profiling a message execution that induces processes that may, in turn, send messages, thus calling the same initial function, hopefully with different parameter values.

As a result, this graph is more difficult to analyze. We are still going to expand the message management function in order to see if we can find anything unusual (see Figure 5-40).

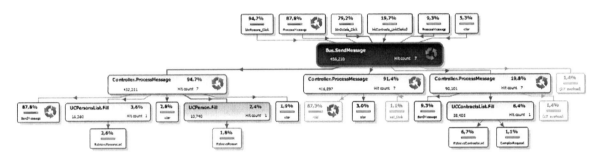

Figure 5-40: The expanded call graph.

There is nothing particular to note on this graph: indeed, the methods that take most of the execution time are the calls to web services, which is no surprise, and the time values displayed are not excessive. Anyway, these calls will be analyzed in more detail in the next chapter, when we will switch to server side.

C.7 Initializing web services clients

C.7.a Analysis

Let's come back to our list of functions taking over 30ms, and walk through it. We mostly find the following:

- graphical controls constructors that call business-related functions to perform our scenario automation: these should, of course, be left out of the analysis

- calls to web services: their possible slowness will be studied in more detail in the next chapter about server-side profiling

- WinForms components initializations, which are usually quite slow.

In short, nothing special. However, one particular point should grab our attention: some web service clients (we sometimes call them proxies) are called several times. If we think back to the architecture of controllers, the principle was to initialize a client once and for all, on the call to function `Initialize`, when loading the controller (Listing 5-21).

```
private Stub.ServiceContracts _Client = null;

/// <summary>
/// Initialization of the controller
/// </summary>
/// <returns>true if the initialization went well</returns>
public bool Initialize()
{
    try
    {
        _Client = new Stub.ServiceContracts();
        return true;
    }
    catch
```

```
      {
          return false;
      }
  }
}
```

Listing 5-21

The logical outcome of this should be only one call to the constructor of `Service` and `ServicePersons` classes, which is not what we observe (see Figure 5-41).

PROFI_WIN	Portal..ctor()		1,293	87,832	1
PROFI_WIN.Stub	Service..ctor()		0,738	60,378	2
PROFI_WIN.Prope...	Settings.get_PROFI_WIN_Stub_Service()		0,001	41,561	2

Figure 5-41: Hit counts for `Service` and `ServicePersons` constructors.

Even if the first scenario is not about contracts, we have seen that this business domain is still initialized, as well as the list of contracts for a given person. This means we should also see the instantiation of the web services client related to contracts. In fact, it is much longer, and thus higher in the list. For a custom view (and to demonstrate another functionality that is offered by most profiling tools), we can filter functions in order to better analyze the situation of web services clients. To do so, we enter the word "Service" in the **Find Method** text-box, and the display adapts accordingly (see Figure 5-42).

Namespace	Method Name	Time (ms)	Time With Children ... ▼	Hit Count
PROFI_CONTRACT...	ServiceContracts..ctor()	1,158	1 192,227	2
PROFI_WIN.Stub	Service.Authenticate(string Login, string ...	0,039	669,366	1
PROFI_CONTRACT...	Settings.get_PROFI_CONTRACTS_Stub_S...	0,031	254,809	2
PROFI_WIN.Stub	Service..ctor()	0,738	60,378	2
PROFI_WIN.Prope...	Settings.get_PROFI_WIN_Stub_Service()	0,001	41,561	2
PROFI_CONTRACT...	ServiceContracts.RetrieveContractsList(s...	0,002	30,520	1
PROFI_WIN.Stub	Service.RetrieveServerSetting(string Set...	0,004	26,513	4
PROFI_PERSONS....	ServicePersons..ctor()	0,704	23,877	3

Find Method: Service × ▼

Figure 5-42: Results when using the Find Method box.

It would have been a shame to miss `ServiceContracts..ctor`, which takes 1,192ms for two calls. We have a potential gain of 600ms for the contracts, 30ms for the utility service, and another 16ms (two thirds of 24ms) for the persons, if we can unify the calls into one instance for each type. One whole second, for such a small sample application and a limited scenario like the ones we are using, represents a huge improvement!

C.7.b   Diagnosis

We start by studying the service on contracts. This will first consist of identifying the two calls. To do so, we create a call graph of this function by clicking the corresponding icon, as explained above (see Figure 5-43).

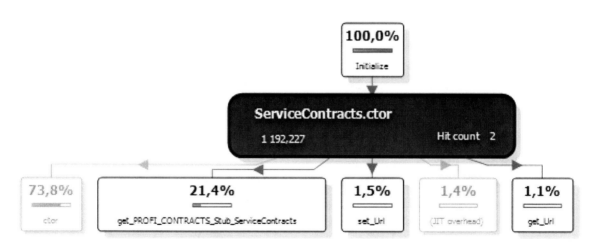

Figure 5-43:   A call graph for `ServiceContracts`.

If we expand the callers, we find the expected call stack but there is still a surprise: the constructor is called twice in total, but we only see one calling entry (see Figure 5-44).

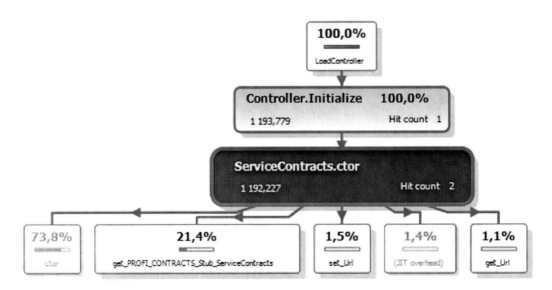

Figure 5-44: Expanded call graph.

In these cases, it is important to remember to clear the **Hide insignificant methods** option, which is typically the reason behind this strange situation. The graph now shows the origin of the two calls (see Figure 5-45).

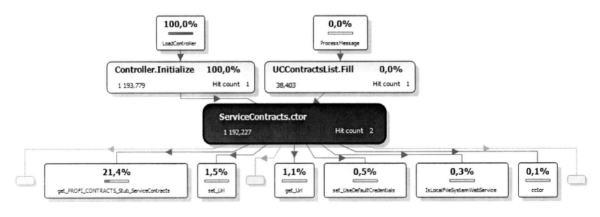

Figure 5-45: Same graph with all functions visible, even the insignificant ones.

However, one of the calls takes almost all the time used by the function, namely the controller initialization. When executing this function, the construction takes nearly 1,200ms, whereas it only takes a few dozen milliseconds when called from `UCContractsList.Fill`. There is almost certainly a cache somewhere, and the gain will be far from the half of the total time spent that we had predicted when analyzing the problem. We are in the same situation as in the case we studied before: loading serialization assemblies and making reflective calls to create the type mappings take a lot of time at the first call.

However, it is not useless to remove the additional calls if possible; firstly, because we may have to do so anyway to achieve our performance goals, and secondly, because it is good practice to eliminate redundancies.

To do so, we find the call in the source code (see Figure 5-46).

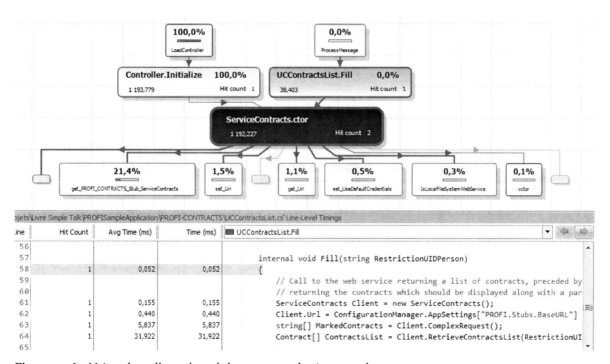

Figure 5-46: Using the call graph and the source code view together.

This is simply a programming mistake: instead of using the instance of client that has been created for unified use, this particular piece of code creates its own client instance. In addition, the `Dispose` function is not even called.

C.7.c   Correction

We are going to correct this problem by writing the code the way it should have been written in accordance with the adopted architecture. To do so, we take the direct call to the web service out of the `UCContractsList` class. Indeed, it should not be in a graphical user control, but rather under the responsibility of the controller.

Architectural rules

This is a difficult point in the development of generic languages like Java or C#: creating a code infra-structure that forces the architectural rules to be followed is complicated. Other than attention given to the build and code reviews, there is nothing to stop a developer from adding references to ADO.NET and calls to a database from a client interface, for example. This is absolutely contrary to the rules of the architecture, since all database calls have to be made from the server-side business-related tier. But apart from putting these rules in place, possibly controlled by tools like FXCop, there is little we can do.

We start by adding the functions to the `Controller` class related to contracts (Listing 5-22).

```
internal string[] ComplexRequest()
{
    return _Client.ComplexRequest();
}

internal Stub.Contract[] RetrieveContractsList(string restrictionOnPersonUID)
{
    return _Client.RetrieveContractsList(restrictionOnPersonUID);
}
```
Listing 5-22

270

These functions are called from `UCContractsList.Fill`, whence we should now access the controller in a simple way, as in Listing 5-23.

```
internal void Fill(string restrictionOnPersonUID)
{
    // Call to the web service that sends the list of contracts,
    // preceded by a call to another method that retrieves the contracts
    // that are marked in a particular way
    string[] markedContracts = Controller.Current.ComplexRequest();
    Contract[] contractsList = Controller.Current.RetrieveContractsList(restriction
                        OnPersonUID);

    [...]
}
```

Listing 5-23

Of course, this modification should be accompanied by the one in Listing 5-24, in the `Controller` class, to be complete.

```
/// <summary>
/// Singleton access to the current controller
/// </summary>
internal static Controller Current = null;

/// <summary>
/// Empty constructor, only there to keep a reference to the instance that
/// has been created
/// </summary>
public Controller()
{
    Current = this;
}
```

Listing 5-24

We have decided to retrieve the controllers from a singleton on the `Controller` class itself rather than linking the business domains and the bus controllers, so that the bus remains as independent as possible from the business domains attached to it. Even if a unique identifier passed at initialization would have done the trick, this still poses problems of non-duplication, typing errors, and so on.

The decision to create a static member that returns the `Controller` instance in order to call instance methods instead of creating static functions is completely arbitrary.

This correction also helped us find another code mistake: the `PROFI.Stubs.BaseURL` setting that we had put in place to simplify switching to another server (a detailed explanation will be given in Section A.4, *Web service URL settings management* in Chapter 6, *Profiling the Sample Application – Server Side*) has not been used on the web service client instance contained in the controller. This can be a source of bugs. Unifying the code helped us to kill two birds with one stone. We modify `Initialize` this way (also adding `using System.Configuration` at the top of the class):

```
public bool Initialize()
{
    try
    {
        _Client = new Stub.ServiceContracts();
        _Client.Url = ConfigurationManager.AppSettings["PROFI.Stubs.BaseURL"]
                    + "ServiceContracts.asmx";
        return true;
    }
    catch
    {
        return false;
    }
}
```

Listing 5-25

All other direct calls are corrected the same way. Those are:

- instantiation of `ServicePersons` from `UCPerson.Fill`

- instantiation of `ServicePersons` from `UCPersonsList.Fill`

- instantiation of `Service` from `Program.Authenticate`

- instantiation of `Service` from the constructor of `Portal.`

In the case of the `Portal`, the controller had no members to store a client to the general-purpose web service that is associated to it. As a consequence, the two calls had to be changed.

Constructor operations display subtleties in ANTS Performance Profiler

When pointing to the constructor, the source code panel in the lower part of ANTS Performance Profiler generally shows the first member being initiated, whereas we would expect the selected line to be the first one in the constructor. This is because the profiler sees what actually gets executed and, when initializing an object, .NET does indeed start by populating the members. This can sometimes make for a strange display where we look for the code of a constructor in a partial file, and actually see the other partial file defining the class. Luckily, we can change the file in a combo.

The method used to look for the callers was, as you would expect, the same as previously, namely using the call graph. Of course, the call stack that passes through `Initialize` was left aside, since this is where we create the unique instance, which should be the only one remaining to serve the other methods. The first graph is for the instantiations of `ServicePersons` (see Figure 5-47).

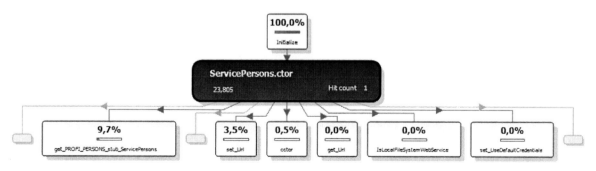

Figure 5-47: Call graph with `ServicePersons` constructor as the chosen method.

The second graph deals with the instantiations of **Service** (see Figure 5-48).

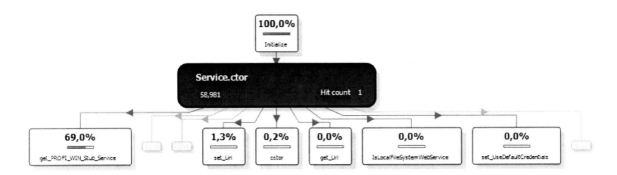

Figure 5-48: Call graph with **Service** constructor as the chosen method.

C.7.d   Results

After working on the code for a few minutes, we obtain the results shown in Figure 5-49. The time is important, since the purpose of this book is to show that performance improvement is mainly a matter of best practice in finding common programming mistakes that are quickly corrected, and not at all a complex operation that only experts can perform.

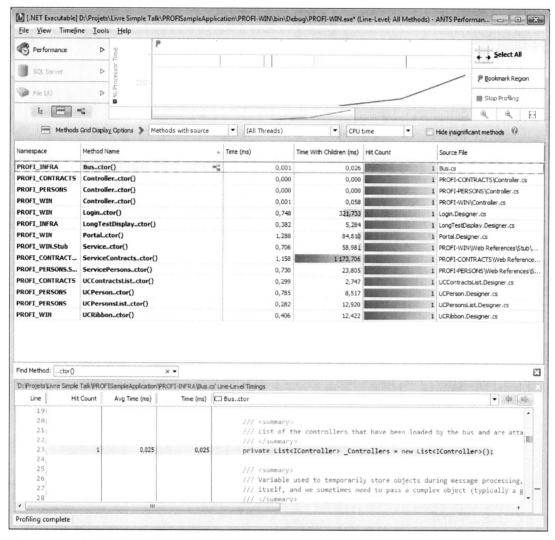

Figure 5-49: Updated profiler results.

We have reached our goal of one single call for each type of proxy. By contrast, results in terms of time saved are disappointing, because the process of the proxy loading could not be optimized, and the gain is almost zero. In fact, it cannot be detected on a single call (we even notice worse results in some cases), and one has to average the time on a dozen scenario executions to notice a gain of a few tens of milliseconds.

Again, this can seem a very feeble advantage, but one should remember we are using an overly-simplistic scenario that runs only six web method calls. On a realistic industrial application, user interactions can originate thousands of calls in a single day, which we should multiply by at least 200 working days in a year. In the end, spending five minutes profiling and correcting the code is an excellent investment.

C.7.e   Additional optimization

We could not conclude this study of the first client-side scenario without proposing a late instantiation of proxies. Indeed, those are always initialized when loading the application. And yet, it is no use creating a proxy before needing it to make a web service call. In order to gain some time, we could replace the controller code by something like the code in Listing 5-26.

```
private Stub.ServicePersons _Client = null;

private Stub.ServicePersons Client
{
    get
    {
        if (_Client == null)
        {
            _Client = new Stub.ServicePersons();
            _Client.Url = ConfigurationManager.AppSettings["PROFI.Stubs.BaseURL"]
                        + "ServicePersons.asmx";
        }
        return _Client;
    }
}

[...]

public bool Initialize()
{
    return true;
}
```

Listing 5-26

This way, the proxy creation will be done as late as possible. The reason why we do not apply this modification is that it would only be worth it for our scenario. Depending on the uses, it could be better to continue creating the client instance early. In particular, this will be so when we load the controllers in parallel with the authentication operations. Again, the optimization of a given scenario can cause a performance drop in another one, hence the importance of keeping a good coverage of the uses of the application by the tests.

C.8   Looking back over the first scenario

Since we had decided to stop at the threshold of 30ms, this section is the last on the first scenario studied on the client side. The remaining functions do not appear to be good sources of improvements, and we are going to switch scenario to study, in more detail, what happens within the business domain of contracts.

Globally, the total scenario time has decreased from 3,360 to 3,072ms. There are several points to note.

- These numbers should not be taken literally: variance in the time spent is inherent to the profiling process.

- However, a difference of half a second is high enough that we cannot treat it as random. Running non-optimized and optimized versions of the scenario several more times shows that this time is stable.

- We could have hoped for more, but 10% more performance in a few hours of work is still an excellent ratio.

- The sample application has been created to show a wide range of coding mistakes. On a real application, a developer will need a bit more time to identify bottlenecks. But previous chapters have shown that profilers are precise enough to identify them quickly.

- Inversely, the sample application executes operations that are so simple in comparison with actual applications that the time spent on loading classes, display and all other infrastructure functions masks the performance gain that has been realized on the business-related functions. In a real case, these would account for a much bigger part, and the relative gain on scenarios would thus be higher.

- Finally, given the small amount of code, we have reached the end of the optimization process quickly. In real studies, it is not unusual to spend days, or even weeks, on profiling. In my experience, and although nothing can be extrapolated in such a sensitive domain as performance, good results have almost always been achieved. It is quite common to divide the time spent in some scenarios by a ratio of two or three, since the coding mistakes cumulate. Ratios of eight to ten have even been observed on some parts of the application dealing mainly with computation and intensive I/O.

D   Analysis of results on the second scenario

D.1   Analysis context

We went through the second scenario at the beginning of this chapter, so we will go straight into the study itself, only reminding readers that the compiling options should be changed from TEST1 to TEST2, and that the solution should be recompiled before profiling.

Contrary to the analysis of the first scenario, in which we have used the different steps to demonstrate profiler functions, we are going to concentrate in this second part of the chapter on actual technical problems. As such, instead of producing the list of time spent in the functions, we will start by looking at this list restricted to functions for which we have the source code (and thus a way to correct if necessary) and for which the time spent is more than 30ms, to keep the same threshold as before (see Figure 5-50).

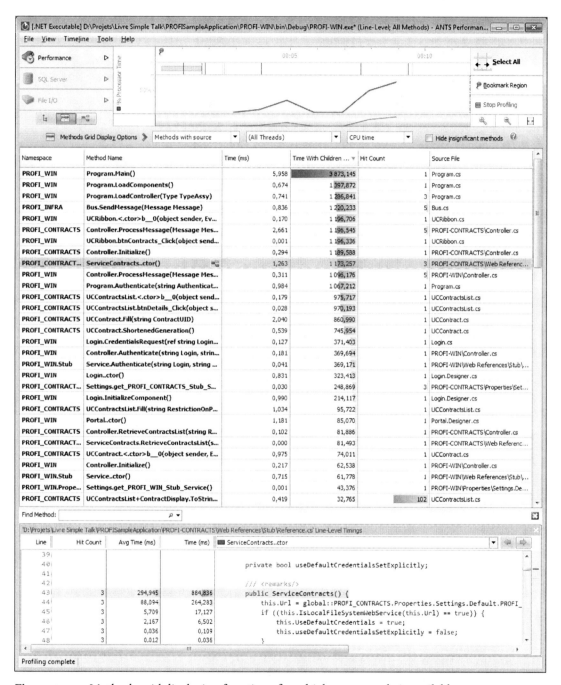

Figure 5-50: Methods grid displaying functions for which source code is available.

Differed time analysis

Almost all profilers allow the user to save the analysis project and the metrics obtained on running a particular scenario independently, in order to analyze them separately. As far as ANTS Performance Profiler is concerned, the results format is binary, which means it can only be manipulated by the tool itself. Nevertheless, exports are possible in XML, HTML and CSV (comma-separated values in a text file). The project format follows an XML grammar, which is very practical for integrating this tool in a software factory. We can indeed automate the preparing of projects depending on the output of an automated build operation, for example. Also, ANTS Performance Profiler can be called from the command line, which facilitates this kind of automation.

As in the first scenario, we are going to start with the longest methods and work our way down to the quicker ones, putting aside functions that are calls from other functions on the same list, as well as the particular cases of slowness due to WinForms.

D.2 Loading the components

As before, the process of loading components is the slowest of all. But since this has already been optimized, we are not going to study these functions again.

However, it remains important to check that the number of calls does not increase, and in fact it has not.

- LoadComponents is still called once and only once.
- LoadController is called three times, once for each business-related domain, namely Portal, Contracts and Persons.

As a result we will not study this function any further. We will put in place another way of optimizing this (because it's always possible to do something quicker), but through a completely different method that will be explained in a later section.

D.3   Instantiation of web services clients

This paragraph logically follows the equivalent one for the first scenario. When optimizing the multiple generations of web service client instances, we had identified the necessary changes to the code so that the scenario does not lead to instance duplication. We used the call graph to correct the callers identified on the given scenario, but we have not gone through the whole code searching for similar uses.

As a consequence, this second scenario on contracts brings up additional cases of useless instantiations, which we will, naturally, correct. This is visible from the fact that there are three calls in the line selected in Figure 5-51.

| PROFI_CONTRACTS | Controller.Initialize() | | 0,294 | 1 189,588 | 1 |
| PROFI_CONTRACT... | ServiceContracts..ctor() | | 1,263 | 1 173,257 | 3 |

Figure 5-51: Hits count for the `ServiceContracts` constructor.

As we have done previously, we use the call graph to find code that will be the target of corrections (see Figure 5-52).

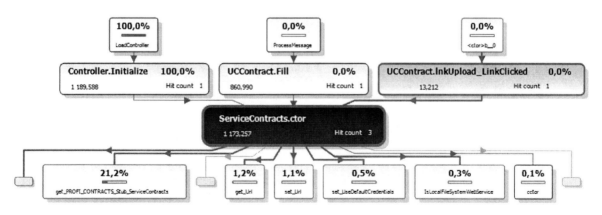

Figure 5-52: The call graph with `ServiceContracts` as the chosen call.

The functions created in the `Controller` class of **PROFI-CONTRACTS** are shown in Listing 5-27.

```
internal void SubscribeUploadSummaryCompleted(Stub.
                                UploadSummaryCompletedEventHandler callbackDelegate)
{
    _Client.UploadSummaryCompleted += callbackDelegate;
}

internal void UploadSummaryAsynchronous(string summaryContent)
{
    _Client.UploadSummaryAsync(summaryContent);
}

internal Stub.Contract RetrieveContract(string contractUID)
{
    return _Client.RetrieveContract(contractUID);
}
```

Listing 5-27

The function `UCContract.lnkUpload_LinkClicked` is modified as in Listing 5-28.

```
private void lnkUpload_LinkClicked(object sender, LinkLabelLinkClickedEventArgs e)
{
    if (_BlockSummary) return;

    //ServiceContracts client = new ServiceContracts();
    //client.Url = ConfigurationManager.AppSettings["PROFI.Stubs.BaseURL"] +
    //"ServiceContracts.asmx";
    try
    {
        // Asynchronous call for sending summary information back to the server
        _BlockSummary = true;
        //client.UploadSummaryCompleted += new UploadSummaryCompletedEventHandler
        //(delegate(object s, AsyncCompletedEventArgs a) { _BlockSummary = false;
        //});
        //client.UploadSummaryAsync(File.ReadAllText(_SummaryFile));
```

```
              Controller.Current.SubscribeUploadSummaryCompleted
                        (new UploadSummaryCompletedEventHandler(delegate(object s,
                        AsyncCompletedEventArgs a) { _BlockSummary = false; }));
              Controller.Current.UploadSummaryAsynchronous(File.ReadAllText(_SummaryFile));
        }
        catch
        {
            _BlockSummary = false;
        }
    }
}
```
Listing 5-28

As far as the call in `UCContract.Fill` is concerned (remember that, in the first scenario, only the call from the class `UCContractsList` was corrected), Listing 5-29 shows it in its corrected form.

```
internal void Fill(string contractUID)
{
    // Retrieving contract definition from its identifier, using the web service
    //ServiceContracts client = new ServiceContracts();
    //client.Url = ConfigurationManager.AppSettings["PROFI.Stubs.BaseURL"] +
    //"ServiceContracts.asmx";
    //_Contract = client.RetrieveContract(contractUID);
    _Contract = Controller.Current.RetrieveContract(contractUID);

    [...]
}
```
Listing 5-29

As in the analysis of the first scenario, we have only made a small gain in total time, but we have reduced to one the number of service instantiations, thus consuming fewer resources. As we usually do, we validate the modification by running the scenario again. The results show a reduced time to execute the method, which is what is expected (see Figure 5-53).

PROFI_CONTRACTS	UCContractsListEventHandlers_Click(object s...	0,027	33,003	1
PROFI_CONTRACTS	UCContract.Fill(string ContractUID)	1,912	832,540	1
PROFI_CONTRACTS	UCContract.ShortenedGeneration()	0,527	725,604	1

Figure 5-53: Hit count for `UCContract.Fill`.

D.4 Loading a contract

D.4.a Analysis

We now go to the next interesting line in our functions list: `UCContract.Fill` took 861ms (and then 833ms during the second call we did to validate the correction above): it is a good candidate for performance optimization.

As usual, we start with a global analysis of the call graph (see Figure 5-54).

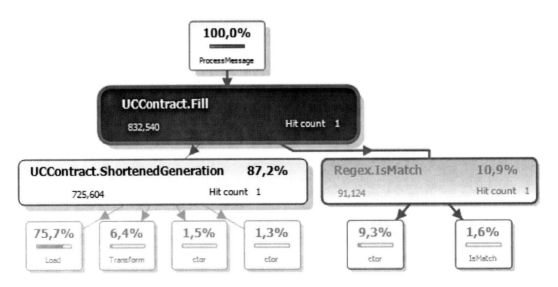

Figure 5-54: The call graph with `UCContract.Fill` as the chosen call.

Contrary to most of the preceding examples, here we have two possible ways of improving performance. We are going to explore them one after the other, hoping at least one will offer a simple solution to accelerate the process.

Why a "simple" solution?

The adjective "simple" in the previous sentence was used deliberately. In fact, we could even say it summarizes the philosophy behind this book. We are not trying to reach maximal performance here, but only to make quick and simple modifications. We simply notice suboptimal or badly coded code portions, and we replace them with quicker versions, without taking the least risk of introducing a regression. If we do not find anything, that does not mean the function cannot be accelerated (all computer-based processes can be, one way or another). Put simply, we are not in an algorithm tuning operation here.

D.4.b   XSL/T transformation

While exploring `UCContract.ShortenedGeneration`, we realized the two functions `Load` and `Transform` shown by the profiler related to the two steps of an XSL/T transformation of an XML document. At first sight, this can look like bad news: those are .NET BCL functions, and these are generally well optimized (and even if they weren't, changing the code is not an option). This is like seeing the glass half-empty.

Luckily the glass can also be seen as half-full. Indeed, based on the hypothesis that .NET functions are fully optimized, we can draw two possible conclusions.

- Either the operation we are processing has such a high inherent complexity that the only way to get it done quicker would be to parallelize it or use a completely different architecture. In this case, the conclusion is easy: this falls within tuning and is irrelevant here.

- Or the way we call .NET functions is the culprit. This can be to do with the way we call them, or because we call them too often, or even simply because the tools are too sophisticated for the job.

We will concentrate on the second hypothesis. To study it, it is better to start from the source code (Listing 5-30).

```
private void ShortenedGeneration()
{
    XslCompiledTransform engine = new XslCompiledTransform();
    using (Stream flux = this.GetType().Assembly.GetManifestResourceStream
                    ("PROFI_CONTRACTS.StylesExtraction.xslt"))
    using (XmlTextReader reader = new XmlTextReader(flux))
        engine.Load(reader);

    StringWriter scribe = new StringWriter();
    ZipFile compressedFile = new ZipFile(_DocumentFile);
    using (Stream fluxStyles = compressedFile.GetInputStream
                        (compressedFile.GetEntry("word/styles.xml")))
    using (XmlReader xslReader = new XmlTextReader(fluxStyles))
    using (XmlWriter xslScribe = new XmlTextWriter(scribe))
        engine.Transform(xslReader, xslScribe);

    File.WriteAllText(_SummaryFile, scribe.ToString());
}
```

Listing 5-30

The engine is loaded with the content of resource **StylesExtraction.xslt**, which we are then going to study. The file is included as an embedded resource in the Visual Studio project, which is the best way for it to follow the life cycle of the .NET assembly it belongs to, since nobody will be able to modify it short of compiling the assembly again. The content of the file is shown in Listing 5-31.

```
<?xml version="1.0" encoding="utf-8"?>
<xsl:stylesheet version="1.0"
                xmlns:xsl="http://www.w3.org/1999/XSL/Transform"
                xmlns:msxsl="urn:schemas-microsoft-com:xslt"
                xmlns:w="http://schemas.openxmlformats.org/wordprocessingml/
                    2006/main"
                exclude-result-prefixes="msxsl">
  <xsl:output method="xml" indent="yes"/>
  <xsl:key name="grouping" match="w:lsdException" use="@w:uiPriority"/>
```

```
  <xsl:template match="/">
    <xsl:element name="root">
      <xsl:for-each select="//w:lsdException[generate-id(.)=generate-
                            id(key('grouping', @w:uiPriority)[1])]">
        <xsl:sort select="@w:uiPriority"/>
        <xsl:element name="group">
          <xsl:attribute name="prio">
            <xsl:value-of select="@w:uiPriority"/>
          </xsl:attribute>
          <xsl:for-each select="key('grouping', @w:uiPriority)">
            <xsl:sort select="@w:name"/>
            <xsl:element name="name">
              <xsl:attribute name="value">
                <xsl:value-of select="@w:name"/>
              </xsl:attribute>
            </xsl:element>
          </xsl:for-each>
        </xsl:element>
      </xsl:for-each>
    </xsl:element>
  </xsl:template>
</xsl:stylesheet>
```

Listing 5-31

XSL/T experts will certainly have noticed the distinctive expression on `for-each`, which is typical of a Muench method (a method to create groups in data through XSL/T). We will try and confirm this by debugging the application in order to retrieve input and output XML content. This is much simpler than going through the code and analyzing where the data comes from and how to get it. We see that the file stored in `_DocumentFile` is a compressed archive in which we find a `word/styles.xml` file. But there is no use looking for its origin for now: instead, we are going to use the variable content to copy the file and decompress it.

WordML and zip files

This file structure is typical of a Word 2007+ or OpenOffice file. They are, in fact, zip archives with a modified extension. This allows them to be composed of several files, generally in XML, while still appearing as single files, and the reduction in size is a huge benefit as well. Another benefit of this format is that it allows reverse engineering, which means developers can easily modify their content.

Setting a breakpoint on the closing brace of the function, we have time to copy the files C:\Temp\tmp3DBF.tmp (value of _DocumentFile) and C:\Temp\tmp3DD0.tmp (value of _SummaryFile). These copies (the file names are, of course, subject to change) allow us to observe the XML content in more detail. Renaming the file with a zip extension enables us to search the internal word directory for the styles.xml file we are interested in. Figure 5-55 shows an extract of this file.

```xml
<?xml version="1.0" encoding="UTF-8" standalone="yes" ?>
<w:styles xmlns:r="http://schemas.openxmlformats.org/officeDocument/2006/relationships"
  xmlns:w="http://schemas.openxmlformats.org/wordprocessingml/2006/main">
 <w:docDefaults>
  <w:rPrDefault>
   <w:rPr>
    <w:rFonts w:asciiTheme="minorHAnsi" w:eastAsiaTheme="minorHAnsi" w:hAnsiTheme="minorHAnsi"
      w:cstheme="minorBidi" />
    <w:sz w:val="22" />
    <w:szCs w:val="22" />
    <w:lang w:val="fr-FR" w:eastAsia="en-US" w:bidi="ar-SA" />
   </w:rPr>
  </w:rPrDefault>
  <w:pPrDefault>
   <w:pPr>
    <w:spacing w:after="200" w:line="276" w:lineRule="auto" />
   </w:pPr>
  </w:pPrDefault>
 </w:docDefaults>
 <w:latentStyles w:defLockedState="0" w:defUIPriority="99" w:defSemiHidden="1" w:defUnhideWhenUsed="1"
   w:defQFormat="0" w:count="267">
  <w:lsdException w:name="Normal" w:semiHidden="0" w:uiPriority="0" w:unhideWhenUsed="0" w:qFormat="1" />
  <w:lsdException w:name="heading 1" w:semiHidden="0" w:uiPriority="9" w:unhideWhenUsed="0" w:qFormat="1" />
  <w:lsdException w:name="heading 2" w:uiPriority="9" w:qFormat="1" />
  <w:lsdException w:name="heading 3" w:uiPriority="9" w:qFormat="1" />
  <w:lsdException w:name="heading 4" w:uiPriority="9" w:qFormat="1" />
  <w:lsdException w:name="heading 5" w:uiPriority="9" w:qFormat="1" />
  <w:lsdException w:name="heading 6" w:uiPriority="9" w:qFormat="1" />
  <w:lsdException w:name="heading 7" w:uiPriority="9" w:qFormat="1" />
  <w:lsdException w:name="heading 8" w:uiPriority="9" w:qFormat="1" />
  <w:lsdException w:name="heading 9" w:uiPriority="9" w:qFormat="1" />
  <w:lsdException w:name="toc 1" w:uiPriority="39" />
  <w:lsdException w:name="toc 2" w:uiPriority="39" />
  <w:lsdException w:name="toc 3" w:uiPriority="39" />
  <w:lsdException w:name="toc 4" w:uiPriority="39" />
  <w:lsdException w:name="toc 5" w:uiPriority="39" />
  <w:lsdException w:name="toc 6" w:uiPriority="39" />
  <w:lsdException w:name="toc 7" w:uiPriority="39" />
  <w:lsdException w:name="toc 8" w:uiPriority="39" />
  <w:lsdException w:name="toc 9" w:uiPriority="39" />
  <w:lsdException w:name="caption" w:uiPriority="35" w:qFormat="1" />
  <w:lsdException w:name="Title" w:semiHidden="0" w:uiPriority="10" w:unhideWhenUsed="0" w:qFormat="1" />
  <w:lsdException w:name="Default Paragraph Font" w:uiPriority="1" />
  <w:lsdException w:name="Subtitle" w:semiHidden="0" w:uiPriority="11" w:unhideWhenUsed="0" w:qFormat="1" />
  <w:lsdException w:name="Strong" w:semiHidden="0" w:uiPriority="22" w:unhideWhenUsed="0" w:qFormat="1" />
  <w:lsdException w:name="Emphasis" w:semiHidden="0" w:uiPriority="20" w:unhideWhenUsed="0" w:qFormat="1" />
  <w:lsdException w:name="Table Grid" w:semiHidden="0" w:uiPriority="59" w:unhideWhenUsed="0" />
  <w:lsdException w:name="Placeholder Text" w:unhideWhenUsed="0" />
  <w:lsdException w:name="No Spacing" w:semiHidden="0" w:uiPriority="1" w:unhideWhenUsed="0" w:qFormat="1" />
  <w:lsdException w:name="Light Shading" w:semiHidden="0" w:uiPriority="60" w:unhideWhenUsed="0" />
  <w:lsdException w:name="Light List" w:semiHidden="0" w:uiPriority="61" w:unhideWhenUsed="0" />
  <w:lsdException w:name="Light Grid" w:semiHidden="0" w:uiPriority="62" w:unhideWhenUsed="0" />
  <w:lsdException w:name="Medium Shading 1" w:semiHidden="0" w:uiPriority="63" w:unhideWhenUsed="0" />
  <w:lsdException w:name="Medium Shading 2" w:semiHidden="0" w:uiPriority="64" w:unhideWhenUsed="0" />
  <w:lsdException w:name="Medium List 1" w:semiHidden="0" w:uiPriority="65" w:unhideWhenUsed="0" />
  <w:lsdException w:name="Medium List 2" w:semiHidden="0" w:uiPriority="66" w:unhideWhenUsed="0" />
  <w:lsdException w:name="Medium Grid 1" w:semiHidden="0" w:uiPriority="67" w:unhideWhenUsed="0" />
  <w:lsdException w:name="Medium Grid 2" w:semiHidden="0" w:uiPriority="68" w:unhideWhenUsed="0" />
  <w:lsdException w:name="Medium Grid 3" w:semiHidden="0" w:uiPriority="69" w:unhideWhenUsed="0" />
  <w:lsdException w:name="Dark List" w:semiHidden="0" w:uiPriority="70" w:unhideWhenUsed="0" />
```

Figure 5-55: Extract from `styles.xml`.

To explain what we are going to do with it, it is not necessary to show the whole file. Muench grouping is only applied to `lsdException` elements. This is confirmed by analyzing the content of the file that results from the XSL/T transformation. Again, we only need to look at part of the file (see Figure 5-56).

Figure 5-56: Extract from the results of the XSL/T transformation.

D.4.c   Possible optimization

Explaining the Muench method is beyond the scope of this book. Interested readers may find the following page helpful: HTTP://WWW.JENITENNISON.COM/XSLT/GROUPING/. Overall, the idea is to generate groups of data, which is what we find in the output file. We observe, in the XSL/T code, the initial creation of a key that gives the `w:lsdException` elements based on the `w:uiPriority` property:

```
<xsl:key name="grouping" match="w:lsdException" use="@w:uiPriority"/>
```

Listing 5-32

We then use a loop from the transformation code to retrieve all the unique values of `w:uiPriority`, followed by a sorting operation so that the grouping values are displayed in ascending order:

```
<xsl:for-each select="//w:lsdException[generate-id(.)=generate-id
                      (key('grouping', @w:uiPriority)[1])]">
  <xsl:sort select="@w:uiPriority"/>
```

Listing 5-33

Finally, another part of the Muench method allows the developer to use the key to retrieve all the `w:lsdException` elements that use the current values of `w:uiPriority`:

```
<xsl:for-each select="key('grouping', @w:uiPriority)">
  <xsl:sort select="@w:name"/>
```

Listing 5-34

The content of this transformation concludes with a simple creation of an element called `name`, with an attribute called `value` that itself contains the value of attribute `w:name` of the element `w:lsdException`:

```
<xsl:element name="name">
  <xsl:attribute name="value">
    <xsl:value-of select="@w:name"/>
  </xsl:attribute>
</xsl:element>
```

Listing 5-35

Nothing very complex and, given the small volumes, we could certainly accelerate this operation by doing it in the code. This can also be a way of optimizing a process.

In practical terms, we are trying to replace the content of the target function by a new code in which the grouping operation will be done purely in C#. In the first part, (Listing 5-36) we walk through the XML file decompressed in memory by an `XmlReader`. The difference, compared to what was done before, is that this walk-through is now only used to store the data in a `SortedDictionary`.

```
StringWriter scribe = new StringWriter();
ZipFile compressedFile = new ZipFile(_DocumentFile);
SortedDictionary<int, List<string>> stylesPerPriority = new SortedDictionary
                                            <int, List<string>>();
using (Stream stylesStream = compressedFile.GetInputStream(compressedFile.
                      GetEntry("word/styles.xml")))
using (XmlReader xslReader = new XmlTextReader(stylesStream))
{
    while (xslReader.Read())
    {
        if (xslReader.LocalName == "lsdException" && xslReader.NamespaceURI ==
                "http://schemas.openxmlformats.org/wordprocessingml/2006/main")
        {
            xslReader.MoveToAttribute("name", "http://schemas.openxmlformats.org/
                            wordprocessingml/2006/main");
            string styleName = xslReader.Value;
            if (xslReader.MoveToAttribute("uiPriority", "http://schemas.
                            openxmlformats.org/wordprocessingml/2006/main"))
            {
                int priority = int.Parse(xslReader.Value);
                if (stylesPerPriority.ContainsKey(priority))
                    stylesPerPriority[priority].Add(styleName);
                else
```

```
                    stylesPerPriority.Add(priority, new List<string>
                              (new string[] { styleName }));
                }
            }
        }
    }
}
```

Listing 5-36

Then, we use the dictionary that has been generated to create the output file with the same format as what was done using XSL/T. An `XmlTextWriter` is of course used in order to optimize the file writing (Listing 5-37).

```
using (XmlWriter scribeXSL = new XmlTextWriter(scribe))
{
    scribeXSL.WriteStartDocument();
    scribeXSL.WriteStartElement("root");
    foreach (KeyValuePair<int, List<string>> couple in stylesPerPriority)
    {
        scribeXSL.WriteStartElement("group");
        scribeXSL.WriteAttributeString("prio", couple.Key.ToString());
        foreach (string style in couple.Value)
        {
            scribeXSL.WriteStartElement("name");
            scribeXSL.WriteAttributeString("value", style);
            scribeXSL.WriteEndElement();
        }
        scribeXSL.WriteEndElement();
    }
    scribeXSL.WriteEndElement();
}
File.WriteAllText(_SummaryFile, scribe.ToString());
```

Listing 5-37

Performance in XML reading and writing

Every time we need performance in XML manipulation, we should use `XmlReader` *and* `XmlWriter`, *which have been specifically designed to read and write XML without having to load the entire content in memory, contrary to what we would do with* `XmlDocument`. *The larger the volume of data, the more important this recommendation is. Indeed,* `XmlReader` *and* `XmlWriter` *classes walk through the XML content as a stream. They advance linearly on the XML elements, keeping only in memory the node currently pointed at. By contrast, an* `XmlDocument` *will load the entire XML content into memory as a Domain Object Model. The DOM approach is of course more flexible because it is easy to go backwards, group objects together, etc. But the necessary amount of RAM makes it impossible to load a file of a few hundred megabytes while maintaining good performance or enough remaining resource.*

D.4.d Results of the optimization on the XSL/T transformation

The test scenarios are run again to observe the improvement to performance. But, before that, it is essential to check that the new function gives the same results as the original one. This is roughly the case (see Figure 5-57).

An experienced eye (or even better, a tool that calculates differences between two files) will note that the content is mainly the same, but that the order of priorities has changed. It simply turns out that this optimization also corrected a problem that existed in the XSL/T: the sort operation was under a text format which, for example, would place 10 before 9.

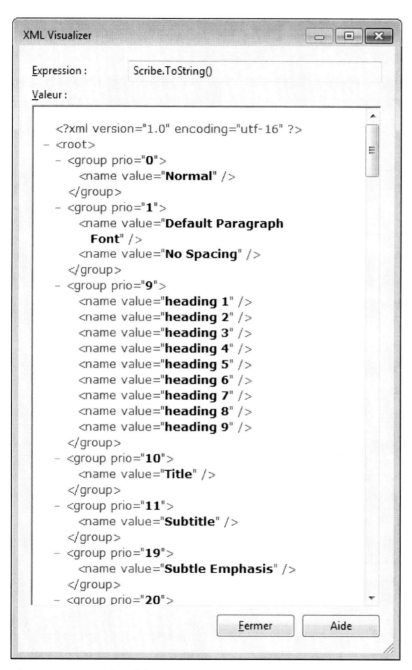

Figure 5-57: Results of the optimized transformation.

Since we have used a dictionary that is based on an integer-type key, we do not have this problem any longer. Obviously, we need to check that the files are exactly the same if we align the algorithms. We could do so by replacing our key with a string, but it seems more logical to take advantage of this to correct the old version. This means modifying the XSL/T file in order for it to sort on the priority as a numeric (which will put 10 after 9) as in Listing 5-38.

```
<xsl:for-each select="//w:lsdException[generate-id(.)=generate-id(key('grouping',
                @w:uiPriority)[1])]">
  <xsl:sort select="@w:uiPriority" data-type="number"/>
```

Listing 5-38

This problem is now solved, and we can launch another profiling session, in order to check that the time spent in this particular process is lower than before.

The improvement exceeds our expectations, with a generation time that has dropped below 65ms (see Figure 5-58). Starting from 726 ms, this is an excellent ratio, particularly if we consider the volume of data was not very high!

Performance or maintenance ease?

The optimization above is only meaningful if performance is the number one success factor for our application. Should ease of process customization have been more important than performance, we would have kept the XSL/T file. In fact, we would even have extracted this file from resources and placed it as an external file, in order to make it easy to modify it without having to build and release a new version. In our case it just so happened that the XSL/T file was more complex to maintain than the corresponding .NET code, even if no rule can be derived from such a particular case.

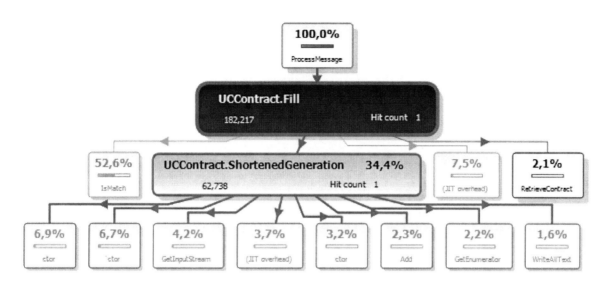

Figure 5-58: Call graph after optimizing.

D.4.e   Use of the regular expression

We now examine the second part of UCContract.Fill, which contains a call to Regex.
IsMatch. A person used to performance profiling will know immediately that they can
squeeze some time out of this. Regular expressions have been implemented very well in
.NET, and they can even be precompiled in assemblies contained in memory for better
performance. Yet, this method is still a generic algorithm and, as such, condemned to
remain less optimized than dedicated algorithms written directly in .NET code.

The same argument about ease of maintenance for XSL/T transformations holds
true. Indeed, it can be very useful in some cases to store a regular expression in a text
parameter, when a user will often need to change the associated behavior. It is much
easier than creating a code plug-in to obtain the same result. Still, regular expressions
need a more technical approach: a non-expert customer will be able to make small
modifications to an XSL/T stylesheet, but will generally lack the skills to intervene in a
moderately-complex regular expression.

Again, we look at the code that calls the **Regex** class to understand what it actually does, and decide whether we could recompile it in C# for better performance:

```
if (!string.IsNullOrEmpty(_Contract.Discount) && Regex.IsMatch(_Contract.Discount,
            @"\[\:?.+\]", RegexOptions.IgnoreCase | RegexOptions.Compiled))
    [...]
```

Listing 5-39

It seems a shame to lose time on this kind of code, because the regular expression has been hard-coded (so there is no excuse in terms of ease of maintenance) and when it could very easily be replaced by a C# condition (Listing 5-40).

```
if (!string.IsNullOrEmpty(_Contract.Discount)
    && _Contract.Discount.StartsWith("[:")
    && _Contract.Discount.EndsWith("]")
    && _Contract.Discount.Length > 3)
    [...]
```

Listing 5-40

At first sight, this code will be much quicker, as .NET automatically uses an optimized operator evaluation approach to ensure no redundant comparison operations are performed.

Operator evaluation within conditional statements

In .NET as in any other modern language, the execution of Boolean expressions is optimized. For example, when the first predicate in an AND operation is valued at false, there is no need to calculate the remaining part of the expression, as the final result will always be false. The inverse is also true with an OR expression and a true value. This is all automatic in .NET. It was not so in Visual Basic 6, where the developer had to explicitly request such behavior by using ANDALSO and ORELSE instead of AND and OR operators.

D.4.f   Results of optimizing the regular expression

As in the previous case, the gain is considerable. In fact, the time spent has literally vanished from the collected metrics (see Figure 5-59).

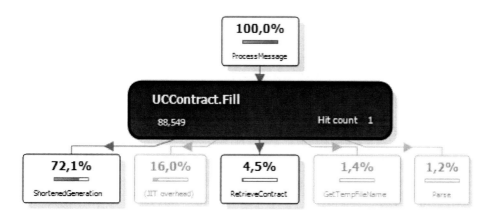

Figure 5-59:   Call graph after optimizing.

The filling of the control based on a contract now takes only 89ms. We are close enough to our objective of 30ms to choose to stop this part of the optimization process here, and move on to another possible source of improvements.

Looking at the content of the call graph in a more detailed view helps convince us to do so (see Figure 5-60).

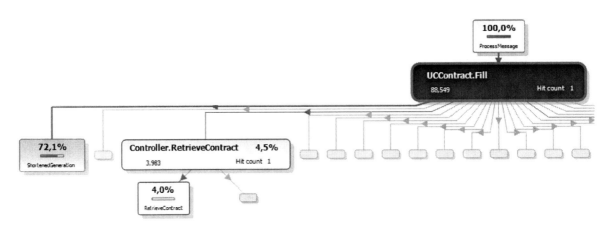

Figure 5-60: A more detailed view of the call graph.

This type of function spread, where no function clearly stands out, and where all of them use a few percent of the total time is typical of a situation where no simple optimization remains. `RetrieveContract` is a call to a web service, and this kind of method is inherently long, due to serialization, network layers, etc. As far as the content of `UCContract.ShortenedGeneration` is concerned, there are only .NET base functions. We could certainly find other ways to optimize some more by using another class instead of `SortedDictionary`, but we would then be venturing into tuning, which is not the goal of this book (although it will be mentioned briefly later on).

D.5   Filling the list of contracts

Our next candidate for time-reduction is the function that fills the list of contracts, even if it has already been covered in part when profiling the first scenario. With a total of 237ms spent in the function, it still remains potentially worthwhile to check whether there could be points on which the first scenario has not thrown any light.

Sadly, there does not seem to be anything more than what we had seen before. The function is not used in a different way from the first scenario. A look at the code confirms that only a restriction on the beneficiary of contracts was made in addition to what happens in the present scenario.

In the end, nothing can be improved for now, since the web service call takes up most of the time (see Figure 5-61).

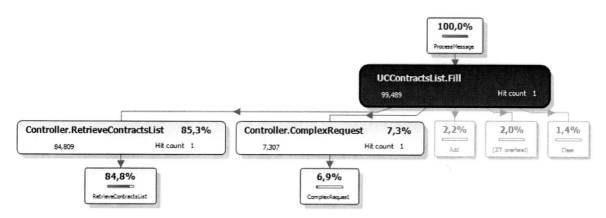

Figure 5-61: Time taken by the web service call.

We will have more opportunities to reduce the process time when working on the server side.

D.6 Additional checks

D.6.a Concept

You will certainly have noticed that the top of the profiler window contains a graphical representation of the CPU consumption during execution of the profiled scenario. The relevant websites will provide more details but, generally speaking, most good profilers allow the user to view the metrics alongside the values of Windows performance counters.

In ANTS Performance Profiler, the timeline at the top of the interface not only gives an overview of resource consumption, but also enables us, in long scenarios, to select a period of time to study (see Figure 5-62).

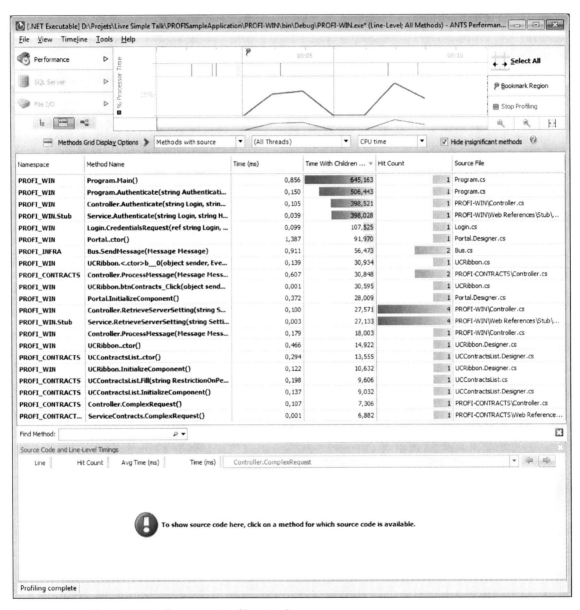

Figure 5-62: The ANTS Performance Profiler timeline.

The screenshot in Figure 5-62 shows that the profiler also retrieves information about exceptions detected while the scenario was executing (a small vertical red line denotes an exception being thrown). This is very helpful, because throwing an exception is extremely resource-consuming. If too many exceptions are thrown, typically because they are generated inside a loop, performance can be greatly affected. We should thus keep an eye on the density of exceptions in this graph, even if, when there are too many, we will certainly see it in the time metrics as well.

D.6.b   Preparing the counters

The content of this graph can be adjusted by selecting different performance counters. When run from Visual Studio, the profiler uses default values, but once in the ANTS Performance Profiler GUI, there is nothing to stop us from running an analysis again after changing the parameters. To do so, we open the **File** menu and click **New Profiling Session**. In the dialog box that appears, the values corresponding to the application are as expected (see Figure 5-63).

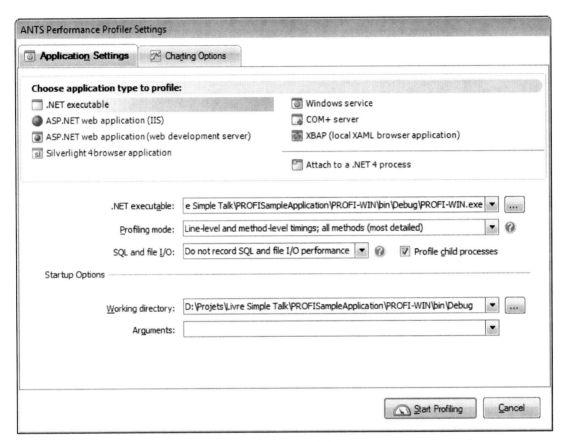

Figure 5-63: The ANTS Performance Profiler Settings dialog box.

Maybe you have noticed that, in the previous profiling sessions, the SQL Server and File I/O tabs were always unavailable, as in Figure 5-64.

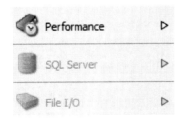

Figure 5-64: The ANTS Performance Profiler profiling type options.

We will change that by running the second scenario again with the **Record SQL and file I/O performance** option selected from the **SQL and file I/O** list (see Figure 5-63).

There are a few potentially interesting counters on the **Charting Options** tab of the Settings dialog box (see Figure 5-65).

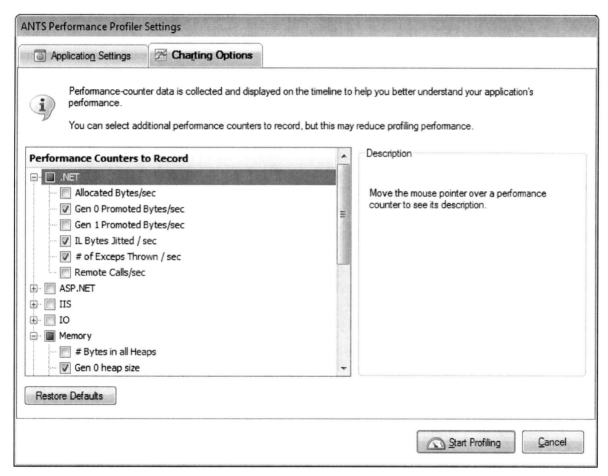

Figure 5-65: The Charting Options tab of the ANTS Performance Profiler Settings dialog box.

For this profiling session, we will add a few performance counters that we will discuss later. Then, we only need to run the profiling process again by clicking **Start Profiling**, and (as usual) waiting for the results to display.

__Reminder about non-interaction__

In case you did not pick up this point earlier in the book (or have since forgotten), it is very important not to interact with the computer when the automated test scenarios are run on the sample application. Test automation as we have done it sends messages to the application that is in the foreground, expecting this to still be PROFI. Changing the active application during the scenario could result in the active application being closed. The scenario would fail, but we might also lose unsaved data from the application we had started using.

D.6.c   Metrics analysis

The upper part of the interface now looks more like Figure 5-66.

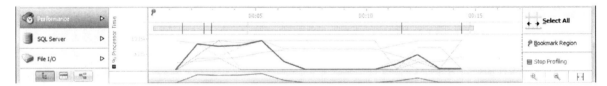

Figure 5-66: The timeline pane in ANTS Performance Profiler.

Clicking the arrow in the Performance tab displays the list of counters that have been recorded, and a contextual help (see Figure 5-67).

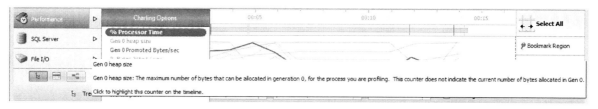

Figure 5-67: List of counters.

Choosing the desired entry displays the evolution of the corresponding metrics (see Figure 5-68). We will study a few of them below.

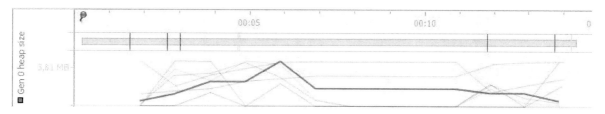

Figure 5-68: Results for the Generation 0 heap size counter.

Gen 0 heap size corresponds to the memory reserved by Generation 0 of .NET CLR, namely, all objects that have not been moved higher by the previous executions of the garbage collector (see Figure 5-68). On such short scenarios as the ones we have put in place, it is rare to see surprising events in the memory management. But we could modify the scenario definitions to generate higher loads.

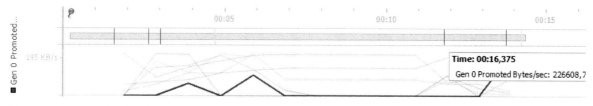

Figure 5-69: Results for the Generation 0 Promoted Bytes/sec counter.

The number of bytes promoted from Generation 0 per second, which we can see in Figure 5-69, does not show anything significant: bytes are promoted to Generation 1, but the rate is very reasonable. To give you a concrete example, an investigation is only necessary when this rate reaches several megabytes per second. In our case, the peak is only around 200 KB/s.

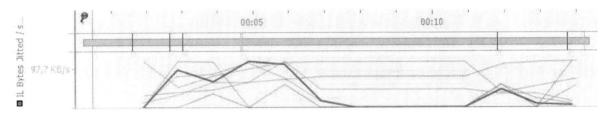

Figure 5-70: Results for the IL Bytes Jitted/sec counter.

The metrics in Figure 5-70 (number of IL bytes compiled into machine language by the JIT per second) shows a logical peak at the beginning of the scenario: this corresponds to the loading of assemblies that can contain a controller, through the mechanism of PROFI start-up. The second peak towards the end of the scenario is less easily understandable. To have a better idea, we select the time around this event, and switch to the method grid view (see Figure 5-71).

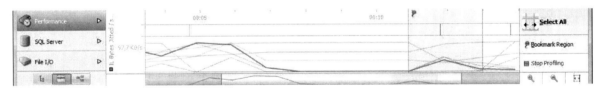

Figure 5-71: Analysis of the second peak in the profiler results.

The portion of the scenario in which the contracts are loaded has been selected: the JIT compiling thus certainly corresponds to the preparation of IL code to perform those operations. The fact that this peak is quite large could be explained by the fact that web services are going to be called, and they need serialization assemblies that can be large.

308

We will talk again about these **XmlSerializer** assemblies later in the book. For now, we only explain the peak in the graph by their existence and loading through the JIT.

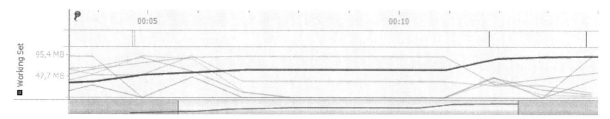

Figure 5-72: Results for the Working Set counter.

The evolution of the Working Set shown in Figure 5-72 corresponds to the extent of the memory pages that have been used recently, which is stable. Nothing worthy of note. To see memory consumption more clearly, it is more useful to look at the Private Bytes performance counter (see Figure 5-73).

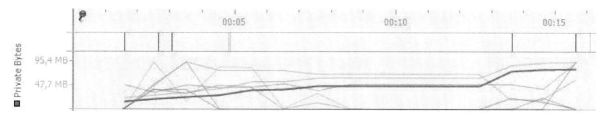

Figure 5-73: Results for the Private Bytes counter.

This is certainly one of the most complicated counters, and it is almost impossible to analyze independently of the others. As we have seen in the section about .NET memory management, it is absolutely normal for the memory used by a process to grow continuously, as long as there is no memory pressure. But, if we want to justify this behavior, the activity of the GC should be non-existent during this time. This is the next counter we will check (see Figure 5-74).

Figure 5-74: Results for the garbage collector activity, in terms of % time spent in the GC.

This confirms the previous hypothesis: the GC activity is basically zero, which means the continuous increase in memory use is nothing to worry about. It simply happens in this scenario that .NET has no memory pressure from the OS, and has decided not to lose time running the GC, since it has plenty of RAM at its disposal.

If, on the contrary, an intense GC activity had been recorded, we could have been facing two potential problems.

- Had the memory been increasing at the same time, we would have been confronted with a memory leak, or with a continuous increase of the working set due to intrinsic needs of the business-related process. In both cases, we would need to find out where it came from, otherwise an OutOfMemoryException would eventually be thrown.

- Had the memory use remained stable, this would mean we had defined activities that spent a lot of time creating and releasing objects in memory instead of running useful activities. A solution to this kind of problem can be to use pooling or even re-entrance, with sets of objects that are continuously reused in successive contexts, instead of creating new objects for every need.

For more information about performance counters and how to use and interpret them, see TechNet: HTTP://TECHNET.MICROSOFT.COM/EN-US/LIBRARY/BB734903.ASPX. MSDN also provides a reference to performance counters: HTTP://MSDN.MICROSOFT.COM/EN-US/LIBRARY/W8F5KW2E%28V=VS.100%29.ASPX.

E   What's next?

This chapter has demonstrated profiling on the client of our sample application. We have learned how to set up a profiler and study the output metrics. We learned a few tricks to analyze these metrics and already saw a few of the most frequent code mistakes that account for performance loss.

In the next chapter, we will apply our experience of profilers to the server, thus extending our study of the application as a whole. We have found bottlenecks in the client, but some have their roots on the server side and we will pick up the trail there. Most of the techniques we will be using have been presented here, but you will see that server profiling has its own peculiarities.

Chapter 6: Profiling the Sample Application – Server Side

A   Configuring the target web application

A.1   Debugging mode

The first thing to do when profiling an application is to set the compilation mode to **DEBUG**, if it is not already set. Profilers need debug links to be activated and available in `.pdb` files in order to display the bottlenecks directly in the code. Displaying the location of a problem in the IL code would make it much more difficult to analyze.

Typically, a display like that in Figure 6-1 indicates that the application has not been compiled with the debugging files. Note the message beginning, "The profiler did not find any methods with source code...".

Beware of the possible confusion between debug compilation mode and the actual generation of `.pdb` files, particularly if you started programming .NET using the first versions of Visual Studio in which, by default, the release configuration did not create `.pdb` files.

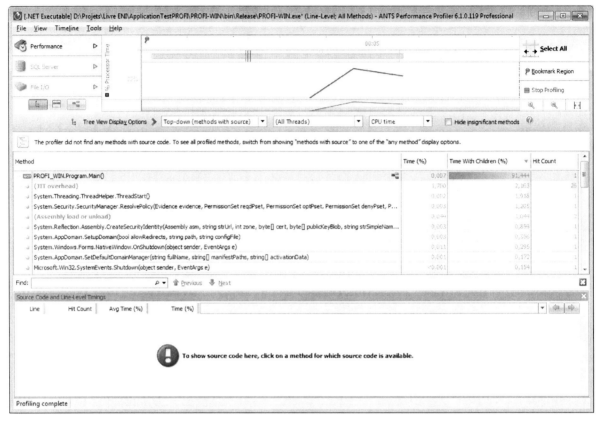

Figure 6-1: Error message when profiling in non-debug mode.

What the profilers really need is for the debugging file generation option to be set to **pdb-only** or **full**, whether the configuration is Debug or Release. To check this is correct, open the properties panel for the Visual Studio project, go to the **Build** tab, and click **Advanced**. The dialog box shown in Figure 6-2 is then displayed, which allows us to set the debugging information generated. However, it should be noted that, in recent versions of Visual Studio, the **.pdb** files are generated by default, in Debug and in Release configuration.

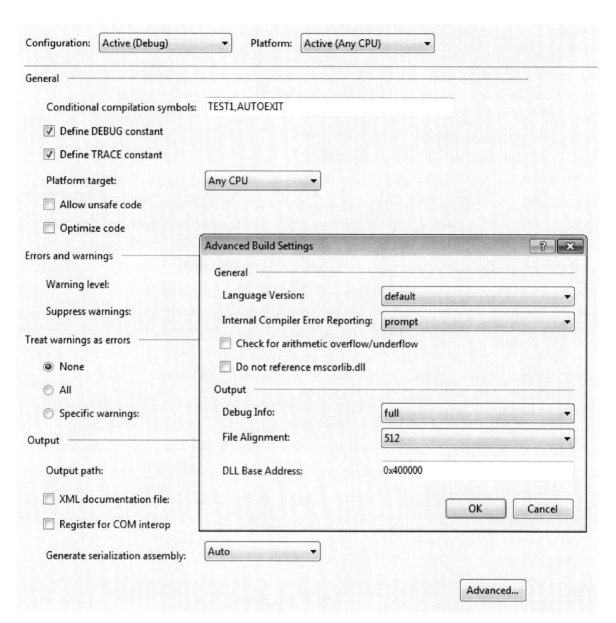

Figure 6-2:   Advanced Build Settings dialog box in Project Properties.

A.2 Optional authentication

Authentication often needs particular attention when deploying ASP.NET solutions, even for pure development. In the case of profilers, the problem is even more significant because high privileges are required, whereas OSs and web servers increasingly tend to reduce the necessary rights.

With Windows, using integrated authentication helps mitigate this problem, but we still have to pay attention to the browsers, as Internet Explorer and other browsers do not manage Windows authentication in the same way. Firefox needs a change in its configuration, which can be performed by using **about:config** as the URL, and then adding the authorized websites in the **network.automatic-ntlm-auth.trusted-uris** key.

Care should also be taken when switching from a development context to a "true" web server like IIS. The security context will no longer be the one for the current user, but the one associated with the default user of the IIS application pool we are using. The kind of error message shown in Figure 6-3 is sometimes encountered because of this.

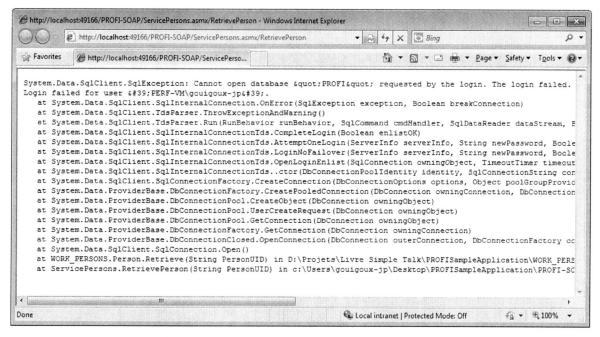

```
System.Data.SqlClient.SqlException: Cannot open database &quot;PROFI&quot; requested by the login. The login failed.
Login failed for user &#39;PERF-VM\gouigoux-jp&#39;.
   at System.Data.SqlClient.SqlInternalConnection.OnError(SqlException exception, Boolean breakConnection)
   at System.Data.SqlClient.TdsParser.ThrowExceptionAndWarning()
   at System.Data.SqlClient.TdsParser.Run(RunBehavior runBehavior, SqlCommand cmdHandler, SqlDataReader dataStream, E
   at System.Data.SqlClient.SqlInternalConnectionTds.CompleteLogin(Boolean enlistOK)
   at System.Data.SqlClient.SqlInternalConnectionTds.AttemptOneLogin(ServerInfo serverInfo, String newPassword, Boole
   at System.Data.SqlClient.SqlInternalConnectionTds.LoginNoFailover(ServerInfo serverInfo, String newPassword, Boole
   at System.Data.SqlClient.SqlInternalConnectionTds.OpenLoginEnlist(SqlConnection owningObject, TimeoutTimer timeout
   at System.Data.SqlClient.SqlInternalConnectionTds..ctor(DbConnectionPoolIdentity identity, SqlConnectionString con
   at System.Data.SqlClient.SqlConnectionFactory.CreateConnection(DbConnectionOptions options, Object poolGroupProvid
   at System.Data.ProviderBase.DbConnectionFactory.CreatePooledConnection(DbConnection owningConnection, DbConnection
   at System.Data.ProviderBase.DbConnectionPool.CreateObject(DbConnection owningObject)
   at System.Data.ProviderBase.DbConnectionPool.UserCreateRequest(DbConnection owningObject)
   at System.Data.ProviderBase.DbConnectionPool.GetConnection(DbConnection owningObject)
   at System.Data.ProviderBase.DbConnectionFactory.GetConnection(DbConnection owningConnection)
   at System.Data.ProviderBase.DbConnectionClosed.OpenConnection(DbConnection outerConnection, DbConnectionFactory cc
   at System.Data.SqlClient.SqlConnection.Open()
   at WORK_PERSONS.Person.Retrieve(String PersonUID) in D:\Projets\Livre Simple Talk\PROFISampleApplication\WORK_PERS
   at ServicePersons.RetrievePerson(String PersonUID) in c:\Users\gouigoux-jp\Desktop\PROFISampleApplication\PROFI-SC
```

Figure 6-3:   Error message when the process user has no associated SQL Server user name.

In this particular case, the problem came from the fact that Cassini uses the current user as its process owner, and that this user had access rights to the database, whereas the user associated with the application pool we used in IIS (**APPPOOL\DefaultAppPool**) did not have these rights. We can solve this in various ways.

- Give the necessary rights to the user associated with the application pool, for example by associating it to a database user.

- Modify the user associated with the IIS application pool. In fact, it is even better practice to create a new application pool with the right user. This way, we will also improve memory compartmentalization, and be able to use more RAM (a worker process is limited to 1.5 GB).

- Impersonate the ASP.NET process, in order to place the worker process under the context of another user, which has the necessary rights.

In our sample application, the simplest solution has been chosen, namely activating impersonation in the `web.config` file as shown in Listing 6-1.

```xml
<?xml version="1.0"?>
<configuration>
     <appSettings>
            <add key="PROFI.Authentication.Mode" value="LoginForm"/>
            <add key="PROFI.ServerDescription" value="Test server - Local mode"/>
     </appSettings>
     <connectionStrings>
            <add name="DBConnection" connectionString="Data Source=.\
                      SQLExpress;Initial Catalog=PROFI;Integrated Security=True"/>
     </connectionStrings>
     <system.web>
   [...]
   <identity impersonate="true" userName="gouigoux" password=
                           "UnobfuscatedPassword"/>
   [...]
  </system.web>
</configuration>
```

Listing 6-1

Using out-of-the-box authentication methods

It is essential to test as early as possible the authentication mode our customers will use. In fact, an even better practice is to ensure our application correctly interfaces with the few standard authentication modes provided by ASP.NET. If possible, it should completely delegate its authentication to these APIs. This is the best guarantee against side effects due to tight coupling between business-related and authentication-related code.

A.3 Using administrator mode

Administrative rights are needed for server profiling when using Windows Vista or 7. The problem is the same as with debugging: in theory, a set of rights could be enough, but it is so large that, most of the time, software editors simply require an administrator role for simplicity's sake.

When starting ANTS Performance Profiler, if we forget to run as an administrator, the **Start Profiling** button will show a recognizable icon requesting higher privileges, the User Account Control shield, as in Figure 6-4.

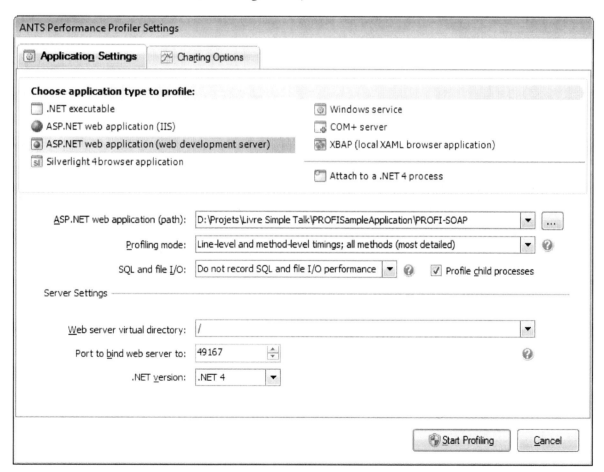

Figure 6-4: Icon on the Start Profiling button, indicating that administrator privileges are required.

In addition, we will get a message asking for privilege elevation, as shown in Figure 6-5.

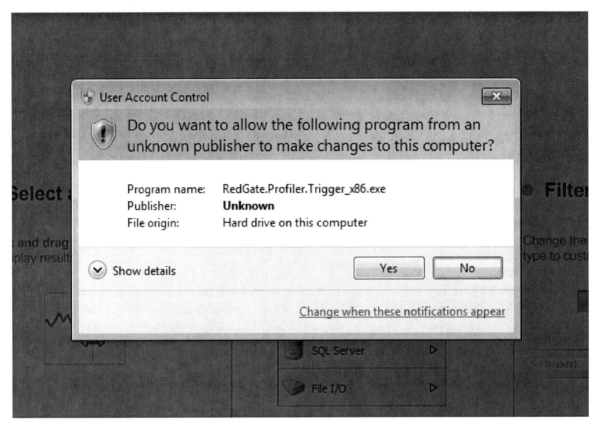

Figure 6-5:   User Account Control dialog.

Adaptive profiler

It should be noted that ANTS Performance Profiler is capable of deducing from the Visual Studio execution context whether profiling should be run in ASP.NET mode or within an executable process. This is very handy, since you only have to modify the start-up project in Visual Studio and run the analysis from the ANTS menu to profile the corresponding project.

To prevent this message from being displayed every time we run a profiling session, we need to run everything under administrative rights. Since, most of the time, we start a profiling session from Visual Studio, which will transfer the administrative privileges to ANTS Performance Profiler, the easiest solution is to use the **Run as administrator** command, as shown in Figure 6-6.

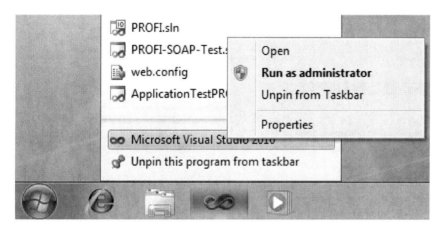

Figure 6-6:   Running Visual Studio with administrative rights.

In order to avoid forgetting this, it is possible to modify the short-cut properties so as to make this the default behavior. This can be done by clicking **Properties** as in Figure 6-6, which will display the dialog shown in Figure 6-7.

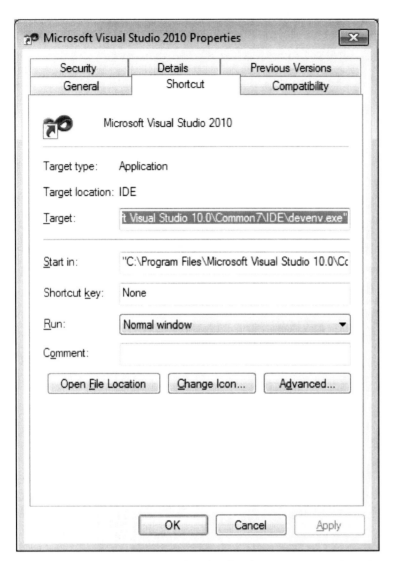

Figure 6-7: Properties dialog box for the short cut to Visual Studio.

By clicking **Advanced** we obtain the dialog shown in Figure 6-8, in which we select the first option, to ensure we always run as an administrator.

Figure 6-8: Activating the option "Run as administrator" for the short cut to Visual Studio.

It will soon be noticed that selecting this option will not prevent the user from having to confirm at every execution that the administrator mode should be used. This is a security feature, in order to validate that a real user is behind this command. But still, this option helps us make sure we will not forget to run the IDE under an administrator context.

Once this is done, Visual Studio has the necessary rights to open Port 49167 (or any other port that is chosen by the application or the developer). The profiler informs us of the presence of required rights through the absence of the User Account Control shield on the Start Profiling button (see Figure 6-9).

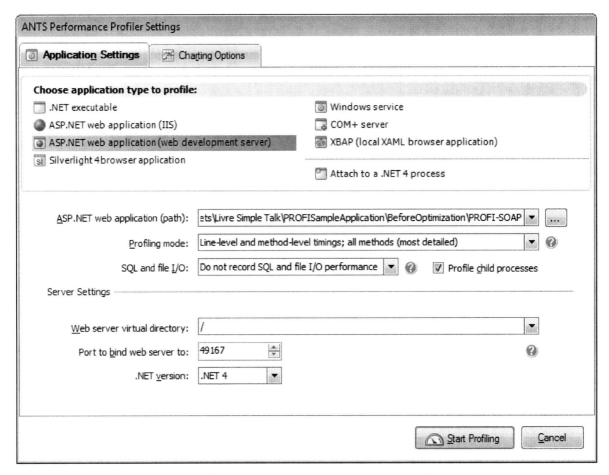

Figure 6-9: Icon on the Start Profiling button, showing administrator privileges are present.

This way, no problem arises, either with running the server on the specified port, or with communicating with the web development server: the expected content is returned correctly, as shown in Figure 6-10.

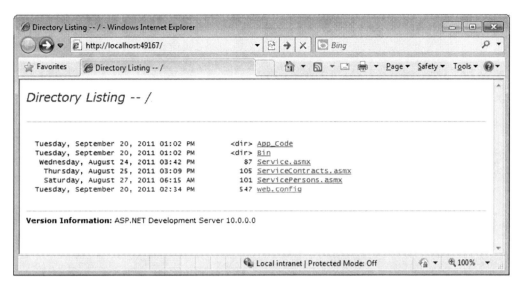

Figure 6-10: Content of the virtual directory for PROFI-SOAP.

This allows us to choose the service we want to test. We will start with **ServicePersons.asmx**, which will bring us to the screen shown in Figure 6-11.

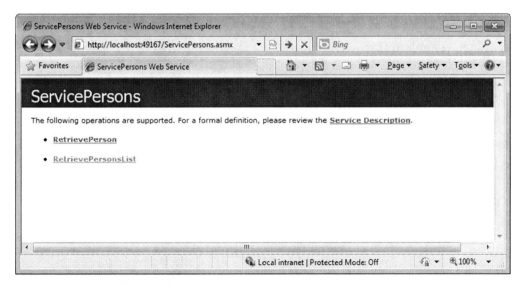

Figure 6-11: List of methods in the **ServicePersons** web service.

325

The web method that we are going to test is the second one, namely
RetrievePersonsList (see Figure 6-12).

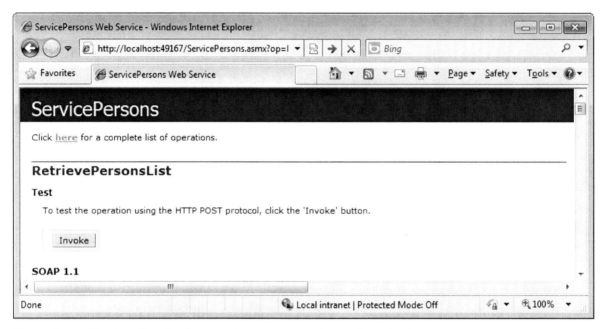

Figure 6-12: Test interface for the RetrievePersonsList web method.

Since all rights-related problems are now solved, we can run our test to the end and
invoke the web method using the **Invoke** button. The expected result is displayed in
Figure 6-13.

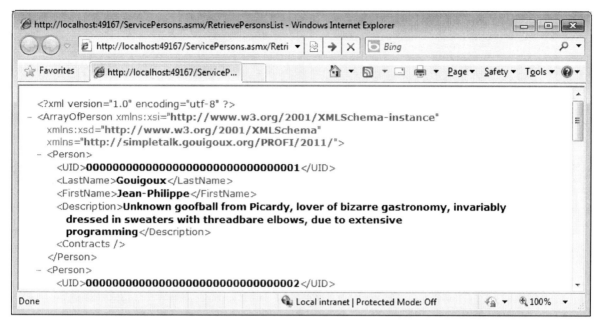

Figure 6-13: Results of calling the RetrievePersonsList web method.

Keeping the browser window open

The browser that the profiler opens when it is run should not be closed before all interactions we wish to profile have completely finished. Indeed, closing this window instructs ANTS Performance Profiler to stop the profiling session. Therefore, it is important to keep it open throughout the analysis. Also be aware that, when a target port number is specified, the port will be closed at the same time that the profiling stops. If the client application continues calling the server, an exception will be thrown.

The results obtained are shown in Figure 6-14.

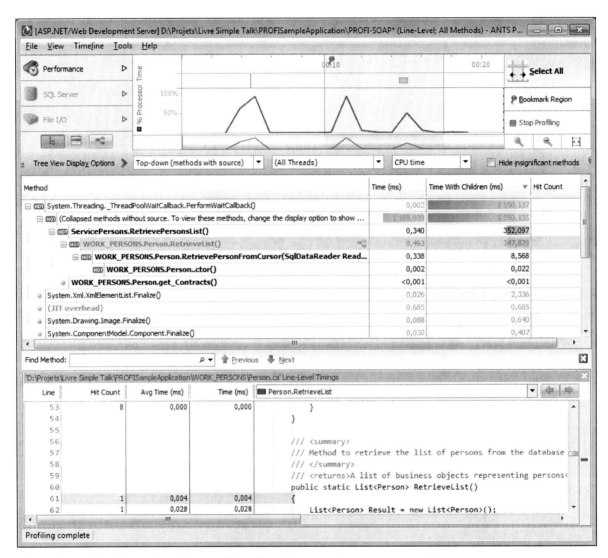

Figure 6-14: Profiler results when profiling the call to `RetrievePersonsList`.

A.4   Web service URL settings management

The sample application uses several web services clients, the code of which is automatically generated. The first one of those is directly in the PROFI-WIN executable assembly, but another one is, for example, located in a referenced assembly, namely PROFI-PERSONS. This can cause a problem during the use of a profiler, among other situations. The modification of the URL contained in the `app.config` generated by Visual Studio when adding the web reference will not have any effect on the execution of the application.

The issue arises if we want to use another port when profiling on a web server. This whole section can be safely skipped if you intend to profile your web server on the original port number.

There is no problem as far as the `app.config` created in PROFI-WIN is concerned: the modification is correctly taken into account. But for a particular reason (that will be explained shortly), the same change in the `app.config` located in PROFI-PERSONS does not produce any visible effect, and the client pointing to `ServicePersons` keeps its default value, namely the one used when initializing the client. We could modify the URL in the web reference inside Visual Studio, but it seems strange that these two settings, although very similar, do not work in the same way. This issue exists even though the proxy in question has been defined correctly with **dynamic** as its mode. Incidentally, this is the default behavior of Visual Studio when creating a web reference, which is precisely what caused the configuration file section we are talking about to appear.

Figure 6-15 shows the Solution Explorer panel with two projects, in which we can see the client that has been generated to call the associated web service. Both are called Stub, and we can also see the two configuration files.

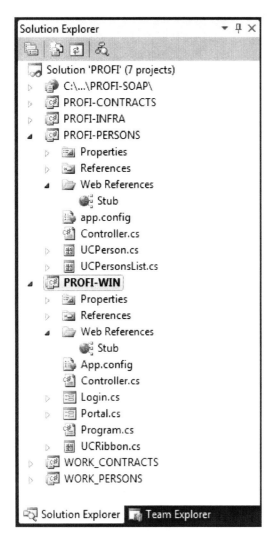

Figure 6-15: PROFI structure in Visual Studio's solution explorer.

For each of the web service clients, we should open the **Properties** pane to check that we are using dynamic mode (see Figure 6-16).

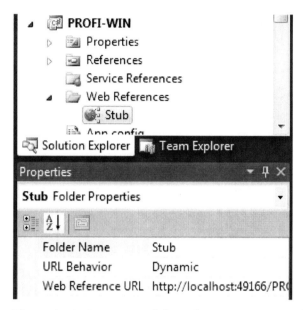

Figure 6-16: Properties of the web service proxies, called "Stub."

The two proxies are generated from a web development server address, which is pointing to the local port number 49166. This means that, when profiling the server, we should use parameters as shown in Figure 6-17.

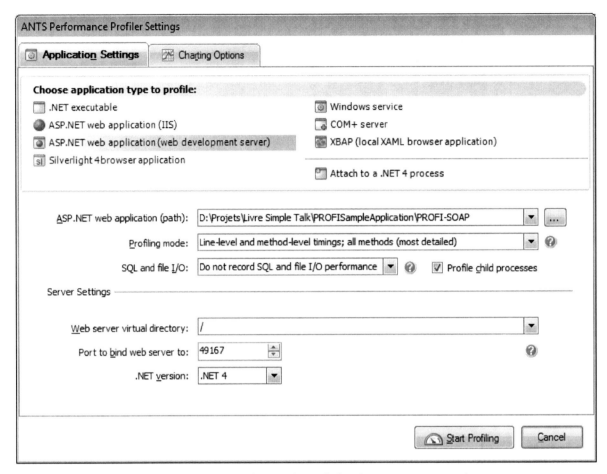

Figure 6-17: Using ANTS Performance Profiler in the web development server mode.

In particular, if we want to profile on the web server by using a specified port number (in our example, 49167), we have to modify both configuration files so that the two client classes called `Stub` point to this modified port number.

The modification for the file `app.config` of PROFI-WIN is shown in Figure 6-18.

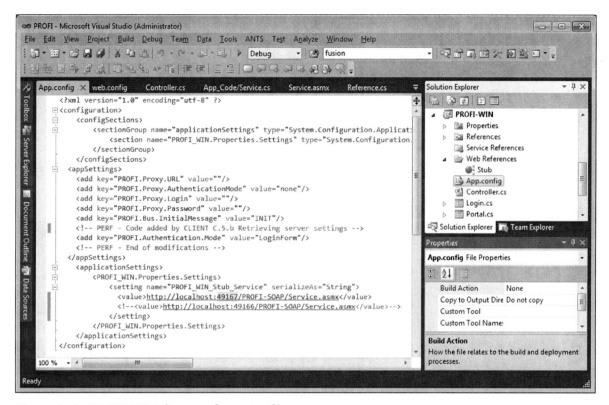

Figure 6-18: PROFI-WIN client configuration file.

The `app.config` file of PROFI-PERSONS is also modified (see Figure 6-19).

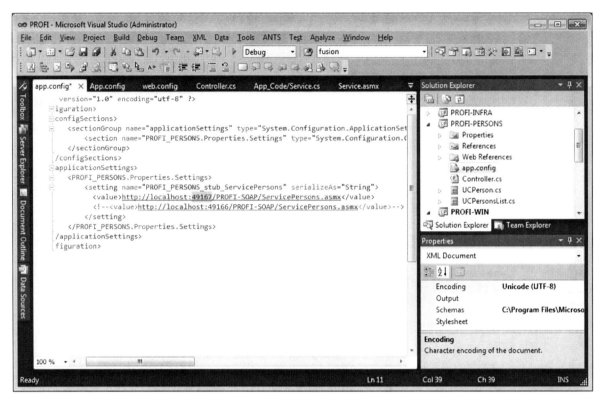

Figure 6-19: `app.config` file for the PROFI-PERSONS project.

We will now show more precisely the problem we have talked about above: when watching the URL member of the client class in debugging mode, we notice that the value has been correctly changed on the one for PROFI-WIN, but not on the second one (see Figure 6-20).

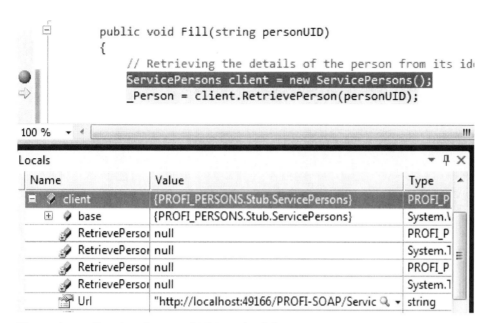

```
public void Fill(string personUID)
{
    // Retrieving the details of the person from its id
    ServicePersons client = new ServicePersons();
    _Person = client.RetrievePerson(personUID);
```

Name	Value	Type
⊟ client	{PROFI_PERSONS.Stub.ServicePersons}	PROFI_P
⊞ base	{PROFI_PERSONS.Stub.ServicePersons}	System.\
RetrievePersor	null	PROFI_P
RetrievePersor	null	System.1
RetrievePersor	null	PROFI_P
RetrievePersor	null	System.1
Url	"http://localhost:49166/PROFI-SOAP/Servic	string

Figure 6-20: Showing the actual URL in the debugger.

The problem comes from the fact that the configuration file should not be modified directly: this method works fine on an executable, but not on a referenced library. The correct way to apply this modification is to use the settings editor, by double-clicking on the file Settings.settings, which was created with an entry for the service URL when we added the web reference. This setting is shown in Figure 6-21.

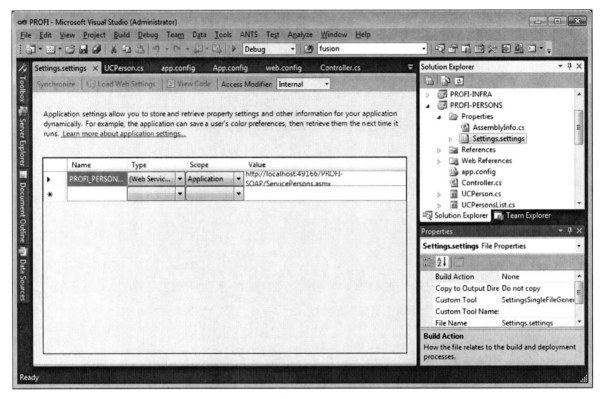

Figure 6-21: Interface to manage the content of the `Settings.settings` file.

In practice, we do not have any settings files in the deployed execution directory: Visual Studio updates the configuration file with the content of the settings files.

As if it was not complicated enough already, if the settings editor and the configuration file are opened simultaneously in Visual Studio, or if the latter has been modified after updating the former, they cannot be synchronized, except if we accept the message that the editor brings up in this case (see Figure 6-22).

336

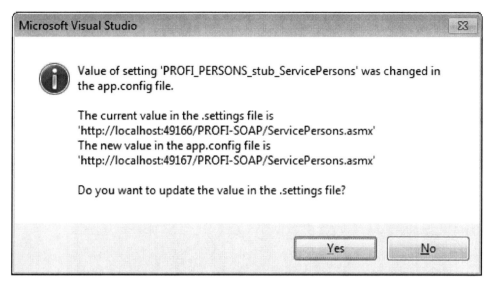

Figure 6-22: Warning message about synchronization of the settings content.

In addition, the more different web services we use, the more locations we will have to remember to update. Still, it is quite useful to expose several web services on the same web application, in order to have a clear separation of business-related domains. In conclusion, it is a good idea to put in place an architecture that allows the base URL for the web services to be centralized. I propose creating a new application setting called **PROFI:Stubs:BaseURL**, as shown in Listing 6-2.

```xml
<?xml version="1.0" encoding="utf-8" ?>
<configuration>
    <configSections>
        <sectionGroup name="applicationSettings" type="System.Configuration.
                        ApplicationSettingsGroup, System, Version=4.0.0.0,
                        Culture=neutral, PublicKeyToken=b77a5c561934e089" >
            <section name="PROFI_WIN.Properties.Settings" type="System.
                        Configuration.ClientSettingsSection, System,
                        Version=4.0.0.0, Culture=neutral, PublicKeyToken=
                        b77a5c561934e089" requirePermission="false" />
        </sectionGroup>
    </configSections>
  <appSettings>
```

337

```
        <add key="PROFI.Proxy.URL" value=""/>
        <add key="PROFI.Proxy.AuthenticationMode" value="none"/>
        <add key="PROFI.Proxy.Login" value=""/>
        <add key="PROFI.Proxy.Password" value=""/>
        <add key="PROFI.Bus.InitialMessage" value="INIT"/>
        <add key="PROFI.Stubs.BaseURL" value="http://localhost:49167/PROFI-SOAP/"/>
        <!--<add key="PROFI.Stubs.BaseURL" value="http://127.0.0.1:49167/"/>-->
        <!--<add key="PROFI.Stubs.BaseURL" value="http://localhost/PROFI-IIS/"/>-->
        <!--<add key="PROFI.Stubs.BaseURL" value="http://antares/PROFI-IIS/"/>-->
    </appSettings>
    <applicationSettings>
        <PROFI_WIN.Properties.Settings>
            <setting name="PROFI_WIN_Stub_Service" serializeAs="String">
                <value>http://localhost:49166/PROFI-SOAP/Service.asmx</value>
            </setting>
        </PROFI_WIN.Properties.Settings>
    </applicationSettings>
</configuration>
```

Listing 6-2

Every new instantiation of Stub will be followed by an instruction to update the URL with the centralized value of the setting. Listing 6-3 shows an example for UCPerson.

```
ServicePersons client = new ServicePersons();
client.Url = ConfigurationManager.AppSettings["PROFI.Stubs.BaseURL"] +
            "ServicePersons.asmx";
```

Listing 6-3

In the class called Portal, which is part of PROFI-WIN, we will have the same code, except for the name of the .asmx entry point (see Listing 6-4).

```
ServicePersons client = new Service ();
client.Url = ConfigurationManager.AppSettings["PROFI.Stubs.BaseURL"] +
            "Service.asmx";
```

Listing 6-4

Version of the code

The code shown above is the initial version of PROFI, before its optimization following the results of the client profiling process explained in the previous chapter.

B   Profiling the first scenario

B.1   Memory profiling

I have decided to restrict this book to pure bottleneck-hunting, and to leave memory analysis aside. Memory profiling is a subject in itself, and it would take another book to explain it properly. Time-based profiling has the advantage of being a slightly more pragmatic approach. In the end, there is a strong relationship between fair memory use and performance, but there are two ways of finding problems: by looking at the time and number of uses of functions, or by measuring memory use. This book takes the first approach.

Right now, sheer time-based performance still has more value than low resource consumption. However, this could change in the coming years, owing to the Green IT movement. The resource savings possible from a software modification are increasingly worth investigating because they affect every level of the system: CPU, time spent using a computer, electricity, number of machines required, cooling, physical storage, and more.

For now, we will limit ourselves to pure visible performance.

B.2   Step by step instructions

Everything that was explained above should be enough but, in order to be sure there be no problem in starting the scenario, the steps are detailed here click by click.

- Run Visual Studio .NET in administrative mode.

- In the ANTS menu, click Launch ANTS Performance Profiler.

- Choose the ASP.NET Web application (web development server) option in the dialog box.

- The parameter called ASP.NET web application (path) is set on the PROFl-SOAP directory.

- Make a note of the value for the parameter Port to bind web server to.

- Coming back to Visual Studio, modify the `app.config` file so that it points to this server URL.

- Click Start Profiling. If the privilege elevation dialog is displayed, accept the use of administrator rights. Wait for the browser window to appear. When it appears, the profiler is active.

- Return to Visual Studio and run the automatic test scenario with the client, so as to generate the activity on the server, which is what we want to analyze.

- When the client application has finished executing the test scenario, we can stop the profiler.

- The results are displayed automatically, but can take some time to come up as the scenario is quite complex.

B.3   First results

The entire configuration is now done, and we can run the application client in its TEST1 automatic test scenario. Results are shown in Figure 6-23.

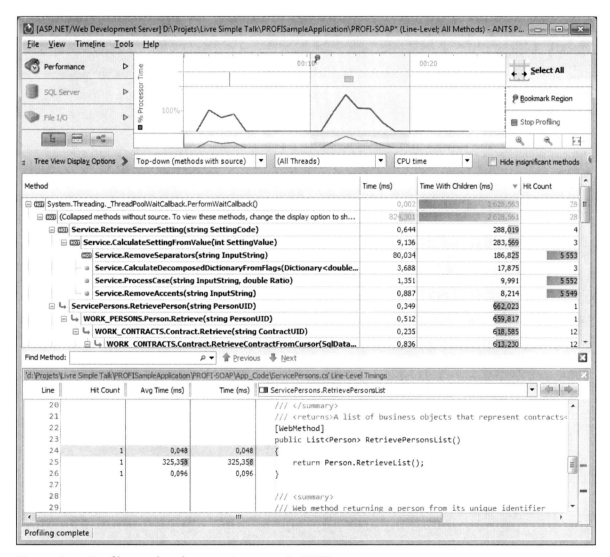

Figure 6-23:   Profiler results when running scenario TEST1.

The application should finish the scenario on its own, without any user interaction, if the `AUTOEXIT` compiling option has been activated. This means we only have to click Stop Profiling or close the browser window, which has the same effect.

Calls to web services are clearly visible, as well as some long "standard" function calls.

Note that we have used the option offered by ANTS Performance Profiler to select only a part of the capture time, by selecting the part where the timeline shows activity. The first CPU peak simply corresponds to the ASP.NET server start-up, and loading the page displayed in the browser, and we are not interested in profiling this part. We concentrate on the server functions that are triggered by the execution of the test scenario on the client.

B.4   Analysis method

Bottleneck analysis does not necessarily start with the slowest method: we should also take into account the number of calls. Luckily, most profilers provide metrics on both the intrinsic unit time of the function, and the total time spent in this function by cumulating all the calls to it.

The rest of this chapter is composed of analyses of performance bottlenecks that we have found running this first scenario or others that will be presented as needed.

Release version

In theory, we should work with a Release version of the server code, so as to benefit from .NET code optimizations and also avoid the weight of debugging information. In practice, it is no more complicated to profile the Debug version, which is the main target for a developer anyway. .NET optimizations will be an additional benefit once the profiling has lowered the execution times to acceptable values. In my experience, optimization in Debug mode always produces equivalent results in Release mode. In theory the results could vary, and this does sometimes happen when finely tuning applications. But again, this is not the approach we are taking in this book, where we are looking for the 20% of programming errors that are responsible for 80% of the time lost. And in this situation, the benefits all add up.

As we did for the client-side profiling, we will simply go down the list of functions that have been identified by the profiler as potential bottlenecks, starting, of course, with the longest ones (taking into account all the calls, as we explained above), which generally offer the most potential for improvement.

At first, we will only analyze functions for which the source code is available. But we will see below that we will soon end up looking at every function to get more details.

B.5   Retrieving server settings

B.5.a   Analysis

It is interesting to notice that the `RetrieveServerSetting` method is called four times. For such a simple scenario, this is a lot, and we will see to it that this number goes down. No use looking at the callers, since the function is called from a web service: we will only get the technical stack, and not the actual calls from the client, which is another process, namely the PROFI-WIN executable. Out of curiosity, we take a look at it anyway, just to appreciate that the stack of methods necessary to execute an ASP.NET web method is very deep (see Figure 6-24). This partly explains the heaviness of web method calls, even if the network transportation remains the slowest part.

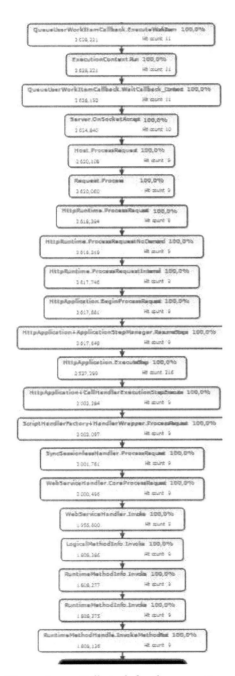

Figure 6-24: Call stack for the execution of an ASP.NET web method (excerpt).

B.5.b   Multiple calls to useless web methods

Let us come back to the analysis of the function itself. First, we can find the different calls which were counted in the metrics, and this can be done without the profiler's help. Maybe there will be a way to group them into one call, or at least reduce the number of occurrences. We find all of the calls are located in the same client function, namely the `Portal` class constructor, as shown in Listing 6-5.

```
public Portal()
{
    InitializeComponent();

    [...]

    string serverDescription = client.RetrieveServerSetting("PROFI.ServerDescription");

    [...]

    string settingValueForCode100 = Controller.Current.RetrieveServerSetting("*100");
    string settingValueForCodeDefault = Controller.Current.RetrieveServerSetting("*");
    string settingValueForCode10K = Controller.Current.RetrieveServerSetting("*10000");

    [...]
}
```
Listing 6-5

This is not a case where all parameters are the same, and we can simply get rid of the last three calls. That would be absurd inside a single function, but similar calls can sometimes be found across the application code. This is more common when code is large, with many developers working on it, and when it is split up into independent modules. Still, it is the software architect's job to suggest common services that will unify this kind of code, and make them available to all modules.

This is clearly the case we are in right here. The function calls are made from the `Portal` class, which is the main class in PROFI-WIN, and the retrieved settings are obviously destined to be used for the rest of the process's life. Hence, it would be worth making only one call out of the present code.

Multiple calls are justified by the fact that several setting values are calculated but, given that the return type of the web method is a plain string, it is feasible to simply unify several calls for different values into one call of a method that would take a list in, and send a corresponding list out. This is what brings us to the following new web method signature in `Service.asmx` (see Listing 6-6).

```
[WebMethod]
public string[] RetrieveServerSettingsList(string[] settingCodes)
{
    List<string> resultsList = new List<string>();
    foreach (string atom in settingCodes)
        resultsList.Add(RetrieveServerSetting(atom));
    return resultsList.ToArray();
}
```

Listing 6-6

In passing, we stop exposing `RetrieveServerSetting` as a web method, and we can also reduce its access to `private` (see Listing 6-7).

```
//[WebMethod]
private string RetrieveServerSetting(string settingCode)
{
    [...]
}
```

Listing 6-7

This second modification is potentially as important as grouping calls on a single web method call. Indeed, we have seen in the previous chapter that the loading of proxy clients for the calls to web services were very slow operations. It turns out that the time spent loading them is more or less proportional to the number of methods and types exposed in the WSDL contract of the web service. It is thus particularly good for performance to be able to get rid of a method. This also means that improvements we are making during server profiling can also benefit the client. This section is still part of the chapter on server-side profiling, since we have discovered it by profiling the ASP.NET process. We sometimes find ways to improve one module by taking a look at another one, and this has nothing to do with dependencies or order of calls.

In order for the calls to be correct, we now modify the **Portal** constructor code as shown in Listing 6-8.

```
public Portal()
{
    [...]

    string[] serverSettings = Controller.Current.RetrieveServerSettingsList
                        ("PROFI.ServerDescription", "*100", "*", "*10000");
    string serverDescription = serverSettings[0];

    [...]

    string code100SettingValue = serverSettings[1];
    string defaultCodeSettingValue = serverSettings[2];
    string code10KSettingValue = serverSettings[3];

    [...]
}
```

Listing 6-8

The method `RetrieveServerSetting` in the `Controller` class is also replaced with the one shown in Listing 6-9.

```
internal string[] RetrieveServerSettingsList(params string[] settingCodes)
{
    return _Client.RetrieveServerSettingsList(settingCodes);
}
```

Listing 6-9

Recompiling

When recompiling the whole application, remember to also refresh the web references when the web method signatures have changed.

The outcome of this modification depends very much on the type of network used by the client and the server to communicate. On a local network, the fact that web methods go through HTTP is not really an issue: latency is low, bandwidth is high. But let us imagine that the server is a remotely hosted platform, and that the client uses a general-purpose 512 KB/s line. Cutting these three calls, even if the total payload remains the same, will result in lower bandwidth consumption because of the SOAP overhead avoided, as well as a decrease of the total latency by a factor of four. In the most extreme context, we are talking about more than a second, which is huge for such a simple piece of software.

This issue has been highlighted because it is one of the main problems of PROFI-WIN in its version loaded with all possible programming errors. Yet, we diagnosed this error with very little help from the profiler: we simply tried to work out whether there was a good reason for this web method to be called several times. Had we followed a set of interactions, it would have been more difficult to separate the justifiable calls from those that were not. This is also one reason for using simple test scenarios. Since they are associated with roughly one use case, they make multiple web method calls immediately suspect. Generally speaking, every network communication is a relatively low-performing operation and should be used as little as possible.

But how can such a mistake be possible?

We have talked about the fact that several developers could work on the application code. This can explain why several identical calls are made in different parts of the application. But why would a developer not check whether the call has already been made in some other part of the application? It could be that the modules are strictly separated and that developers only have access to their own module's source code. It is also possible that calling a web service has been made so easy by automatically generated proxies that the developer will not bother checking in the rest of the code. Of course, we should not reject these methods and ask developers to code the generation of SOAP content themselves. But it cannot be denied that exposing a web method, which is complex and resource-costly, by simply adding an attribute to a method has made all this so easy that the whole process has become commonplace; developers sometimes do not realize how big a call is in terms of resource consumption. If these errors happen often in a given software project, it can be useful to rename the proxies (or the utility class that centralizes calls to them, like in our example) with a name that clearly states the potential heaviness of calls to it.

B.5.c   Complexity of the settings calculation

While we are in this function about retrieving settings values for the server, we might as well dig deeper, just to see if there is more scope for performance improvement. The new globalized method still uses almost half a second and a dutiful developer cannot pass such a function without taking a look at why it takes so long (see Figure 6-25).

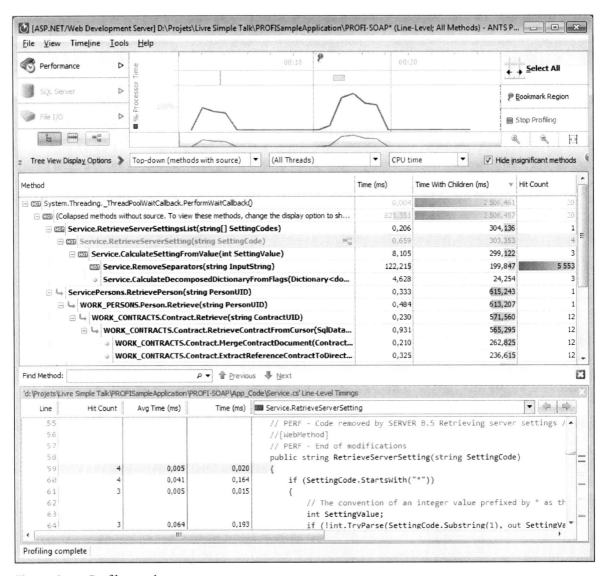

Figure 6-25: Profiler results.

As we are now used to (at least if you have read everything above and, in particular, the chapter about client-side profiling), we open the call graph (see Figure 6-26).

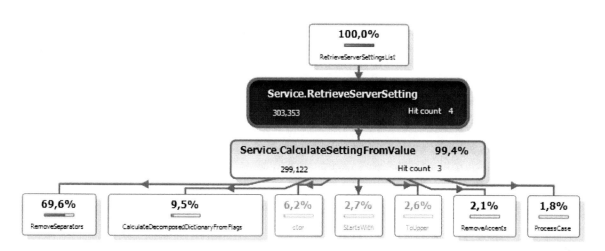

Figure 6-26: Call graph for `CalculateSettingFromValue`.

The difference between the number of calls to `RetrieveServerSetting` and the number of calls to `CalculateSettingFromValue` should draw our attention: there are four instead of three. This means that, in some cases, we will not go through the second function. Yet, the total amounts of time spent are so close (303 and 299ms) that this particular case is extremely quick: as little as 4ms. What could make one particular call last only 4ms in some cases, and make the three others take a total of 299ms, which is over 20 times longer per call on average?

In order to answer that, the simplest thing to do is to analyze the code directly (see Listing 6-10).

```
public string RetrieveServerSetting(string settingCode)
{
    if (settingCode.StartsWith("*"))
    {
        // The convention of an integer value prefixed by * as the setting code
        // triggers specific processing
        int settingValue;
        if (!int.TryParse(settingCode.Substring(1), out settingValue))
            settingValue = 1000;
```

```
        return CalculateSettingFromValue(settingValue);
    }
    else
        return ConfigurationManager.AppSettings[settingCode];
}
```

Listing 6-10

For once, there is a completely acceptable explanation for this behavior: a particular business rule justifies two different processes. In consequence, we continue the analysis only on the function called `CalculateSettingFromValue`.

> ### Not always lucky!
>
> *This is just to show that you are very often going to find functions that are very resource intensive, but for which you will not come up with a quick improvement. Leave them unmodified and do not worry too much: you will find some other places with a higher yield, and in the odd case where this is not enough to reach the level of performance you require, it will be time to come back to these previous functions and spend more time finding a sophisticated solution. Always keep in mind that our goal is to achieve the improvements with the best ratio between the execution time saved and the time spent analyzing and correcting.*

B.5.d   Inefficient string manipulation

We start with the function that takes the most time to calculate the value associated with a setting, namely `RemoveSeparators`. When we expand the call graph, we notice that a fair amount of time is spent only concatenating strings, with a huge number of calls to `String.Concat` (more than 1,000,000, as shown in Figure 6-27).

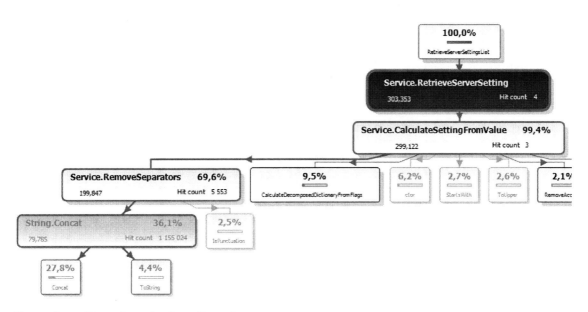

Figure 6-27: Deep down in the call graph.

This must be the most common smell (the inverse of a best practice) that I see in performance-related code reviews. When concatenating strings (and this applies to any other immutable type), a new instance is created for each operation, thus resulting in high memory and GC use when called in loops, causing a drop in performance. The presence in the profiler metrics of a high number of calls to the string concatenation function should ring alarm bells.

The problem is present in the code (see Listing 6-11).

```
private string RemoveSeparators(string inputString)
{
    string result = string.Empty;
    foreach (char car in inputString)
        if (!char.IsPunctuation(car))
            result += car;
    return result;
}
```

Listing 6-11

This code absolutely must be replaced with that in Listing 6-12.

```
private string RemoveSeparators(string inputString)
{
    StringBuilder result = new StringBuilder();
    foreach (char car in inputString)
        if (!char.IsPunctuation(car))
            result.Append(car);
    return result.ToString();
}
```

Listing 6-12

To be perfect, we could even take advantage of the fact that we know the maximum size of the output (it cannot be more than the size of the input string, as we are only removing some characters) and initiate the `StringBuilder` instance with an adequate size, as shown in Listing 6-13.

```
private string RemoveSeparators(string inputString)
{
    StringBuilder result = new StringBuilder(inputString.Length);
    foreach (char car in inputString)
        if (!char.IsPunctuation(car))
            result.Append(car);
    return result.ToString();
}
```

Listing 6-13

How often can this happen?

This code mistake is one of the classic ones. With any luck, diffusion of best practice should confine it to bad-quality code. But this is something that is often seen in code reviews when developers have just been trained to program, rather than to program efficiently.

B.5.e   Aside on StringBuilder

I have often been asked about the threshold under which the use of a `StringBuilder` is not quicker than string concatenations. If we consider the parameters to be the number of concatenation operations and the size of strings to assemble, we can use the code in Listing 6-14 to search for this or these threshold values.

```csharp
using System;
using System.Diagnostics;
using System.Text;
using System.IO;

namespace BenchmarkStringBuilder
{
    class Program
    {
        static void Main(string[] args)
        {
            int numberOfTurns = 100;

            foreach (int stringSize in new int[] { 0, 10, 20, 100, 1000, 10000 })
            {
                if (stringSize != 0)
                    Console.Write(stringSize);
                Console.Write('\t');
                foreach (int numberOfStrings in new int[] { 2, 5, 7, 10, 15, 20 })
                {
                    if (stringSize == 0)
                    {
                        Console.Write(numberOfStrings);
                        Console.Write('\t');
                        continue;
                    }

                    string testString = new string('*', stringSize);

                    Stopwatch chronoConcat = Stopwatch.StartNew();
                    for (int turn = 0; turn < numberOfTurns; turn++)
                    {
                        string resultConcat = string.Empty;
                        for (int index = 0; index < numberOfStrings; index++)
```

```
                    resultConcat += testString;
        }
        chronoConcat.Stop();

        Stopwatch chronoStringBuilder = Stopwatch.StartNew();
        for (int turn = 0; turn < numberOfTurns; turn++)
        {
            StringBuilder resultStringBuilder = new StringBuilder();
            for (int index = 0; index < numberOfStrings; index++)
                resultStringBuilder.Append(testString);
        }
        chronoStringBuilder.Stop();

        Stopwatch chronoInitializedStringBuilder = Stopwatch.StartNew();
        for (int turn = 0; turn < numberOfTurns; turn++)
        {
            StringBuilder resultInitStringBuilder = new
                        StringBuilder(stringSize * numberOfStrings);
            for (int index = 0; index < numberOfStrings; index++)
                resultInitStringBuilder.Append(testString);
        }
        chronoInitializedStringBuilder.Stop();

        Console.Write(chronoConcat.Elapsed < chronoStringBuilder.
                        Elapsed ? '-' : '+');

        if (chronoInitializedStringBuilder.ElapsedTicks <
                        chronoStringBuilder.ElapsedTicks)
            Console.Write("(!)");
        Console.Write('\t');
    }
    Console.WriteLine();
        }
      }
    }
}
```

Listing 6-14

Results from my machine are shown in Figure 6-28. The number of strings to concatenate is indicated in the columns, and the size of strings in the rows. A minus sign
indicates String.Concat is quicker, a plus sign indicates StringBuilder is quicker.

356

An exclamation mark shows where the initial buffer reservation for `StringBuilder` improves the results.

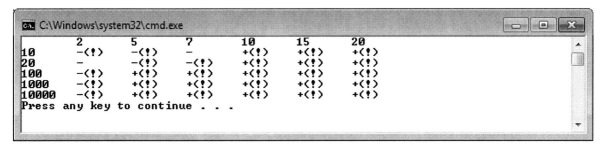

Figure 6-28: Results for the string concatenation to `StringBuilder` comparative benchmark.

Clearly, except for a few cases where the parameter values are small, it is always an advantage to initialize the buffer size if we have a good idea of it.

However, as far as the difference in performance between the two operations is concerned, only one result is clear: beyond ten operations, `StringBuilder` is quicker. Below this, the results are not sufficiently refined. As far as the second parameter, namely the string size, is concerned it will also be necessary to run a more detailed test.

Dependence of the results on the machine

You may find somewhat different results on your machine. On a powerful machine that I have access to, this benchmark showed that the advantage in buffer initialization was not as strong when reaching high numbers. But generally speaking, the most important point is that this benchmark will show on any machine that `StringBuilder` is always quicker past a certain number of concatenations.

A more advanced version of this program can be found on the Simple Talk website (www.simple-talk.com/RedGateBooks/JPGouigoux/CodeDownload.zip), in the project `BenchmarkStringBuilder`, under the UtilitySolutions directory. It uses the same principles as the code shown in Listing 6-13, but tests more values for the two parameters, and also calculates an average based on more cases. The output is also set to a CSV file in order to allow for easier and deeper analysis of the results.

This benchmark project outputs such a table, which is basically the same metrics, but more detailed (see Figure 6-29).

	1	2	3	4	5	6	7	8	9	10	12	15	20	30	50	100
5	-	-	-	-	-	+	+	+	+	+	+	+	+	+	+	+
10	-	-	-	-	-	-	-	+	-	+	+	+	+	+	+	+
15	-	-	-	-	-	-	+	+	-	+	+	+	+	+	+	+
20	-	-	-	-	-	+	-	+	-	+	+	+	+	+	+	+
50	-	-	+	+	-	+	+	+	+	+	-	+	+	+	+	+
100	-	+	-	-	+	-	+	+	+	+	+	+	+	+	+	+
200	-	-	+	-	-	+	+	+	+	+	+	+	+	+	+	+
500	-	-	-	+	-	+	+	+	+	+	+	+	+	+	+	+
1000	-	-	-	-	-	-	-	-	-	+	+	+	+	+	+	+

Figure 6-29: Refined results for the string concatenation to `StringBuilder` comparative benchmark.

The threshold for concatenation operations can be seen more easily, and is between five and ten operations. As for the relationship between performance and the size of strings, it is very subtle.

In conclusion, the necessity of using `StringBuilder.Append` instead of `String.Concat` (the same holds true for `StringBuilder.Remove` instead of `String.Remove`) is not linked to the size of strings, but depends heavily on the number of operations. The limit is between five and ten strings.

Of course one should be careful with benchmarks. Not only will the results not be the same on another machine or with a different memory context, but also the difference seen with small numbers of strings is actually so small that, unless we are required to reach the ultimate performance of a given code, we should simply use `StringBuilder` all the time.

A pragmatic approach to the problem could be to have the simplest message for the developers, and this should be: use `StringBuilder` in every case of string manipulation, except when the operations are so compacted and limited that a plus sign will actually make the code more readable. This means `String.Concat` should be reserved for simple cases like in Listing 6-14 and never be written out in full.

```
string Greeting = "Hello, " + firstname + ". How is " + spouse.firstname + "
doing?";
```
Listing 6-15

And when you think about it a little more, this kind of string would be much more elegantly generated using `String.Format`.

Making it easy

If you have to train a team of developers who are beginners in C#, or you are asked to write programming norms for such a team, I recommend you do not expose them to this threshold but simply tell them to use the plus sign when it will never be performed in a loop, and to use `StringBuilder` *in every other case.*

B.5.f   Setting a cache mechanism

We now come back to where we left the settings generation code, namely after we solved the problem in the RemoveSeparators function.

We use the functionality of the profiler that enables us to create a new call graph from a particular node (see Figure 6-30), in our case CalculateDecomposedDictionary-FromFlags, which is the method that takes the most time after RemoveSeparators (hint: they are always ordered by use of time from left to right).

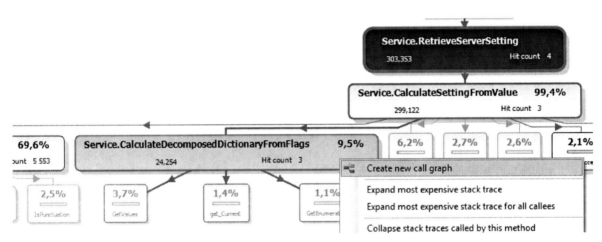

Figure 6-30: How to create a new call graph centered on the node from an existing one.

This brings up a new graph, in which we adjust the parameters to see all the functions called (see Figure 6-31).

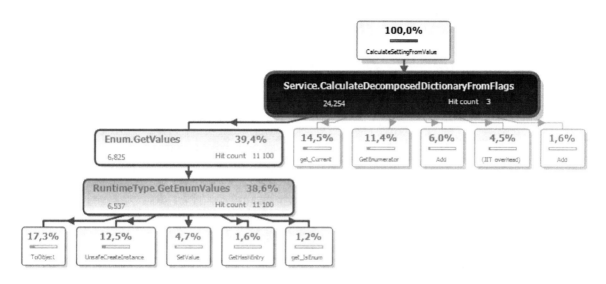

Figure 6-31: New call graph based on the selected node.

The `Enum.GetValues` function takes a major part of the time spent in the function. Moreover it is called 11,100 times. The number in itself is easy to understand: since the optimization target, namely the `CalculateDecomposedDictionaryFromFlags` function, is called three times with values 100, 1,000 and 10,000 for the parameter, 11,100 logically corresponds to the sum of these values. What is much less logical is that the line in question always uses the same enumeration (see Listing 6-16).

```
foreach (SettingMode v in Enum.GetValues(typeof(SettingMode)))
```

Listing 6-16

Yet this enumeration only contains four values, as we see in Listing 6-17!

```
[Flags]
private enum SettingMode : byte
{
    NONE = 0,
    ACCENTS = 1,
```

```
    CASE = 2,
    SEPARATORS = 4,
}
```

Listing 6-17

It is thus abnormal that 11,100 calls to this function are performed in a single function call. There is clearly an advantage in realizing the calls only the necessary number of times, which means putting a cache in place.

But wait! The right reaction in this situation is to first go up the calls progressively and check whether the cache could not be located even higher in the call stack. This is made necessary because the profiler will show methods that take the most time, but cannot know whether some calls can be unified, or if they are always called with different parameter values and cannot. Only a human eye can distinguish this kind of thing, at least for now.

In our example, we go up until we reach the (unique) call to the function, and find the code shown in Listing 6-18.

```
// We start by creating a dictionary randomly filled with values and settings
Dictionary<double, SettingMode> flagsDictionary = new Dictionary<double,
                                SettingMode>();
for (int index = 0; index < settingValue; index++)
{
    Random engine = new Random(index);
    flagsDictionary.Add(engine.NextDouble(), (SettingMode)engine.Next(8));
}

// The values of this dictionary are translated into lists of settings
Dictionary<double, List<SettingMode>> decomposedDictionary =
                        CalculateDecomposedDictionaryFromFlags(flagsDictionary);
```

Listing 6-18

Further in the code, we find the only use of the dictionary generated with the CalculateDecomposedDictionaryFromFlags function, and it is a simple walk-through .

This dictionary appears to have been created simply because of too large a separation of the process steps: maybe two developers were put in charge of this function and divided the work into two tasks that were too isolated from each other.

When debugging the code, a review of the content before and after confirms our analysis. The content of flagsDictionary as generated with 100 values is shown in Figure 6-32.

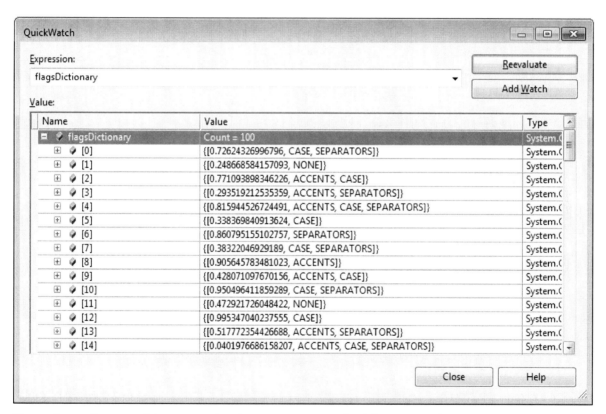

Figure 6-32: Content of the flagsDictionary, as seen in the debugger watches.

The content of `decomposedDictionary` is the same except that, for each line, the "flags style" enumeration has been broken down into its atomic values (see Figure 6-33).

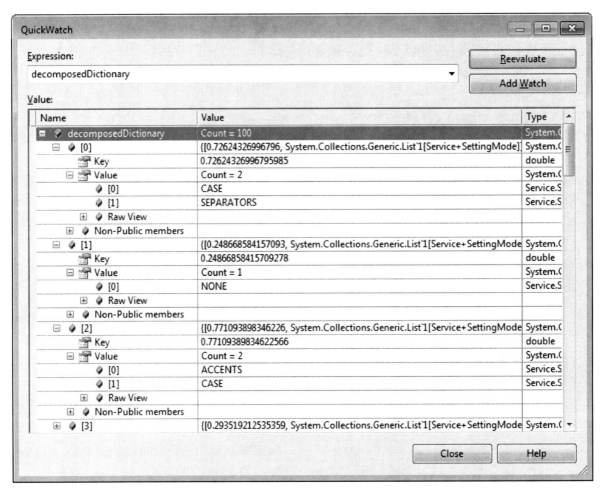

Figure 6-33: Detail of the content of `decomposedDictionary`, as seen in the debugger (excerpt).

Thus, it is possible to kill two birds with one stone, by using a cache and removing the intermediate dictionary generation at the same time. To do so, we are going to refactor the code in two steps. First, we simply loop over `flagsDictionary`, and execute at the beginning of the loop the process that was done for each entry in `CalculateDecomposedDictionaryFromFlags` (see Listing 6-18).

```
private string CalculateSettingFromValue(int settingValue)
{
    [...]

    foreach (KeyValuePair<double, SettingMode> couple in flagsDictionary)
    {
        List<SettingMode> decomposedList = new List<SettingMode>();
        foreach (SettingMode v in Enum.GetValues(typeof(SettingMode)))
            if ((couple.Value & v) == v && v != SettingMode.NONE)
                decomposedList.Add(v);
        if (decomposedList.Count == 0) decomposedList.Add(SettingMode.NONE);

        // Processing the required operations : in the rest of the method code, we
        // replace Couple.Value with DecomposedList

        [...]
    }

    [...]
}
```

Listing 6-19

This first refactoring step allows us to simplify the code. For example, the line in Listing 6-20 does not need to use a decomposed list anymore.

```
if (decomposedList.Contains(SettingMode.CASE))
```

Listing 6-20

Indeed, knowing which test is actually done, we could replace this code with the line in Listing 6-21.

```
if ((couple.Value & SettingMode.CASE) == SettingMode.CASE)
```

Listing 6-21

The same simplification can be made to other uses of `decomposedList` and the `switch` code can simply be replaced with the line in Listing 6-21 (see Listing 6-22).

```
if ((couple.Value & SettingMode.ACCENTS) == SettingMode.ACCENTS)
    modifString = RemoveAccents(modifString);
if ((couple.Value & SettingMode.CASE) == SettingMode.CASE)
    modifString = ProcessCase(modifString, couple.Key);
if ((couple.Value & SettingMode.SEPARATORS) == SettingMode.SEPARATORS)
    modifString = RemoveSeparators(modifString);
```

Listing 6-22

The `couple` variable now corresponds to an entry in `flagsDictionary`, and not an entry in `decomposedDictionary`. This means we can suppress the latter and the `CalculateDecomposedDictionaryFromFlags` function altogether.

But, most importantly, since the simplifications removed all calls to `decomposedList`, which was introduced in the first step of refactoring, we can also remove the lines we had moved from the dictionary transformation function.

We have indeed solved two problems with one code modification. Merging the operations has solved the problem of the high number of calls to `Enum.GetValue`, and the cache is, in fact, not necessary.

B.5.g   The limits of the cache approach

Not needing the cache is good news for another reason: it is always difficult to strike the right balance between better performance and higher memory use. After grouping the calls to this function, then watching which part of it took most time (and we will continue this further), we study the calls in general.

Indeed, our profiling scenarios have a significant limitation: we only execute one instance of the client to profile the server, which is quite far from real use with many clients in various numbers over time. There are practical reasons for this: it is much simpler to track improvements in terms of server execution time with a fixed set of requests. Remember the basic profiling rules? We have to be able to measure improvement and, in order to have precise metrics, we need an environment that is stable and as neutral as possible. This is why we generally profile a server using one client only.

Still, the server is destined to be called by several clients, and the question of a cache mechanism arises again, in order to rapidly send results of the settings calculations. Several aspects have to be taken into account.

- Firstly, the random aspect of the process: when taking a look at the code, it appears that a random number generator is used to populate dictionary data. In consequence, should a cache be used, only the initial generation would be random, when starting the server. Then, every subsequent call would send the same value. Only business rules of the application will tell us if this is acceptable. The random part may have been used to introduce variance between clients, and the cache mechanism will be useless. By contrast, if the server only needed to generate random numbers once for every client, we can store the initial results and improve calculation time.

- Secondly, the case of clients calling the server many times with the same parameter value can also arise. When this happens, it can be advantageous for the client itself to manage a cache. But the client may prefer to always ask the server, in order to guarantee that it gets fresh data. In this case, the server could also decide to create a per-client cache. Again, a balance has to be struck between sparing CPU and consuming more memory. In particular, if a user session uses dozens of megabytes, we will encounter memory problems.

- Thirdly, another aspect of the problem is estimating the size of what we would have to put into memory. How many parameter values are possible? In our test scenario, we are only called with *100, *1,000 and *10,000, but are those the only possible values? If this is so, there is a clear interest in not repeating the complex calculation that we have started to optimize above. Moreover, the result is very small and will not take much memory to store. But if the software requirements state that all integer values between 1 and 100,000 will be called with roughly equal frequency, we clearly should not cache the data.

Typically, in the last case, the code shown in Listing 6-23 can rapidly induce memory saturation, particularly since it does not impose any limit, either in terms of number of entries or in terms of time before refreshing calculated data.

```
if (!settingDictionary.ContainsKey(settingValue))
    settingDictionary.Add(settingValue, CalculateSettingFromValue(settingValue));
return settingDictionary[settingValue];
```

Listing 6-23

In short, a cache mechanism in the web server is too complex for this book's approach. We will store the result of a calculation in memory during request processing, and not during the ASP.NET application's life. However, it is obvious that a server profiling campaign should put aside some time to validate improvements under load/stress. As explained before, profiling itself is hard to perform under load, because too much variance will make the metrics less precise. But our goal still remains to improve global performance on realistic scenarios, and we will show at the end of this chapter an approach to validate the code improvements on a more realistic use of the server, using many simulated clients.

B.5.h   Additional aside

The corrections above have suppressed every reference to the Count property of a generic list and to the Length property of a System.Array, but we should, however, make a small note on these. Their apparent simplicity can lead the developer to think the call will be instantaneous.

The code shown in Listing 6-24 is quite natural.

```
for (int i = 0; i < ProductsList.Count; i+)
{
    [...]
}
```
Listing 6-24

Yet, except if the loop is stopped for other reasons, this particular code will call the Count property a number of times that equates to its initial value. Admittedly, there are cases where this is necessary for the algorithm to work properly: if the list we use evolves along with the iterations, the size will vary, and so will the number of iterations. This is the benefit of such code: at each iteration the loop will check anew that it has not passed the end of the list.

But if we have a functional guarantee that the list will not change in size during the loop, which is extremely common, we can write the code like in Listing 6-25 and reduce the calls to Count to only one.

```
int size = ProductsList.Count;
for (int i = 0; i < size; i+)
{
    [...]
}
```
Listing 6-25

It may look like a minor improvement, but the effects are not negligible. In the example of a loop over 64 elements, which was called 56,000 times (thus resulting in approximately 3 million calls to the property), the time improvement was around 700ms. Of course, we should first check that these 56,000 calls are really necessary, but if they are due to the inherent complexity of the algorithm, reducing the execution time by a factor of eight will still have a substantial impact, as was the case in this real-life situation.

B.5.i   Case processing

Normally, we should now study the next function in the list ordered by total time taken. But, in an attempt to make reading this more fluid, we will first finish off with the optimization of the settings retrieval functionality. In practice, what follows falls between profiling and tuning. But since the solution is based on best practices, we are still within the philosophy of the book.

The functions called **ProcessCase** and **RemoveAccents** are called several thousand times (see Figure 6-34). As such, they are an ideal target for profiling.

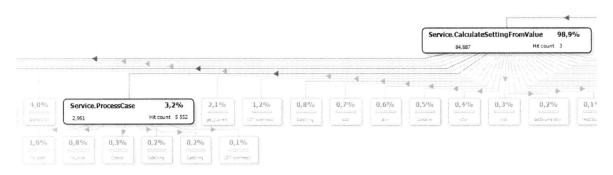

Figure 6-34: Call graph around the **ProcessCase** function.

You could be a bit surprised that we are spending time on functions that only account for a few tens of milliseconds, but there are several good reasons for doing so.

- Even if we would not necessarily spend time on this sort of optimization in an industrial context (or maybe only as a last resort), the aim of this book is not only to explain the art of profiling, but also to show the "traditional" cases of poor code performance.

- In some cases, gaining those last few percent could be worthwhile in order to fulfill our measured goals in terms of time spent in a given scenario.

- Last but not least, the scenario we based our study on is extremely small for practical reasons. On a real application with hundreds of users working several hours a day, the time saved can quickly amount to several minutes instead of the 30 or so milliseconds measured here.

We start our study with the function `ProcessCase`, which spends over a fifth of its time in `String.ToUpper` (see Figure 6-35). Perhaps there will be a way to reduce this number of calls?

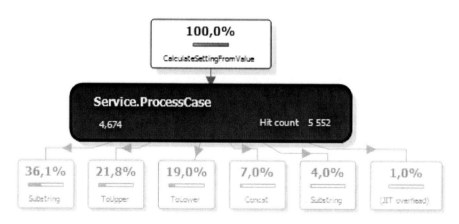

Figure 6-35: Call graph centered on `ProcessCase`.

Analyzing the code in Listing 6-26 shows that each call uses the function only once.

```
private string ProcessCase(string inputString, double ratio)
{
    int indexOfLastModifiedCharacter = (int)(inputString.Length * ratio);
    if (indexOfLastModifiedCharacter < inputString.Length)
        return inputString.Substring(0, indexOfLastModifiedCharacter).ToUpper() +
                inputString.Substring(indexOfLastModifiedCharacter).ToLower();
    else
        return inputString;
}
```

Listing 6-26

Thus, it seems difficult to optimize anything in this function. But there is still something we can do, considering the variable `indexOfLastModifiedCharacter` is used in the `Substring` operation on the input string. Indeed, this variable comes from multiplying the string length by a randomly-generated ratio that comes from `Random.NextDouble`. This function returns numbers between 0 and 1 (excluded). Hence, the `if` test is useless, since the position can only be smaller than the size of the input string. Therefore we can write this function with a simpler code shown in Listing 6-27.

```
private string ProcessCase(string inputString, double ratio)
{
    int positionLastModifiedCharacter = (int)(inputString.Length * ratio);

    return inputString.Substring(0, positionLastModifiedCharacter).ToUpper() +
            inputString.Substring(positionLastModifiedCharacter).ToLower();
}
```

Listing 6-27

This will not greatly affect performance, but it is always good practice to make the code simpler. Even if it does not bring any visible results immediately, a better understanding of the code helps to reduce coding errors (which are potentially harmful to performance), and that is already a good thing.

We are now going to study `CalculateSettingFromValue`, the caller of this function, (see Listing 6-28).

```
foreach (KeyValuePair<double, SettingMode> couple in flagsDictionary)
{
    string modifString = refString;
    if ((couple.Value & SettingMode.ACCENTS) == SettingMode.ACCENTS)
        modifString = RemoveAccents(modifString);
    if ((couple.Value & SettingMode.CASE) == SettingMode.CASE)
        modifString = ProcessCase(modifString, couple.Key);
    if ((couple.Value & SettingMode.SEPARATORS) == SettingMode.SEPARATORS)
        modifString = RemoveSeparators(modifString);

    // Additional string modification
    if ((couple.Value & SettingMode.CASE) == SettingMode.CASE)
    {
        if (modifString.StartsWith(refString.ToUpper().Substring(0, 90)))
            modifString = modifString.Substring(0, 90);
        else if (modifString.StartsWith(refString.ToUpper().Substring(0, 60)))
            modifString = modifString.Substring(0, 60);
        else if (modifString.StartsWith(refString.ToUpper().Substring(0, 30)))
            modifString = modifString.Substring(0, 30);
    }

    listModifiedStrings.Add(modifString);
}
```

Listing 6-28

The first remark we can make is that, when the value of Couple.Value is SettingMode. NONE, we could save some time by avoiding the additional tests, and going directly to the last instruction of the loop, as shown in Listing 6-29.

```
foreach (KeyValuePair<double, SettingMode> couple in flagsDictionary)
{
    // Author's note : if you see the error in this code, do not immediately
    // jump to the next section. It is part of the sequence of investigation we
    // want to demonstrate.
    if (couple.Value == SettingMode.NONE)
    {
        listModifiedStrings.Add(refString);
        break;
    }
```

```
    string modifString = refString;
    if ((couple.Value & SettingMode.ACCENTS) == SettingMode.ACCENTS)
        modifString = RemoveAccents(modifString);

    […]

    listModifiedStrings.Add(modifString);
}
```

Listing 6-29

Code duplication

The last instruction of adding a string in a list is a duplication of the code. In practice, the code is not exactly the same because the string variable is different, but a purist would prefer to put the content of the loop in an if statement. If we are more into code simplicity, the code above has the advantage of better showing the intention of the developer, namely cutting short the useless tests if possible.

Again, there is little performance improvement to be obtained from this modification, but it is important in the sense that it forces us to have a better understanding of the code. We now notice that the string that is passed to **ProcessCase** is always based on a fixed reference string, which can only be processed in terms of case beforehand. Not only does this function create two cases instead of one but, in addition, case modification and accent removal are independent activities if we process the capital accented characters. Listing 6-30 shows this is the case.

```
private string RemoveAccents(string inputString)
{
    return inputString.Replace('î', 'i').Replace('é', 'e').Replace('è', 'e').
        Replace('Î', 'I').Replace('É', 'E').Replace('È', 'E');
}
```

Listing 6-30

Difference from the real world

We are only modifying the accents that are actually in our hard-coded sample string. Of course, in the real world, we would take all possible accents into account, but this will be discussed a bit later. Also, since the string is hard-coded, we could have simply removed this function by hard-coding an additional version of the reference string without accented characters. However, this function was an opportunity to show optimization tricks in a bit more detail. The same remark applies to `RemoveSeparators`.

It may also be worth noting that the `InputString.Replace` calls in the previous method are inefficient (as mentioned in the `StringBuilder` section) and could be replaced with code similar to that in Listing 6-31 to get better performance.

```
private static string RemoveAccentsPerf(string inputString)
{
        StringBuilder sb = new StringBuilder(inputString);
        sb.Replace('î', 'i');
        sb.Replace('é', 'e');
        sb.Replace('è', 'e');
        sb.Replace('Î', 'I');
        sb.Replace('É', 'E');
        sb.Replace('È', 'E');
        return sb.ToString();
}
```
Listing 6-31

Mention should also be made of the Task Parallel Library (TPL) with .NET which can be used in this scenario to speed up execution of this code exponentially on a multicore computer. A simple modification could be:

```
Parallel.For(0, iterations, (i) =>
{
        var replacedData = RemoveAccentsPerf(TestData);
});
```
Listing 6-32

In a loop with millions of calls, this code is much faster than the original.

We now come back to the function `CalculateSettingFromValue`, the code of which has been modified to resemble Listing 6-33.

```
List<string> listModifiedStrings = new List<string>();
string refString = "Hard-coded string (chaîne in French) simply there to
demonstrate (démontrer) performance problems (problèmes) on a simulated (simulé)
process on internationalized strings (hence the parentheses with accented
characters).";
foreach (KeyValuePair<double, SettingMode> couple in flagsDictionary)
{
    if (couple.Value == SettingMode.NONE)
    {
        listModifiedStrings.Add(refString);
        break;
    }

    // Performing the requested processes
    string modifString = refString;
    if ((couple.Value & SettingMode.CASE) == SettingMode.CASE)
        modifString = ProcessCase(modifString, couple.Key);
    if ((couple.Value & SettingMode.ACCENTS) == SettingMode.ACCENTS)
        modifString = RemoveAccents(modifString);
    if ((couple.Value & SettingMode.SEPARATORS) == SettingMode.SEPARATORS)
        modifString = RemoveSeparators(modifString);

    [...]

    listModifiedStrings.Add(modifString);
}
```

Listing 6-33

We know the first parameter of `ProcessCase` is now a fixed value, but the second parameter can have any double-precision value between 0 and 1, which is obviously too large to use a cache. But let us take a look at what changes if we move the first instruction out of the body of `ProcessCase`. The calling code is now shown in Listing 6-34.

```
if ((couple.Value & SettingMode.CASE) == SettingMode.CASE)
{
    int positionLastModifiedCharacter = (int)(modifString.Length * couple.Key);
    modifString = ProcessCase(modifString, positionLastModifiedCharacter);
}
if ((couple.Value & SettingMode.ACCENTS) == SettingMode.ACCENTS)
    modifString = RemoveAccents(modifString);
```

Listing 6-34

As for the function itself, it is now so simple that we could have doubts about its usefulness (see Listing 6-35).

```
private string ProcessCase(string inputString, int positionLastModifiedCharacter)
{
    return inputString.Substring(0, positionLastModifiedCharacter).ToUpper() +
            inputString.Substring(positionLastModifiedCharacter).ToLower();
}
```

Listing 6-35

But what is more interesting is that only a limited number of different calls are possible to this function. And since it is deterministic (the same inputs will always produce the same output), we can cache the results as shown in Listing 6-36.

```
private List<string> _PreprocessedStrings = null;

private string ProcessCase(string inputString, int positionLastModifiedCharacter)
{
    if (_PreprocessedStrings == null)
    {
        _PreprocessedStrings = new List<string>();
        for (int index = 0; index < inputString.Length; index++)
            _PreprocessedStrings.Add(
                inputString.Substring(0, index).ToUpper()
                + inputString.Substring(index).ToLower());
    }
    return _PreprocessedStrings[positionLastModifiedCharacter];
}
```

Listing 6-36

Not such a real-world application

Again, I ask you to make the imaginative leap from this oversimplistic code to a real-world application. It is obvious that, in industrial software, such an accumulation of errors and multiple calculations on a hard-coded string would be impossible. But when the code complexity increases, a developer can forget or even be unable to walk up the call stack in order to verify that calls are not made with identical parameters.

The profiler shows the improvement in metrics (Figure 6-36).

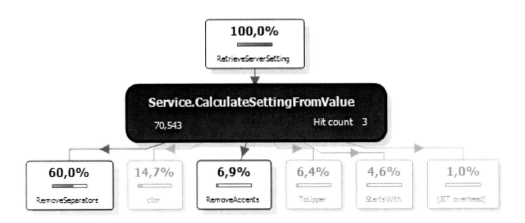

Figure 6-36: Call graph centered on `CalculateSettingFromValue`.

The function `ProcessCase` is simply no longer seen in the calls from `CalculateSettingFromValue`, which means it now accounts for less than one percent of the total execution time of the calling function. We have to clear the **Hide insignificant methods** option to see it, bearing a small 0.6% of the total execution time (see Figure 6-37).

Figure 6-37: Call graph centered on `CalculateSettingFromValue`, but with the "Hide insignificant methods" option cleared.

A problem arises: we do not see any calls to the `RemoveAccents` function, which was next in line for our optimization process. After searching for a few minutes (remember to switch to the original port number in order to debug the server application), it turns out that the code modification to exit `CalculateSettingFromValue` as soon as possible with `SettingMode` is `NONE` was incorrect. I used `break` instead of `continue`, which changes the algorithm.

Why keep this incorrect code?

I made this error when coding the sample application, and thought it was worth keeping it in the book because, in my view, it serves two additional purposes. First, it warns against untested code modifications. When optimizing, always try to have as much test coverage as possible before profiling. Second, it shows the profiler can have a role, albeit a minor one, in debugging. To check that a number of calls to a function is zero, one can put a breakpoint on it and wait, but this may be risky (if the `.pdb` files are not there, for example). On the other hand, the profiler will give better assurance if zero is displayed in the metrics.

After correcting this code, the metrics should be recaptured, and the refreshed results shown in Figure 6-38 seem closer to what was expected. The function `RemoveAccents` has actually come back.

Figure 6-38: Same graph as before, with the `RemoveAccents` method now back in the graph.

The results are quite interesting: `ProcessCase` now only takes 0.432ms instead of 4.674ms as before, which amounts to a factor of more than ten! This kind of time, less than a millisecond, seems to conform more to what should be expected. We can now study the following function, namely `RemoveAccents`.

B.5.j   Accents removal

You should now have the hang of profiling, and we are only going to show the possible optimizations in this function, without going into the details of the analysis that brought us there.

The initial code is shown in Listing 6-37.

```
private string RemoveAccents(string inputString)
{
    return inputString.Replace('î', 'i').Replace('é', 'e').Replace('è', 'e').
                Replace('Î', 'I').Replace('É', 'E').Replace('È', 'E');
}
```

Listing 6-37

When executed 2.5 million times, the total execution time is around 85 seconds. A first possible optimization consists of using a method based on Unicode, which will perform the same operation, but in only 9.5 seconds. The corresponding code is shown in Listing 6-38.

```
private string RemoveAccents(string inputString)
{
    string normalizedString = inputString.Normalize(NormalizationForm.FormD);
    StringBuilder builder = new StringBuilder();
    for (int cpt = 0; cpt < normalizedString.Length; cpt++)
    {
        char character = normalizedString[cpt];
        if (CharUnicodeInfo.GetUnicodeCategory(character) != UnicodeCategory.
                    NonSpacingMark)
            builder.Append(character);
    }
    return builder.ToString();
}
```

Listing 6-38

Moreover, this method is much more robust than the previous one, where it was easy to forget one accented character in the list of possible ones. This also means the difference in performance would have been even bigger, had the initial code not been limited to only the three accented characters used in our hard-coded string. Another possible optimization uses encodings to achieve the same results (see Listing 6-39).

```
private string RemoveAccents(string inputString)
{
    return Encoding.ASCII.GetString(Encoding.GetEncoding(1251).
        GetBytes(inputString));
}
```

Listing 6-39

This time, the time spent on the same number of calls is only 8.5 seconds. In short, we have reached a division by a factor of ten, which is very appreciable when manipulating massive amounts of accented characters.

> ***Keep It Simple, Stupid!***
>
> *It is interesting to note that, as is often the case, the simplest code performs the best. Yet another reason to stick with the KISS principle.*

We could push the optimization further by transforming the input string into a character array (function `ToCharArray`), on which we would loop to replace the accented characters. This method can reduce the time spent by an additional factor of four. But it is not generic and we would have to enter all the accents by hand, which is error-prone. This should only be used as a last resort, when fine-tuning is needed, and we are willing to compromise on the maintainability of the code.

An extreme example of this would be speeding up `ToLower` and `ToUpper` functions by shifting the ASCII codes by 32 units. This is, of course, quicker, but it also means not taking into account accents or other special characters. In short, this type of optimization would not work in an internationalized context, and would cause great problems when making the application available to other cultures. There is a greater chance of this problem being overlooked when companies in English-speaking countries create software: not only do they produce software using OSs and programming architectures that are natively in English, but in addition they use an alphabet without accents, and may not fully appreciate the possible subtleties of other languages.

B.5.k   Final output of the string

This analysis would not be complete without noting the general process of string composition used to create the result of the function `CalculateSettingFromValue`. We show this in a schematic form in Listing 6-40.

```
List<string> listModifiedStrings = new List<string>();
foreach (KeyValuePair<double, SettingMode> couple in flagsDictionary)
{
    [...]

    string modifString = refString;

    [...]

    listModifiedStrings.Add(modifString);
}

return string.Join(" - ," listModifiedStrings.ToArray());
```

Listing 6-40

We could concatenate the resulting string along with loop iterations, preferably using a `StringBuilder` instance in order to keep performance acceptable. Instead, `String.Join` has been chosen because it better shows the intention of the developer and, as an optimized method itself, it is as quick as using `StringBuilder`.

*****The notion of "intention of the developer"*****

This consists of making clear what the developer wants to achieve, rather than how. For example, an alternative to the code in Listing 6-40 would have been to append a " – " string at the beginning of each loop iteration except the first one. Another developer reading the code (or its creator looking at it a few years later) might have spent a few minutes figuring out the need for such a behavior. On the other hand, the code using the `String.Join` function shows this in only one instruction, which makes it quicker and easier to understand.

B.5.l   The final word on settings

A simple function, which was not even the longest in the profiled scenarios, has taken up a major part of the current section, but this approach was important because it showed a wide range of profiling cases and the corresponding code problems.

Finally, a last run of the scenario, results of which are shown in Figure 6-39, will provide a global view of the improvements.

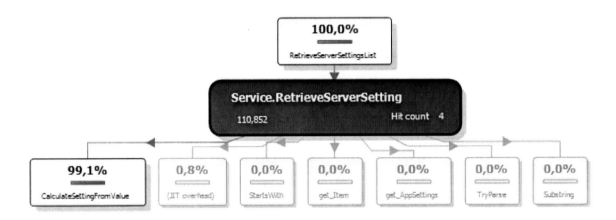

Figure 6-39: Call graph showing the results of the modification.

The total time spent has gone from 303 to 110ms. Simple code modifications have divided the time spent generating settings values for the client by almost three. The return on investment is excellent.

As a final note, you may have noticed that the algorithm above could be optimized still further. The goal of the present section was not to show a full optimization, particularly since we explained at the beginning of this book that this is bad practice. Our investigation time is better spent finding methods offering potentially large improvements. Our purpose here was to provide techniques, promote good habits and demonstrate a new way of efficiently profiling an application. If you see some more ways of improving the code, this goal has been reached. As an exercise, I encourage you to follow the optimization process with RemoveSeparators. Beware that there is a trap in there, because the case-processing operation has been put at the beginning of the function code.

B.6 Reading contract data

We continue the analysis with the slowest function in the scenario, namely `Retrieve-ContractFromCursor` (see Figure 6-40).

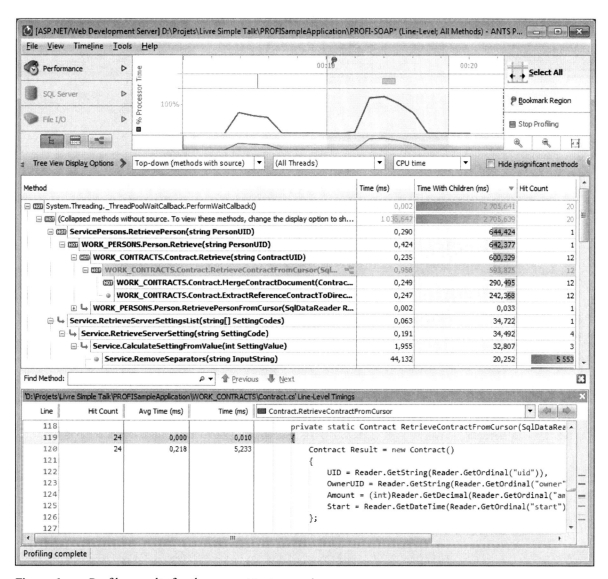

Figure 6-40: Profiler results for the current test scenario.

As the call graph in Figure 6-41 shows, this function is called by the two web services called `RetrievePerson` and `RetrieveContractsList`.

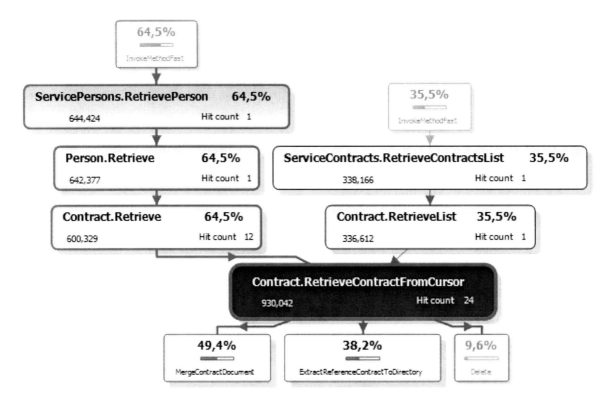

Figure 6-41: Call graph centered on the `RetrieveContractFromCursor` function.

`Person.Retrieve` and `Contract.Retrieve` seem to be semantically close to those two web methods, and the functions below `RetrieveContractFromCursor` are also visible in the list of longest functions. We can deduce that the ten or so lines at the top of the list in Figure 6-40 are in fact the same problem, namely that `MergeContractDocument` and `ExtractReferenceContractToDirectory` are slow. The problem may also be that they are each called 24 times.

We are thus going to investigate these two methods, as well as the `File.Delete` operation that takes almost 10% of the time spent in the target function, which amounts to 90ms.

B.6.a   Removing temporary files

We start with the `File.Delete` function, the calling context of which is shown in Listing 6-41.

```
string tempDir = ExtractReferenceContractToDirectory();

string mergeFile = MergeContractDocument(result, tempDir);
result.DocumentBase64 = Convert.ToBase64String(File.ReadAllBytes(mergeFile));

File.Delete(mergeFile);
Directory.Delete(tempDir, true);
```
Listing 6-41

The extraction function which creates the to-be-deleted content of `TempDir` is defined by Listing 6-42.

```
private static string ExtractReferenceContractToDirectory()
{
    string tempDir = Path.GetTempFileName();
    File.Delete(tempDir);
    Directory.CreateDirectory(tempDir);
    using (Stream flux = typeof(Contract).Assembly.GetManifestResourceStream
                    ("WORK_CONTRACTS.ReferenceContract.docx"))
        new FastZip().ExtractZip(flux, tempDir, FastZip.Overwrite.Always, null,
                                        ".*", ".*", false, true);
    return tempDir;
}
```
Listing 6-42

In plain English, the resource file with extension **.docx**, which is in fact a zip archive, is simply uncompressed into a temporary directory. We will analyze what is done in this directory by **MergeContractDocument** in order to try and find possible improvements to the extraction process. The code of **MergeContractDocument** is shown in Listing 6-43.

```
private static string MergeContractDocument(Contract result, string tempDir)
{
    string documentFile = Path.Combine(tempDir, @"word\document.xml");
    XmlDocument dom = new XmlDocument();
    dom.Load(documentFile);

    XmlNamespaceManager nsMgr = new XmlNamespaceManager(dom.NameTable);
    nsMgr.AddNamespace("w", "http://schemas.openxmlformats.org/
                    wordprocessingml/2006/main");
    foreach (XmlNode nodeMerge in dom.SelectNodes("//w:t[contains(., '[MERGE_')]",
                    nsMgr))
    {
        nodeMerge.InnerText = nodeMerge.InnerText.Replace("[MERGE_uid]", result.
                    UID);
        nodeMerge.InnerText = nodeMerge.InnerText.Replace("[MERGE_amount]", result.
                    Amount.ToString("C"));
        nodeMerge.InnerText = nodeMerge.InnerText.Replace("[MERGE_start]", result.
                    Start.ToLongDateString());
    }

    dom.Save(documentFile);

    string mergeFile = Path.GetTempFileName();
    new FastZip().CreateZip(mergeFile, tempDir, true, ".*");
    return mergeFile;
}
```
Listing 6-43

It turns out that only the uncompressed file called word\document.xml is used by this algorithm so it is a shame to unzip the entire archive. A possible optimization would be to use the partial extraction capabilities of **SharpZipLib** to reduce the unzipping time.

But we can do even better: since the function is called 24 times without the file changing, we could simply store the uncompressed word\document.xml file. No memory issue will arise in this case, because the cache will only store a unique content, and we will not risk losing control of the memory used by the cache if several callers need this content.

B.6.b   Merging the contract document

To put in place the optimization we just talked about, we begin by modifying Merge-ContractDocument so that it takes a file rather than a directory as a parameter. This means we can be sure that our diagnosis was correct when refactoring. Indeed, if the function uses the content of the directory for something else, build errors will warn us about the situation.

The function is modified by changing the second input parameter, and removing the first instruction that has no more use. The result is shown in Listing 6-44.

```
private static string MergeContractDocument(Contract result, string documentFile)
{
    XmlDocument dom = new XmlDocument();
    dom.Load(documentFile);

    XmlNamespaceManager nsMgr = new XmlNamespaceManager(dom.NameTable);
    nsMgr.AddNamespace("w", "http://schemas.openxmlformats.org/
                            wordprocessingml/2006/main");
    foreach (XmlNode nodeMerge in dom.SelectNodes("//w:t[contains(., '[MERGE_')]",
                            nsMgr))
    {
        nodeMerge.InnerText = nodeMerge.InnerText.Replace("[MERGE_uid]", result.
                            UID);
        nodeMerge.InnerText = nodeMerge.InnerText.Replace("[MERGE_amount]", result.
                            Amount.ToString("C"));
        nodeMerge.InnerText = nodeMerge.InnerText.Replace("[MERGE_start]", result.
                            Start.ToLongDateString());
    }

    dom.Save(documentFile);
```

```
      string mergeFile = Path.GetTempFileName();
      new FastZip().CreateZip(mergeFile, TempDir, true, ".*");
      return mergeFile;
}
```

Listing 6-44

Recompiling shows an error, as **TempDir** was used, not only in the file modification, but also in the creation of an archive from the complete content of the directory. We have to adapt the code a bit more than was planned, but a major optimization remains possible because the directory is only used to generate an archive with the file we have modified. It is thus possible to put the entire content of the directory in cache and have a single decompression stage, provided that two ASP.NET threads do not simultaneously modify the word\document.xml file.

This means a second modification of the function, namely the creation of an archive based on a directory that is now stored as a public member. While we are at it, we extend the logic to doing the same operation with the **DocumentFile** parameter, the content of which will be kept in cache instead of having a link to a file. This improves performance a bit more. The modified function is shown in Listing 6-45.

```
private static string MergeContractDocument(Contract result)
{
    XmlDocument dom = new XmlDocument();
    dom.LoadXml(DocumentFileContent);

    XmlNamespaceManager nsMgr = new XmlNamespaceManager(dom.NameTable);
    nsMgr.AddNamespace("w", "http://schemas.openxmlformats.org/
                              wordprocessingml/2006/main");
    foreach (XmlNode nodeMerge in dom.SelectNodes("//w:t[contains(., '[MERGE_')]",
                              nsMgr))
    {
        nodeMerge.InnerText = nodeMerge.InnerText.Replace("[MERGE_uid]", result.
                              UID);
        nodeMerge.InnerText = nodeMerge.InnerText.Replace("[MERGE_amount]", result.
                              Amount.ToString("C"));
        nodeMerge.InnerText = nodeMerge.InnerText.Replace("[MERGE_start]", result.
                              Start.ToLongDateString());
```

```
    }

    dom.Save(Path.Combine(MergeDir, @"word\document.xml"));

    string mergeFile = Path.GetTempFileName();
    new FastZip().CreateZip(mergeFile, MergeDir, true, ".*");
    return mergeFile;
}
```
Listing 6-45

Obviously, we have to add the following code so that the previous one becomes fully functional. Two static members are put in place as singletons (see Listing 6-46).

```
private static string _DocumentFileContent = null;

private static string DocumentFileContent
{
    get
    {
        if (_DocumentFileContent == null)
            LoadingSingletonsValues();
        return _DocumentFileContent;
    }
}

private static string _MergeDir = null;

private static string MergeDir
{
    get
    {
        if (_MergeDir == null)
            LoadingSingletonsValues();
        return _MergeDir;
    }
}

private static void LoadingSingletonsValues()
{
    _MergeDir = Path.GetTempFileName();
    File.Delete(_MergeDir);
```

```
    Directory.CreateDirectory(_MergeDir);
    using (Stream flux = typeof(Contract).Assembly.GetManifestResourceStream
                ("WORK_CONTRACTS.ReferenceContract.docx"))
        new FastZip().ExtractZip(flux, _MergeDir, FastZip.Overwrite.Always, null,
                ".*", ".*", false, true);

    string documentFile = Path.Combine(_MergeDir, @"word\document.xml");
    _DocumentFileContent = File.ReadAllText(documentFile);
}
```

Listing 6-46

For the second singleton to work it had to call the logic of the function `ExtractRefer`-`enceContractIntoDirectory`, so we have decided to copy it completely, which means the original function can be removed. However it is necessary to load both singleton values at the same time. Otherwise, we run the risk of the word/document.xml file being modified before we have read its initial content, which will serve as a reference for all the contract merge operations.

This being set, the code for `RetrieveContractFromCursor` can now be rewritten without any reference to `ExtractReferenceContractToDirectory`, as shown in Listing 6-47.

```
private static Contract RetrieveContractFromCursor(SqlDataReader reader)
{
    Contract result = new Contract()
    {
        UID = reader.GetString(reader.GetOrdinal("uid")),
        OwnerUID = reader.GetString(reader.GetOrdinal("owner")),
        Amount = (int)reader.GetDecimal(reader.GetOrdinal("amount")),
        Start = reader.GetDateTime(reader.GetOrdinal("start")),
    };

    if (!reader.IsDBNull(reader.GetOrdinal("discount")))
        result.Discount = reader.GetString(reader.GetOrdinal("discount"));

    // Execution of a document merge to put the contract Word document at the
    // disposal of the business-related object
    string mergeFile = MergeContractDocument(result);
```

```
result.DocumentBase64 = Convert.ToBase64String(File.ReadAllBytes(mergeFile));
File.Delete(mergeFile);

return result;
}
```

Listing 6-47

Finally, we should add the code to avoid concurrent calls to the merge process, in order to avoid potential data loss due to two parallel operations on the same ASP.NET server writing the same file content. This can be done using a static lock somewhere in the `Contract` class, as shown in Listing 6-48.

```
private static object _MergeLock = new object();
```

Listing 6-48

We then have to make one last modification to the code calling the merge process in order to prevent simultaneous operations. We use the `lock` keyword for that, as shown in Listing 6-49.

```
lock (_MergeLock)
{
    string mergeFile = MergeContractDocument(result);
    result.DocumentBase64 = Convert.ToBase64String(File.ReadAllBytes(mergeFile));
    File.Delete(mergeFile);
}
```

Listing 6-49

In practice

Anybody with a bit of knowledge of parallel processing will immediately identify the limits of such an approach: we should never use static members in a web application, we should take into account the possible modification of the reference file and refresh the cache accordingly; we should set a time limit for the lock; and finally, we should check that the processing time does not become a bottleneck for several parallel operations. In our case, we stick to a simple approach, because the file has a fixed and limited size. Moreover, the fact that it is an embedded resource in the library prevents it from being modified during the application's execution. Lastly, if static members are read-only and they are used to simulate a simple cache, this is generally not a problem, provided we use a `ReaderWriterLock`*. We favor an Agile approach, where a simple and quick operation is preferred to the full application of strict rules. Sometimes, when trying to prevent errors that in fact have almost zero chance of appearing, these rules can cause us to over-architect systems, which is one of the surest ways of getting low application performance.*

We do not even need detailed explanations: a quick look at the profiling results in Figure 6-42 shows that performance is, indeed, going up.

Again, a one-hour-long modification has enabled us to greatly reduce the reference time of a scenario! An expert developer could argue that the development error was simple to spot, but it is so only because the sample application is extremely compact, with all business-related work performed in a single class. Finding this kind of overconsumption of temporary files is much more complex in a real application with dozens of classes potentially dealing with common resources like the merge source in our example. Only a profiling session can show this kind of information without too much work.

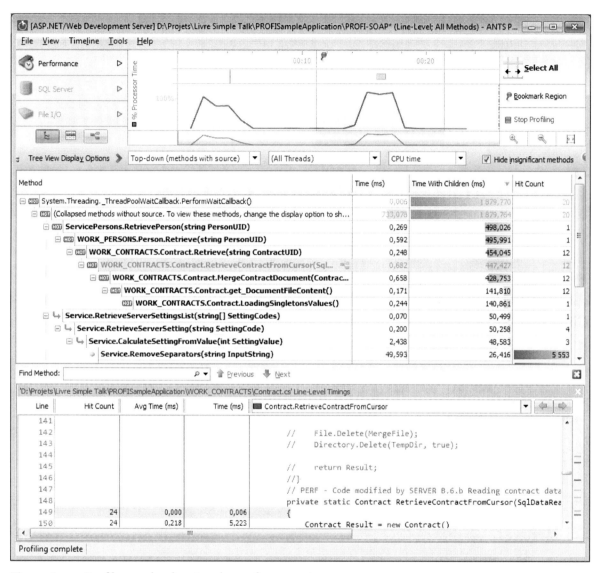

Figure 6-42: Profiler results showing the performance improvement.

Ratio of improvement is highly dependent on the machine

It should be stressed that I used a very powerful machine for these tests: two physical CPUs with four cores each. HyperThreading has been deactivated (its effects on parallelizing and performance vary with the algorithm), but it still amounts to eight cores! This means the ratio may be a bit biased. Indeed, when using my old computer (two cores instead of eight), I obtained a much higher performance gain through this code optimization, by a factor of more than three (instead of the 20 percent improvement here).

B.6.c   Extraction of the reference contract

In the case above, we needed to extract all the files from the compressed archive, but we can imagine cases where it would not be useful, and we suggested that only single files could be extracted using the advanced functions of `SharpZipLib`. If you remember, this method was used when optimizing the client-side of our sample application (see Chapter 5). We show in Listing 6-50 the code in question for information, knowing that it cannot be used for the reasons given above.

```
StringWriter scribe = new StringWriter();
ZipFile compressedFile = new ZipFile(_DocumentFile);
SortedDictionary<int, List<string>> stylesPerPriority = new SortedDictionary<int,
                List<string>>();
using (Stream stylesStream = compressedFile.GetInputStream(compressedFile.
                GetEntry("word/styles.xml")))
using (XmlReader xslReader = new XmlTextReader(stylesStream))
{
    while (xslReader.Read())
    {
        […]
    }
}
```

Listing 6-50

B.6.d   Merge by XML manipulation

The document merge process can certainly be improved further. Indeed, we have used a singleton to store the content formatted as text, but given that it is systematically loaded into an XmlDocument, why not only do this once as well? With this, we could suppress the 3.1% of time spent in LoadXml (see Figure 6-43).

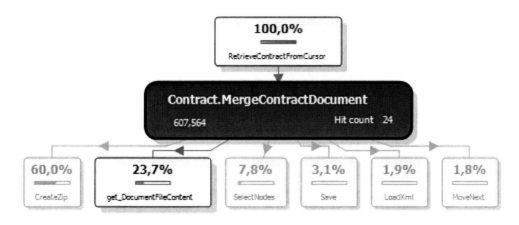

Figure 6-43: Call graph centered on the MergeContractDocument function.

While we are studying this function, we could also pre-select XML nodes on which we are going to base the merge process, which would reduce the 7.8% of time spent on the function SelectNodes.

To do so, we modify the MergeContractDocument function as shown in Listing 6-51.

```
private static string MergeContractDocument(Contract result)
{
    foreach (XmlNode nodeMerge in NodesMerge)
    {
        nodeMerge.InnerText = nodeMerge.InnerText.Replace("[MERGE_uid]", result.
                       UID);
        nodeMerge.InnerText = nodeMerge.InnerText.Replace("[MERGE_amount]", result.
                       Amount.ToString("C"));
```

```
        nodeMerge.InnerText = nodeMerge.InnerText.Replace("[MERGE_start]", result.
                        Start.ToLongDateString());
    }

    DomMerge.Save(Path.Combine(MergeDir, @"word\document.xml"));

    string mergeFile = Path.GetTempFileName();
    new FastZip().CreateZip(mergeFile, MergeDir, true, ".*");
    return mergeFile;
}
```

Listing 6-51

Of course, the code that manages the singletons has to change as well (see Listing 6-52).

```
private static void LoadingSingletonsValues()
{
    _MergeDir = Path.GetTempFileName();
    File.Delete(_MergeDir);
    Directory.CreateDirectory(_MergeDir);
    using (Stream flux = typeof(Contract).Assembly.GetManifestResourceStream
                    ("WORK_CONTRACTS.ReferenceContract.docx"))
        new FastZip().ExtractZip(flux, _MergeDir, FastZip.Overwrite.Always, null,
                            ".*", ".*", false, true);

    string documentFile = Path.Combine(_MergeDir, @"word\document.xml");
    _DocumentFileContent = File.ReadAllText(documentFile);

    _DomMerge = new XmlDocument();
    _DomMerge.LoadXml(_DocumentFileContent);

    XmlNamespaceManager nsMgr = new XmlNamespaceManager(_DomMerge.NameTable);
    nsMgr.AddNamespace("w", "http://schemas.openxmlformats.org/
                            wordprocessingml/2006/main");
    _NodesMerge = _DomMerge.SelectNodes("//w:t[contains(., '[MERGE_')]", nsMgr);
}
```

Listing 6-52

We also add the following singletons (see Listing 6-53), with the locks needed to keep their construction thread-safe.

```
private static XmlDocument _DomMerge = null;

private static object LockDom = new object();

private static XmlDocument DomMerge
{
    get
    {
        if (_DomMerge == null)
            lock (LockDom)
                if (_DomMerge == null)
                    LoadingSingletonsValues();
        return _DomMerge;
    }
}

private static XmlNodeList _NodesMerge = null;

private static object _LockNodes = new object();

private static XmlNodeList NodesMerge
{
    get
    {
        if (_NodesMerge == null)
            lock (_LockNodes)
                if (_NodesMerge == null)
                    LoadingSingletonsValues();
        return _NodesMerge;
    }
}
```

Listing 6-53

Given the reference scenario, which uses a given path, we could certainly write a simpler code with fewer accessors. But this would not help performance, so we leave the code as it is.

B.6.e   Merge in textual mode

Let us push the performance logic as far as possible: since loading an XML Domain Object Model is only about replacing text entries by values when they start with [MERGE_, why not simply replace these entries directly in the text?

Purists will definitely frown on this idea. If the developer who originated the XML format went to the trouble of building the schema, it seems wrong to treat this as pure text and not take into account the hierarchical dimension that the XML grammar conveys. However, we can apply the principle of simplicity here because the format of the merge entries is itself based on a text-based convention. If an XML attribute had been used to request the merge, we could not have performed the operation on plain text: too many unknown parameters would have appeared, like the order of the attributes, the presence of significant white spaces, etc.

But since a convention has been created to locate the merge spaces in the document (and the presence of special characters like "[" and "_" clearly shows that the confusion with other text has been taken care of), we can replace the merge code by the one in Listing 6-54.

```
private static string MergeContractDocument(Contract result)
{
    string modifiedContent = DocumentFileContent.Replace("[MERGE_uid]", result.
                          UID);
    modifiedContent = modifiedContent.Replace("[MERGE_amount]", result.Amount.
                          ToString("C"));
    modifiedContent = modifiedContent.Replace("[MERGE_start]", result.Start.
                          ToLongDateString());
    File.WriteAllText(Path.Combine(MergeDir, @"word\document.xml"),
                          modifiedContent);

    string mergeFile = Path.GetTempFileName();
    new FastZip().CreateZip(mergeFile, MergeDir, true, ".*");
    return mergeFile;
}
```

Listing 6-54

This enables us to get rid of the singletons `DomMerge` and `NodesMerge`, as well as removing their initialization from the loading functions, the new version of which is shown in Listing 6-55.

```
private static void LoadingSingletonsValues()
{
    _MergeDir = Path.GetTempFileName();
    File.Delete(_MergeDir);
    Directory.CreateDirectory(_MergeDir);
    using (Stream flux = typeof(Contract).Assembly.GetManifestResourceStream("WORK_
                    CONTRACTS.ReferenceContract.docx"))
        new FastZip().ExtractZip(flux, _MergeDir, FastZip.Overwrite.Always, null,
                        ".*", ".*", false, true);

    string documentFile = Path.Combine(_MergeDir, @"word\document.xml");
    _DocumentFileContent = File.ReadAllText(documentFile);
}
```

Listing 6-55

On such a simple example, execution will hardly change at all, but the principle is interesting and it is important to demonstrate this optimization even if only for the almost philosophical approach of the choice "XML versus text." Indeed, many developers will argue that text-based transformation is not robust enough, and that XML will take all the possible cases into account. This thinking would certainly be true if the XML grammar had been used to structure the data but, in our case, the merge structure was dictated by a text-based convention inside an XML element.

If, despite this explanation, you still feel reluctant, or fellow colleagues refuse to go for it, remember that the elegance of the code should always come second to simplicity. Most of the time, the two go hand in hand but, when they do not, the latter should always prevail. Performance is a much more important argument to a customer than design robustness. Again, this is not true for software used in critical functions. But any marketer trying to sell a simple business management solution will confirm without hesitation that they prefer to sell a quick application with a small bug than a perfectly robust but slow one.

B.6.f   Usefulness of the initial contract merge

We could go on and optimize strings replacement. The effect of immutability is that every replacement will create as many strings as there are instances of merge keywords in the document. But the results are already good enough (see Figure 6-44).

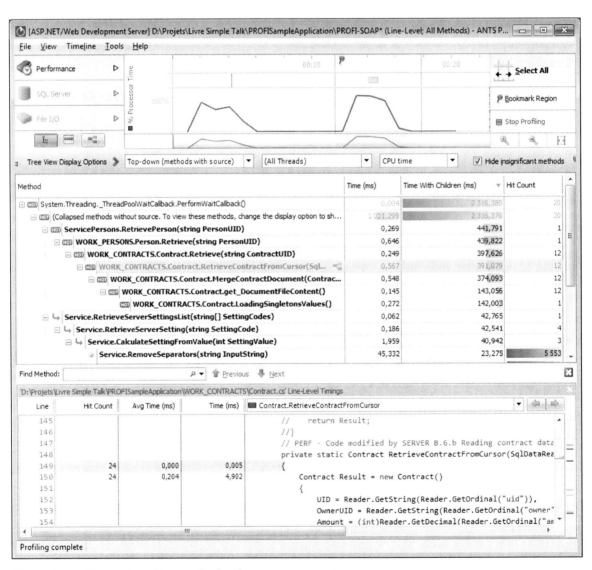

Figure 6-44: Updated profiler results for the current scenario.

However, we are still bumping into the **CreateZip** problem: since the merge process is about creating a compressed archive with extension **.docx** and this document is different for each contract, we simply cannot unify the calls to this function. And yet, this process represents a major part of the time spent in **MergeContractDocument** by a long way (see Figure 6-45).

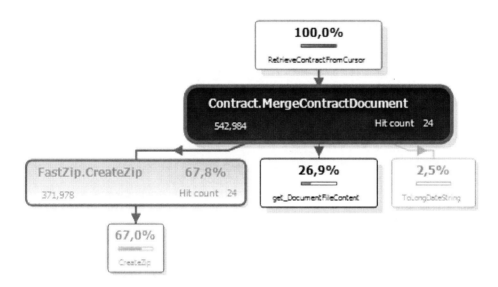

Figure 6-45: Call graph around **MergeContractDocument**.

In these situations, the best approach is to return to the basic options for reducing the time spent in a method: removing it if possible, removing calls to it, or reducing the number of instructions in it. In our case, are all the calls really necessary? When executing the method, yes, but how about going up a few levels in the stack and addressing this from the client perspective? When the web method of contract retrieval is called, the interface in Figure 6-46 is displayed.

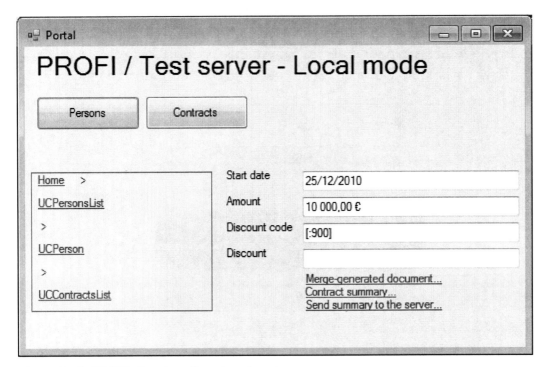

Figure 6-46: PROFI client interface after choosing a contract.

No document is displayed! So it is no use merging the Word document when we send the list of contracts to the client, since it could be generated only upon request, when the user clicks the **Merge-generated document** link. Waiting a few tenths of a second when the document is actually needed will definitely be much more acceptable than a 1.5 second delay during every initial display of the contract properties. Moreover, the latter time will keep growing with the volume of contracts, whereas the former will remain constant.

In consequence, we can simply remove the generation of a merged contract document when creating a `Contract` object on the server, and add a web method, dedicated to merge, that we will call from the client. We start by simplifying the server side, as shown in Listing 6-56.

```
private static Contract RetrieveContractFromCursor(SqlDataReader reader)
{
    Contract result = new Contract()
    {
        UID = reader.GetString(reader.GetOrdinal("uid")),
        OwnerUID = reader.GetString(reader.GetOrdinal("owner")),
        Amount = (int)reader.GetDecimal(reader.GetOrdinal("amount")),
        Start = reader.GetDateTime(reader.GetOrdinal("start")),
    };

    if (!reader.IsDBNull(reader.GetOrdinal("discount")))
        result.Discount = reader.GetString(reader.GetOrdinal("discount"));

    // No need to merge the contract document here anymore!
    return result;
}
```
Listing 6-56

The MergeContractDocument function, which now includes the merge itself
and the calling code, can be made non-static since we now call it by passing an
instance of Contract that has just been created. This also means the function
should become public.

```
public void MergeContractDocument()
{
    lock (_MergeLock)
    {
        string modifiedContent = DocumentFileContent.Replace("[MERGE_uid]", UID);
        modifiedContent = modifiedContent.Replace("[MERGE_amount]", Amount.
                    ToString("C"));
        modifiedContent = modifiedContent.Replace("[MERGE_start]", Start.
                    ToLongDateString());
        File.WriteAllText(Path.Combine(MergeDir, @"word\document.xml"),
                    modifiedContent);

        string mergeFile = Path.GetTempFileName();
        new FastZip().CreateZip(mergeFile, MergeDir, true, ".*");
```

```
        DocumentBase64 = Convert.ToBase64String(File.ReadAllBytes(mergeFile));
        File.Delete(mergeFile);
    }
}
```

Listing 6-57

A good sign

This kind of drastic simplification is generally a good sign that an important step has been taken in the process of optimization and associated refactoring.

The web method created to request the merged document is shown in Listing 6-58.

```
[WebMethod]
public string RetrieveMergeDocument(string contractUID)
{
    Contract target = Contract.Retrieve(contractUID);
    target.MergeContractDocument();
    return target.DocumentBase64;
}
```

Listing 6-58

It would certainly be possible to produce even quicker code by only retrieving values for the contract that are actually used in the merge process. However, this is a typical case of a little less data making almost no difference to performance, while creating maintenance problems if we add a merge field to the document template without knowing whether the value in question has been retrieved from the database.

On the client side, the controller gets a new function to call the web method. This is shown in Listing 6-59.

```
internal string RetrieveMergeDocument(string contractUID)
{
    return _Client.RetrieveMergeDocument(contractUID);
}
```
Listing 6-59

The old version of the code for the management of the event associated with clicking the link was very simple, as seen in Listing 6-60.

```
private void lnkDocument_LinkClicked(object sender, LinkLabelLinkClickedEventArgs e)
{
    if (_DocumentFile != null)
        Process.Start(_DocumentFile);
}
```
Listing 6-60

It is now a bit more complex, since we add some logic for the late generation of the merge document (Listing 6-61).

```
private void lnkDocument_LinkClicked(object sender, LinkLabelLinkClickedEventArgs
e)
{
    if (_DocumentFile == null)
    {
        // Deserializing the contract under a Word document format
        _Contract.DocumentBase64 = Controller.Current.RetrieveMergeDocument
                            (_Contract.UID);
        _DocumentFile = Path.GetTempFileName();
        File.Move(_DocumentFile, _DocumentFile + ".docx");
        _DocumentFile += ".docx";
        File.WriteAllBytes(_DocumentFile, Convert.FromBase64String(_Contract.
                            DocumentBase64));
    }
    Process.Start(_DocumentFile);
}
```
Listing 6-61

What about data consistency?

We have chosen here to retrieve only the result of the merge operation, but let us suppose that the business object has changed between its initial reading from the client and the request for a merged document by the user. The interface would still use the old version, whereas the merged document would show a different amount, for example. In some cases, the customer organization can result in business objects being allocated to single software users, and this situation is then impossible. Inversely, if the data is being actively refreshed by several users, it would be better to retrieve, not only the merged document, but also the refreshed instance of contract business objects, so that the display always matches the Word document. As we could take advantage of the existing round trip between the client and the server, this would not impact performance very much.

B.6.g Dead code

When executing unit tests to validate that the modification shown above has not created any nasty side effects, we get a bad surprise, namely an exception being thrown when calling UCContract.ShortenedGeneration. This is the ideal moment to explain that this code is actually completely useless! Indeed, the unique call to it is surrounded by code like that shown in Listing 6-62.

```
_SummaryFile = Path.GetTempFileName();
ShortenedGeneration();

using (XmlTextWriter scribe = new XmlTextWriter(_SummaryFile, Encoding.UTF8))
{
    scribe.WriteStartDocument();
    scribe.WriteStartElement("root");
    scribe.WriteStartElement("contract");
    scribe.WriteAttributeString("uid", _Contract.UID);
    scribe.WriteAttributeString("start", _Contract.Start.ToShortDateString());
    scribe.WriteAttributeString("amount", _Contract.Amount.ToString("C"));
    scribe.WriteEndElement();
    scribe.WriteEndElement();
    scribe.WriteEndDocument();
}
```

Listing 6-62

However, it turns out that the only member modified by function `ShortenedGener-ation` is in fact `_SummaryFile`, as shown in Listing 6-63.

```
private void ShortenedGeneration()
{
    [...]

    File.WriteAllText(_SummaryFile, scribe.ToString());
}
```

Listing 6-63

Since the content of `_SummaryFile` is modified by another method immediately after it has been generated, we can deduce that the call to `ShortenedGeneration` is not useful. As this is the only call in the code, the conclusion is that the function is altogether useless. This is called dead code (technically speaking, it is said to have zero Afferent Coupling).

Again, this case could seem highly specious to a developer: what are the chances that absolutely useless code is present in an application? In fact, chances are far from nothing, and several code reviews done with NDepend, even on well-known Open Source applications, have shown some percentage of dead code.

Dead code is dead easy to create: typically, a developer adds a new and simpler version of a function. Not knowing the details of the callers to this function, they will prefer to leave the old code in place rather than taking the risk of removing it. After all, it may be called by a foreign module, or even through reflection. In this case, they would not receive any compile error from the automated build. In order not to make any faux pas, developers tend to leave the dead code behind, particularly since the impact is so small: additional IL size is quite limited, and the risk of side effects is almost non-existent. This happens very often with method overloading: everybody adds their own signature, but nobody takes the time necessary to remove the useless ones because it takes time to review every possible case of use, including loose coupling, and you will get no credit for it.

All these reasons mean that, contrary to what people may think, it is far from rare to find dead code in an application's libraries. The best preventive solution is to share the code responsibility, in order for each developer in a team to feel empowered and competent enough to suppress a function they have not written themselves, while keeping a reasonable idea of the potential effects. Again, this is a good practice of Agile methods.

Possible optimization

Had the generation code for `_SummaryFile` *not been so simple, it would have been good to use the same approach as per the contract document merge operation, namely generating it only when the corresponding link was clicked on the client.*

These last modifications, which have led to creating merged documents only when they are needed (when the user asks for it to be displayed, which is never in this test scenario, but will be done once in the second one), gave excellent results (presented in Figure 6-47).

We are even obliged to clear the Hide insignificant methods option to see `RetrieveContractFromCursor` again. Despite its 24 calls, it now only takes a few tens of milliseconds.

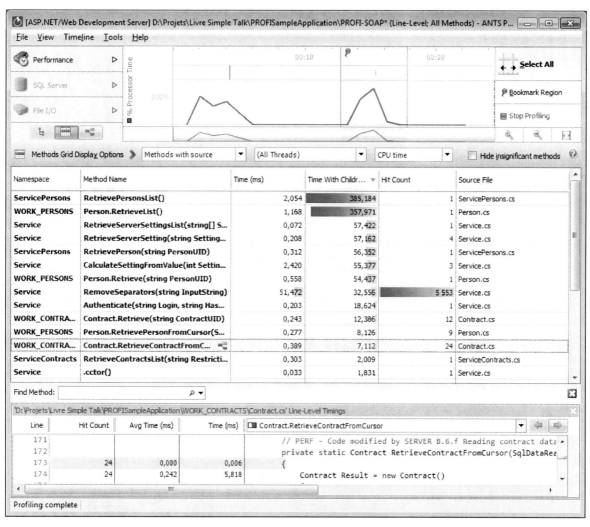

Figure 6-47: Updated profiler results after the latest modifications.

B.7   Reading data on the persons

The profiler metrics show that the last function to analyze in this scenario is the retrieval of the list of persons, which takes almost half a second. The call graph in Figure 6-48 shows that almost all of this time is spent in unique calls to the connections management API and in the requests sent to the SQL Server database.

Figure 6-48: Call graph showing the time spent in database-related operations.

There is, therefore, little chance that we can improve these calls, and we will conclude our optimization attempts on this first scenario. The total server time has been more than halved, which is very nice given the limited time we spent on this. Moreover, the present modifications will fully express themselves in the periods of high server load, since our scenario was simple and based on only a few tens of persons and contracts.

B.8   Weight of the web services conversations

B.8.a   Recording method

Before switching to the second test scenario, we will demonstrate a simple way of analyzing network consumption in terms of size of messages. We could use one of the specially-designed tools like SoapTrace (very simple) or WireShark (much more comprehensive, but also complex). But in the case of an IIS web server, there is an even simpler solution: using the logs to retrieve the size of conversations.

To use this feature, we need to enter the IIS configuration service and select the Logging option as shown in Figure 6-49.

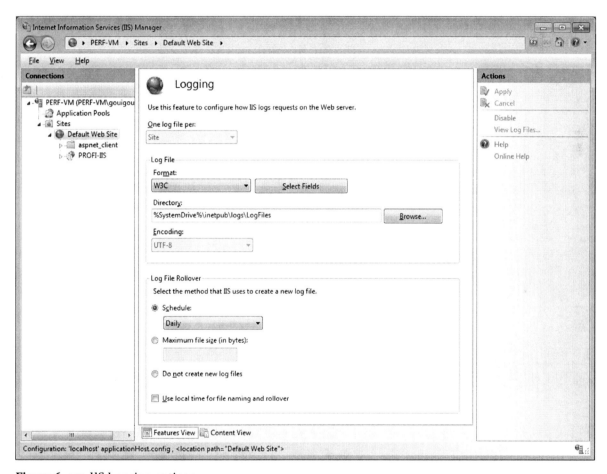

Figure 6-49: IIS Logging options.

We then use the Select Fields button to add the entries called **Bytes Sent** and **Bytes Received** (see Figure 6-50).

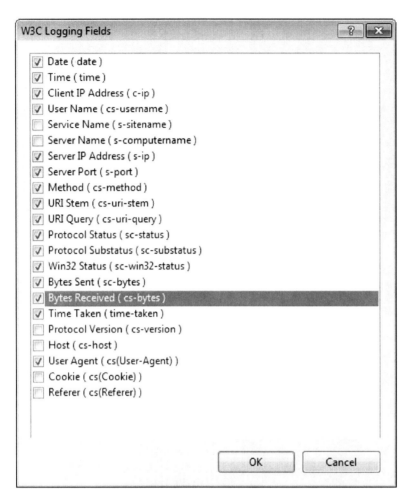

Figure 6-50: List of fields to be recorded through logging.

The IIS logs will then display the number of bytes coming in and going out. For example, Listing 6-64 shows the line of the log that corresponds on my machine to the call to the authentication web method.

```
2011-01-25 23:46:22 W3SVC223085719 192.168.1.10 POST /PROFI-IIS/Service.asmx - 80 -
192.168.1.10 PROFI-WIN 200 0 0 643 2100 392
```

Listing 6-64

What emerges from this is that 643 bytes have been received by IIS and 392 bytes have been sent back (the order of parameters in the log is given in the header of the log file), that the 192.168.1.10 machine was the origin and the destination, and that the returned HTTP code was 200 (OK), etc.

Of course, there are several other valid ways of retrieving these values, and they are sometimes more efficient, particularly SoapTrace, SOAPUI, WebLOAD, and others. Even Visual Studio provides a performance and load testing tool, though it is only available in the high-end versions.

B.8.b   Results on the scenario

After gathering all the required lines, we obtain the following summary table. This time, we have only recorded the data size of the SOAP messages. This is more relevant to our goals, since the HTTP header is not something we can change. The results are shown in Figure 6-51.

Method	Bytes received	Bytes sent
Authenticate	453	380
RetrieveServerSettingsList	487	1,228,634
RetrievePersonsList	317	2,235
RetrievePerson	388	990,489
ComplexRequest	309	1,564
RetrieveContractsList	420	990,209

Figure 6-51: Results of the bandwidth consumption per function analysis.

In the end, it appears that server settings are more important than we expected, but this is mainly due to the fact that the sample application's behavior is not realistic from this point of view.

On the other hand, responses on `RetrievePerson` and `RetrieveContractsList` are quite high, with more than 900 kilobytes sent back every time, because these metrics were taken before we decided to stop sending the merged document and to wait for it to be requested explicitly. After that improvement, these messages are only 2,985 and 2,705 bytes respectively, which amounts to a division by 300!

In fact, this metric may be the one that best shows the huge improvement made through this last optimization. Indeed, halving the execution time could almost look normal, and this ratio is quite small compared to the effort required. But all tests have been done in local mode. Let us now imagine the application is deployed with a remote client using ADSL to call the server: the gains would be positively huge.

In practice

In fact, the application in its non-optimized form would have been totally unusable outside a local network. This is why it is advisable to perform a complete deployment and test in conditions close to actual future use as soon as possible in the development process. Typically, if we make the effort of putting in place a bandwidth reduction tool (e.g. NetBalancer), we will be able to see the problem right from the function's first local test.

B.8.c   Tools for resource limitation

For information, NetBalancer (HTTP://SERIOUSBIT.COM/NETBALANCER/) is a network surveillance and use control tool. Its main interface lists the processes that are using the network (see Figure 6-52).

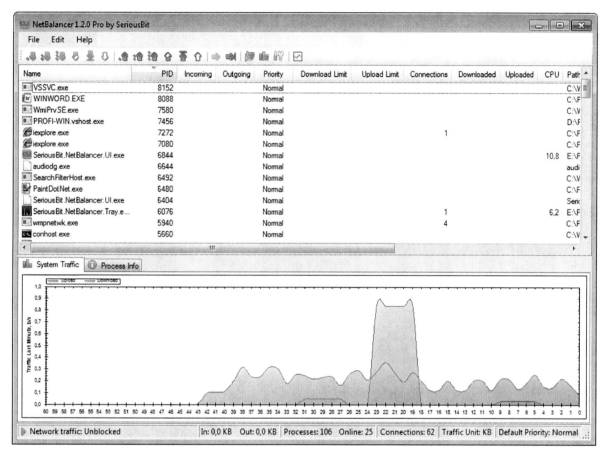

Figure 6-52: NetBalancer interface.

The **Settings** command in the **Edit** menu opens a window that allows the user to limit the download and upload traffic, which is very useful for emulating slow networks (see Figure 6-53).

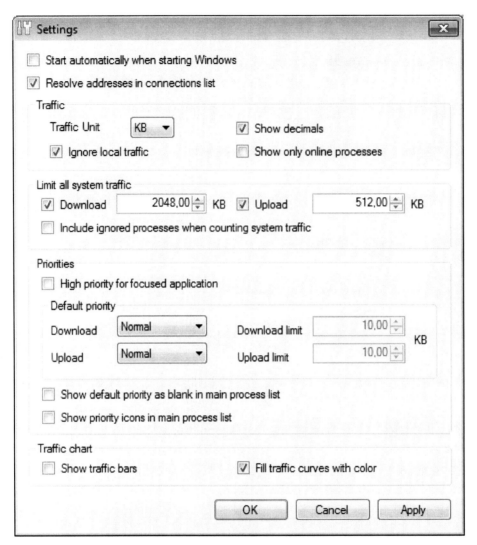

Figure 6-53: NetBalancer Settings dialog box.

There are also utilities for CPU or RAM limitation. MemAlloc , for example, (HTTP://WWW.SOFT.TAHIONIC.COM/DOWNLOAD-MEMALLOC/INDEX.HTML) lets us reserve memory, in order to artificially lower the available memory (see Figure 6-54).

418

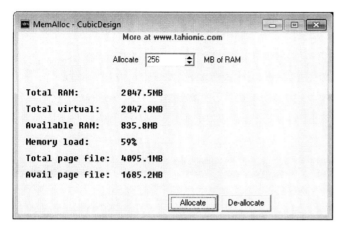

Figure 6-54: MemAlloc interface.

C Running profiling on the second scenario

C.1 Context

Before running the analysis on the second scenario, it should be stressed that several web methods (authentication and settings retrieval, for example) are common to both scenarios. Therefore it makes sense that we should have much less work than for the first scenario, where we started from scratch.

Moreover, since we are taking advantage of the optimizations that have been done on the first scenario, we should see in a more salient way the problems that remain in the second one.

C.2   Initial profiling

After modifying the compilation options for the four interface-related projects in PROFI so that they use **TEST2**, **AUTOEXIT**, then rebuilding the client, we can start server profiling and run the second scenario client side. The first metrics are reported in Figure 6-55.

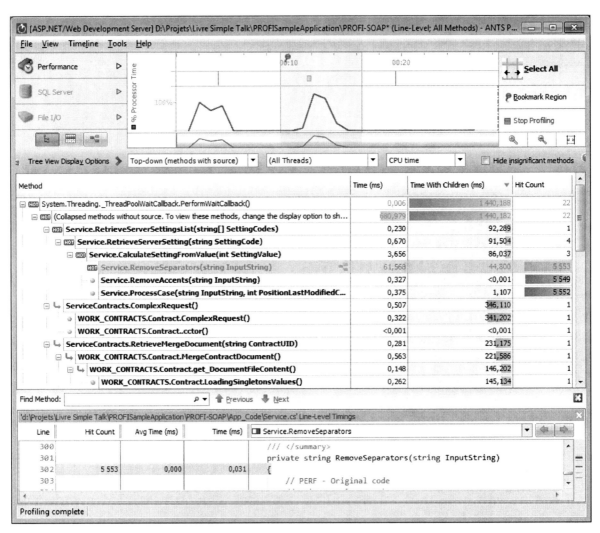

Figure 6-55: Initial profiler results for the second test scenario.

Before getting to the heart of the subject, there are a few points to note.

- `ServiceContracts.ComplexRequest` and `Contract.ComplexRequest` clearly relate to the same functionality: same method name, almost same time spent in the function. They will definitely be the web service method and its implementation in the business tier.

- Settings retrieval still takes a lot of time, but we have already pushed the optimization process quite far.

- The `RetrieveMergeDocument` operation is indeed called by this TEST2 scenario, as we had anticipated when putting in place the delayed merge of the Word document. This scenario confirms that the service works as expected, and that the hit count (i.e. number of calls) is now 1, instead of 24 as before.

- All the other visible functions are linked to business functions that have already been optimized during the first test scenario analysis.

C.3 Complex SQL request

C.3.a Diagnosis

The call graph for `ComplexRequest` is shown in Figure 6-56.

It seems that the vast majority of execution time is spent in functions linked to the SQL Server ADO.NET provider, and not in .NET code that is purely related to the PROFl application tier.

In this case, the calling code is not the problem, and only the request has a performance problem. SQL optimization is a subject of its own and outside of the scope of this book (see HTTP://WWW.SIMPLE-TALK.COM/SQL/PERFORMANCE/ for more information), but we will still take the opportunity to give a few hints on how to integrate SQL analysis into standard profiling.

Figure 6-56: Call graph for the ComplexRequest method.

C.3.b   A poor man's SQL profiler

As a preliminary remark, most profilers will not specifically process SQL activities. In this case, a solution is to look for the time spent in SQLCommand.ExecuteReader functions, for example, but this is clearly a very limited approach.

- We should also take into account ExecuteNonQuery, ExecuteScalar and ExecuteXmlReader, and summing the times would have to be a manual operation.

- The SqlDataAdapter instances used to fill the datasets should be treated in a differentiated manner, in order to get complete results.

- A major limitation would be that the SQL requests cannot be segregated: we would only obtain the time for executing them in general.

- All these problems will be multiplied by the number of ADO.NET providers in the case of an application using multiple databases.

The simplest way to solve these difficulties is to create an additional layer of code, through which all the SQL commands will go, and add instrumentation capabilities to this layer. For example, the code shown in Listing 6-65 will log all the SQL execution requests together with their execution time, in a dedicated category called "SQL" in the traces.

```
public static SqlDataReader ExecuteReader(string Request, SqlParameter[]
Parameters)
{
    SqlConnection Conn = new SqlConnection(ConfigurationManager.ConnectionStrings
                    ["DBConnexion"].ConnectionString);
    SqlCommand Command = new SqlCommand(Request, Conn);
    Command.Parameters.AddRange(Parameters);
    Conn.Open();
    try
    {
        Stopwatch Chrono = Stopwatch.StartNew();
        SqlDataReader Reader = Command.ExecuteReader(CommandBehavior.
                    CloseConnection);
        Chrono.Stop();
        Trace.WriteLine(string.Format("Request {0} executed in {1} ms", Request,
                    Chrono.ElapsedMilliseconds), "SQL");
        return Reader;
    }
    catch
    {
        Trace.WriteLine(string.Format("Error when executing request {0}", Request),
                    "SQL");
        throw;
    }
}
```

Listing 6-65

C.3.c   SQL capabilities of Profilers

ANTS Performance Profiler is one of the rare affordable tools that specifically profiles SQL requests, as well as file I/O. The results of SQL profiling are shown in Figure 6-57.

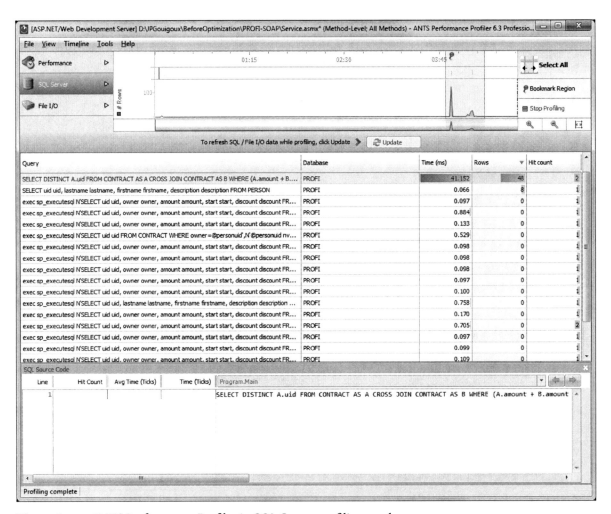

Figure 6-57: ANTS Performance Profiler in SQL Server profiling mode.

This example enables us to find the complex SQL request that we had placed inside PROF1 to show the case of a heavy SQL operation. The code-level profiling would also have shown a slow .NET operation, but this approach, with a clear separation between .NET and SQL is very useful when profiling applications that have a heavy use of databases (which basically means all management applications).

ANTS Performance Profiler also has an I/O profiling function that can retrieve results such as those shown in Figure 6-58.

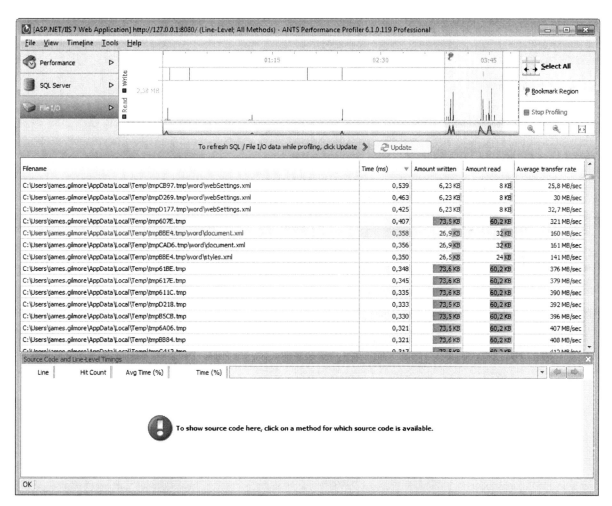

Figure 6-58: ANTS Performance Profiler in I/O profiling mode.

Again, it is generally interesting to separate I/O from the code metrics. In the example above, we could add up all the times spent in files from the TEMP directory, and draw the appropriate conclusions. For example, lots of small files could lead us to execute the corresponding algorithms in memory instead, which would bring more performance while still being sustainable in terms of resource consumption.

D   Running scenarios under load

D.1   Concepts

As promised in Section B.5.g, *The limits of the cache approach*, we are now going to try and validate the performance improvements that have been realized on unit scenarios under load. To do so, we are going to simulate several clients communicating with the server during the profiling operations.

It is extremely rare for a performance improvement to a single scenario not to result in an improvement on a set of parallel heterogeneous scenarios. However, a code modification may improve a given resource but degrade another one. This is typically the case when a cache is not correctly implemented, and the CPU savings result in a huge amount of memory consumption. Generally speaking, though, with a well-balanced code modification, what is true for a unique call will be true for multiple calls. As a corollary, a drop in a test scenario's execution time will almost always lead to an improvement of the server capacity in terms of the number of clients that can be served together.

We have explained several times that a profiling operation must be carried out with a stable reference scenario in order to obtain comparable metrics. But that does not mean an additional test under load should not be executed after each profiling campaign, in order to validate improvements in a more realistic use case. To do so, we are going to use a stress tool.

D.2   Caveat

The goal of this part of the book is only to provide you with tools so that you can carry out load tests after a profiling campaign. We are not going to start another analysis and optimization step using the results of the stress tests. Indeed, it is extremely rare that simple code errors are made visible by a stress test without having been seen in unit tests. In fact, I have never seen it happen in more than ten years in my developer / software architect job. This means the stress tests are basically there to confirm the performance improvement on load scenarios, and show what ratio can be obtained in real life. A 1:2 ratio in unit execution time will sometimes amount to only a 3:4 ratio under massive load. By contrast, it may sometimes bring a ratio of 1:5 or more under the same context. Only tests will tell.

A stress test may show performance problems that a profiling session using a single client does not show, but this is rarely due to the kind of programming errors we are looking for when profiling. Concurrency issues may come to light, and memory overconsumption will be more obvious under stress. But an experienced developer with a critical eye on memory use has a good chance of spotting these in a unit test scenario. And if this overconsumption is too light to be detected under normal load, we are venturing into tuning, and this is not our aim.

D.3   Introducing WebLOAD

Lots of different tools exist to perform web server load tests. Visual Studio, JMeter, OpenSTA and Selenium are such applications, but in my humble opinion, two utilities stand out of the crowd, namely SOAPUI and RadView's WebLOAD. We are going to use the latter in our examples. Although it has become a commercial tool, a free version still exists at HTTP://WWW.WEBLOAD.ORG/.

The choice of WebLOAD is dictated by simplicity. The recorder is easy to configure, as is the load ramp. The commercial version provides a metrics analysis tool that is quite useful. SOAPUI is more oriented towards pure scenario replay, and its management of load tests is rudimentary, but it lets the user set the parameters with more details. The other tools that have been cited are also good ones, but they take longer to get used to. In short, WebLOAD is to stress test managers what ANTS Performance Profiler is to profilers: a good compromise in a non-expert approach, which is why it was chosen for this book.

Using WebLOAD involves three steps, each of them linked to a given executable in the software suite from RadView.

- **WebLOAD IDE** lets the user create test scenarios in the form of recorded HTTP requests, together with a script language that can set parameters in these requests, in order to simulate different users during a stress test. Take the example of a web method that needs a parameter that will become a unique identifier in the database. We cannot send this value hard-coded in the WebLOAD script, otherwise only the first call will work, and all the following ones will result in an exception, thus altering the metrics.

- **WebLOAD Console** creates stress campaigns by mixing several scripts from WebLOAD IDE, and executing them in parallel through injectors that simulate clients' behavior. These injectors can be dispatched on several machines to obtain high server loads without being limited by the power of the injector itself.

- **WebLOAD Analytics** allows the user to group the metrics resulting from the previous module into aggregated reports. This module is supposed to have an intelligent approach that will help a non-expert to spot errors, but this seems quite exaggerated. Reports only signal, through a different color, the performance counters for which a parameterized threshold has been reached, and do not really offer any explanation.

These three steps are going to be shown below on the PROFI sample application.

D.4   Recording scenarios

First, we have to record the HTTP requests that are sent to the server during our test scenarios. Indeed, WebLOAD injectors send HTTP content directly to simulate a client's activity. Thus, we have to start by recording this content when playing the client scenarios on which we have based our profiling activity.

The simplest way of doing this is to use the integrated recorder of WebLOAD IDE. However, we have to configure the software prior to recording. When running WebLOAD IDE, the dialog in Figure 6-59 appears.

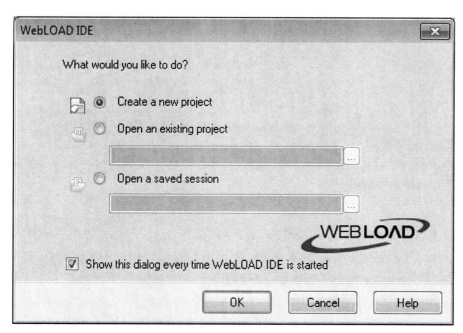

Figure 6-59: WebLOAD IDE Welcome screen.

The **Create a new project** option brings us to the main window of WebLOAD IDE, which should look similar to Figure 6-60.

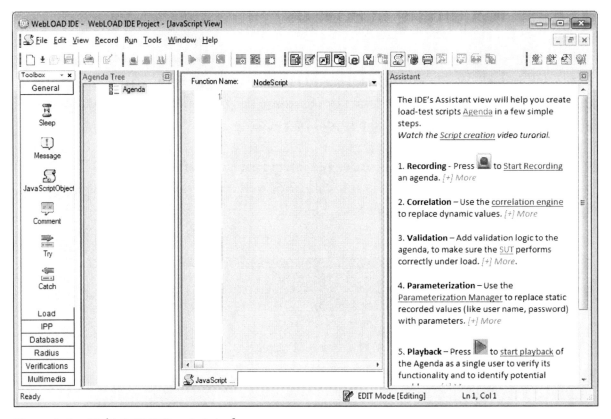

Figure 6-60: WebLOAD IDE main interface.

The wizard in the right-hand pane shows the steps to create a load scenario. We are not going to go into this in much detail, since the aim is not to master WebLOAD, but to show how it can be used to validate the results of a profiling campaign.

Before starting the actual recording, we have to configure two options to be able to record HTTP exchanges. WebLOAD works by placing a recording proxy between client and server. But this product is typically used with Internet browsers as a client, so we have to change a few things. First, we go to the **Tools** menu and choose **Recording and script generation options**, which brings up the **Options** dialog box shown in Figure 6-61.

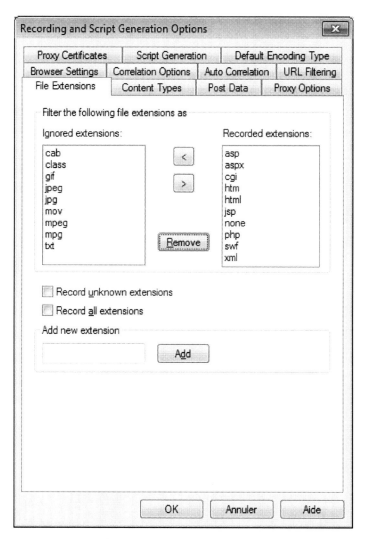

Figure 6-61: WebLOAD IDE File Extensions Options dialog box.

For our application, we need to support `.asmx` extensions, so we enter this in the text-box under **Add new extension**, and click **Add**. We must then send this extension to the right-hand-side list in order for the web services to be taken into account by the recording service. We can safely ignore the other extensions. After modification, the **File Extensions** tab should look as in Figure 6-62.

431

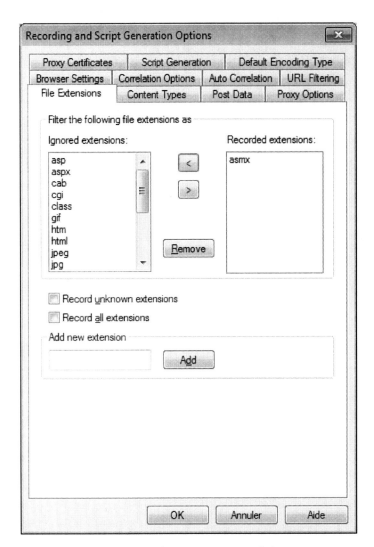

Figure 6-62: Selecting only `asmx` as a recorded extension.

An even simpler solution, if the machine is dedicated to testing, is simply to select the
Record all extensions option.

We then go to the following tab, **Content Types**. Again, we can use the easy way by selecting **Record all types**, or be a little more elegant and register **text/xml**, since we are recording SOAP calls. The result is shown in Figure 6-63.

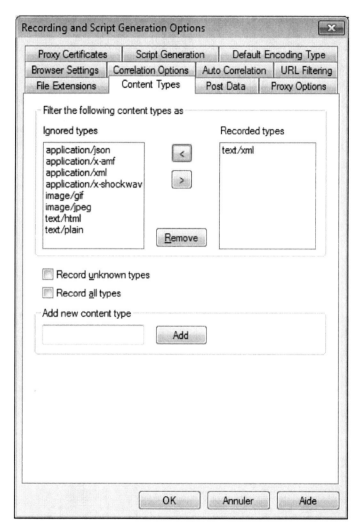

Figure 6-63: Selecting only text/xml in the WebLOAD IDE Content Types Options dialog box.

A third tab needs our attention, namely **Browser Settings**. As we have explained, our client will not be a simple web browser, but rather the PROFI-WIN executable process.

Therefore we select the **Other browser** option, and point it to **PROFI-WIN.exe**, as shown in Figure 6-64.

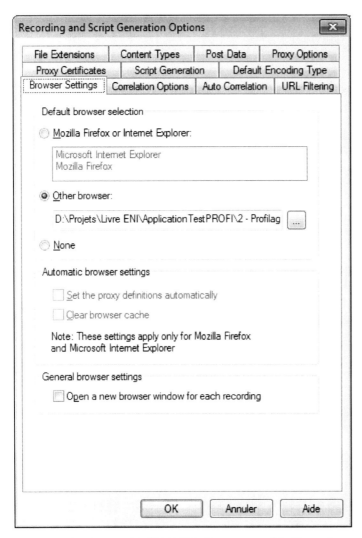

Figure 6-64: Setting PROFI-WIN client executable file as the recorded browser in WebLOAD IDE Browser Settings Options dialog box.

We finish with a look at the **Proxy Options** tab. We are not going to make any changes there, but just read the port number of the recording proxy to which our application should point. The display is more or less like Figure 6-65, with possible variations depending on the context.

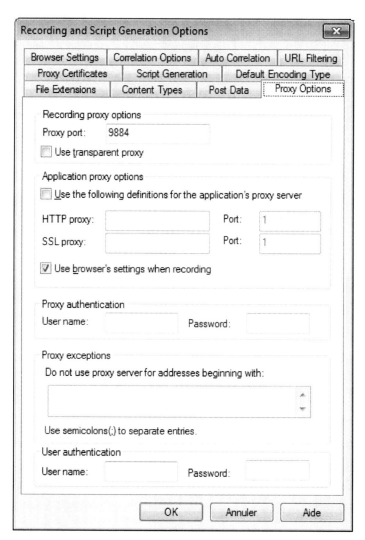

Figure 6-65: WebLOAD IDE Proxy Options dialog box.

We are then going to modify the source code of PROFI so that each of the controllers uses this proxy. Be careful not to forget any of the three, otherwise we will only record part of the scenario. The two lines about proxy should be added into the initialization functions for the client (`Controller` classes), as shown in Listing 6-66.

```
public bool Initialize()
{
    try
    {
        _Client = new Stub.Service();
        _Client.Url = ConfigurationManager.AppSettings["PROFI:Stubs:BaseURL"] +
                    "Service.asmx";
        _Client.Proxy = new System.Net.WebProxy("localhost", 9884);
        _Client.Proxy.Credentials = System.Net.CredentialCache.DefaultCredentials;
        return true;
    }
    catch
    {
        return false;
    }
}
```
Listing 6-66

We could have written code to use the default proxy, since WebLOAD changes it on the fly, but the code in Listing 6-66 is more explicit, which is hopefully clearer.

No duplicated code

It would also have been possible to make this a single operation, by declaring the proxy parameters in the <system.net> *section of the client configuration file. Of course, this is what we would do in a professional application. However, it seemed interesting to show that this could also be done in the code, since profiling sometimes needs quick and localized context changes.*

A final change has to be made to the client configuration file. Indeed, the profiling will be done using IIS, but WebLOAD does not support `localhost` addresses, because the loopback network cannot be recorded. Thus we need to use the actual machine name or the IP address in the `PROFI:Stubs:BaseURL` setting, as shown in Listing 6-67.

```
<appSettings>
  <add key="PROFI:Proxy:URL" value=""/>
  <add key="PROFI:Proxy:AuthenticationMode" value="none"/>
  <add key="PROFI:Proxy:Login" value=""/>
  <add key="PROFI:Proxy:Password" value=""/>
  <add key="PROFI:Bus:InitialMessage" value="INIT"/>
  <add key="PROFI:Stubs:BaseURL" value="http://192.168.1.10/PROFI-IIS/"/>
  <add key="PROFI:Authentication:Mode" value="LoginForm"/>
</appSettings>
```

Listing 6-67

Once all of these parameters are set, we can finally run the recording of the first test scenario, by recompiling the four client modules of PROFI with TEST1 as a build option, and clicking **Start recording** in the **Record** menu. Once the application has finished, we stop the recording, and the display should contain a script roughly similar to the one shown in Figure 6-66 (the wizard has been hidden to provide a better view of the script).

This script allows us to replay the method chains on the server without needing the PROFI-WIN client any longer. We record it under the name scenario1.wlp, and do the exact same operation to create scenario2.wlp, which corresponds to the build option TEST2 in PROFI-WIN.

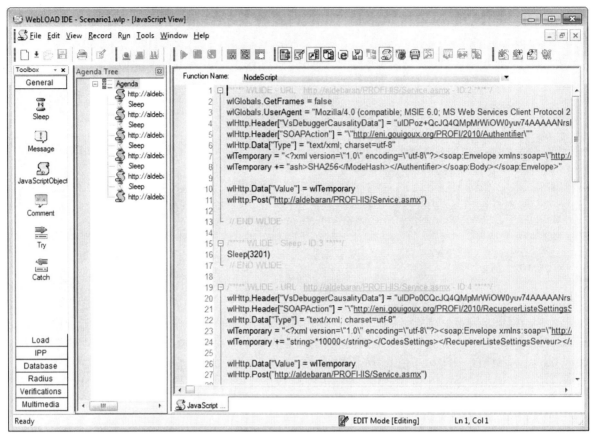

Figure 6-66: Script generated by WebLOAD after recording scenario TEST1.

VsDebuggerCausalityData

This HTTP header (which appears in the script) is used for remote debugging. It was sent because the example has been run from the **PROFI-WIN.vshost.exe** *process, which is initialized by Visual Studio for debugging (this is not a problem for WebLOAD, even if* **PROFI-WIN.exe** *was the file set as navigation client). We can safely remove this header from the script. In fact, we should do so, because it is known to become quite heavy and can cause problems. If we wish to block this behavior in the application, so as not to have to remove all instances of the header by hand next time we record a scenario, we can add the content of Listing 6-68 to the application configuration file.*

```
<configuration>
  <system.diagnostics>
    <switches>
      <add name="Remote.Disable" value="1" />
    </switches>
  </system.diagnostics>
</configuration>
```

Listing 6-68

D.5   Creating the load session

The two scripts that correspond to the test scenarios are now generated, so we can simulate a load session using them. In some cases it can be useful to create stress tests based on one scenario. However, in general, we want to create something as realistic as possible, and thus we should create a session based on several scenarios in accordance with the uses that different users will make of the applications. When starting WebLOAD Console, a dialog is displayed (Figure 6-67). By default, it offers to use a wizard to create the template, and this is what we are going to do.

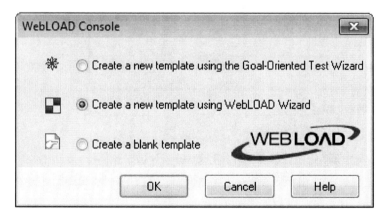

Figure 6-67: WebLOAD Console start-up screen.

The first screen of the wizard is a simple welcome screen, but it describes well what we are going to create, so I have included it in Figure 6-68.

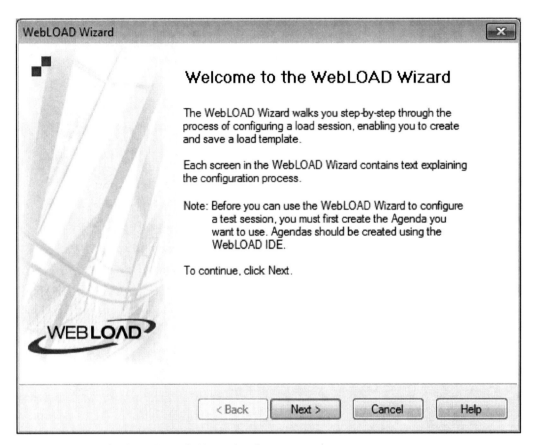

Figure 6-68: WebLOAD Console Wizard welcome screen.

In the second step (Figure 6-69), we choose a **Mix of Agendas**, which will allow us to use several scenarios. The result will be more realistic, since not all the users of an application use it in exactly the same way, depending on their respective roles.

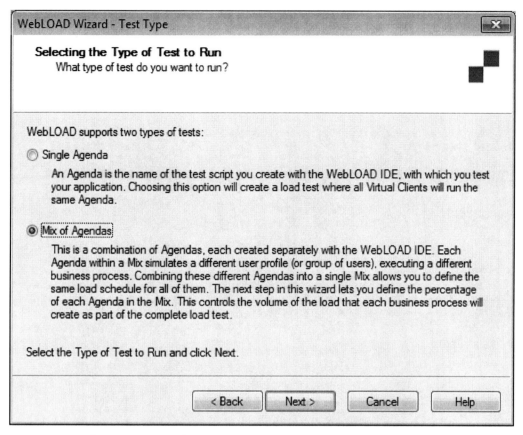

Figure 6-69: Choosing a type of test in the WebLOAD Console Wizard.

Since we had not previously created a mix of agendas, which is a group of scenarios that have been assigned relative weights, we are going to generate it from the wizard. But before moving to the next step, we will specify statistics for our template by clicking **Measurements Manager** (see Figure 6-70).

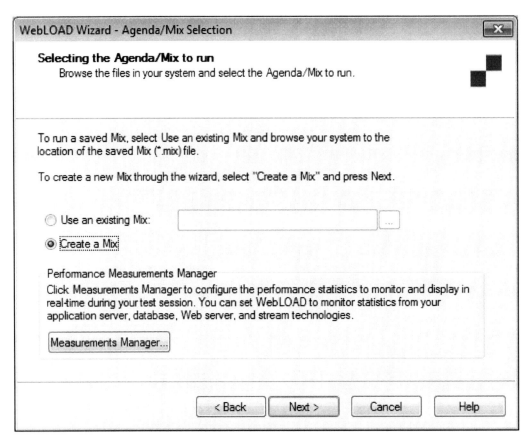

Figure 6-70: Selecting agendas to run in the WebLOAD Console Wizard.

The Measurements Manager is a module that allows us to choose the Windows counters we wish to record when playing the stress test. It is highly recommended, after carefully selecting the performance counters, to create an export of this list, in order to avoid having to re-create it next time we create a template.

The Manager initially looks like Figure 6-71.

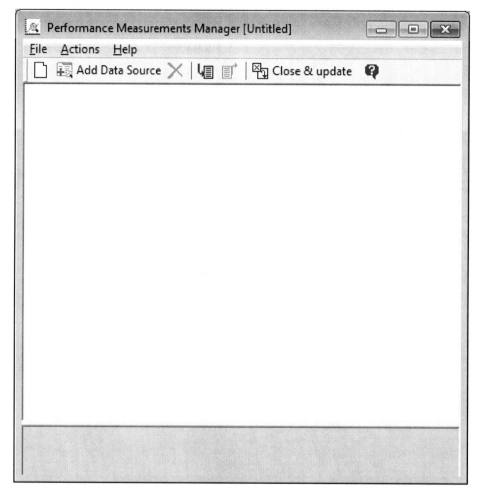

Figure 6-71: The Performance Measurements Manager dialog in the WebLOAD Console Wizard.

Add Data Source will display a predefined list in which we will choose the indicators we want to follow. WebLOAD offers the Windows counters, but also several specific counters (such as JMS, SNMP, JBoss and WebSphere) that will be very welcome to professionals. Figure 6-72 shows a few of them.

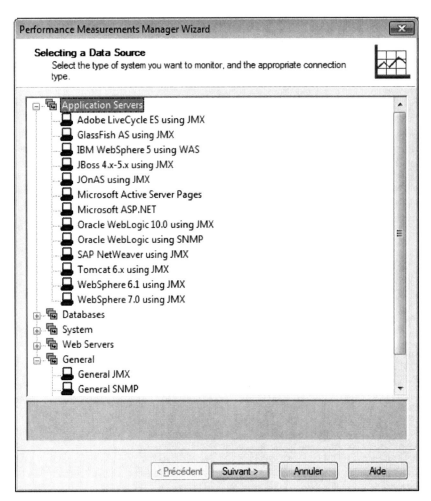

Figure 6-72: List of available data sources in the WebLOAD Console Wizard.

When choosing a type of counter, the wizard then gives us the choice of the machine on which to collect the associated metrics, and the possibility to refine the options. Once the choice has been made, we are back in the Measurements Manager and can add another one, not forgetting to export our selection before clicking **Close and Update** to return to the main wizard. Figure 6-73 shows my selection of counters.

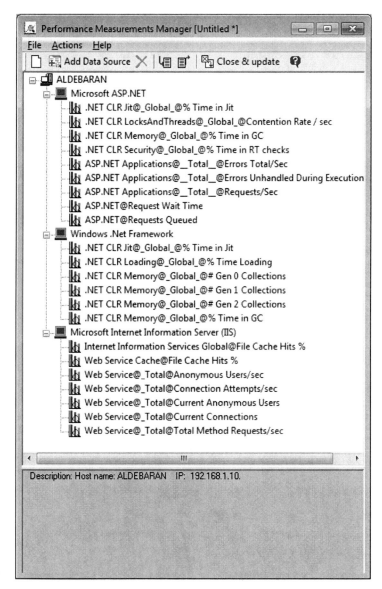

Figure 6-73: A selection of data sources in the WebLOAD Console Wizard.

The following step of the wizard consists of adding agendas and dividing them up by percent. For example, Figure 6-74 shows we have decided that 60% of the PROFl users execute Scenario 1, while 40% use Scenario 2. This is obviously an arbitrary choice on a

445

sample application. On real-life software, it can be interesting to survey the use of the software or ask our customers about this distribution. This parameter can also be saved, in order to avoid re-creating it for another load template, which can be handy if dozens of scenarios with complex percentages are used.

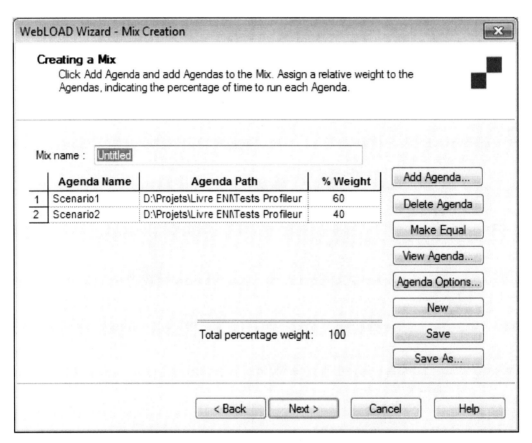

Figure 6-74: Establishing the mix of agendas in the WebLOAD Console Wizard.

The next step is used to allocate load machines (servers) and probing client machines (injectors). In our case, we will use the same machine, but using different names in order to trick WebLOAD into thinking they are different (see Figure 6-75).

By default, WebLOAD does not accept that a machine can be an injector and a target server at the same time. Indeed, this will mean competition for resources, and the supported load will not be the same as if the server was independent. In the example used for this book, the trial version was used and only allowed five virtual clients, so this was not really a problem (an injector can handle hundreds of clients). It is obviously bad practice in an industrial context, but, with only one physical machine available, one sometimes has to resort to some tricks. We can use the counters to validate that the impact of this remains small.

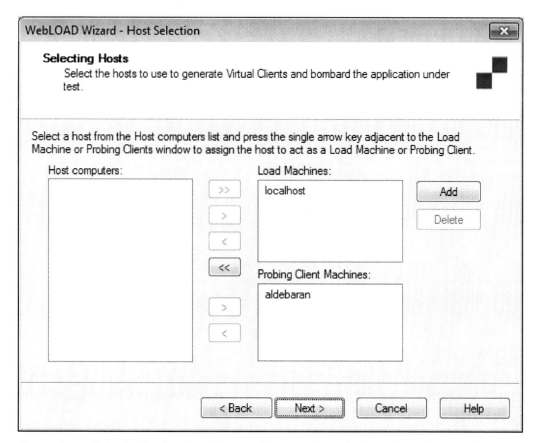

Figure 6-75: Selecting load and probing machines in the WebLOAD Console Wizard.

Once this step is finished, we are going to define the loading itself (see Figure 6-76).

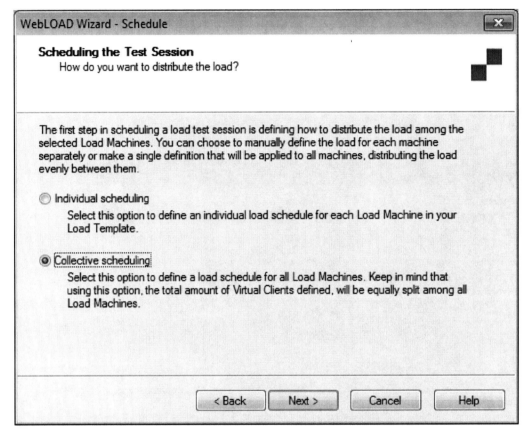

Figure 6-76: Scheduling the test session in the WebLOAD Console Wizard.

We choose the **Collective scheduling** option which, in fact, does not change anything since we are using a single machine. For the content of this scheduling, we are not going to use the default mode, but rather change it by clicking **Load Profiler** (on the right-hand side in Figure 6-77).

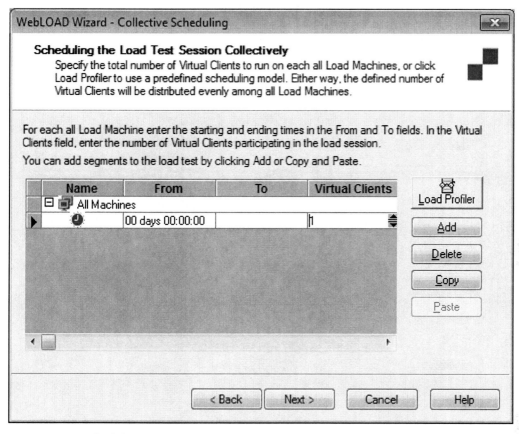

Figure 6-77: Scheduling options in the WebLOAD Console Wizard.

We select a ramp that will progressively increase from one to five users in two minutes, then keep a plateau for four minutes, and finally decrease back to one user in the remaining two minutes. Such a progressive increase is necessary to avoid creating an unrealistic situation on the server. In no company will all the employees start working at exactly the same second, and this is lucky, since most application servers would burst under this sudden load.

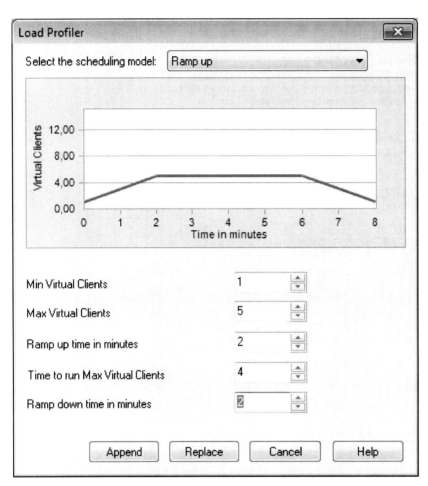

Figure 6-78: Setting a ramp for the load session in the WebLOAD Console Wizard.

Clicking **Replace** will bring us back to the load test plan definition, and the next step is the end of the wizard, with an option to run the test immediately (see Figure 6-79).

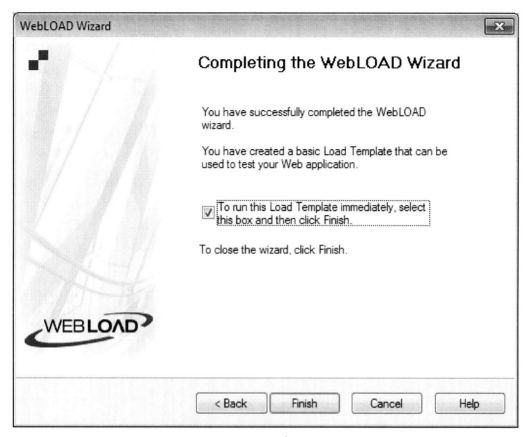

Figure 6-79: Final wizard screen in the WebLOAD Console Wizard.

We should then have a little patience and try to interfere as little as possible with the machine. After a few minutes (in our case) or a few hours (in a more realistic setup), we will obtain our first metrics and a graph that summarizes the results of the test, as in Figure 6-80.

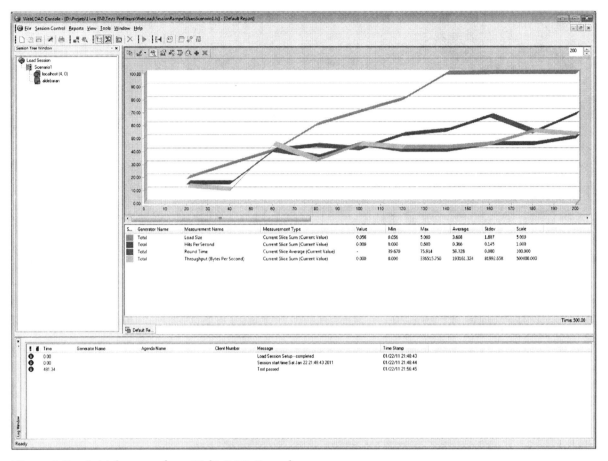

Figure 6-80: Initial reports from WebLOAD Console.

D.6 Analysis of the WebLOAD results

A dialog should appear to lead us to the third module of WebLOAD, the Analytics module, in order to analyze the results in more detail. Accepting this brings up a display that should be similar to Figure 6-81.

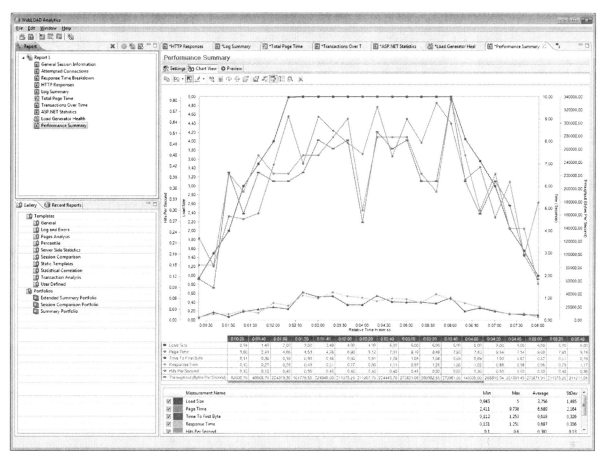

Figure 6-81: WebLOAD Analytics main interface.

As stated above, we are not going to start another round of analysis and optimization using these metrics. I simply want to show what such a tool can offer in terms of validation of the performance improvements through a more realistic scenario. Generally speaking, running load and stress tests should be reserved for a second round of profiling, after a first pass has been made with single-user profiling. Indeed, we should always start with the bigger bottlenecks, and these are often apparent without stressing the application. If there aren't any, it is indeed time to stress the server to identify where it fails in terms of performance.

D.7 Mixing WebLOAD and ANTS Performance Profiler

Connecting the load generator, which becomes the client, to a profiler positioned in front of the IIS server in order to supplement the load generator metrics with those of the profiler can be an interesting exercise. Such a setup may look a bit overloaded, but it is definitely feasible.

To start with, we open ANTS Performance Profiler and configure it as in Figure 6-82.

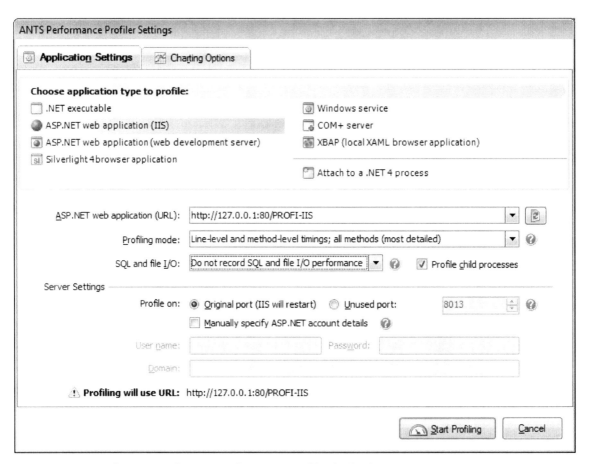

Figure 6-82: Configuration of ANTS Performance Profiler for load tests.

A sensitive setup

I recommend that you use exactly the same settings as in Figure 6-82. Profilers, as well as load generators, are sensitive tools and parameterizing them, which is very closely related to the network configuration, can sometimes be a little tricky.

Despite the two applications working very closely to the system, the combination works fine, and we obtain our metrics in parallel during the execution of the agenda, as shown in Figure 6-83.

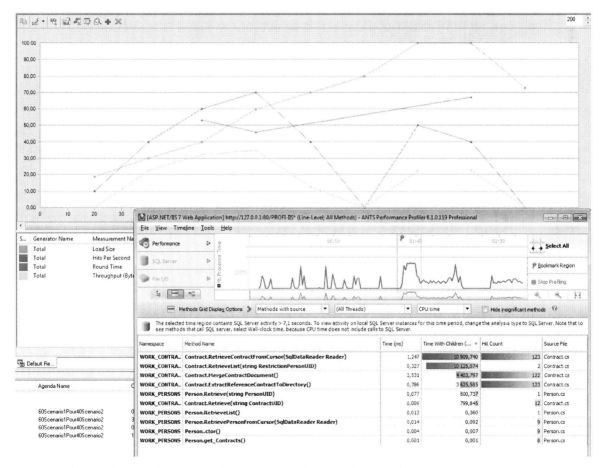

Figure 6-83: Working with ANTS Performance Profiler and WebLOAD at the same time.

However, there are a few things to note.

- Other than using the actual wall time, it is impossible to aggregate the counters coming from both applications, which makes it difficult to use the results together.

- On a small-to-average machine, the profiler and stress-generator can take a fair amount of CPU and RAM, and performance indicators will then be a little distorted. But profilers always have an impact anyway, and at the moment they cannot work remotely.

- We have simulated sets of scenarios containing a connection to the application as well as a few interactions. Had we decided to be more realistic, we would have created a connection scenario and given it 10 percent or less of the agenda. This would better reflect an actual use of the application, since no user would reconnect to the application every minute. But this would cause a problem for the remaining 90 percent, which would have to work without authentication. Recording long scenarios (for example, half a working day) to get round this is quite a complex solution. A simpler solution could be to create a transparent authentication plug-in just for our tests.

D.8   Correction of the Random problem

Profiling under load also helped us to see a design error that was located too deep in the stack to be seen in unit test scenarios. This is not very common, but this time, the path seen as the "hottest" by the profiler leads directly to the code error (see Figure 6-84): the `System.Random` constructor is called half a million times!

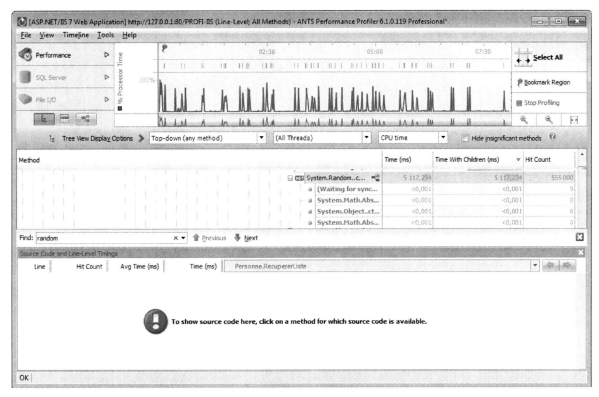

Figure 6-84: Observing the `System.Random` problem in profiler results.

A quick look at the code shows the source of the problem (see Listing 6-69).

```
Dictionary<double, SettingMode> flagsDictionary = new Dictionary<double,
SettingMode>();
for (int index = 0; index < settingValue; index++)
{
    Random engine = new Random(index);
    flagsDictionary.Add(engine.NextDouble(), (SettingMode)engine.Next(8));
}
```

Listing 6-69

The developer of this piece of code certainly thought that generating an instance of System.Random and calling the function Next formed a single operation. This is not so, and there is a good reason why .NET separates these two operations: the instantiation initiates the engine (in particular the seed the Random is based on), while the calls to Next use the engine to extract random values. Each random value uses the previous one to add entropy. The class is in charge of this, in order to reduce the predictability of the values generated.

The code must be modified as shown in Listing 6-70, so that the class is only instantiated once. While we are at it, we use the millisecond value of the current time to initiate the seed, in order to add some more entropy (the original code used the index of the loop, which was much more deterministic).

```
Dictionary<double, SettingMode> flagsDictionary = new Dictionary<double,
                 SettingMode>();
Random engine = new Random(DateTime.Now.Millisecond);
for (int index = 0; index < settingValue; index++)
{
    flagsDictionary.Add(engine.NextDouble(), (SettingMode)engine.Next(8));
}
```

Listing 6-70

Again, this kind of mistake can look like it would never happen in an industrial application, but it is only obvious here because the code has been compressed into four lines in order to keep the sample application small. In a more complex methods stack, where function responsibilities are more diluted, the two parts (the loop and the random number use) of this functionality can be very far from each other. Thus, the problem will be more difficult to spot than in PROFI. Of course, part of the problem still lies in the lack of proper developer training, which is the source of this kind of error.

D.9   Final results analysis

The results obtained by a profiler when scenarios are played with a load simulation led to a deeper understanding of our sample application.

First, the load tester is very efficient at removing noise in the metrics: we only see web methods and functions that actually correspond to an important server activity, which helps us in analyzing the list of functions more quickly.

Then the hit counts give a more realistic idea of what happens on the server. This is a big change: until now, the only analysis we had used them in was checking that there was a reason for their value being higher than one, should the case arise.

The evolution of the profiler graph compared to the load manager graph allows us to validate the behavior of the application under stress. If we add the CPU counter on the load generator, we have another way, even if it is very imprecise, of putting the two graphs in parallel.

Finally, if we look back at Section B.5.c, *Complexity of the settings calculation*, we notice that the function `RetrieveContractFromCursor` is still the longest one. But, comparatively, optimizing the function `RetrieveList` is now almost as important.

This means that profiling under load can, in some cases, alter the order of priority in which functions should be optimized. On several occasions we have seen that it is essential to give priority to significant gains, where a short analysis will bring large improvements. Of course this depends on the relative amount of time spent executing different functions.

In consequence, having a mix of scenarios as close as possible to the actual use of the software will give us more precision in the choice of which function should be optimized first. The main risk of an analysis based on unit scenarios is that satisfying one user may lead to frustration of many others. On the contrary, using the right mix of scenarios will give a globally satisfying result, even if not optimal for each of the uses. Figures 6-85 and 6-86 show the two profiling sessions again, in single execution mode and under stress respectively. This helps us to see the difference in the long functions distribution.

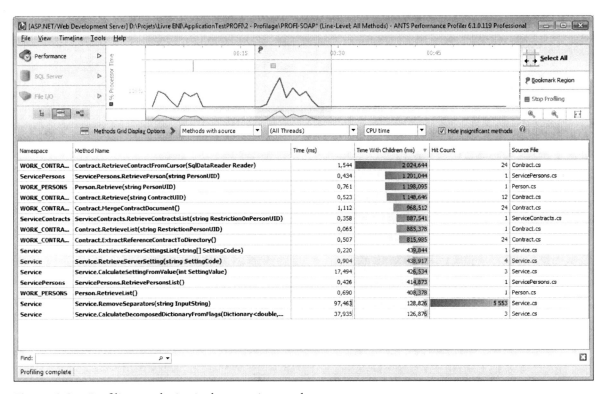

Figure 6-85: Profiling results in single execution mode.

Figure 6-86, which corresponds to scenarios under load, plainly shows a more clear-cut distribution.

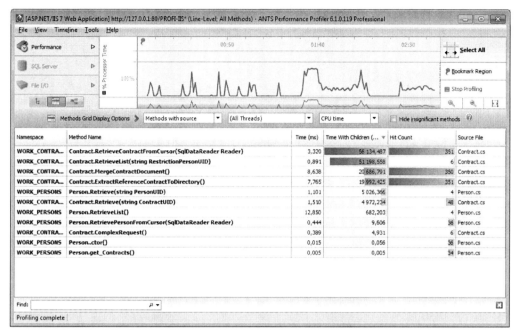

Figure 6-86: Profiling results in an execution of the server under stress.

In conclusion, this kind of analysis under stress, even if it is not traditionally seen as part of profiling, is quite helpful and reveals the actual level of performance obtained. If it is not possible to carry out this type of test throughout the optimization process, it should, at the very least, be done once at the end of each campaign.

Quick optimizations

Sometimes, the time necessary to execute such stress scenarios can get in the way of the quick optimization process I have been talking about since the beginning of this book. On code improvements that need half an hour of analysis and ten minutes of actual programming, it is difficult (except if we have large resources) to prepare and run tests that can span hours to validate the impact. In addition, several hours are needed on industrial applications to simulate a satisfying ramp with multiple servers. For a full explanation of stress and load testing, see .NET Performance Testing and Optimization – The Complete Guide by Paul Glavich and Chris Farrell (Simple Talk Publishing, 2010).

461

D.10   Comparison with the non-optimized server

D.10.a   Collecting results

To complete the first part of the analysis above, we replay the ramp, in conditions as similar as possible, on servers with and without optimization. To do so, we use the same setup with 60% Scenario 1 and 40% Scenario 2, and run the tests in a neutral context (no Internet connection, no antivirus, and no other foreground or background applications).

In order for the non-optimized mode to work correctly, we will have to record our WebLOAD sessions again, starting from the beginning, namely the automated client scenarios. Indeed, optimizations have led us to modify web service signatures (e.g. when grouping settings retrieval operations) and it is thus necessary to modify the HTTP WebLOAD scripts accordingly.

If we forget to update the scenario together with the server, here are the kinds of results that await us. We see in Figure 6-87 red bars that represent all the exceptions we would receive. And of course, it is impossible to judge the performance of a web server when the methods do not actually execute but simply send back errors.

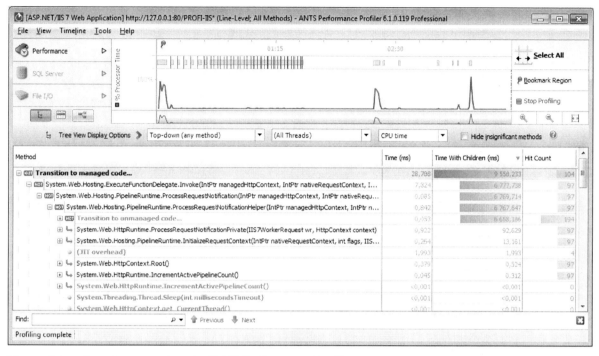

Figure 6-87: Showing exceptions in ANTS Performance Profiler.

Republishing

Do not forget, when switching from one version to another, not just to recompile, but also to republish the website we are using as profiling target.

Having run the two studies we obtain the following results. Figures 6-88 and 6-89 show the WebLOAD summary graph and the ANTS Performance Profiler metrics for an optimized server. Figures 6-90 and 6-91 show the same graphs, but with a load scenarios mix played on the original code before optimization.

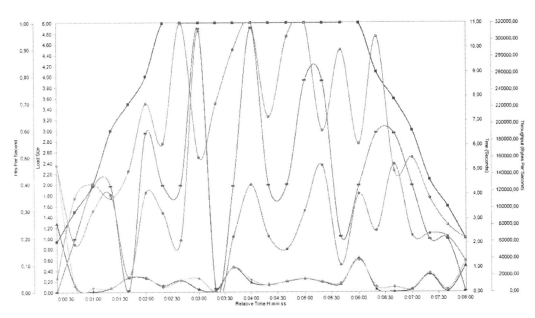

Figure 6-88: WebLOAD Analytics results for a load on optimized code.

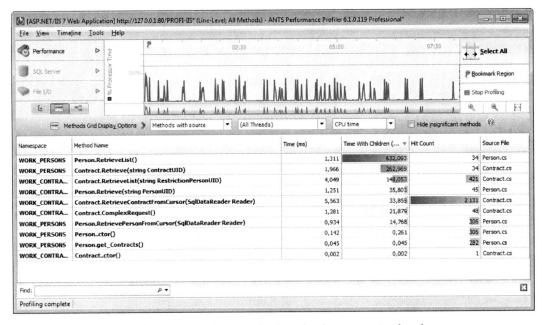

Figure 6-89: ANTS Performance Profiler results for a load on optimized code.

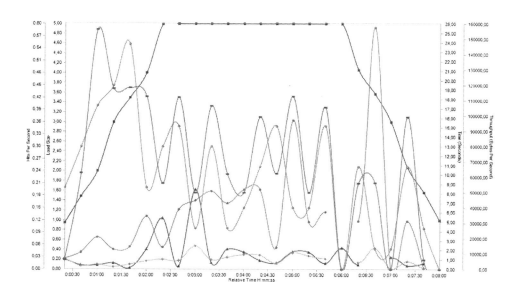

Figure 6-90: WebLOAD Analytics results for a load on non-optimized code.

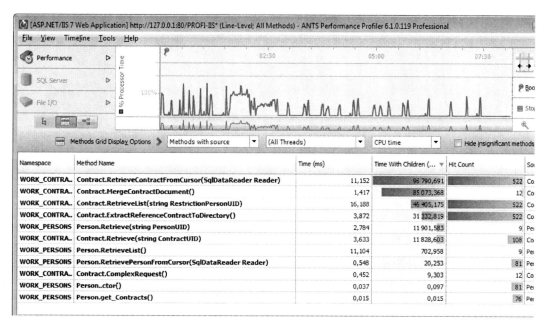

Figure 6-91: ANTS Performance Profiler results for a load on non-optimized code.

D.10.b WebLOAD results comparison

What kind of conclusion can we draw from these graphs?

Starting with the WebLOAD graphs, at first glance, they seem equally unstable, with peaks on most of the metrics. However, there is a huge difference between the optimized server and the one based on the original code. Indeed, the scale of the graphs (which is set automatically) is not the same in the two sessions.

Let us look at the throughput curve first (this can be roughly defined as the aggregate amount of data going in and out of the server against time; in short, the mass of data it can process and deliver under load). On the graph for a non-optimized server (Figure 6-92), the maximum is 160,000 bytes per second.

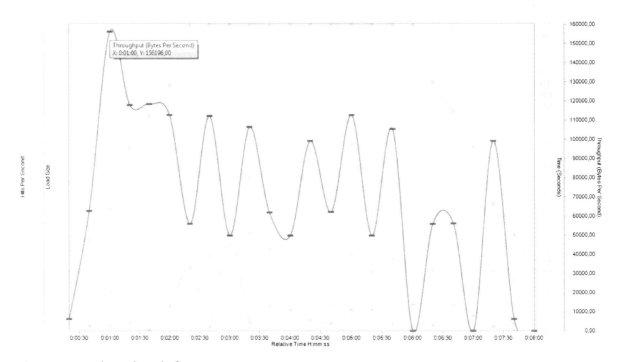

Figure 6-92: Throughput before optimization.

If we look at the optimized version, however, the curve looks quite similar, but in fact the throughput is twice as good, since the scale is now set to the maximum at 320,000 bytes per second! (See Figure 6-93.)

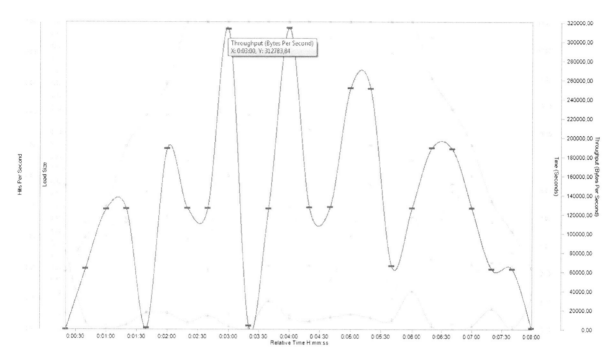

Figure 6-93: Throughput after optimization.

If we now compare the curves for request output time (this metric basically corresponds to the server's reactivity, namely its speed for processing a single call), the same observation can be made on the scale. Indeed, the high point on the graph without optimization (Figure 6-94) is 26 seconds.

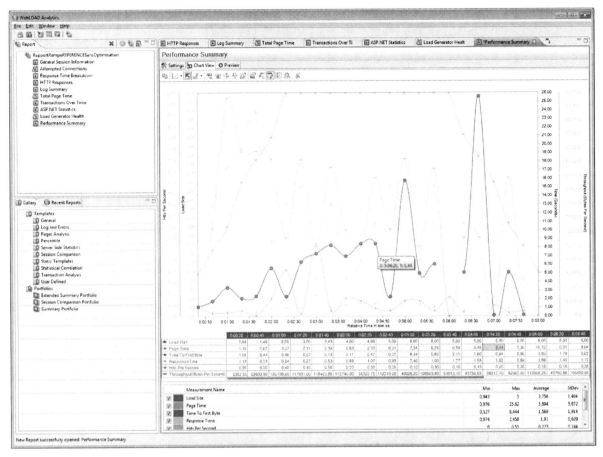

Figure 6-94: Request output time before optimization.

On the other hand, the high point on the graph showing the results for the optimized server (Figure 6-95) is only 11 seconds, which is much better.

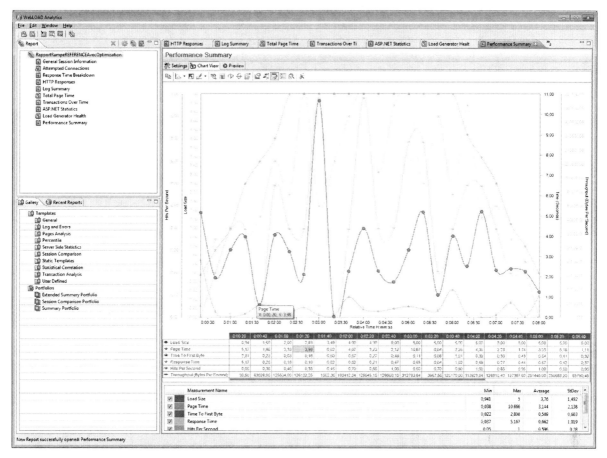

Figure 6-95: Request output time after optimization.

Again, the graphs look roughly similar, whereas they actually show very different values, with processing times on average 2.5 times lower after optimization.

What about fixing the scales?

Unfortunately, WebLOAD does not allow us to explicitly specify the graph scales. But it is possible to export results in raw format in order to create our own reports.

D.10.c   ANTS Performance Profiler results comparison

We could stop at comparing WebLOAD graphs: they already largely justify the optimizations that have been done on the server side. But it is still interesting to take a look at what ANTS Performance Profiler shows.

It goes without saying that numerical results are excellent: 97 seconds spent in the longest function without optimization dropped to only 632ms for the longest one after optimization. But those are only isolated measurements. They will create an overall improvement in the end, but it is more interesting to take a look at metrics at a higher level.

To do so, we compare the CPU graph before (top) and after (bottom) optimization. The result is shown in Figure 6-96.

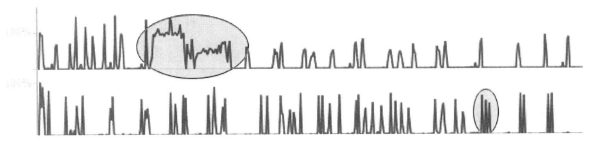

Figure 6-96: Comparing CPU use before and after optimization.

We do not see much difference in terms of CPU peaks: they are as numerous and, as we explained in the first part of the book, it is quite normal for CPU use to go up to 80%, provided that it is for limited periods. This is the case for most of the parts of the scenario, except at the end of the first quarter in non-optimized mode (see the bubble in the top left of Figure 6-96). We clearly see a plateau that corresponds to an intensive and sustained use of resources.

Thus, optimization also has an effect on resource consumption: in optimized mode, even if some clients were running their scenarios in very close succession, the peaks were close but did not form a plateau (see, for example, the bubble in the bottom right). By contrast, in non-optimized mode, when several clients request a server operation at precisely the same time, the application will use all available resources.

This might be even more important than the results from WebLOAD. Indeed, we are far from a real stress test here: the evaluation version of WebLOAD we are using is limited to a ramp of five simultaneous virtual clients. Obviously such a server application should serve at least a few hundred simultaneous clients. If we notice CPU plateaus with only five users, a real stress test would certainly have been catastrophic. We would not have a simple drop in performance, but a complete breakdown of the server.

Using the right server

Stress tests should always be done using real, production-like environments. In particular, IIS should be used instead of Cassini. The latter will already be down when the former is just getting comfortable with the activity. IIS in particular caches the compiled ASP.NET code and is adapted to high loads, whereas Cassini is really just a developer tool.

E   Additional remarks

We are almost at the end of this chapter, and I still have a few remarks to make on server-side profiling, that did not fit into the previous sections.

E.1   Profiler warning

ANTS Performance Profiler sometimes displays warnings such as the one in Figure 6-97, which reads, *The selected time region contains SQL Server activity > 1.5 seconds. To view activity on local SQL Server instances for this time period, change the analysis type to SQL Server. Note that to see methods that call SQL Server, select Wall-clock time, because CPU time does not include calls to SQL Server.*

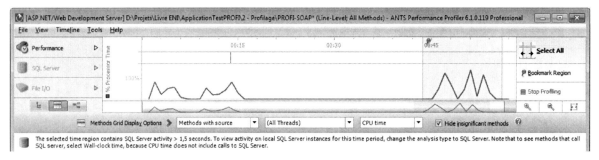

Figure 6-97: Profiler warning when database calls are detected.

This is due to the fact that, even if the SQL and I/O data collection is not active, this profiling tool keeps an eye on the time spent in the ADO.NET classes, in order to report behaviors that require additional analysis.

Simultaneous analysis: a word from the expert

SQL and I/O profiling cannot be activated independently from each other. Andrew Hunter, from Red Gate, explains: "The reason is fairly prosaic: the performance hit of profiling both isn't significant, so there's no reason not to profile both simultaneously. This enables us to have one less check box to configure. The check box really turns on or off collection of data through the Event Tracing for Windows mechanism (which is not always available, so does actually need to be configurable). Part of the design philosophy behind ANTS Performance Profiler is to leave analyzing data until after the application has been profiled: it should never be necessary to rerun a session to perform a different analysis on the same task. The main way we achieve this is by using the timeline control instead of a snapshot mechanism, but another part of this is to collect as much data as possible, so if the profiling session does lead in an unexpected direction, it's possible to investigate without needing to create another session and potentially spending a long time reproducing the issue."

E.2   Using other profilers

In order to maintain coherence in the profiling process demonstration, I preferred to use the same profiler throughout, and the one from Red Gate has been chosen for reasons of simplicity. However, the complete process has also been carried out using JetBrains dotTrace in order to validate that the results were coherent. It is only fair to stress that both have systematically confirmed what ANTS Performance Profiler recorded.

E.3   Start-up side effects

Although I have not shown this, to avoid cluttering up the reports, profiling operations on a server that had just been started were always preceded by a "blank" scenario shot, in order to get rid of the start-up times of ASP.NET, JIT compiling effects, etc.

E.4   Security issue in the authentication process

If you have experience in software security, you might have noticed that the SHA-256 hash applied to the password did not use any salt. This was done in order not to overcomplicate the code for readers who do not know about this concept. It was important to keep the content of this book focused on performance problems, but it is equally important to inform you that this code is not really secure.

Chapter 7: Beyond Profiling

A   Introduction

After two chapters focusing on client and server profiling respectively, this one follows up the performance analysis of our sample application, but without using a profiler.

To begin with, we will simply continue analyzing PROFI, trying to find other leads for improvements. We will be looking for issues that typically cannot be found with automated tools, for example problems related to display or loading application libraries, and we will try to suggest innovative solutions to improve the user's perceived performance.

We left tuning aside for the main part of the book, but this chapter will provide a few hints for the cases where you are at the end of the profiling phase but still need a bit more performance.

After that, we will talk about the last resort in performance improvement: when profiling does not identify any more bottlenecks, and tuning is not enough, only re-architecting the application will offer a solution. We generally iterate over these three steps. In this section, we will talk about hardware scaling, then innovative architectures that can replace traditional ones when performance is of paramount importance.

B   Remaining improvement methods

B.1   Introduction

Before re-architecting the entire solution, though, we still have a lot of places in PROFI where we can improve performance without fundamentally modifying the software.

In the previous two chapters, we tried as much as possible to show traditional coding errors related to performance. Our goal was to show that a lack of performance does not necessarily need expertise to find a solution, but often comes down to a few well-known programming errors.

Numerous other cases exist which, although they may not be identified during profiling, are still coding errors known to affect performance, but which are not common enough to merit a chapter of their own. The aim is not to provide an exhaustive list of potential improvements (which would be impossible) but simply to show some concrete cases, and improve your comprehension of performance as a whole.

The goal of this section is also to propose a few simple ways of improving an application's performance, without necessarily correcting the error, but without amounting to real tuning either, given the simplicity of the solutions put forward.

I will not provide detailed instructions, but just offer feedback on particular technologies, together with advice on using them.

B.2   Display speed

Managing the performance of application display in Windows could fill a book in itself. We will not provide any technical analysis but only one important piece of advice on the GUI technology: if your applications still use WinForms and suffer from flickering and long refresh intervals, you may benefit from migrating to Windows Presentation Foundation, which uses hardware acceleration. This does not mean you will magically get rid of performance problems when adopting WPF, but its general architecture is definitely a big step forward compared to WinForms. Incidentally, Microsoft no longer provides any support for WinForms, either in general or for display problems in particular.

If some applications cannot be migrated for any reason, here is some useful information on the performance of WinForms.

- Display reactivity is extremely different from one CPU type to another, even within comparable product ranges. I have performed tests as part of my job that showed a ratio of 1:2 between AMD and Intel CPUs, despite overall equivalent configuration: almost same processor and bus frequency, same number of cores and amount of in-chip cache, etc. WinForms is highly sensitive to CPU, and your performance testing should take this into consideration.

- Use transparency with caution: WinForms manages it in a software way, and this can lead to surprises if we use this feature instead of the visibility of a control to mask portions of the GUI. On a relatively simple form with a dozen controls, replacing code that set the `Opacity` property to 0 by code setting property `Visible` to **False** led to a 500ms improvement to reaction times!

- Nesting too many panels within one another is the main cause of flickering when the controls are then resized. To put some figures on it, eight levels of layout generally do not pose a problem. But when reaching 12 levels with complex layout relationships that require moving up and down the hierarchy to calculate the actual size and positions of controls, delays start to appear, as well as flickering when resizing the forms.

A possible solution to this last problem is to use such code as in Listing 7-1.

```
/// <summary>
/// We hide all the controls during resizing
/// </summary>
private void Portal_ResizeBegin(object sender, EventArgs e)
{
    RecursiveModifyVisibility(tlpGlobal, true);
}

/// <summary>
/// At the end of the resizing operation, we can display the controls
/// </summary>
private void Portal_ResizeEnd(object sender, EventArgs e)
{
    RecursiveModifyVisibility(tlpGlobal, false);
}

/// <summary>
/// Utility function helping to set the visibility for all the controls
/// in the window
/// </summary>
private void RecursiveModifyVisibility(Control targetControl, bool hide)
{
    foreach (Control childControl in targetControl.Controls)
        RecursiveModifyVisibility(childControl, hide);
    targetControl.Visible = !hide;
}
```

Listing 7-1

This code recursively hides controls during a resizing operation, then displays them again when done. In short, it enables us to go back to the good old days of Windows 95, where the content of a window was hidden during resizing and moving operations, in order to make for a more fluid display. Since continuous refreshing during modification of the display context is simply a visual comfort, forcing this feature to be temporarily inactive can be justified.

Let's use this small code modification to profile a scenario during which we resize the main window of PROFI. The results are shown in Figure 7-1.

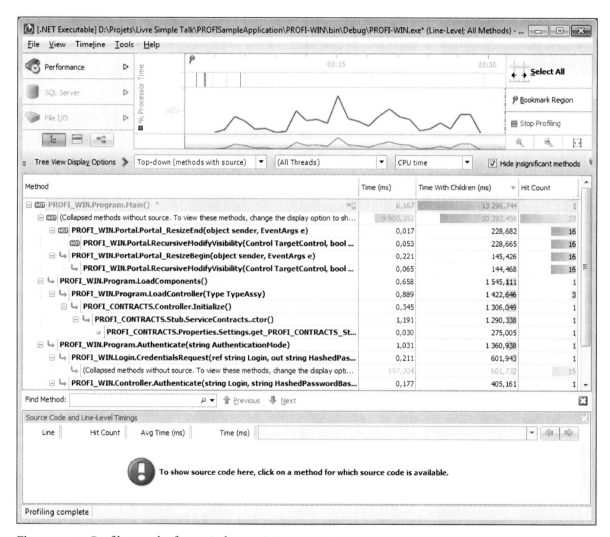

Figure 7-1: Profiler results for a window-resizing scenario.

The results show that we spend too much time in the recursive function. This is not surprising, as the developer who created this function did not know that a container's visibility is automatically propagated by WinForms to all the child controls. A simple modification as shown in Listing 7-2 makes for a reduction of the calls from 16 to only 4 in this scenario.

```
/// <summary>
/// We hide all the controls during resizing
/// </summary>
private void Portal_ResizeBegin(object sender, EventArgs e)
{
    RecursiveModifyVisibility(tlpGlobal, true);
}

/// <summary>
/// At the end of the resizing operation, we can display the controls
/// </summary>
private void Portal_ResizeEnd(object sender, EventArgs e)
{
    RecursiveModifyVisibility(tlpGlobal, false);
}

/// <summary>
/// Utility function helping to set the visibility for all the controls in
/// the window
/// </summary>
private void RecursiveModifyVisibility(Control targetControl, bool hide)
{
    targetControl.Visible = !hide;
}
```
Listing 7-2

Code modification tags

Changes to the code based on improvements discussed in this chapter are surrounded by tags with the code SUP followed by the section number, instead of CLIENT and SERVER like in the preceding chapters. This helps you follow the changes that we are explaining in the book in the code of PROFI.

This remark, in addition to being related to performance, also forces us to think about code modification in general. What will a developer do when they see this code and are pretty sure that the recursion call is useless? Since they have a good opinion of their colleagues, they will often think that there might be a case they have not thought of where this is actually necessary.

In the worst case, communication among developers is bad or limited, and the person who saw the problem will not take the risk of introducing a regression because they have not fully understood the rationale (or its absence) behind the code. Performance comes after functionality, and the code will remain as it is.

With a bit of luck, the developer will file a bug on a display slowdown for which they have created a particular test scenario, and the developer in charge of this part of the application will modify the code if they think it necessary.

The best case, of course, is when the development team has good internal communication. The developer will talk about the potential problem at the next meeting with their peers (typically at the daily meeting in Agile teams), and the person who created the code will confirm it was a mistake and that the code can be modified safely.

The moral of the story is this: to work efficiently on an application's performance (and this is true for any other development activity) we need good ideas and good communication, but also humble developers.

B.3   Application load time

B.3.a   NGen

NGEN.exe is a tool provided by .NET SDK to precompile .NET assemblies into machine code. In a way, it does the JIT compiler job in advance and produces the binaries as they will be executed by the processor (Microsoft uses the expression "native images"). These native images are different from one machine to another. As a consequence, NGEN cannot be executed on an application before it is installed, but should be done at the very end of the deployment process.

To use NGEN on PROFI, we simply call the following command-line instruction:

```
ngen.exe install PROFI-WIN.exe
```

Listing 7-3

NGEN also processes dependencies of the assembly which we passed to it as a parameter, but since PROFI loads its controller libraries by reflection, we have to run the additional commands from Listing 7-4.

```
ngen.exe install PROFI-PERSONS.dll /ExeConfig:PROFI-WIN.exe.config
ngen.exe install PROFI-CONTRACTS.dll /ExeConfig:PROFI-WIN.exe.config
```

Listing 7-4

NGEN is supposed to improve .NET assemblies' loading time and to have no effect on pure application execution times. In theory, however, since the application does not need to JIT compile the classes upon first use, NGEN could have a positive impact on runtime performance. In practice, this impact will be zero as soon as the scenario is run a second time and, since we often run a blank scenario first when profiling, the effect will not be noticed.

In three different attempts at improving loading times on very different industrial applications, I have never seen any significant improvement after using NGEN. It seems a lot of other people have had the same experience. In order not to be overly critical, I will just give two links, below, to relevant resources.

- *Can C# be as fast as C++?* on .NET Monster (February 2008): HTTP://WWW.DOTNET-MONSTER.COM/UWE/FORUM.ASPX/DOTNET-CSHARP/80694/CAN-C-BE-AS-FAST-AS-C

- *Which is faster? VB 6 or VB.NET?* on About.com: HTTP://VISUALBASIC.ABOUT.COM/OD/IMHOINMYHUMBLEOPINION/SS/VB6VSVBNET_8.HTM.

Even Microsoft's own documentation on the subject (available on MSDN at HTTP://MSDN.MICROSOFT.COM/EN-US/LIBRARY/6T9T5WCF%28V=VS.80%29.ASPX) is not really encouraging. It states:

> *Precompiling assemblies with Ngen.exe can improve the start-up time for some applications. In general, gains can be made when applications share component assemblies because after the first application has been started the shared components are already loaded for subsequent applications. Cold start-up, in which all the assemblies in an application must be loaded from the hard disk, does not benefit as much from native images because the hard disk access time predominates.*

In conclusion, NGEN exists and may be helpful with application loading problems. However, I recommend seriously evaluating gains on deployment targets before using this tool throughout your applications.

B.3.b   XmlSerializers

.NET offers another generic method for improving performance, namely automatic generation of assemblies containing specialized serialization classes (which are necessary for web service proxies). We have seen during client profiling that creating a proxy client to a web service was a costly operation. This is because these objects must adapt dynamically to any request or response structure contained in the WSDL contract. This needs classes for serialization and de-serialization, and since this operation includes lots of reflective calls, it takes a lot of time.

These classes can be generated in advance and put in dedicated assemblies to save the time their dynamic generation would take at runtime. The simplest way of activating the corresponding option, is to use the Visual Studio properties for the project that contains the reference to the web services, and set the **Generate serialization assembly** option to **On** (see Figure 7-2). The default mode is **Auto**, but I have never seen any `*.XmlSerializers.dll` being produced without setting it to **On**.

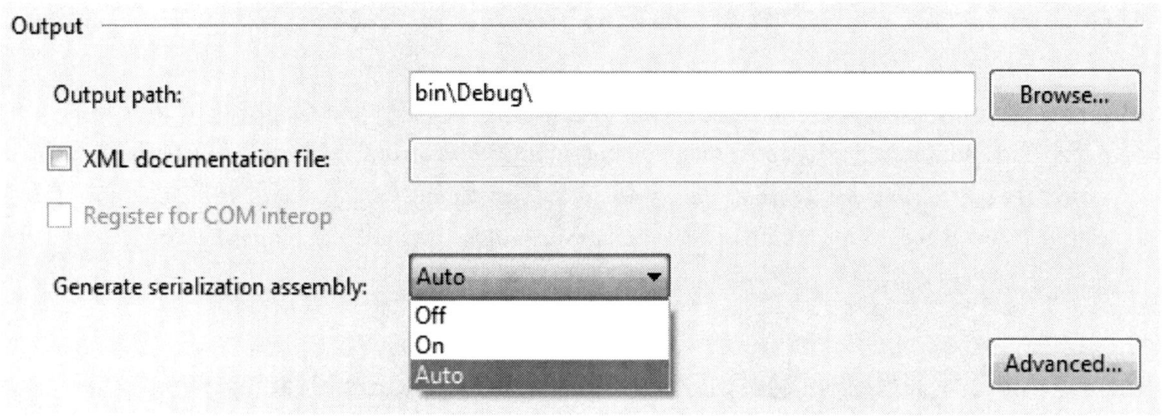

Figure 7-2:   Options for serialization assembly generation.

If you want to integrate this function to an automated build process, the corresponding SDK utility is **SGEN.exe**. For details about use and options, see HTTP://MSDN.MICROSOFT. COM/EN-US/LIBRARY/BK3W6240%28V=VS.80%29.ASPX.

An option for this tool limits generation of serialization classes to those used by web services client proxies. But the default behavior is to generate classes for every use of `System.Xml.Serialization.XmlSerialize` in the target assembly.

For an application like PROFI, the improvement is nil. Sadly, just as with NGEN, I have not been able to produce any convincing improvements, even with bigger clients with more than ten different proxies, each of them embedding dozens of functions, sometimes with huge class hierarchies to serialize. Again, this means I cannot really recommend the tool, but only suggest that you try it and see the results in your particular context.

To come back to simple optimizations (which is the philosophy of this book), one piece of advice: instead of trying to reach small improvements through the use of SGEN, spend a bit of time checking that all web methods are actually used by the client. If only half of the methods exposed are indeed called, performance can be greatly improved by splitting the web service into two parts and only loading the proxy for the part that is actually used. Proxies loading time is proportional in a quasi-linear way to the number of serialized classes, and since the times are quite large, any removal of a method or a type has a considerable effect.

The importance of communication

Once again, this leads us to the importance of communication between developers. A too strong separation of teams increases the probability of duplication of services, or at least of methods with signatures that are so similar they can easily be merged into one. By contrast, if developers are comfortable enough to ask the service team for an evolution, and if the latter delivers changes quickly enough, the increase in number of methods will be better contained, as will the proxies loading time.

B.4 Improving perceived performance

B.4.a Actual and perceived performance

Developers may have a good opinion of their application's performance, backed up with benchmark results, while the customer using it thinks the application is too slow. There are lots of reasons that can lead to such a difference of views. First, it may be that the developer only works on the server side of the application, and considers that if the process related to business requirements is quick enough, then so is the whole application.

It can also be that developers and users take measurements differently, even when taking into account the additional client processing time. A developer will tend to set a stopwatch instance inside their code, and trust this metric without taking into account the complexity of the interfaces and the corresponding display times. If the stopwatch stops at the time the form has finished loading, there may be up to one second (two in the worst cases) until the actual end of the display refresh in WinForms.

But this shift in perception can sometimes be turned to our advantage. Let us imagine a process that lasts three seconds, with not much variation, and that sends a message to the user when complete. A trick can be to display the dialog before the actual end of the process, as soon as we have the necessary data to display it. This way, while the user looks at this dialog and clicks on the button to close it, the application has had some more time to finish the second part of the process (and refresh the display, for example). In the end, if we ask the user about the time taken to execute this operation, they will tend to think it was quicker than without the trick.

Similarly, a gauge that scrolls very quickly gives the illusion of a faster process than if the exact same time had been spent without any feedback to the user. The gauge, and if possible text describing the content of the process steps, together with a percentage, gives the user an idea of the complexity of the operations executed behind the interface, and conditions them to accept more easily a delay in their interaction.

To summarize, it is essential to work on perceived performance at least as much as on actual process performance. Again, we are not strictly within the subject of the book, but we will nevertheless give a few leads for making improvements.

B.4.b   Asynchronous processes

The difference between the actual time spent in a process and the time perceived by the user can be put to use by anticipating further operations during the time spent in user interactions.

Let us take the example of what is done in the `Main` function of `Program` in PROFI-WIN (Listing 7-5).

```
[STAThread]
static void Main()
{
    Application.EnableVisualStyles();
    Application.SetCompatibleTextRenderingDefault(false);

    // Starting the bus
    new Bus();

    // Loading components and attaching them to the message bus
    LoadComponents();

    string authenticationMode = ConfigurationManager.AppSettings["PROFI.
                        Authentication.Mode"];

    // Before even entering the main Windows loop, we must authenticate
    Authenticate(authenticationMode);
    Application.Run(new Portal());
}
```

Listing 7-5

A timeline of this code's execution is shown in Figure 7-3.

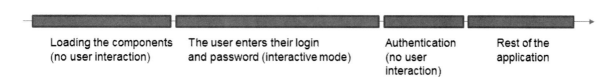

Loading the components (no user interaction) | The user enters their login and password (interactive mode) | Authentication (no user interaction) | Rest of the application

Figure 7-3: Sequential code chronology.

To gain some time (and we are not talking about a perceived gain, but a genuinely faster display of the authentication dialog), we could use the fact that the whole first part of the start-up process does not need access to components loaded into the bus. This means a timeline such as that shown in Figure 7-4 is possible in functional terms.

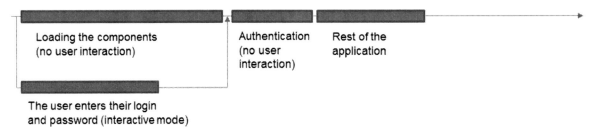

Figure 7-4: Parallelized code chronology.

Parallelizing these asynchronous processes consists of creating a thread in the Main function (Listing 7-6).

```
[STAThread]
static void Main()
{
    Application.EnableVisualStyles();
    Application.SetCompatibleTextRenderingDefault(false);

    _LoadingProcess = new Thread(new ThreadStart(StartBusAndComponents));
    _LoadingProcess.Start();

    string authenticationMode = ConfigurationManager.AppSettings["PROFI.
                        Authentication.Mode"];

    // Before even entering the main Windows loop, we must  authenticate
    Authenticate(authenticationMode);
    Application.Run(new Portal());
}
```

Listing 7-6

In order for the code in Listing 7-6 to compile, we need to add a method to the class Program that will be called at the start of the thread, and that executes the actual process. This is shown in Listing 7-7.

```
private static Thread _LoadingProcess = null;

private static void StartBusAndComponents()
{
    // Starting the message bus
    new Bus();

    // Loading the components and attaching them to the message bus
    LoadComponents();
}
```
Listing 7-7

At the first manual test, the code seems to work: while we enter the login and password, the libraries are loading, and then the rest of the application works as usual. However, automated test scenarios will show an anomaly, namely an exception thrown from the code in Listing 7-8, which is part of the function `Authenticate`.

```
isAuthenticated = Controller.Current.Authenticate(login, hashedPasswordBase64,
"SHA256");
```
Listing 7-8

This exception indicates that `Controller.Current` is `null`, and as a consequence, it is impossible to call the server-side authentication method. What happened? This is simply proof of the difficulty of asynchronous programming: nothing guarantees that the time spent in the login form will always be enough for all the components to be loaded in parallel.

Indeed, when executing the automated scenarios, the code shown in Listing 7-9 is responsible for entering credentials.

```
#if TEST1 || TEST2
this.Activated += delegate(object sender, EventArgs e)
{
    txtLogin.Text = "abc";
    SecuredPassword.AppendChar('c');
```

```
        SecuredPassword.AppendChar('b');
        SecuredPassword.AppendChar('a');
        this.DialogResult = DialogResult.OK;
        this.Close();
    };
    #endif
```

Listing 7-9

Obviously, automating such an operation will be at least a thousand times quicker than any user typing on a physical keyboard to achieve the same operation. In consequence, the timeline in this case looks more like Figure 7-5.

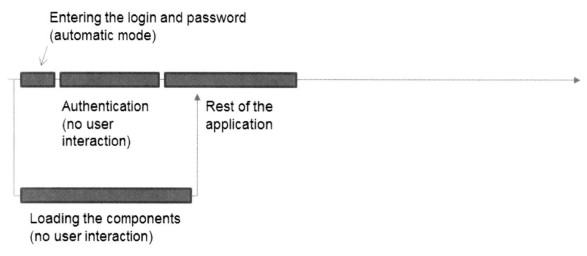

Figure 7-5: Possible problem when parallelizing code.

The authentication code is run before the loading of the components is finished. But this second process is responsible for generating controllers' instances. This explains the `NullReferenceException`: the code tries to call a method on an instance that has not yet been activated.

The solution consists of adding a condition to the execution of the non-interactive part of the authentication, by inserting an instruction that waits for the complete loading of the components before it allows use of the controllers. To do so, we add a `Thread.Join` instruction to `Authenticate`, as shown in Listing 7-10

```
if (loginDialog.CredentialsRequest(ref login, out hashedPasswordBase64))
{
    _LoadingProcess.Join();

    // The administrator password is hard-coded to "hiya"
    if (string.Compare(login, "ADMIN", true) == 0 && string.
Compare(hashedPasswordBase64, "EOXt5HFcgIhb9Mpvnqh9hBy9JM0La9GvXx7cm1YQUt4=") == 0)
    {
        // The good old backdoor, obviously removed from production code
        isAuthenticated = true;
    }
    else
    {
        // Server call to check the validity of the password
        isAuthenticated = Controller.Current.Authenticate(login,
                    hashedPasswordBase64, "SHA256");
    }
}
```

Listing 7-10

The effect on the timeline can be illustrated as shown in Figure 7-6.

The `Join` instruction forces the main thread to wait for the end of the secondary thread and thus the complete loading of components and instantiating of controllers, in order to use them for functional operations.

To push the optimization a bit further, we could have used one additional level of threading to asynchronously load the controller needed for the authentication and all the others in a separate thread.

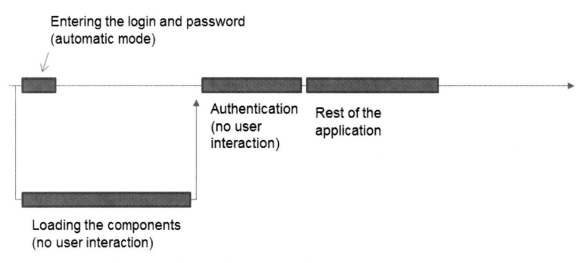

Figure 7-6:   Code chronology after introducing a thread join.

But this is where asynchronous programming shows its difficulty. Manually coding single thread synchronization to the main program is quite easy, even if the maintenance remains hard. Other developers may integrate some code into a thread that depends on resources potentially handled by another thread. The code may even pass the tests correctly, and fail in another context, since there is no certainty as to which thread the CLR will favor at a given time.

Extending this method to many threads causes some real programming headaches. In a company I used to work for, a team was entirely dedicated to asynchronous/multi-threaded programming and, most of all, debugging. The developers in this team were considered very skilled programmers.

Async

Microsoft offers a modern asynchronous management framework called Async, which reduces the difficulty of asynchronous programming. However, one should not expect miracles from this technology: it will not replace the developer's intelligence. Even if Async can detect simple dependencies between resources and help write much cleaner and more concise code, only a human developer will be able to create the initial decomposition into parallel tasks. Details on Async, which is bound to be part of the next version of Visual Studio, can be found at HTTP://MSDN.MICROSOFT.COM/EN-US/VSTUDIO/GG316360. *Microsoft also provides debugging tools that are specific to multithreaded application, enabling pausing and managing threads. Even more than Async and the associated syntactic sugar, these tools will truly help to achieve efficient asynchrony.*

B.4.c   Lazy-loading

As is often the case, moderation is called for when running processes during user interactions: we should only choose operations that will be run at some point anyway, and that are most of the time quicker than the interaction that will mask them. Lazy-loading should be used when possible: only loading objects when we actually need them (even if exceptions to this, such as the one above, can be worthwhile).

For example, applying the "lazy" principle could result in changing the point at which the parameters dictionary is instantiated in the class called `Message`. The original code is shown in Listing 7-11.

```
public class Message
{
    private string _Order;

    public string Order
    {
        get
        {
            return _Order;
        }
```

```
    }

    public readonly Dictionary<string, string> Parameters = new Dictionary<string,
                  string>();

    public Message(string order)
    {
        _Order = order;
    }

    public void AddParameter(string code, string value)
    {
        Parameters.Add(code, value);
    }
}
```

Listing 7-11

In order to avoid creating an instance of dictionary that would be useless if no parameter is added to the message, we could modify the code as shown in Listing 7-12.

```
public class Message
{
    private string _Order;

    public string Order
    {
        get
        {
            return _Order;
        }
    }

    public Dictionary<string, string> Parameters = null;

    public Message(string order)
    {
        _Order = order;
    }

    public void AddParameter(string code, string value)
    {
```

```
        if (Parameters == null)
            Parameters = new Dictionary<string, string>();
        Parameters.Add(code, value);
    }
}
```

Listing 7-12

This kind of optimization can seem basic but, applied to an application where every single interaction causes the creation of many messages to communicate between the different controls of the interface, the gain in memory and GC activity can be appreciable.

B.4.d   Splash screens

.NET provides a class that handles splash screens. These are welcome screens that come up as soon as possible when starting an application, and display information about start-up, thus allowing for better perceived performance. This class is contained in the namespace `Microsoft.VisualBasic.ApplicationServices`, but it can still be used in C#, despite what the name may suggest.

The class we are interested in is called `WindowsFormsApplicationBase`, and can be used by inheriting it in a class on which we will reference the instances of the main application window and of the splash screen form. The corresponding code is shown in Listing 7-13.

```
using System;
using Microsoft.VisualBasic.ApplicationServices;

namespace ApplicationWithSplashScreen
{
    public class Window
    {
    }

    public class Splash
    {
```

```
    }

    public class SpecializedApplication : WindowsFormsApplicationBase
    {
        public SpecializedApplication()
        {
            // We have to assign the main window here instead of the usual
            // Application.Run(new MainWindow()) in the Main method
            MainForm = new Window();

            // The Microsoft documentation says this should not be useful, but it
            // actually is for removing the splash screen at the end of the start
            // up (http://msdn.microsoft.com/en-us/library/microsoft.visualbasic.
            // applicationservices.windowsformsapplicationbase.hidesplashscreen.
            // aspx)
            MainForm.Shown += new EventHandler(MainForm_Shown);

            // The splash screen is assigned here
            SplashScreen = new Splash();
        }

        void MainForm_Shown(object sender, EventArgs e)
        {
            HideSplashScreen();
        }
    }
}
```

Listing 7-13

For the code above to be called, we have to modify the way the `Program` class runs the WinForms application, as shown in Listing 7-14.

```
using System;
using System.Windows.Forms;

namespace ApplicationWithSplashScreen
{
    static class Program
    {
        /// <summary>
        /// Main entry point for the application
```

```
        /// </summary>
        [STAThread]
        static void Main()
        {
            Application.EnableVisualStyles();
            Application.SetCompatibleTextRenderingDefault(false);

            SpecializedApplication Appli = new SpecializedApplication();
            Appli.Run(Environment.GetCommandLineArgs());
        }
    }
}
```

Listing 7-14

Allowing only a single instance of application

The class `WindowsFormsApplicationBase` *can also be used to restrict the user to only one instance of the application running at the same time. An event called* `StartupNextInstance` *will enable the developer to catch attempts to start a new instance and adapt behavior of the current instance, for example through the use of the new set of arguments.*

B.4.e   Show the process complexity

Users can tolerate a long execution time if they find it justified by an inherent complexity. Waiting a few seconds for an authentication operation or the display of a simple dialog may seem long. On the other hand, the bulk processing of thousands of business objects will be recognized as something so complicated that minutes or even hours of processing time are justified.

It is the developer's responsibility to communicate the complexity of processes taking place behind the GUI, thus helping the user to accept potential slowdowns that are justified by the functional complexity. For example, for a complex mathematical analysis we can display a wait screen (this can be the splash screen, which typically contains a `Status` property for this purpose). By displaying this screen, instead of just changing the cursor, the user will understand that the associated process is a heavy one, and may be willing to wait for a few more seconds.

B.5 A few remaining problems

As a last step in studying performance-related coding errors, I will show a few cases that would be detected by a profiler, but that I did not find useful to integrate into PROFI, as they are easy to understand.

B.5.a Correct logs management

Performance problems, even if generally small, can arise when verbose logs are activated. This will, of course, be as much a problem as the density of tracing instructions in the application is high. If traces are associated to every single function, the slowdown can be quite significant.

Particular attention should be paid to deactivating logging when it is no longer necessary. It is also important to use the different levels of trace that .NET provides (error, warning, information, verbose) in order to reduce the size of logs when possible. Only messages of paramount importance (notice of a potential security breach, non-transactional process cancellation, etc.) should always remain active.

Stopwatch

While discussing logs it is worth reiterating that the simplest of all profiler tools just consists of integrating stopwatches into the traces, by surrounding the steps to study with `System.Diagnostics.Stopwatch.StartNew()` *and* `Stop()` *operations. Short of an Aspect Oriented Programming framework, it is impossible to place stopwatches everywhere in the code, but when we have a fair idea of the source of the performance problems, this can be a quick and useful ad hoc solution.*

B.5.b   Duplication of SQL requests

This is certainly the main cause of performance problems in the code of a server linked to a database engine. Execution of the server application may result, in some cases, in looping over SQL calls. Just like for web services, even simple SQL requests are heavy operations, as they require handlers, connection to a database engine, network bandwidth, marshaling results, etc. Looping over them is naturally one of the worst cases for performance. There is an example of this in **Person.Retrieve** (see Listing 7-15).

```
public static Person Retrieve(string personUID)
{
    SqlConnection conn = new SqlConnection(ConfigurationManager.ConnectionStrings
                    ["DBConnection"].ConnectionString);
    SqlCommand command = new SqlCommand("SELECT uid uid, lastname lastname,
                    firstname firstname, description description FROM PERSON
                    WHERE uid=@personuid", conn);
    command.Parameters.Add(new SqlParameter("personuid", personUID));
    conn.Open();
    Person result = null;
    using (SqlDataReader reader = command.ExecuteReader(CommandBehavior.
                    CloseConnection))
        if (reader.Read())
            result = RetrievePersonFromCursor(reader);

    // If we found the person, we add the associated contracts
    if (result != null)
    {
        command = new SqlCommand("SELECT uid uid FROM CONTRACT WHERE
                        owner=@personuid", conn);
        command.Parameters.Add(new SqlParameter("personuid", personUID));
        conn.Open();
        using (SqlDataReader reader = command.ExecuteReader(CommandBehavior.
                    CloseConnection))
            while (reader.Read())
                result._Contracts.Add(Contract.Retrieve(reader.GetString(reader.
                            GetOrdinal("uid"))));
    }

    return result;
}
```

Listing 7-15

499

Instead of executing a single SQL request with a join operation between PERSON and CONTRACT to retrieve a complete set of data, the code in Listing 7-15 makes a first SQL request to retrieve the characteristics of the `Person`-type object, and then runs a SQL request in a loop for each contract associated to this instance of `Person`. This is catastrophic from the point of view of performance, since executing a SQL request takes 100 to 1,000 times longer than reading the same amount of data from memory.

This kind of code is often found where functionality has been written through many successive code modifications, particularly when methods encapsulate calls to the database, thus making this error much more difficult to spot than in Listing 7-15. A consequence of this is that a developer might forget to check the typical unit calls execution time. Finally, this problem is made even bigger when business objects automatically fill their children instances recursively.

The example in Listing 7-15 made the error almost immediately obvious to anyone concerned with good coding. But this is only true because the code shown is that of a sample application that concentrates as many errors as possible into the fewest lines of code. In a more realistic context, the faulty code might be lost in lots of code, or even split into two functions that are quite far from one another in terms of code structure. This is why it is so important to reduce this distance by clearly separating responsibilities between different components, as well as to refactor code as soon as necessary.

SOLID programming

The Single Responsibility principle described above is one of the SOLID principles, along with the Open/Closed, Liskov Substitution, Interface Segregation and Dependency Inversion principles. These five best practices help achieve robust object-oriented code. More explanation can be found at HTTP://WWW. CODEPROJECT.COM/ARTICLES/60845/THE-S-O-L-I-D-OBJECT-ORIENTED-PROGRAMMING-OOP-PRIN *or* HTTP://WWW.SLIDESHARE.NET/IONKRUGER/SOLID-SOFTWARE-DESIGN-PRINCIPLES.

B.5.c   Avoid over-architecting

Although this has already been mentioned briefly, a short paragraph about over-architecture is justified by the fact that this is still one of the major causes of performance problems. An example on the web method Authenticate is shown in Listing 7-16.

```
[WebMethod]
public bool Authenticate(string login, string hashedPasswordBase64, string
hashMode)
{
    if (string.Compare(hashMode, "sha256", true) == 0)
    {
        // Sample implementation : the password is the login in reverse
        string password = new string(login.ToCharArray().Reverse().ToArray());
        SHA256 engine = SHA256Managed.Create();
        byte[] hash = engine.ComputeHash(Encoding.UTF8.GetBytes(password));
        return string.Compare(hashedPasswordBase64, Convert.ToBase64String(hash))
                == 0;
    }
    else
    {
        // For such a simple application, no need to support other hash methods
        throw new NotSupportedException("Unsupported hash mode");
    }
}
```

Listing 7-16

A developer with a tendency to over-architect may wish to modify this code so that it uses a plug-in mechanism for the different hash methods. They will typically argue that this will allow new hash methods to be deployed at runtime, remove the need to recompile the code, and also avoid authentication failures due to a badly-written hash mode.

Let us debunk these arguments: it's not as if new security-related methods are added to servers every morning and, given the long validation steps for everything that is related to security, it is absolute nonsense that restarting the application could be a problem.

As far as the risks of rejection of a badly-written hash mode are concerned, one only needs to remark that end-users will not enter the mode themselves: it will be generated by a list, a setting, an entry in the database, all ways that are extremely stable in time. Since it is unthinkable that such an error in the application parameters could go unnoticed during the integration tests, there is absolutely no objective reason why writing this parameter incorrectly could cause problems in production.

Avoiding over-architecting code is a state of mind that goes against lots of IT practices. I have personally seen architects using UML diagrams to explain a simple application with two or three business rules, sometimes even to generate huge amounts of code, 10% of which at most was actually used in production. Another pathological case is a developer who has recently been taught injection and uses it everywhere, even to inject interfaces for which we will never in the world have a different implementation. Given the levels of complexity reached by some IT systems, simplicity and pragmatism are certainly the best possible advantages to keep high-performance processes. In fact, these qualities will be far more efficient than all the solutions exposed in this book, which remain technical.

B.5.d   Do not forget temporary files

When operations needing temporary files are executed, it is important to purge these files at the end of the process, in order to avoid saturating the disk space. The risk may seem limited on home computers that commonly have a capacity of 500 gigabytes these days. But business computers often have quotas per user profile. On a server computer with many clients, the problem is even more present, and disks can quickly get filled if developers do not pay attention to purging the files.

Of course, server machines will be under the supervision of administrators, which helps mitigate the risk of running out of space. But it is clearly not good practice to leave it to an outside process to clean up your old files. This should always be the responsibility of the code that created these files, as no other algorithm can better know their life cycle and the best time to delete them.

The real problem is knowing when to remove these files.

- In a synchronous way at the end of the associated process, just before coming back to the caller function, whether it be the client for the server or the user for the client application? This is the most logical and widespread method, but it takes some time and needs to be coded carefully, so that files are purged even in case of an exception (typically, removing temporary files is done in a `finally` section).

- Implementing this asynchronously may be interesting, as the cleaning code will be run while the results are sent back to the caller, which allows for an early response. But this kind of code is typically a fair bit more complex to implement.

- If the server should remain as quick as possible during periods of intense use, and also have frequent periods of low activity, it can be better to clean temporary files at a given time, by using a batch, for example. On a client application, a good method is to remove the temporary files upon closing the application. This avoids losing some time during GUI use by keeping all this cleaning process for the end. Also, provided a clear message is sent to the user when closing the application, stating that the software is cleaning its working files and that the application will stop in a few minutes without any further interaction, the process is very acceptable. If necessary, it is even possible to offer a cancellation option, and operate the clean-up process at the next closure of the application.

The code in `UCContract.OnLeave`, for example, is called when the application exits the control (Listing 7-17).

```
protected override void OnLeave(EventArgs e)
{
    foreach (string TempFile in new string[] { _DocumentFile, _SummaryFile })
        if (TempFile != null && File.Exists(TempFile))
            try { File.Delete(TempFile); }
            catch { }
}
```

Listing 7-17

The problem with this kind of code is that we do not have much guarantee that it will get called. For example, in PROFI, going to another interface does not remove the former screens, because it should remain possible to go back to them using the history links on the right-hand side of the screen. In consequence, controls are not suppressed while the application is being used, and temporary files pile up. It is better to purge them at the end of the application itself.

Limitations of `System.IO.Path.GetTempFileName`

If many calls are made to this .NET function that generates temporary files, and under certain circumstances only (reproduced in Windows XP), it is possible that this method will get slower, and that it may send two similar file names in a row.

B.5.e   Paginating results

Another best practice to limit the size of data exchanges is to systematically use pagination in the sending of lists. Not doing so is a risk for a server, because that means one client alone can take the server out by asking for a huge number of results because of an uncontrolled request. In the worst cases, this can block all other clients.

Generally speaking, any option allowing pagination to be temporarily disabled should not be included. Indeed, if the goal is to display the data, the user will not be able to interpret the results anyway. And if a bulk process is done to this data, a separate channel should be used for this kind of operation.

B.5.f   Garbage Collection takes some time

In Chapter 2, *.Profiling a .NET Application*, we detailed at length the way the GC works, and talked about its impact on the memory available to the application.

We should not forget that the GC not only influences memory, but can have a great impact on time-based performance. Indeed, if an algorithm creates a lot of objects that are almost immediately not referenced anymore, the GC will succeed in coping with memory pressure by firing more often and recycling the corresponding memory use, but this will take some time, and this time will increase with the speed of instantiation of the faulty algorithm.

It is possible to use a profiler, or even simply Windows performance counters (in the .NET category), to read the percentage of time spent in the GC. Starting at 10%, we definitely should have a look at memory allocation and correct the defective code.

A typical case of this is the operation of concatenating strings in loops with `String. Concat` (or the + operator, which is the same in C#), instead of using an instance of `StringBuilder`.

The reason why the former method is slower than the latter is that strings are immutable in .NET: when we add String B to String A, .NET starts by creating a third string the length of which is the sum of the lengths of A and B, then fills it with the content of A then B, and finally assigns this new memory block to variable A. The old value of A can then be recycled since no other reference points to it. If this kind of mechanism is done in loops, the time spent in the GC can increase to a high level. The role of `StringBuilder` is precisely to allocate, from the start, a large buffer in order to add characters to it without creating a new string at every instruction.

To push it further (but this is definitely tuning), we could even use the constructor of `StringBuilder` that accepts passing of the initial buffer size. `StringBuilder` generally does a great job of optimizing the initial size of the buffer, and the size of the steps of additional reservation, but no algorithm can be better than using the exact right size from the beginning, if we know it in the code. This also helps to keep the memory consumption as low as possible.

B.5.g   Limit exceptions to truly exceptional circumstances

A programming error often appears in samples of code that extract a numerical value from a string that can represent a number, but in some regular cases can be something else. An example of such problematic code is shown in Listing 7-18.

```
try { discount = decimal.Parse(_Contract.Discount) * _Contract.Amount; }
catch { }
```

Listing 7-18

Exception throwing and handling are extremely complex and resource-greedy processes. This is why functions like `TryParse` have been added to the BCL in order to allow for analysis of an incorrect string without necessarily noticing errors through an exception. A better version of code from Listing 7-18 is shown in Listing 7-19.

```
if (decimal.TryParse(_Contract.Discount, out discount))
    discount *= _Contract.Amount;
```

Listing 7-19

Functions like `TryParse` exist on numeric types, and if you have to create a function that extracts some data from a string, it is good practice to create this function along with `Parse`, which should only be used if invalid values are exceptional and relate to severe problems in the application.

Error in PROFI

This coding error appears in PROFI, but was not detected during profiling because it is not performed in a loop, so the impact in absolute time is quite low. But had it been in a loop, it would certainly have appeared at the top of the longest methods.

A very common error

The fact that this is talked about almost at the end of the book does not mean that it is a negligible case. Quite the contrary, in fact: auditing code written by a programmer who is a .NET beginner often shows this error. As a consequence of the huge time cost of an exception (between 100 and 1,000 times the time necessary for a functionally-equivalent condition), slowdowns can appear quickly, in fact as soon as a given scenario with ten or so operations causes more than one or two exceptions. A normal test should never throw any exceptions. It is, of course, possible to test scenarios that will simulate a context where an exception should be thrown (for example, we could shut down a service during the test and validate the data consistency, and thus the transactional aspect of the code, when the service is turned on again). But the normal course of an integration test is not to throw a single exception.

B.5.h   Equals and GetHashCode functions

An incorrect implementation of `GetHashCode` can pose serious performance problems when the class is used in a hash table (e.g. using generic class `HashSet<T>`). The goal of `GetHashCode` is to accelerate the search for an equal key, simulating the behavior of an index. The fact that two hash codes are the same does not mean the two objects are equivalent, and we should then use the `Equals` function to get some certainty. However, a different hash code does mean the objects are different. Since comparing a hash code string is much quicker than comparing the complete content of two objects, this function makes searching for a key in a hash table much quicker. The algorithm will only compare the objects that have the same hash code, thus gaining a lot of time.

Yet, in order to fully benefit from this, the `GetHashCode` function should be wrong as rarely as possible, while remaining as quick as possible. One extreme is that `GetHashCode` only tests the main property of the object, and `Equals` will be called very often. The other extreme is that `GetHashCode` compares all the properties of the object. In this case, `Equals` will not be called very often, if at all, but the time gained will be nil, or even negative.

If the improvement to performance from using a hash table is in doubt, it can be interesting to compare the number of calls for these two functions. If `Equals` is called almost the same number of times as `GetHashCode`, the algorithm behind the latter function is not precise enough.

However, be careful not to compare the average execution time for the two functions. Indeed, `Equals` is potentially called at each comparison, whereas a hash code is generated once through `GetHashCode` for an object, and can take longer on average, without this being a problem, since it will only be called once for a given object when populating a hash table.

B.5.i   AddRange operation

To conclude this section of the chapter, I have one last recommendation regarding coding for performance: when adding the content of a list to another one, it is important to use `AddRange`.

Let us start with a sample code (Listing 7-20).

```
using System;
using System.Collections.Generic;
using System.Diagnostics;

namespace AddRangeBenchmark
{
    class Program
    {
        static void Main(string[] args)
        {
            List<string> numbers = new List<string>();
            for (int i = 0; i < 100000; i++)
                numbers.Add("Number " + i.ToString());

            List<string> target = new List<string>();
            Stopwatch chrono = Stopwatch.StartNew();
            foreach (string value in numbers)
```

```
                    target.Add(value);
                chrono.Stop();
                Console.WriteLine("Add in loops: " + chrono.ElapsedTicks);
            }
        }
}
```
Listing 7-20

This application, on my machine, uses 115,166 ticks. Let us then modify the code as shown in Listing 7-21.

```
using System;
using System.Collections.Generic;
using System.Diagnostics;

namespace AddRangeBenchmark
{
    class Program
    {
        static void Main(string[] args)
        {
            List<string> numbers = new List<string>();
            for (int i = 0; i < 100000; i++)
                numbers.Add("Number " + i.ToString());

            List<string> target = new List<string>();
            Stopwatch chrono = Stopwatch.StartNew();
            target.AddRange(numbers);
            chrono.Stop();
            Console.WriteLine("AddRange: " + chrono.ElapsedTicks);
        }
    }
}
```
Listing 7-21

The time spent now amounts to only 3,689 ticks. The improvement is significant, and will increase even more with the number of concatenated strings, and also to a lesser extent with their size.

B.6 Using more modern frameworks

B.6.a New and improved often does not mean more performance

You may have found it strange that PROFI is not based on modern frameworks like Windows Presentation Foundation (WPF) and Windows Communication Foundation (WCF). The reasons why PROFI uses WinForms and ASMX web services are two-fold.

First, it had been decided from the beginning to show performance problems that actually happened in production with an industrial application. It would have been artificial to migrate a large part of this application just to be up to date with technology.

Second, most of the performance problems that can be seen are shared between WinForms and WPF, or between WCF and ASMX. Sure, there are some issues that are specific to one technology or another but, when we reach this level of analysis, we have generally entered the stage of tuning. Most of the performance-related recommendations hold for any framework. The only real difference is that the more modern one sometimes provides a few additional ways around the problem than the older one.

Vendors are not lying when they claim the new version of such or such software is faster than the old one: they just happen to provide numbers based on benchmarks, where their software is used by its creators, who are experts at using it. But the actual problem is when another developer is using it in a non-optimized way. Sure, WPF can be hardware-accelerated, but if one does not know that the use of some functions will force it back to software rendering, the level of performance will not be as expected.

As a result, do not expect to improve performance just by adopting a more modern framework: it might even result in lower performance if you do not have the time to learn how to use it in the best conditions. There simply is no silver bullet in the domain of software performance.

B.6.b Windows Presentation Foundation

When writing this book, I considered migrating PROFI's client code from WinForms to WPF. The reasons I have not done so have been explained above, but there are still a few comments to be made on WPF.

First, whatever the technology, the main source of slowdowns in rich interface frameworks remains too many nested panels in the layouts. WPF uses hardware rendering, but the interface composition step is realized before the rendering, and does not gain much from this improvement. Try to keep the number of nested panels reasonable: six or seven levels should be more than enough to create any kind of GUI. The trick is only to use nesting as needed for the interface composition, and not for the modularity of the application. So:

- if you need a layout because resizing elements should change the view, it is used well

- if you use a layout to keep two lists of controls logically separated, and they do not need different layout behaviors, you are lowering composition performance for no good reason.

Still on the subject of layouts, try to compose your application so that the direction of layouts composition remains, as far as possible, the same. Some layouts apply constraints from the container down to the content. For example, when using a `StackLayout`, the contained controls will be reorganized to fit the preferred size of the panel. The direction of layouts composition is down. Whereas a `GridLayout`, for example, uses the opposite composition direction: its size is generated from the size of its content. In order to limit the complexity of the calculation that the WPF layout engine has to make, it is good practice to reduce the changes in composition direction along the hierarchy of layouts as much as possible.

Another performance area where WPF brings some interesting functions is the use of background threads. Using such threads for performing operations separated from the GUI refresh is a good use of threads, in WPF just as in WinForms. But WPF provides a few more tools to make this easier than in WinForms, in particular the class called `System.Windows.Threading.Dispatcher`. The subject has been covered in great detail on the Internet (for example, HTTP://MSDN.MICROSOFT.COM/EN-US/MAGAZINE/CC163328.ASPX), so I am not going to discuss it further here. Just note that this is the number one class that should be used to obtain applications that react quickly.

Comparison of multithread asynchronous work with a paper-based office

I often use the analogy of an application process with the work in a paper-based office to explain the need for multithread asynchronous behavior in an application. When secretaries gives their boss a paper file to read through and sign, they do not wait in front of the desk until they get it back. They will go back to their own desks and continue with other work during that time, perhaps only getting the initial file back at the end of the day. If everybody in a paper-based office worked synchronously, everybody would soon spend their time waiting for others, and no work would be done. The same applies to client applications: it simply does not make sense to use a single thread for UI and processing.

In addition to common recommendations, there are some that are specific to WPF.

In particular, resources are used more heavily in WPF than in WinForms. In the latter, they were mainly used for text whereas in the former, resources are used for much more: storing text and binary resources, certainly, but also templates, styles, or even controls. It becomes more important to have a loading policy for them, the key being not to load everything at the start-up of the application.

Hardware rendering improves performance but, to really benefit from it, one should be aware of which actions will revert to software rendering, in order to avoid them as much as possible. For example, transparency can cause an application window to be software rendered. The exact context for this to happen is beyond the subject of this book, but can easily be found on the Internet. The main resource about WPF performance optimization is HTTP://MSDN.MICROSOFT.COM/EN-US/LIBRARY/AA970683.ASPX. There, you will find additional tricks like object freezing, `DependencyProperty` optimizations, controls recycling, start-up time improvement, and more.

To conclude this section about WPF, there is a dedicated software suite for WPF performance management, simply called *WPF Performance Suite*. This is a free tool created by Microsoft and can be obtained from HTTP://MSDN.MICROSOFT.COM/EN-US/LIBRARY/ AA969767.ASPX. Although it is quite a sophisticated tool, one can benefit from it without understanding it in depth.

B.6.c   Windows Communication Foundation

The same reasons stand for PROFI not being migrated to WCF, and remaining on good old ASMX web service.

There is one reason, though, why WCF may be a good choice for performance, even for beginners: the fact that it uses a new and improved serializer. Wait a minute: I told you above that this does not necessarily make for an actual performance improvement! Indeed, but that does not contradict what we are talking about with WCF. We are not interested in the sheer execution speed of the serialization engine, but in the fact that it radically changes the way it handles serializable classes.

Had `DataContractSerializer` just been quicker than `XmlSerializer`, I would have warned you that this would not necessarily lead to visible performance improvements in scenario execution times. But there is much more: whereas `XmlSerializer` used to process every public property in a class by default, letting one choose what not to serialize, `DataContractSerializer` uses the inverse approach. And this is great news for performance, since the default behavior is now the quickest one: the developer has to manually pick what they want to serialize. Instead of using bloat as the normal behavior, and counting on the developer's expertise to reduce the weight of the messages, WCF starts with the quickest possible behavior (processing nothing) and forces developers to decide what they actually want to serialize.

Of course, there might still be some cases where lazy developers do not care at all, and mark everything as serializable, but this approach makes it much less likely that an object could be fully serialized whereas only part of the data was useful.

WCF is a very good framework in the sense that it defaults to reasonable behaviors. Sure, you will find lots of articles about WCF performance, by adapting concurrency, using throttling, cache, TCP binding, and so on. But those are about tuning, and it is quite a good sign that there is not much to say about possible performance-hindering ways of using WCF. This is the mark of a well-thought-out framework, where you can tune the performance contextually, but where the default behavior is already good and the settings will not let you impair the execution time.

C   Tuning

C.1   Caveat

What more can we do when we have gone through all the "classical" profiling steps shown in the previous chapters, and we still need some more performance? When the code no longer contains any application bottlenecks, it is time to turn to tuning: we will finely adjust parameters, identify system bottlenecks, and generally put in a lot of effort to squeeze out these last few drops of performance. This is where performance optimization's reputation for complexity comes from. But in the vast majority of cases you will not have to go through this step, since the first stage of profiling will generally bring more than enough improvement.

I have repeated this multiple times throughout the book: in 99% of cases, there are much safer and easier ways to improve an application's performance than tuning it. Profiling has already been explained in great detail, and we will discuss re-architecture, which is the third step after tuning, in due course. For now, we will talk briefly about tuning, but the following is more about warning you against its limitations than an encouragement. Unfortunately, if you need to go into tuning further, you will find a lot of literature on the Internet. In my opinion, the adverb "unfortunately" is justified by a number of facts.

- The fact that too many articles about performance are in fact limited to tuning. This is understandable because people are more likely to publish a blog post on expert high-added-value subjects than on general recommendations. But this damages the whole subject of optimization by reinforcing the opinion that performance is an expert field, despite the fact that a good developer with the right profiler can solve most performance problems without any particularly expert knowledge.

- The fact is that this abundance of articles sometimes even leads to opposing recommendations, mainly because the contexts are different for every writer. Actually, this is the major inconvenience of tuning: the proposed solutions are very brittle. Activating specific options or tuning memory management may improve performance in some cases, but may also degrade it in another situation, sometimes even with the same target application. This means there is generally little interest in articles about tuning, because the outcome is not transferable to another context. The only thing that can be useful is when the methodology is explained in enough detail, so that someone else can carry out the same study and find their own optimized parameters.

C.2   The basics: compiling in Release mode

The Release configuration activates some code optimizations by default. These can also be activated in Debug mode, but this is neither common practice nor recommended. Since the debugger .pdb files are generated by default even in Release mode, these optimizations are basically the only difference in terms of performance between the Visual Studio configurations. Incidentally, getting rid of these files will not improve performance.

Activating code optimizations is done in the project properties dialog, as shown in Figure 7-7.

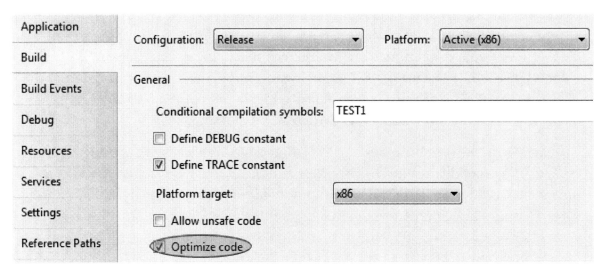

Figure 7-7:   Code optimization option in Visual Studio project properties dialog.

This is clearly a question of tuning, as it generally lowers execution times by a few percent at most. Moreover, if these optimizations were based on best practice, they would also be present by default in Debug mode. In fact, they are so complex that they can actually affect the way the debugger works. In short, these are not actual optimizations, but code tuning.

C.3   Playing with consistency

C.3.a   BASE instead of ACID

We developers have been raised with the indisputable idea that a transaction should be ACID: Atomic, Consistent, Isolated, and Durable. But this guarantee of consistency comes at a high price. There is a good reason why the default isolation level for ADO.NET providers is not "Serializable" (the highest level, allowing for completely ACID transactions) but "ReadCommited" (a lower, but much quicker isolation level).

What is not clear is the need for such continuously perfect consistency across transactions. Let us look at two examples to explain the concept of "eventual consistency."

In the first scenario, we change the street and the city of an address in a database. These two modifications must be made in one transaction, because it is unthinkable that a user of the application could retrieve incomplete information and send a letter that would be addressed to the right street in the wrong city.

In the second scenario, we imagine that a change is needed to the first name of the person, which was spelled incorrectly in the database. Generally a developer will include this modification in the same transaction: the business object corresponding to the person and address will be treated as a single atomic entity, with guaranteed consistency.

However, adding operations to a transaction increases the risk that another transaction will be blocked because of the first one's locks. Eventually, too many locks and waiting for their release will make for a performance drop in the application. All this is done to guarantee that the address and the person's first name are changed at once.

But, when you think about it, creating two separate transactions would help performance by distributing locks and keeping them short, without posing any real consistency problem. What is the worst situation that could happen? If another user retrieves the person data right between the two transactions, the address will be the new one, but the first name will be the incorrect one. This will not prevent correct delivery of the letter. Even if the order is reversed (correct name and wrong address), the effect will not be very different from the case where this user had queried the database just a few seconds before, prior to the first change being committed. In short, the negative effects of splitting the operations in two transactions are negligible.

This approach is called BASE, as opposed to ACID. BASE stands for Basically Available, Soft state, Eventually consistent. We are particularly interested in the last part of the acronym, which we have explained with the example above. Eventual consistency means we are not committed to consistency at all times during processes, but only at the end of their global execution.

The Basically Available part can be seen as a consequence or a strategic improvement of BASE: since we are lowering the frequency of locks, the database will be available for modifications more often. The concept of BASE pushes this to the limit, and considers the database should accept modifications at all times, even if this means that the user eventually realizes that consistency is no longer maintained, and that a compensation mechanism should be used to retrieve it.

C.3.b   Another example

In order to try and give a good understanding of the BASE concept and, in particular, the compensation mechanism to obtain eventual consistency, I will use another example on the running of builds in a software integration factory.

The ACID approach consists of treating every developer commit as a separate transaction, that will need recompiling, playing of the tests, and could be rejected depending on the results of these two operations. Thus, if three developers deliver code modifications in a row, three different complete build processes will be executed. If the first delivery is correct, code modifications will be accepted. Then, the second one will be built with its own modifications plus the ones from the first delivery. Supposing there are errors, this second delivery will be rejected, which means the third one will be compiled with its own modifications plus the ones from the first delivery only.

In this case, the database has never contained code that is not correct in terms of build or tests. But, if a build and its unit tests takes ten minutes, this means that the last developer in the queue will wait half an hour to find out if their code modifications are accepted or not.

The BASE approach to this scenario would consist of accelerating as much as possible the compiling by grouping the three different modifications set. Typically, this would be done by accepting modifications until a particular threshold is reached that would trigger the actual build, be it the number of changes or a maximum time since the first code delivery.

This could even be done manually, with a convention that the last person to deliver code runs the build. The result is that the process would always run in ten minutes.

A lot of us, educated with the concept of consistency, would tend to think it is dangerous not to be able to identify which code delivery has broken the integration.

By contrast, the BASE practitioner takes a more pragmatic approach, and will argue that, in the vast majority of cases, developers work on different modules of code, and that compiling errors or unit tests will clearly show where the problem comes from. At worst, two developers work on the same blocks of code, in which case they will almost certainly be communicating about it. If this is not the case, well, forcing them to do so is another advantage of this approach! It can only be beneficial to the product as a whole.

Isolation in sandboxes

Yes, I know modern software factories will not encounter the problem described above, since they run each build on a new sandbox. But honestly, isn't this one of the examples of resource hogs we are trying to hunt down? Also, such an approach is also limited, since it will not test the interaction of the different sets of modifications before the next nightly build. Why not do this right away? The sacred consistency of the code database is much more dependent on good unit test practices than actual granularity of the commits.

C.3.c   Change PROFI's code to BASE

BASE is not an absolute opposite of ACID – it just introduces a bit more flexibility to processes where losing some consistency will not be a problem, but will dramatically improve performance.

In PROFI's code, there is a particular case of code where we have adopted an ACID approach: when we navigate from the list of persons to the detailed characteristics of a person (and the same interaction on the contracts), we call a web service that brings refreshed data from the server. Clicking on the link to see the details creates a message in UCPersonsList, with the selected person identifier as a parameter (see Listing 7-22).

```
private void btnDetails_Click(object sender, EventArgs e)
{
    if (lstPersons.SelectedItem != null)
    {
        PROFI_INFRA.Message detailsMessage = new PROFI_INFRA.
                Message("PERSONDETAILS");
        detailsMessage.AddParameter("PersonUID", (lstPersons.SelectedItem as
                PersonDisplay).Payload.UID);
        Bus.Current.SendMessage(detailsMessage);
    }
}
```

Listing 7-22

Then, in the `Controller` class, we create the control to display the person and call the method to fill it with the person's identifier. The buffer on the bus is only used to store the graphical control we just created, so that it can be used later when the displaying message will be processed. This is shown in the code in Listing 7-23.

```
public void ProcessMessage(Message message)
{
    PROFI_INFRA.Message displayMessage = new Message("DISPLAYCONTROL");
    switch (message.Order)
    {
        case "PERSONDETAILS":
            UCPerson personDetails = new UCPerson();
            personDetails.Fill(message.Parameters["PersonUID"]);
            Bus.Current.Store(personDetails);
            displayMessage.AddParameter("Target", "Content");
            Bus.Current.SendMessage(displayMessage);
            break;

        [...]
    }
}
```

Listing 7-23

Finally, in `UCPerson`, we implemented the `Fill` function by calling the web service that reads the data for the person (as shown in Listing 7-24).

```
public void Fill(string personUID)
{
    _Person = Controller.Current.RetrievePerson(personUID);
    DisplayPerson();
    lnkDescription.LinkClicked += new LinkLabelLinkClickedEventHandler
                (lnkDescription_LinkClicked);
    lnkContracts.LinkClicked += new LinkLabelLinkClickedEventHandler
                (lnkContracts_LinkClicked);
}
```

Listing 7-24

Another way would be to use the instance of **Person** that was contained in the list. Indeed, when calling the function to populate the list, we created a list of **Person-Display**. This class, as its name indicates, is used mainly to overload the **ToString** function in order to display the lines in the list with the requested level of information (see Listing 7-25).

```
internal class PersonDisplay
{
    internal Person Payload;

    public PersonDisplay(Person payload)
    {
        this.Payload = payload;
    }

    public override string ToString()
    {
        return string.Concat(Payload.LastName, " ", Payload.FirstName);
    }
}
```

Listing 7-25

The instance of this class still contains the instance of **Person** in the field called **Payload**. We could thus modify the event manager on the Details link so that it sends the whole person definition to the bus, instead of only the identifier.

To do so, we will use the same mechanism as for the passing of a graphical control, namely putting it on a buffer of the bus (called `Slot`), as is shown in Listing 7-26. As a result, the message will not carry a parameter anymore.

```
private void btnDetails_Click(object sender, EventArgs e)
{
    if (lstPersons.SelectedItem != null)
    {
        Bus.Current.Store((lstPersons.SelectedItem as PersonDisplay).Payload);
        PROFI_INFRA.Message detailsMessage = new PROFI_INFRA.
                Message("PERSONDETAILS");
        Bus.Current.SendMessage(detailsMessage);
    }
}
```
Listing 7-26

In the `Controller` class, we will not call a `Fill` function with a parameter string anymore, but an overloaded signature that will accept a `Person` as its parameter (see Listing 7-27).

```
public void ProcessMessage(Message message)
{
    PROFI_INFRA.Message displayMessage = new Message("DISPLAYCONTROL");
    switch (message.Order)
    {
        case "PERSONDETAILS":
            UCPerson personDetails = new UCPerson();
            personDetails.Fill(Bus.Current.ReadStoredObject() as Person);
            Bus.Current.Store(personDetails);
            displayMessage.AddParameter("Target", "Content");
            Bus.Current.SendMessage(displayMessage);
            break;

        [...]
    }
}
```
Listing 7-27

Finally, in the class `UCPerson`, the new `Fill` signature would simply not call a web service anymore, because the necessary data would be complete (see Listing 7-28).

```
public void Fill(Person person)
{
    _Person = person;
    DisplayPerson();
    lnkDescription.LinkClicked += new LinkLabelLinkClickedEventHandler
                (lnkDescription_LinkClicked);
    lnkContracts.LinkClicked += new LinkLabelLinkClickedEventHandler
                (lnkContracts_LinkClicked);
}
```

Listing 7-28

Again, a developer used to the principles of strict consistency will object that the definition of the person might have changed between the loading of the list and the user accessing the details of the corresponding line.

In practice, lots of arguments can be used to show this is not such a problem, and that the expected advantages of fresh data are perhaps not worth round-tripping to the server every time, which is extremely costly in terms of serialization, use of network, and so on.

- First, a user will generally not spend a long time viewing a list of persons. If they call this list, it is generally to locate a person and immediately view their details. This already dramatically reduces the probability of inconsistency.

- Let us now suppose that the user sees an address that is not correct as of one second ago, because a colleague was in the process of correcting it. This could also have happened if the first user had clicked on the link just a few seconds before, so the case should be treated as part of how the application is used (e.g. allocating persons to dedicated users).

- Moreover, if the user decides to create a contract document for this person, the Word document merge process will be run on the server, and the address will then be the latest one. At worst, the user will have a moment of confusion when seeing a different address on the Word document from the one on screen. But simply refreshing the screen will indicate that the data has just been updated.

- In some cases, it could even be considered that changing the data between two views in the same client process could be a problem. Let us suppose a complex mathematical calculation has to be derived from the characteristics of the person. Wouldn't it be better to have a correct, even if outdated, result rather than a completely erroneous one? In this case, the consistency of the process might go against the consistency of data.

Using the modified code above means one web service call can be avoided, which is excellent for the performance of the application.

What about contracts?

This optimization has not been made to the contracts in the final version of the code containing all optimizations, because it would have meant refactoring a lot of code, thus moving all the other modifications. This would have made it difficult for you to find the modifications we made to the code in the profiling chapters. But carrying out the modification above on contracts does not pose any practical problems.

C.4 Hard-code HTTP calls

In Chapter 5, *Profiling the Sample Application – Client Side*, we left Section C.3, *Creating web service clients* after carrying out interesting performance improvements, but with the time required to prepare the web service proxies still high. Indeed, serialization, reflective calls and loading dynamic assemblies are operations that are intrinsically complex.

There exists an efficient, albeit radical, way of suppressing the time spent in these ancillary operations. We could remove the web reference, and create an HTTP client dealing with hard-coded SOAP requests and responses. The outgoing XML content would simply be used after replacing parameters with the right values, and the incoming XML parsed in a DOM to analyze the response from the server.

Code such as that in Listing 7-29 could be used to do so.

```
HttpWebRequest request = (HttpWebRequest)WebRequest.Create("http://localhost:2959/
WebSite1/Service.asmx");
request.Method = "POST";
request.ContentType = "text/xml; charset=utf-8";

string content = "<?xml version=\"1.0\" encoding=\"utf-8\"?>"
    + " <soap:Envelope xmlns:xsi=\"http://www.w3.org/2001/XMLSchema-instance\"
                xmlns:xsd=\"http://www.w3.org/2001/XMLSchema\"
                xmlns:soap=\"http://schemas.xmlsoap.org/soap/envelope/\">"
    + "  <soap:Body>"
    + "    <RetrievePerson xmlns=\"http://simpletalk.gouigoux.org/PROFI/2011/\">"
    + "      <PersonUID>" + PersonUID + "</PersonUID>"
    + "    </RetrievePerson >"
    + "  </soap:Body>"
    + "</soap:Envelope>";

byte[] data = Encoding.UTF8.GetBytes(content);
request.ContentLength = data.Length;

Stream scribe = request.GetRequestStream();
scribe.Write(data, 0, data.Length);

WebResponse response = request.GetResponse();
StreamReader reader = new
StreamReader(response.GetResponseStream());
string result = reader.ReadToEnd();

Console.Out.WriteLine(result);
Console.In.ReadLine();

XmlDocument dom = new XmlDocument();
dom.LoadXml(result);
XmlNamespaceManager ns = new XmlNamespaceManager(dom.NameTable);
ns.AddNamespace("soap", "http://schemas.xmlsoap.org/soap/envelope/");
ns.AddNamespace("x", "http://simpletalk.gouigoux.org/PROFI/2011/");
```

```
Console.Out.WriteLine(dom.DocumentElement.SelectSingleNode("/soap:Envelope/
              soap:Body/x:RetrievePersonResponse/x:RetrievePersonResult/
              x:LastName", ns).InnerText);
```

Listing 7-29

When talking about how radical this change was, it is worth recognizing everything we sacrificed to speed:

- no automatic update when the WSDL changes

- no support for dynamic URLs

- need to modify the XPath requests if the service changes

- risk of error in the XML generated

- possible problems with the namespaces

- and more.

However, performance is excellent, since we restrict the web service operation time to almost just the time for network exchange and server processing (which could also be hard-coded, for the non-business-related part). But the price to pay is so high in terms of robustness and functionality that it is definitely a question of tuning. This should only be carried out on completely stable platforms on which performance is of uttermost importance.

String concatenation

The content of the request is created in the code above through string concatenation. We explained before that it is better to use StringBuilder, *but an attentive look at the code above shows that there are actually only two concatenation operations, around the insertion of the* PersonUID *variable. All the other + operators will be removed by the compiler, which will create one single constant for each of the two message parts around the variable. This code is thus not less optimized than if using* String-Builder, *even if it could have been better to do so, if only to standardize coding rules.*

C.5   Globalized asynchrony

In the paragraph above, on asynchronous processing, we talked about modifying some parts of an application to make them asynchronous. It is possible to extend this behavior to almost all interactions in a client. This should be thought of in a global way, and is a difficult task. Indeed, the presence of callbacks for each of the calls tends to diffuse the code for activating a function and reacting to its completion all over the classes, and make it difficult to read and maintain. However, strict norms and use of dedicated frameworks help to mitigate this risk.

Again, if high performance is absolutely essential and if an additional improvement justifies difficult rewriting of the application, it is possible to use Async, Reactive Extensions or other such technologies to write globally asynchronous code, but this is a daunting task.

C.6   Limit reflection

Another coding trick that can be considered as tuning consists of replacing the reflective calls on the assemblies using `System.Reflection` classes with those from `Mono.Cecil`. Cecil is an Open Source project that is integrated with Mono (the Open Source .NET implementation, maintained by Novell, and now Xamarin), which allows for reflection without loading the whole class. Cecil uses only the assemblies' manifest to do so, thus obtaining much better performance than the "official" Microsoft .NET methods.

It should be noted that, just like other Mono libraries, Cecil is not limited to Linux and works perfectly under Windows, including under a Microsoft CLR.

C.7 Advice on ASP.NET

ASP.NET includes functions for session management and page state management. These are very useful for turning a fundamentally disconnected application into one that reacts as if it was connected. However, these functionalities are extremely resource-greedy, and it is highly recommended they are disabled if the developer does not use them.

This consists of three steps:

- disable session management (in the configuration file)

- disable viewstate management (globally or per-page)

- then, use the `Page.IsPostBack` test as much as possible in order to find out whether this is the first call to a page, so as to limit loading processes to this first call, and avoid repeating them at every round trip from the client to the server.

Of course, there are times when these features are truly necessary and can be used, as long as it is done with care. When doing so, one should use them in the best possible way. For example, when session management is used, it should be used in the `InProc` mode, where everything is stored in memory, rather than in `ServerState` or `SqlServer-State`. These modes are indeed slower because session content has to be serialized in order to be stored on another machine or in a remote database, respectively.

C.8 Using weak references

Microsoft has published a complete performance tuning guide for managed code (HTTP://MSDN.MICROSOFT.COM/EN-US/LIBRARY/MS998547). This document is an excellent accompaniment to the present book, and it provides expert technical solutions. I am not going to copy it here, but I wish to stress one point in particular: the value of using weak references in an application that generates a high memory turnover of objects.

When a program uses objects that are potentially complex to initiate and occupy lots of memory, it can be frustrating to only have the choice between always keeping a reference to them (thus blocking memory reuse) and releasing every reference to them for the GC to collect them, knowing there is a risk one will have to initiate a similar object just a few moments later, depending on the context.

Weak references offer a compromise between the two approaches, by keeping a reference to an object, while letting the GC recycle it if necessary. If another use of the object appears before the GC has kicked in, the weak reference enables the developer to retrieve a strong reference to it and manipulate it as any other instance. If the object has been recycled, the weak reference will inform the calling code that it will have to re-initiate the instance.

The class to be used is `WeakReference`. It exposes members `IsAlive` to find out if the object is still available, and `Target` to retrieve a reference on it if this is so.

This approach should be classified as tuning, because it works on particular applicative cases when it may allow a gain of a few percent at most. However, the gain in terms of memory can be bigger (up to a few tens of percent) if the objects have a rapid turnover.

C.9   Beware of extreme tuning

C.9.a   The limits of tuning

Talking about extreme tuning may be a tautology: tuning in itself can be considered an extreme, and even unreasonable, programming technique. I am personally not far from thinking so, hence the brevity of the section on tuning in this book. I will illustrate the risks associated with tuning using three examples in the sections below.

C.9.b   Struct instead of class

First, we will look into the use of structures instead of classes. The risk in tuning is of transforming all classes into structures when the objects in question are simply used for data storage in big quantities. Indeed there is no absolute guarantee that it will actually improve an application's performance: only precise measurements on dedicated scenarios will show whether this is so. The parameters (memory occupation, size of objects, size of the lists, etc.) are too numerous to be able to predict whether such a modification will be worthwhile.

Generally speaking, structures are not better than classes, provided the latter are reused as much as possible. Immutability is indeed great for limiting bugs, but also consumes lots of memory. Transforming a `class` into a `struct` means creating immutable copies every time the instances are passed to a function. In the end, the scenario could execute a bit quicker, but with a big impact on memory.

Sometimes, using non-immutable classes instead of structures is actually a more effective form of tuning. For example, let us come back to the processing of accented characters that we talked about in Chapter 6 on server-side profiling, and imagine some letters must be replaced with an asterisk. The current code is as shown in Listing 7-30.

```
foreach (char Character in CharactersList)
    Result = Result.Replace(Character, '*');
```
Listing 7-30

The immutability of strings implies that we are going to create as many new instances of string as there are characters in the list to be processed, thus leaving it to the GC to recycle that many strings. If the code is used intensively, it can be worth upgrading to some more complex, but less memory-greedy, code like the one shown in Listing 7-31.

```
char[] TableString = Result.ToCharArray();
for (int Index = 0; Index < Result.Length; Index++)
    foreach (char Character in CharactersList)
        if (TableString[Index] == Character)
        {
            TableString[Index] = '*';
            break;
        }
Result = new string(TableString);
```

Listing 7-31

This code provides the further advantage that it will not go on searching in the list of characters once one entry has already caused it to be turned into an asterisk.

All this shows that tuning should not be pushed too far, because there are risks of losing performance while we are trying to improve it. Each tuning activity must be evaluated with care, in all possible scenarios, and taking into account not only the speed of execution but also other application health indicators. If speed increases by a few percent but memory use is doubled at the same time, it goes without saying that, except in extremely rare cases, it is better to revert to the original code.

C.9.c   Late instantiation and early release

This is another example of tuning. We will not come back to the principles behind this, as they have been explained in Chapter 2, Section A.8.a, *Criteria for memory collection*. This section is only to stress the fact, if need be, that this is clearly a tuning-related modification. We could even use the redundant expression "extreme tuning," as results are extremely hard to demonstrate.

The only advantage of these two techniques is that they cannot have an adverse effect. The performance improvement due to their use in the code may be extremely limited, but it cannot be negative. To be perfectly honest, I have never succeeded in finding actual production code where using late instantiation and early release helped to noticeably reduce execution time, memory use or GC activity.

C.9.d   Byte instead of int in enumerations?

Our last example will show that tuning, in addition to having low or sometimes even negative impact, can also be dangerous because it is difficult to master. Profiling is a very down-to-earth activity, where common sense is as important as observation. Tuning, on the other hand, can sometimes seem to be in opposition to logic.

For example: is it better to code an enumeration with only a few values using a `byte`? In terms of code, which of the two codes in Listing 7-32 is the best (knowing that, when no class is specified, an enumeration uses `Int32`)?

```
private enum SettingMode32
{
    NONE = 0,
    ACCENTS = 1,
    CASE = 2,
    SEPARATORS = 4,
}

private enum SettingMode8 : byte
{
    NONE = 0,
    ACCENTS = 1,
    CASE = 2,
    SEPARATORS = 4,
}
```

Listing 7-32

In functional terms, both versions do exactly the same thing but `SettingMode8` uses only one byte for storing values. It should thus be more efficient, but the opposite is actually true!

Indeed, Microsoft has optimized the enumerations since version 2.0 of .NET, so that they are aligned on 32 bits, which was the standard width of a processor bus a few years ago. However, that does not mean it will be the same for the next versions of .NET.

This is why tuning is so difficult: common sense has nothing to do with reality in tuning, and it is very easy to end up with useless or even counterproductive modifications that we think are useful without actually having proven them to be so.

D   Going further with re-architecture

The previous section was about tuning, and explained that this step should be envisaged after profiling when performance had not been improved sufficiently. From experience, I can tell you this is rarely the case.

But if profiling was not enough and we are sure that the problem is with the intrinsic complexity of the software, what is the point in trying to find a solution with tuning? It can help to improve performance by a few percent, at the price of a lot of effort and being limited to very specific contexts, but it will not radically change the performance of an application.

In this case, it is better to skip to Step 3, which means iterating on the initial architecture activity, rethinking in depth the fundamentals of our application. Is the database limiting us in terms of throughput? Under certain conditions, in-memory databases can provide excellent performance improvements. Simple and innovative architectures can even help us get rid of the database altogether, rendering useless all the associated modules, and dramatically easing persistence.

But re-architecting a system can also start with simply scaling the hardware better.

D.1   Scalability

D.1.a   Concept

Scalability is the capacity of a system to increase its activity to loads that are higher than the ones used as a reference for the integration tests, and in particular doing so in the most efficient manner possible.

For example, a low-scalability system might require twice the power to process only 40% additional data. On the other hand, an application carefully written for scalability might be able to process almost double the size of data in the same conditions.

This is not related to profiling or tuning, because scalability is mainly a question of respecting programming rules and architecture best practices. Scalability is a large subject in its own right, and I will only skim over the subject here with some basic advice.

D.1.b   Scalability modes

First, we should understand the difference between scaling-up and scaling-out. Scaling-up consists of using a more powerful machine. To my knowledge, this kind of operation never causes any performance problems, and most of the time the results can be determined in advance through benchmarks.

The only problems with scaling-up are the following:

- most of the time the application has to be stopped in order to switch to the new hardware infrastructure
- the price of the equipment increases exponentially with its power.

Scaling-out consists of multiplying the number of machines. Generally speaking it has more to commend it because it is not limited to the size of the biggest machine that is available, or that we can afford. However, certain coding recommendations need to be followed to make it worthwhile. We will discuss these in more detail below.

D.1.c   Parallelizing processes

For scaling-out to be possible, we have to use processes that can be parallelized, at least on a coarse-grain basis. Luckily for most developers, web servers can generally do this and are good candidates for scaling-out, due to the utterly disconnected nature of the web, where each request can be treated as independent from the other, and then two of them parallelized without functional issues.

A problem can arise when a session-keeping mechanism breaks this independence for requests coming from the same client. In this case, the allocation of parallel requests has to take into account the session affinity to a given machine.

Except for this limitation (which, admittedly, is considerable), each request can be processed separately, and software suites like IIS or Apache Web Server are naturally highly-scalable. The real problems arise when we try to push the parallelism to a finer granularity, for example by processing a single request in separate parts, each of them allocated to a different machine. The relationships between different parts of the process can make this much more difficult.

D.1.d   Scalability best practices

Even if I do not pretend to any expert knowledge of parallel programming, a few remarks can be made on the link between scalability and performance profiling.

- It is important, when the session mechanism is to be used, to keep the session size as light as possible. If mechanisms for session-sharing between servers are used, one should also take care to place only serializable objects into ASP.NET `Session` and `Application` containers.

- Whenever possible, services should be made re-entrant, which means they are based on objects that will not be recreated for each call, but can serve many calls, even if it is still necessary to go through a short process that quickly adapts them to the context. This is a complex approach, but generally gives excellent results. However, this needs an expert understanding of how the application works. For example, there is no use in trying to make a process that mainly calls the database re-entrant, since the connections pool mechanism already makes this useless, reusability being done by the lower layers.

- Without going as far as complete re-entrance, it is worth keeping services stateless as much as possible. Stateless services are independent of the execution context. The stateless concept is a generalization of the sessionless concept to all objects that can be used when processing a request.

D.1.e   Parallel Linq

A simple example of code shows how easy parallelizing a loop can be with frameworks like Parallel Linq, provided the process is adapted to it (typically, when an iteration of the loop has no relation to the other iterations, i.e. the inner workings are stateless).

```
using System;
using System.Collections.Generic;
using System.Linq;
using System.Text;
using System.Diagnostics;
using System.Threading;
using System.Threading.Tasks;
```

```
namespace PLinqTest
{
    class Program
    {
        static void Main(string[] args)
        {
            List<int> Integers = new List<int>();
            for (int ind = 100000; ind < 120000; ind++)
                Integers.Add(ind);

            Stopwatch Chrono = Stopwatch.StartNew();
            foreach (int Value in Integers)
                if (IsPrime(Value))
                    Console.WriteLine(Value);
            Console.WriteLine("Extraction done in {0} ms", Chrono.Elapsed.
                            Milliseconds);

            Chrono = Stopwatch.StartNew();
            Parallel.ForEach<int>(Integers, i => { if (IsPrime(i)) Console.
                            WriteLine(i); });
            Console.WriteLine("Extraction done in {0} ms", Chrono.Elapsed.
                            Milliseconds);
        }

        private static bool IsPrime(int Number)
        {
            for (int ind = 2; ind < Number - 1; ind++)
                if (Number % ind == 0)
                    return false;
            return true;
        }
    }
}
```

Listing 7-33

This code shows an almost perfect scalability: when using two processor cores instead of one, the processing time is divided by a factor very close to two.

It is particularly interesting to use these techniques to improve an application's performance, since frameworks like Parallel Linq have made this an accessible technique, whereas it required experts a few years ago. This is not a case of tuning, because parallel computing is a large movement that will affect all server-related developments in the coming years. Instead, it should be considered a new programming paradigm.

Making the code thread-safe

Had we needed to store the prime numbers in the code above, it would have been essential to use a list class that supports adding values in a thread-safe manner, which is something generic lists do not do. Instead, we should use classes in the `System.Collections.Concurrent` *namespace.*

D.2   Institutionalize cache use

Using cache mechanisms in an institutionalized manner goes beyond simple tuning, because the generic character bears an architectural approach, needing a well thought-out infrastructure.

D.3   Think Lean/Agile

Lean and Agile approaches apply not only to the code, but also to architecture and design in general. Such pragmatic and simplifying approaches led, for example, to the concept of BASE discussed above. In the same manner, some innovative architecture models can bring sizeable leaps in performance. We will discuss a few of them here.

D.3.a   IMDB

The In-Memory DataBase was launched by SAP and Oracle, even if several software applications were developed before these well-known products. The aim of putting a database in RAM was obviously to improve performance. In the case of applications highly dependent on a database, this solution can bring immediate performance gains. The cost, however, should not be overlooked.

D.3.b   NoSQL

The Not Only SQL movement consists of replacing tabular database structures with better-adapted ones (such as key/value pairs, dictionaries, and tree-like graphs). This translates into a capacity to request data in a more logical language than SQL, and is particularly aimed at increasing scalability. The gains in performance also come from the fact that these approaches often eliminate the need for an Object/Relational Mapping infrastructure, which is generally quite a heavy subsystem.

D.3.c   CQRS

The Command and Query Responsibility Segregation approach is about radically separating the operations related to modifying data from reading operations. CQRS is based on the fact that 80% of operations in most applications are reading, and that it is a shame that the remaining 20% of operations which involve writing to the database slow all other requests down because of locks. The CQRS architecture proposes using two independent pipelines: write operations are serializable commands to a dedicated server linked to the main database, while read operations are sent to several servers in parallel, each of them keeping their data up to date in an asynchronous way.

The slight shift in time to update data after writing is a reasonable sacrifice in terms of consistency, knowing that the scalability improvement is huge. This kind of architecture helps performance a lot, since it can combine scaling-up of the write server and scaling-out of the reporting servers, thus striking a better balance between performance and price than standard client-server architectures can. Consistency is achieved, but at the end rather than at every step of the process, hence the designation of the paradigm as eventual consistency.

D.3.d Object prevalence

Object prevalence is an old technique that came back to life a few years ago with frameworks like Bamboo on .NET, or Prevayler on Java. To put it simply, object prevalence takes the best aspects of IMDB and NoSQL, as illustrated by Figure 7-8.

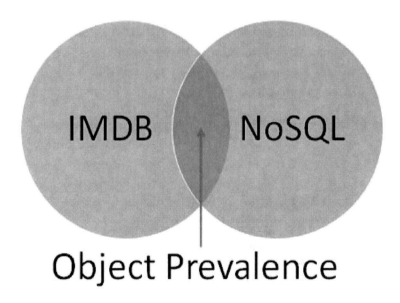

Figure 7-8:   Concepts of object prevalence.

Object prevalence's goal is to not use any persistence structure at all, and to only store data in RAM, directly in the business objects model. Naturally, data will not be lost if the server fails: a persistence operation is carried out, but in the background, based on memory snapshots and logs of the commands applied to the business objects.

In this architecture, the developer can concentrate purely on coding a high-added-value business model, in a Domain Driven Design approach, without wasting time on Object/Relational Mapping operations, or even fitting their design into table structures. Requesting data in .NET object prevalence will use technologies like Linq-To-Objects. The benefits in terms of performance are huge, not only because the data is in memory, but also because they are directly available in the format to process them.

More on object prevalence

Since I have been studying object prevalence and giving lectures on it, I humbly propose my blog as a resource for more details on object prevalence: HTTP://GOUIGOUX.COM/BLOG-FR/?CAT=7.

D.4 Performance of modern architectures

The present book has talked at length about traditional .NET programming errors related to performance on classical n-tier architectures. However, the lessons we have learned from that do not apply to other architectures, where lack of performance can have very different causes, or at least where the most common errors are not the same.

Without going into much detail, the following paragraphs suggest starting points for improvement on a few of the modern architectures we have just talked about. Each technology has its own limitations, and understanding these allows for a better use of the architecture in question.

D.4.a Scale-out

The main problem with scaling-out is that the increase of performance is not proportional to the increase of resources. It leads to a plateau of performance because of the increasing cost of coordinating resources with all machines actively involved in the cluster. What really makes a system architecture better is when this plateau appears only with a high number of machines. However, this is not always a problem, and some applications may have perfect scalability, keeping an almost linear increase of performance with each machine added to the cluster.

D.4.b   Parallelized computation

The difficulty in parallelizing code for performance improvement is linked to the correct management of locks and an efficient orchestration of processes. As was briefly stated above, one should be particularly cautious about thread-safe operations. Despite the fact that some frameworks like Parallel Linq make this more accessible, this is still an expert's job.

D.4.c   Mobility

Mobile terminals often use I/O on memory cards, which are much slower than hard disks. As a result, operations like ZIP-uncompressing can lead to results very different to those seen on a desktop machine. Optimizing a process can thus lead to a radically different decision on a mobile system than on another piece of hardware.

Another example is the use of cache: where we strike the balance will not be the same on a PC with 1 GB of RAM and 500 GB ROM as on a 32 MB SD-Card-based RAM terminal. Bandwidth optimization will clearly be of much higher importance on a 3G phone than on a 1 GB 100% LAN-based client application.

All this should be taken into account when profiling a mobile application, and conclusions on performance will be much more closely related to resource use on such machines. Another piece of advice is not to profile on emulators but on physical devices, in order to get actual metrics. The performance difference between the two can be enormous and, moreover, it may be higher for a given resource while being lower on another one. As such, it is impossible to profile accurately using emulators. Again, this comes back to the general rule that one should always try to put oneself in the customer's shoes.

D.4.d   SOA and ESB

Service Oriented Architectures and Enterprise Service Buses are a completely new field for performance management.

First of all, the basic notion of speed of execution is difficult to grasp on an asynchronous message: you do not know who is going to process it or when it will be done. If the service in charge is busy, the message can wait in line for a few minutes. If it is not, it will be processed the next instant. In short, it is impossible to measure performance of an asynchronous Message Oriented Middleware in terms of time. The number of transactions per second is generally used or, alternatively, throughput.

Putting in place test scenarios in such architectures can be quite difficult, not only because they require complex software and hardware infrastructures, but also because their execution is far less deterministic than that of a simple client-server model.

A few points to think about when profiling the performance of a service bus.

- Bus supervision tools provide metrics that can be used just like we do with system counters when we are profiling standalone applications. Since these tools are mostly compatible with the traditional methods for retrieving probes measurements, using them in a test factory should be straightforward.

- Injectors disseminated in the System Under Test as a whole can be synchronized by using a second bus completely separated from the one under test. This second bus is only used to diffuse test scenario messages to the different servers making up the first bus. This method can help us achieve synchronized stress scenarios that are a realistic use of the bus, provided that the distributed scenarios are granular enough to stay synchronized.

- Tools exist to synchronize logs from separate servers when testing them under load in multiple machine environments. A few modifications should be enough for these tools to be used to collate logs from servers with different responsibilities in the bus, so as to show performance issues between emitters and listeners. These kinds of markers

543

would be very interesting to record on an ESB because, if the times match up, that might mean the coupling is not as loose as it should be. In a way, this is the case with the Query/Response pattern: technically, there are two separate messages and the applications are decoupled but, depending on the method used by the emitter to deal with the response, we can have performance problems. For example, the emitter could block the application in a waiting loop with timeout (this is an extreme case given for the purpose of demonstration).

- The subject of ESB performance is getting bigger, and an Internet search will come up with lots of references to commercial tools. I encourage you to think first in terms of methodology: the priority is to find the bottlenecks. Tools can help you, but they will not do your work. Most of the time, simple logs and some work on it will get you further that any elaborate tool you do not have a good grasp of.

D.4.e   Databases

Database performance in itself could fill many other books, and I have intentionally stayed out of the subject. The reason for this small paragraph is only to bring your attention to several concepts that can help you go much further when performance tuning is just not enough anymore.

- BigData: instead of slowing your centralized database with huge amounts of data, the approach taken by products like Hadoop, Cassandra or Voldemort may be the answer you are waiting for. The Map/Reduce paradigm can provide parallelism at the level of data chunks, and lead to linear performance in the processing of huge data sets.

- Clustering is often seen as a technology that is difficult to set up. Products like SQL Server 2012 and PostgreSQL 8.4 make this a normal administrative task. The associated changes in the development are quite limited most of the time, particularly if you compare this solution with the BigData approach, which requires you to change your whole approach to data, leading to longer time-to-market.

- Sharding and partitioning can be applied to databases in order to put in place a more controlled parallelism than true clustering.

D.5   Going even further

As this book draws to an end, I have a few comments on what you might want to look at next in terms of profiling. Performance is a domain where improvements can extend without any limit. This is why it is so important to set limits and goals at the beginning of a profiling campaign.

Comparing the profiling metrics before and after optimization can provide inspiration for ways of optimizing the application's architecture. You can use JetBrains dotTrace for these operations but, in my experience, a tool like NDepend is better designed for a developer to benefit from this analysis.

The function called **Compare two versions of a code base** allows you to compare two different source code analyses, as shown in Figure 7-9.

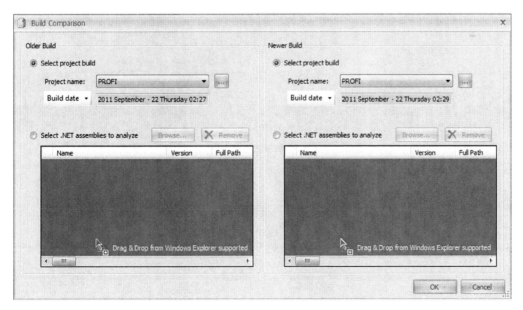

Figure 7-9:   Comparing two versions of a code base in NDepend.

The results obtained when comparing PROFI before and after all the optimizations we have done in the previous chapters are shown in Figure 7-10.

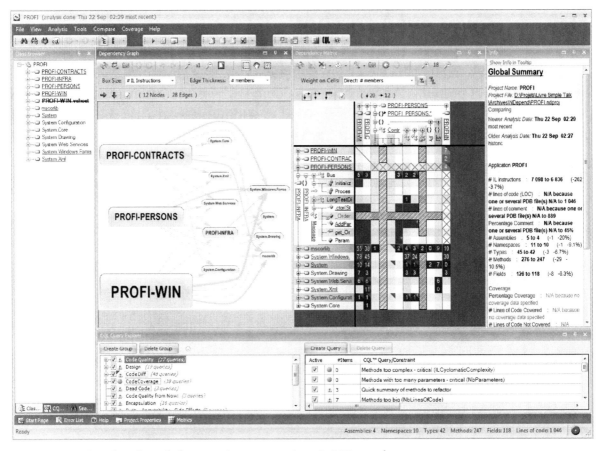

Figure 7-10: Results of a code base versions comparison in NDepend.

We will not go into too much detail, but a quick analysis of the results, in particular the dependencies graph and the matrix showing references before and after the optimizations, allows you to do a number of things.

- Check that the code modifications have not harmed the application architecture in terms of coupling. This is an important point.

- Check that the code quality metrics are also better than before. A good improvement should be simple. If it is not, it is worth refactoring. If it turns out that it is impossible to return to the previous level of code quality, maybe the optimization is too close to tuning.

- Find additional ideas for refactoring classes and modules, which could result in incidental improvements to performance.

- Finally, and this may be the most important benefit, this kind of analysis provides a better grasp of the code and a deeper understanding of the application, which is without any doubt the best guarantee for further optimizations.

Chapter 8: Conclusion

A   Everything can be a performance problem

If one single principle should be put forward at the end of this book, it is that performance issues can come from anywhere. There simply is no miracle recipe for locating bottlenecks, and only careful profiling will show the root of the problem.

It is of uttermost importance, when performance is low, not to run an analysis without preparation, or, even worse, use a debugger. Even a simple unit test is a great way to isolate a problem. Profiling is the same as testing: a small recorded scenario and a profiler is the simple but efficient recipe for solving a performance problem.

This preliminary remark will help you step back and be objective with the checklist I propose below. Writing a limited list of the main .NET coding problems related to performance is highly questionable, precisely since issues can come from everywhere, and each situation is a new one. Nevertheless, well-known cases stand out.

This being said, the profiler is the judge for every case, and you will adjust the list depending on your long-term observations.

B   Checklist

Even though the exercise is bound not to be exhaustive, we will list here the "traditional" code mistakes that can result in low .NET performance.

- The most frequent problems are those related to low control over iterations. Each performance issue can always be discussed, but when a function is called thousands of times in a loop, there is no question: either execution time or number of calls has to be reduced. The typical example of this category of problems is a web method called in a loop, instead of using an equivalent method dealing with all operations at once.

- As a corollary, systematically calculating values that will not change, whether in a loop or over several distinct calls, rather than storing them for further use, is a frequently observed source of slowdowns.

- Loading a complete set of data rather than streaming through it is often much simpler to code, but performance will be lower, especially on big volumes. In particular, `XmlTextReader` should be preferred to `XmlDocument`, `StreamReader` preferred to `File.ReadAllText`, `StreamWriter` preferred to `File.WriteAllText`.

- Strings generally represent a huge part of the memory used by a .NET application. It is important to compose and manipulate them with adequate methods. `StringBuilder` should be used when concatenating more than five strings. Cases of intense modifications should be handled by replacing strings with arrays of characters.

- Bad exception management can be the cause of many problems, either functional or related to performance. Exceptions should be limited to genuinely exceptional cases that will not happen in the normal execution of a user scenario. They should never be used to report simple errors.

- As a consequence, one should never use `Parse` functions in a `try...catch` range if incorrectly formatted values are anything less than exceptional. `TryParse` functions should be used unless we are almost certain that all values will be correct.

- The web services proxies generated by `WSDL.exe` are extremely heavy classes. One should be careful to put as few methods in services as possible, even if this means slicing them into several modules.

- The garbage collector in .NET is extremely efficient, but one should still take care not to overload it. It can get out of most memory use situations, but if the code loops on reserving large memory slots that are almost immediately left unused, it will legitimately take more and more time, thus slowing down the whole process.

Paying particular attention to these rules should help to avoid needing a profiler in most cases. These technical recommendations, however, should be accompanied by a more global warning against over-architecture, which remains the most insidious enemy of performance. We will come back to this a little later, at the very end of the book, to stress the importance of the subject.

C   Root causes of errors

Before concluding, let us look into root causes, namely the reasons why these coding errors appear so frequently. This will help us to avoid them.

- First of all, lack of training in performance coding is undoubtedly the source of lots of problematic situations. One only needs to read outlines of .NET programming courses to realize that very few of them talk about performance except for dedicated sessions advertised as being for experts. I hope I have convinced you that this approach is flawed, and that non-expert developers do not need more than a few tricks to avoid most performance traps. This book should be enough to avoid most of them, at least for non-critical operations. Expert training is only necessary for writing fully-optimized code, which, most of the time, will only bring a few more percent of performance than simple, clean code.

- Performance is also often left to one side during tests. For example, one rarely reads unit tests that take advantage of their execution to collect performance-related metrics about the System Under Test.

- The absence of a culture of software performance is also apparent in requirements analyses. Most requirements analyses only contain a single reference to execution times, stating, for example, that all simple operations should take less than three seconds. At best, they will differentiate long and short interactions. Obviously this is not enough: an authentication process has no reason to last more than one second. On the other hand, the complexity of some mass-treatments sometimes justifies hours of processing. An Agile approach with user stories will be useful for solving this problem, by embedding target execution time, even if expressed approximately.

- Lastly, and this may be the most worrying cause, there is a refusal from some developers or software architects to adopt pragmatic, simple solutions. Using conventions instead of code, for example, is still often discussed, and some applications spend long periods differentiating two situations that could have easily been segregated with a simple convention. The so-called risks associated with the use of conventions rather than handling all situations in the code are mostly a pretext to avoid changing our way of thinking.

Convention over code approach

Convention over code refers to adopting a convention within code (for example, a naming convention) that implies or adopts certain behavior, rather than relying on a more complex, computationally intensive operation to achieve that behavior programmatically. You can learn more about this best practice at HTTP://MSDN.MICROSOFT.COM/EN-US/MAGAZINE/DD419655.ASPX.

All these reasons are made even more important by the fact that application responsiveness is an important criterion for most customers. Honestly, who prefers a slow application without known bugs over a highly-responsive one with a few minor bugs for which there exist workarounds? Moreover, the latter will be easy to improve, simply by correcting the last remaining bugs, whereas the former, in the worst case, can take months of profiling and end up with re-architecting to reach the requested level of performance.

D   Coding lightly

The history of IT resembles geological strata. Twenty years ago, we programmed logical controllers to command liquid crystal displays in order to display a number or a letter. Nowadays, nobody even thinks of these layers of code, although every OS is based on them to display characters. There has been sedimentation, so much in fact that we often do not even remember the name of these old technologies. After 15 years of use, the BIOS will progressively be replaced by some more sophisticated codes: who remembers that this was *a* BIOS, and not *the* BIOS?

The deposit and sedimentation process can become a performance issue. Without going to the extreme and proposing that we code business applications with assembly code in order to improve their performance, the question should be posed, when architecting a solution, of the usefulness of each layer. In the world of the Internet, an application server and an injection framework have become so usual that some projects use them even if they do not need them. In the same way, I have witnessed numerous projects that used a full-blown database system to only persist a few tens of megabytes of data. Some even had only read-only data. What is the point of using a database engine that takes up to 100 MB of RAM only to expose a data set that is actually smaller, and that could simply have been placed in a file?

Over-architecture is clearly the worst enemy of performance in our applications. But it is the very nature of IT to build on stable layers, thus making the architecture more and more complex. When some layers are pure utilities and others are piled on top of them, it becomes more and more difficult to know whether the application really needs this layer or if it can avoid the associated complexity by fulfilling its needs in a simpler way.

This is why the step of architecting is so important. This is also a good recommendation for a simple approach to software design. Methodologies like Lean, although they come from the mechanical industry, can be a great source of inspiration and improvements to IT teams. Also, simplicity in coding and light architectures result in lower resource consumption, thus contributing to greener IT.

At the moment, the ecological gain of a code optimization does not bring significant advantages in financial terms, because the cost of optimization is still much higher than the additional cost of electricity, servers, and resource use. But with increasingly expensive resources, it seems possible that software optimization will come back to the fore sometime in the future. After all, our predecessors could fit a printer driver into 32 KB. A bit closer to us, the demo scene in the early 1990s on Atari, Amiga and even Amstrad (see HTTP://WWW.DEMOSCENE.INFO/THE-DEMOSCENE/), has proven that extreme ingenuity in programming could lead to performance literally unthinkable on standard software. Today, we have all the necessary tools to do the same on industrial applications.

E   Final words

You may have told yourself several times when reading this book that the code mistakes were obvious, and sometimes that they could not appear in a good-quality application. To be honest, I have indeed exaggerated some cases. Sometimes for educational reasons, sometimes to reduce the size of the code we analyzed, and this is why redundancies, for example, appeared so clearly.

But all errors shown here are "classics." Of course, they will not appear in solid code, in critical or semi-critical applications, for which our customer is ready to pay an important additional cost to have the assurance of a highly-tested robustness. But IT is not only about such applications. Simple business applications abound, but they are not sub-applications for all that. For example, they are often very well secured, sometimes much better than mass market applications. Inversely, performance is often not taken into account right from design, and developer teams are not often trained to code for performance, or even in simple use of a profiler tool.

I invite you to read again the notes I suggested you take while studying the code for the sample application presented in Chapter 3. At that time, I had asked you to try and find lines of code that would have a negative impact on performance, only by reading the code. Were all the points we found in the profiling process easy to spot? Chances are they were not. If you have found many of them, you must be an expert at this, because forming an opinion on performance by simply reading the code is extremely difficult. Of course, some cases are relatively easy to spot. But after asking several well-trained developers to take a look at this, it turned out they could only see at best around 50% of the issues hidden in the code. And remember, PROFI is a sample application where performance issues have been concentrated in the smallest possible number of lines of code!

I hope this has convinced you of the utility of a profiler. It is impossible, even for experts, to detect all the bottlenecks in a piece of software by simply looking at its code and imagining what is going to happen from a resources point of view.

On the other hand (and this is the good news carried by this book), profiling can be undertaken by any developer, and brings useful results in most cases. During our profiling process, our sample application went from a jumble of all bad practices to a well-profiled application, in which no bottleneck remains. Now it's your turn...

Happy profiling!

Index

Symbols

W

X

SQL Server
and .NET Tools
from Red Gate Software

Pricing and information about Red Gate tools are correct at the time of
going to print. For the latest information and pricing on all Red Gate's
tools, visit www.red-gate.com

redgate®
ingeniously simple tools

ANTS Memory Profiler $495

Find memory leaks and optimize memory usage

↗ Find memory leaks within minutes

↗ Jump straight to the heart of the problem with intelligent summary information, filtering options and visualizations

↗ Optimize the memory usage of your C# and VB.NET code

"Freaking sweet! We have a known memory leak that took me about four hours to find using our current tool, so I fired up ANTS Memory Profiler and went at it like I didn't know the leak existed. Not only did I come to the conclusion much faster, but I found another one!"

Aaron Smith IT Manager, R.C. Systems Inc.

ANTS Performance Profiler from $395

Profile your .NET code and boost the performance of your application

↗ Identify performance bottlenecks within minutes

↗ Drill down to slow lines of code thanks to line-level code timings

↗ Boost the performance of your .NET code

↗ Get the most complete picture of your application's performance with integrated SQL and File I/O profiling

"ANTS Performance Profiler took us straight to the specific areas of our code which were the cause of our performance issues."

Terry Phillips Sr Developer, Harley-Davidson Dealer Systems

"Thanks to ANTS Performance Profiler, we were able to discover a performance hit in our serialization of XML that was fixed for a 10x performance increase."

Garret Spargo Product Manager, AFHCAN

Visit **www.red-gate.com** for a 14-day, free trial

.NET Reflector ®   From $35

Decompile, browse, analyse and debug .NET code

↗ View, navigate and search through the class hierarchies of any .NET assembly,
  even if you don't have access to the source code.

↗ Decompile and analyse any .NET assembly in C#, Visual Basic and IL

↗ Step straight into decompiled assemblies whilst debugging in Visual Studio, with the same debugging
  techniques you would use on your own code

"One of the most useful, practical debugging
tools that I have ever worked with in .NET! It
provides complete browsing and debugging
features for .NET assemblies, and has clean
integration with Visual Studio."

Tom Baker Consultant Software Engineer, EMC Corporation

"EVERY DEVELOPER
NEEDS THIS TOOL!"

Daniel Larson Software Architect,
NewsGator Technologies

SmartAssembly ®   from $795

.NET obfuscation, automated error reporting and feature usage reporting

↗ **Obfuscation:** Obfuscate your .NET code and protect your IP

↗ **Automated Error Reporting:** Get quick and automatic reports on exceptions your end-users
  encounter and identify unforeseen bugs within hours or days of shipping. Receive detailed reports
  containing a stack trace and values of the local variables, making debugging easier

↗ **Feature Usage Reporting:** Get insight into how your customers are using your application, rely on
  hard data to plan future development, and enhance your users' experience with your software

"Knowing the frequency of problems (especially immediately after
a release) is extremely helpful in prioritizing & triaging bugs that are
reported internally. Additionally, by having the context of where those
errors occurred, including debugging information, really gives you
that leap forward to start troubleshooting and diagnosing the issue."

Ed Blankenship Technical Lead and MVP

Visit **www.red-gate.com** for a 14-day, free trial

SQL Compare® Pro $595

Compare and synchronize SQL Server database schemas

- ↗ Eliminate mistakes migrating database changes from dev, to test, to production
- ↗ Speed up the deployment of new databse schema updates
- ↗ Find and fix errors caused by differences between databases
- ↗ Compare and synchronize within SSMS

> **"Just purchased SQL Compare. With the productivity I'll get out of this tool, it's like buying time."**
> **Robert Sondles** Blueberry Island Media Ltd

SQL Data Compare Pro $595

Compares and synchronizes SQL Server database contents

- ↗ Save time by automatically comparing and synchronizing your data
- ↗ Copy lookup data from development databases to staging or production
- ↗ Quickly fix problems by restoring damaged or missing data to a single row
- ↗ Compare and synchronize data within SSMS

> **"We use SQL Data Compare daily and it has become an indispensable part of delivering our service to our customers. It has also streamlined our daily update process and cut back literally a good solid hour per day."**
> **George Pantela** GPAnalysis.com

Visit **www.red-gate.com** for a 14-day, free trial

SQL Prompt Pro $295

Write, edit, and explore SQL effortlessly

- ↗ Write SQL smoothly, with code-completion and SQL snippets
- ↗ Reformat SQL to a preferred style
- ↗ Keep databases tidy by finding invalid objects automatically
- ↗ Save time and effort with script summaries, smart object renaming and more

> **"SQL Prompt is hands-down one of the coolest applications I've used. Makes querying/developing so much easier and faster."**
> **Jorge Segarra** University Community Hospital

SQL Source Control $295

Connect your existing source control system to SQL Server

- ↗ Bring all the benefits of source control to your database
- ↗ Source control schemas and data within SSMS, not with offline scripts
- ↗ Connect your databases to TFS, SVN, SourceGear Vault, Vault Pro, Mercurial, Perforce, Git, Bazaar, and any source control system with a capable command line
- ↗ Work with shared development databases, or individual copies
- ↗ Track changes to follow who changed what, when, and why
- ↗ Keep teams in sync with easy access to the latest database version
- ↗ View database development history for easy retrieval of specific versions

> **"After using SQL Source Control for several months, I wondered how I got by before. Highly recommended, it has paid for itself several times over."**
> **Ben Ashley** Fast Floor

Visit **www.red-gate.com** for a 28-day, free trial

SQL Backup Pro

$795

Compress, encrypt, and strengthen SQL Server backups

↗ Compress SQL Server database backups by up to 95% for faster, smaller backups

↗ Protect your data with up to 256-bit AES encryption

↗ Strengthen your backups with network resilience to enable a fault-tolerant transfer of backups across flaky networks

↗ Control your backup activities through an intuitive interface, with powerful job management and an interactive timeline

"SQL Backup is an amazing tool that lets us manage and monitor our backups in real time. Red Gate's SQL tools have saved us so much time and work that I am afraid my director will decide that we don't need a DBA anymore!"

Mike Poole Database Administrator, Human Kinetics

Visit **www.red-gate.com** for a 14-day, free trial

SQL Monitor

from **$795**

SQL Server performance monitoring and alerting

- ↗ Intuitive overviews at global, cluster, machine, SQL Server, and database levels for up-to-the-minute performance data

- ↗ Use SQL Monitor's web UI to keep an eye on server performance in real time on desktop machines and mobile devices

- ↗ Intelligent SQL Server alerts via email and an alert inbox in the UI, so you know about problems first

- ↗ Comprehensive historical data, so you can go back in time to identify the source of a problem

- ↗ Generate reports via the UI or with Red Gate's free SSRS Reporting Pack

- ↗ View the top 10 expensive queries for an instance or database based on CPU usage, duration, and reads and writes

- ↗ PagerDuty integration for phone and SMS alerting

- ↗ Fast, simple installation and administration

> **"Being web based, SQL Monitor is readily available to you, wherever you may be on your network. You can check on your servers from almost any location, via most mobile devices that support a web browser."**
>
> **Jonathan Allen** Senior DBA, Careers South West Ltd

Visit **www.red-gate.com** for a 14-day, free trial

SQL Virtual Restore $495

Rapidly mount live, fully functional databases direct from backups

↗ Virtually restoring a backup requires significantly less time and space than a regular physical restore

↗ Databases mounted with SQL Virtual Restore are fully functional and support both read/write operations

↗ SQL Virtual Restore is ACID compliant and gives you access to full, transactionally consistent data, with all objects visible and available

↗ Use SQL Virtual Restore to recover objects, verify your backups with DBCC CHECKDB, create a storage-efficient copy of your production database, and more.

"We find occasions where someone has deleted data accidentally or dropped an index, etc., and with SQL Virtual Restore we can mount last night's backup quickly and easily to get access to the data or the original schema. It even works with all our backups being encrypted. This takes any extra load off our production server. SQL Virtual Restore is a great product."

Brent McCraken Senior Database Administrator/Architect, Kiwibank Limited

SQL Storage Compress $1,595

Silent data compression to optimize SQL Server storage

↗ Reduce the storage footprint of live SQL Server databases by up to 90% to save on space and hardware costs

↗ Databases compressed with SQL Storage Compress are fully functional

↗ Prevent unauthorized access to your live databases with 256-bit AES encryption

↗ Integrates seamlessly with SQL Server and does not require any configuration changes

Visit **www.red-gate.com** for a 14-day, free trial

SQL Toolbelt $1,995

The essential SQL Server tools for database professionals

You can buy our acclaimed SQL Server tools individually or bundled. Our most popular deal is the SQL Toolbelt: fourteen of our SQL Server tools in a single installer, with **a combined value of $5,930 but an actual price of $1,995**, a saving of 66%.

Fully compatible with SQL Server 2000, 2005, and 2008.

SQL Toolbelt contains:

↗ **SQL Compare Pro**

↗ **SQL Data Compare Pro**

↗ **SQL Source Control**

↗ **SQL Backup Pro**

↗ **SQL Monitor**

↗ **SQL Prompt Pro**

↗ **SQL Data Generator**

↗ **SQL Doc**

↗ **SQL Dependency Tracker**

↗ **SQL Packager**

↗ **SQL Multi Script Unlimited**

↗ **SQL Search**

↗ **SQL Comparison SDK**

↗ **SQL Object Level Recovery Native**

> **"The SQL Toolbelt provides tools that database developers, as well as DBAs, should not live without."**
> **William Van Orden** Senior Database Developer, Lockheed Martin

Visit **www.red-gate.com** for a 14-day, free trial

Performance Tuning with SQL Server
Dynamic Management Views
Louis Davidson and Tim Ford

This is the book that will de-mystify the process of using Dynamic Management Views to collect the information you need to troubleshoot SQL Server problems. It will highlight the core techniques and "patterns" that you need to master, and will provide a core set of scripts that you can use and adapt for your own requirements.

ISBN: 978-1-906434-47-2
Published: October 2010

Defensive Database Programming
Alex Kuznetsov

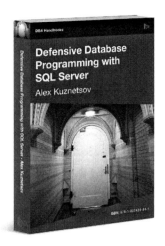

Inside this book, you will find dozens of practical, defensive programming techniques that will improve the quality of your T-SQL code and increase its resilience and robustness.

ISBN: 978-1-906434-49-6
Published: June 2010

Brad's Sure Guide to
SQL Server Maintenance Plans
Brad McGehee

Brad's Sure Guide to SQL Server Maintenance Plans shows you how to use the Maintenance Plan Wizard and Designer to configure and schedule eleven core database maintenance tasks, ranging from integrity checks, to database backups, to index reorganizations
and rebuilds.

ISBN: 978-1-906434-34-2
Published: December 2009

The Red Gate Guide to SQL Server
Team-based Development
Phil Factor, Grant Fritchey, Alex Kuznetsov,
and Mladen Prajdić

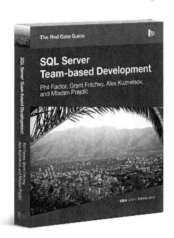

This book shows how to use of mixture of home-grown scripts, native SQL Server tools, and tools from the Red Gate SQL Toolbelt, to successfully develop database applications in a team environment, and make database development as similar as possible to "normal" development.

ISBN: 978-1-906434-59-5
Published: November 2010

CPSIA information can be obtained at www.ICGtesting.com
Printed in the USA
BVOW061634241212

308769BV00004B/5/P